EGOS

Egos

CONNECTING WITH THE
INDIVIDUAL SELF

Don Pierce

Heartwood Path

Contact:
Heartwood Path
info@heartwoodpath.com
805-689-7042
www.heartwoodpath.com

ISBN/SKU: 979-8-9857352-2-2
EISBN: 979-8-9857352-3-9

To my loving parents, Don and Marilyn.

Contents

Read This First

Although anyone may find the practices, challenges, and understandings in this book to be useful it is made available with the understanding that neither the author nor the publisher are engaged in presenting specific medical, psychological, emotional, sexual, or spiritual advice. Nor is anything in this book intended to be a diagnosis, prescription, recommendation, or cure for any specific kind of medical, psychological, emotional, sexual, or spiritual problem. Each person has unique needs and this book cannot take these individual differences into account. Each reader is encouraged to engage in a program of treatment, prevention, and cure only in consultation with a licensed, qualified physician, therapist, or other competent professional.

Introduction

EGOS: CONNECTING WITH THE INDIVIDUAL SELF

Wholeness begins with the individual. Evoked, colored, and interpreted by the uniqueness of each individual person, all of nature, all of the environment, and all of the universe would not be known nor complete without you. You are one of a kind. And your novel perspectives influence both what you perceive and the way the world becomes. For these reasons, we continue our outgoing path of learning with the general topic of each person's novel style, original view, and idiosyncratic approach. These are the some of the best peculiarities that make the world so varied and interesting.

Although not mandatory, if you have not read the first two books in this series, you may find it helpful to purchase and read them. **Kosmos** gives you the overview of the Heartwood Path and important background information. **Logos** presents important and pertinent universal principles, aimed at helping you to prevent swimming upstream in life.

If you prefer to forge ahead, without going back to the previous book, you can always go to www.heartwoodpath.com and press the link for one-on-one guidance. This service makes going down the Heartwood Path even more enjoyable and productive.

The present book—**Egos**—will help you identify and protect the important gifts that you bring to the world. We are honored that you are about to bring these gifts to the world with the help of the Heartwood Path. Proceed by moving to the first waypoint in **Egos**: "Individuation."

1

Individuation

HOLD FIRM TO YOUR UNIQUENESS

With a critical mass of people anchoring their uniqueness in the ways described in this book, we can avoid global tragedy, prevent widespread heartbreak, stem the tide of environmental devastation, and create conditions that will preserve all of our positive agendas. Most people are unaware that we are in the midst of a dark night for all species.

Within this night is the eye of an evolutionary perfect storm, where conditions are coming together that, without bold corrective actions, will cause the demise of billions of fellow earthlings. Fewer still are aware that the Twenty-First Century—a time of quiet horror and pain for humans and non-humans, alike—marks a birth on a massive scale of a time of improved intelligence and grace. All births are painful, including births of renewal.

This renewal can only happen if we do the necessary work, as described in this book and elsewhere. The collective offspring of this birth of renewal needs to be an embodied divine humanity.

We need such folks to grow into the kind of secular saints this series of books aims to develop. Such good folks need to have ensouled bodies, masculine and feminine energies, and the capability to perceive using both *heady* concepts and *bodily* sensations.

They will need to have the fortitude to resist the mainstream, obsessive, dissociated, chilling commitment to thinking in terms of separation, objectivization, and control. By reading this book, you will be given the ability to use a newly acquired free-flowing, supple, intuitive intelligence that comes from a "brain" you probably do not know you have. By changing your "self" in the way described in this book you can become a "midwife" that aids the birth of a more feminine outlook and approach.

This feminized outlook and approach is capable of ending the semi-demented denigration of the wild, both within us and outside of the enclosures (our homes) where we too often waste the bulk of our lives, filling the perceived emptiness of our own company by watching senseless, televised programming.

From television and other sources we are programmed to be dissatisfied, to want more, and to work for others to gain what we think will make us feel better. Over time, we are lulled to accept ruinous divisions such as the separability of mind from body, or the separability of man from nature, or the separability of "self" from "other."

We begin this book in the way most of us currently think—as if the individual can be separated from the whole. Each of us is an individual, and, as people with agency, we have our own uniqueness. This individuality marks half of our being, with integration into the whole— discussed in the next book—making up the rest.

We may not be able to stand alone, but we can learn about our individual aspects; and, in this learning, we will begin to see how by working on ourselves we affect the whole. While this book is about the individual and the Ego, remember: as we relate to our individual bodies, so too do we relate to our world; and as we deepen our experience of the body, so too do we deepen our experience of the world.

This series of books will make it possible for you to tap into the enormous source of intelligence that comes to you via your own newly acquired abilities to feel, deep in your bones, both Nature and a glorious sense of Wholeness. The state of wholeness feels like a lack of injury, like nothing is missing, like everything is complete, like everything is perfect, like everything is unbroken, and like you are in a peaceful state of total unity. It is an immensely satisfying feeling of love that seems native to your Soul. It is a feeling of joy marked by healthiness, satisfaction, and uncut oneness.

You will never perceive this natural unbroken wholeness—this ultimate fulfillment—until you able to feel in a more complete way with your individual body. As we shall see, this feeling of wholeness is difficult because our culture encourages us to focus on the functions of the well-known cranial brain—on concepts, rationality, analysis, and separation—rather than on a blending of the cranial brain with the little-known "brain" at the other end of the spinal column—the enteric brain—which governs feelings and the sense of unity with the whole.

It need not be this way. We need not be mired in abstractions. We can know and use our masculinity (our propensity to be a disembodied doer) but, even as we do, we ought to also keep and use our femininity (our propensity to be a felt body). Simply put, be both the action and the actor.

Our culture could support the yearning to be free, to have creativity, and to be present amid the myriad of things. But it doesn't. And it ought to because we need all three—freedom, creativity, and presence. There is no freedom without creativity and presence, nor is there creativity without freedom and presence, nor is there presence without creativity and freedom. We need to be able to walk around on these three legs, on these three aspects of our wholeness, so that our Selves can be complete, so that we can awaken to the integration into the whole to which our Selves belongs.

There cannot be integration into the whole without an individual being integrated. And there cannot be an individual alone, living without the whole.

You are one of these three-legged individuals—having one-leg yearning for freedom, one-leg yearning for creativity, and one-leg yearning for presence. To put all three of these useful yearnings to good use for yourself and the world, you cannot expect society as a whole to guide you. The guidance that you need requires the individual. Without individuals there is no freedom, no creativity, and no presence. Your "three-leggedness" means that it is you as an individual that has to guide and, therefore, create a better future. You, armed with the three yearnings, are perfectly suited for this role.

You may be a man or you may be a woman; but; either way, you have a mixture of masculine and feminine qualities. The masculine in you makes you a *doer*. The feminine in you makes you a *being*. You are a unity of doing and being. The doer in you streamlines, and gets right to the job at hand. The being in you multitasks, connects, and communicates. It is your feminine side that lives in accordance with the rhythms of nature and seeks to minimize aggression and war.

If you tend to wonder "What should I do?" more than you wonder "How should I be?" the masculine side is likely to be dominant in you. We will discuss more about such gender differences in the Heartwood Path book entitled "**Eros.**" And we will discuss the abiding reality of life, found in one's relationship with the whole, in the next book. Here, we are focusing on the entity that is being related. With a title like "**Egos**" you may suppose that we will be discussing in this course the egregious, hard-to-control impulse to acquire more and more. The subject of that misdirected drive is introduced in this Heartwood Path book and expanded upon in a later book entitled "**Ethos**".

Egregious wealth can be thought of as a measure of one's ability to abuse the world. Certainly, with greater affluence one has the wherewithal to purchase more than one needs. Such consumption often comes at considerable cost to other people and the environment.

Wealth does not measure one's ability to do good. For this reason, we will in this course focus on a better measure of goodness: one's openness of heart, one's ability to transform, and one's yearning to grow in depth by adding layers to one's spiritual development.

You will not need wealth to be successful as you progress down the Heartwood Path. You will need compassion, a sense of justice, and an unswerving commitment to reduce suffering.

We begin with the individual self, as if it stands alone when really it does not. A fabrication, the individual self is part of the "duplicate" world of concepts and words. I say "duplicate" because the individual self is not real, but a duplication of the real that comes in the form of concepts and ideas. The individual self is not made of stuff, but it is a metaphorical process, a man-made character that we shall use for literary clarity.

Despite its fictional nature, the self is extremely important to you as an individual. A fragile conceit, all reality appears to be contingent upon the individual self, which is never out of relationship with the whole. We can only speak and act as if we have no relations. In reality, nothing, including the individual self, exists alone. We can, however, talk about it separately. But let us always remember, the Self has no *perseity*. It is not an actual separate entity. Defined in the English Oxford Dictionary as "the quality or condition of existing independently, *perseity* is a false notion because isolation is a meaningless fantasy. Everything is sustained by the whole. How to overcome "*perseity*"—the false notion upon which the whole of western civilization is established —is addressed in the Heartwood Path book, entitled, **Collectivos**.

How the individual self relates to the whole brings up the notion of rights and responsibilities. An individual's *right* is a possession that one has and typically wants to defend. A responsibility is a relationship with the whole. Such ethical distinctions are discussed in more detail in the Heartwood Path book: "**Ethos**."

Without thinking of it as a fiction, we often place the individual self in the head, in the private isolation chamber of the brain. This placement is our way of getting "ahead" but it is not a good way to achieve enlightenment—that is, all-aware unbroken harmony.

It will as you progress down the Heartwood Path often be acceptable to be empty of ideas so that you can be more in touch with your feelings. The insensate cranial brain, a numbskull, is the center for masculine *doing*. The sensate enteric brain is the center for feminine *being*. At each waypoint you will be asked to create a duplicate world of words. In doing so, always remember that you are creating a replica or re-creation of the real thing.

In the activities for this series of books, use words to record your impressions. Specifically, focus on NNIAAL—the Universe's inner world constitution: Now's Nameless, Intelligent, Alive, Attraction, Love. If truthful, write down your impressions about becoming massively connected, about how you can feel the distinction between abstract substitutes/duplicates/models and the experience of the present. Failing to feel this distinction will put you right back into society's trap, a prison where fear of feminine being leads many of us to become tyrannical doers who placate our typical fear of being with the acquisition of possessions. The upcoming waypoint will help you learn how to correct this planet-wrenching tendency. There, you will learn how to perceive with what can be thought of as your two "heads:" the "head" for the creation of concepts **and** the "head" for bodily sensations. Let me explain:

We have a cranial brain which is the seat of our mental processes. We also have a visceral or enteric brain, located in the pelvis, which is the seat of our nonverbal consciousness. For much of your activity along the Heartwood Path, moderate the use of the brain in your head so that you can allow to come forth the feelings of your visceral brain in your lower body. Doing so will be important because you will be asked, over and over, to minimize conscious thinking and to highlight the feelings of conscious being. This process occurs in the individual, which is why we are addressing the topic of individuation here. As you proceed down the Heartwood Path and later in life, do not allow the head to always be the rightful ruler. And do not allow the masculinity (or any man) to be the supreme creation of the universe. The balancing of the head and the heart and the brain and the pelvis will enable you to develop a consciousness that is axial (head to tail, cranial brain to enteric brain) rather than unipolar (head or tail, cranial brain or enteric brain). It is through your axial consciousness—your ability to both think and feel—that you will become particularly well suited to making sure that for every right there is also responsibility. As you learn to develop such axial consciousness, you will be pleased about how good it feels; and you will realize that to be present in the world means making room within the corridor between the head and the pelvis for the world to be present in you. This room-making is extremely pleasurable, so much so it will make you glad to replace the *known self* that is a fiction made up of duplicate entities and words with a wondrous *felt self* that is made up of one's body, of the revelations of felt currents, and of the expansion of compassion. Once this felt self emerges, the known self falls away. In its place is a grounded abiding presence that is also the blossoming of one's core. And, in its place is a glorious feeling of being connected to all that is.

As you engage in the practices of this series of courses, you will be undergoing a hero's journey aimed at healing the primary wound of our culture: the rupture between thinking and being. As a result of this journey, the self will dilate beyond the boundaries of your skin to include the presence of the universe.

This delightful opening to the whole of the world occurs within the individual, but not within an individual who is crass or brutish. The wonderful feeling of opening up to the whole occurs within a person who is gentle. As it turns out, our sensitivity, more so than our willpower, helps the world. In **Ecclesiasticus,** one of the books of the Apocrypha in the King James Version of the Old Testament, it is written: "Many are in high place, and of renown; but mysteries are revealed unto the meek."

The concept of being meek is a familiar sentiment that is often confused with timidity or a retreating demeanor. By encouraging meekness, I am not suggesting that individuals going the down Heartwood Path need to lack strength. I am instead calling for a grounded presence that allows one to be in the world's stillness in innocence. A meek person can stand tall in humility before Spacious Presence. A meek person can be patient and un-resentful under injury or reproach. A meek person can have a grounded gentleness of heart. She is one who can usher others into a relationship with the present while being fully sensitive to it. To be meek is not to dress or speak in any particular way. It is rather a willingness to be open to the illumination of vivid companionship, open to the mind and hearts' sensitivity, and to use the medium of love for communication with anything. Writes Philip Shepherd:

"The gentler you are with yourself, the more fully you will be present. When you can be gentle with your whole life, your whole life will be present. Of course, gentleness is soft, but its effects are not. It opens the door on the flux of the world, the only reality, which moves with the power of a whirlpool. Not everyone chooses to give over to its pull. If you do make that choice, your grounded gentleness will carry you into an ocean of truth . . .Your ability to respond depends on the yielding spirit of gentleness, and whenever gentleness is offered, your 'responsibility' will be activated" (2010, pp. 314-315).

If we want a peaceful world we as individuals will have to be peaceful. Indeed, the world we make replicates the one we experience within.

In this Heartwood Path book you will learn about how individual and largely unconscious inner world mechanisms underlie the world's ecological predicament. You will also learn how understanding your own psychology and developing your individual self are initial steps towards finding that place where your own deep happiness meets the world's deep hunger for sustainability. Getting to know oneself through inner reflection is the foundation of any spiritual quest.

You will occasionally be looking specifically at the individual, sin-gular Realm of Interiority. This is the realm of your intentions. Here, you find your purpose.

Your purpose, aims, and Will are inner world events that you do not solely produce by yourself. They are part of the Universal Source. Your role is to become attuned to them. Pardon the expression, but I invite you to use your so-called "little mind" to tap into the world's "Big Mind," which is really your own mind expanded. This broader and deeper mind knows what you are to do with your life. The Big Mind directs a friendly universe, one that always works on your behalf.

When you look within, you concentrate all Spirit at your point of attention. In doing so, you will discover that you are much greater than you previously had known. You become what you like to become. The power of intention is revealed as:

1. creativity,
2. kindness,
3. love,
4. the appreciation of beauty (which is wholeness, reverence for life, and truth) and the ever-growing expansiveness of life,
5. unlimited abundance in the nonmaterial realm, and
6. receptivity to receiving and giving guidance. (Dyer, 2005).

As this book progresses, we will be looking at the core of the problem. And, we will address solutions. As we shall see, one cannot just stick an intention into the blank space of the mind because there are some curious occurrences (called "defenses") going on in there. These inner world events may get in the way of a magnificent future, both for oneself and for the world. For this reason, defenses—described subsequently—have to be understood and dealt with before one can begin to think about working out solutions.

For now, however, before working on your defenses, learn to create more beauty by uncovering what is beautiful about yourself and by applying your own beautiful uniqueness into all of your actions. Begin each Heartwood Path Activity in the customary fashion:

1. by going into nature,

2. by seeking out an attractive being found there, a

3. by opening yourself up to Nature through all of your fifty-four natural senses (described subsequently).

Then, as instructed in the following activity, read the text in the left column and answer the questions about yourself in the right column.

To A Positive Self-concept...

HumaNatureConnect Activity

Start-up Protocol

If this is not a day when you prefer to spend time in nature without an agenda, do the Heartwood Path Start-up Protocol found in the Appendix.

Connecting Positively With The Individual Self

For this activity, create a positive self-concept. In the first table, read the statements below (in the left column) and give your related impressions (in the middle column) now and in the right column at the end of this book. Also note that there is another table aimed to encourage you to write down what you hope you will achieve regarding your self-concept by participating in this section of the Heartwood Path. After writing down declarations as instructed in the two tables, place your statements together in an envelope. You will be instructed to open this envelop at the last waypoint for this course. It will be interesting to read what you say after anchoring your individual self as a result of taking this course. Notice in the second table below that you are given space to write down your reactions to your own growth at the end of this course.

Recreate the next two tables below. Fill in your answers and put them in an envelope to be opened at the end of this course.

Statements That Apply To People With Positive Self-concepts.	How, If At All, The Statements Apply To You At The Beginning Of This Course.	How, If At All, The Statements Apply To You At The End Of This Course.
I have self-confidence.		
I accept criticism and I do not become defensive.		
I can set obtainable goals.		
I am willing to take risks and to try new experiences.		

What would you like to get out of this course concerning your own individual self-concept?	What did you actually get out of this course concerning your own individual self-concept?

Follow-up Protocol

For best results, write down your impressions of this activity in your journal using the Heartwood Path Follow-up Protocol found in the Appendix. Afterwards, consider sharing your interpretations with others.

Heartwood Path Axioms

Key Assertions From Waypoint 3.1

3.1.1.

The inner world of individuals underlies the world's ecological predicament.

3.1.2.

Great happiness comes to those who find that place where their own happiness meets the world's hunger for sustainability.

3.1.3.

The way one thinks about one's self shapes who one is and informs the way one makes decisions.

Nocturnal Pilgrimage 3.1

For best results, write down your impressions of each night's dreams in your journal using the Heartwood Path Dreaming Time Protocols found in the Appendix. Afterwards, consider sharing your Dream Tending with others.

A major theme of all of the Nocturnal Pilgrimage sections for this course is "lucid dreaming," You are having a lucid dream when you are aware that you are dreaming.

You are not lucid in your dreams when you are only aware of them as memories after you wake up. That is unconscious dreaming.

Lucid dreaming has some variety to it. Sometimes a person having a lucid dream is only slightly aware of it and can act or make decision within the Dream. Other times a person knows that they are dreaming but still sees the Characters and action as separate from themselves. When you are aware that you are dreaming, see the action and Characters as parts of yourself, and can control the action and outcome of the dream, you are having the type of lucid dream needed and sought by those making a pilgrimage down the Heartwood Path. How to have such dreams, how to keep your lucid dream going, and what to do with your dreaming time power of lucidity will all be imparted to you as you progress from waypoint to waypoint in this book or course. Be patient. Lucid dreaming usually requires the kinds of skills that come from practice. You will get there. But, for now, sleep and dream Tend to your dreams, using the procedures listed in the Before Dreaming, Dreaming, and After Dreaming Protocol plus a few extra suggestions listed here:

Additional Heartwood Path Dream Tending Suggestions

1. Rather than jump to immediate attempts to interpret a dream, pay attention to what is actually presented in the dream itself.
2. Focus your attention on the particularity of the setting for the dream—the dreamscape.
3. During your dream, follow the way the dream is presented to you.
4. Notice the characters and creatures of the dream.
5. Look for similarities, contrasts, and repetitions.
6. Become curious about the dream.
7. Perceive the Dream Images as the voice of the world and/or the dream as the dream of the earth.

8. Interact with the Dream Images as living beings (by having conversations with them, for example).
9. Imagine using all of your senses to communicate and experience the Dream Images, Characters, or Settings.
10. Move with the feelings and rhythms of the Dream Images and let go of such notions as being beautiful or appropriate.

When working to incubate a certain dream—that is, to call forth a particular dream—do not express your desire vaguely or with any length. Your intentions become more powerful with single-pointed clarity and brevity.

With your knowledge of the subject matter of this waypoint—the topics of holding firm to your individuality, lucid dreaming, our Dream Tending protocols, and giving power to your intentions—you are ready to move to the next waypoint, entitled "The Attractive Natural Being Impression." There, you will learn how nature shares its intelligence with you. And, as you make this transition, remember:

Positive change requires positive vision.

Action is blind without vision.

2

The Attractive Natural Being Impression

KEEP YOUR FOCUS ON THE INSEPARABLE COMBINATION OF NATURAL BEINGS *AND* YOUR IMPRESSIONS OF THEM

This waypoint contains a teaching that is critical to making the Heartwood Path work for you. It will also be invaluable to whatever else you do in your life. It begins the work of realizing that the world is not just outside of the mind and the mind is not just separate from the world. This learning is critical to understanding how one comes to know anything.

At this waypoint we will here be addressing two important ways of knowing: 1) knowing that relies on scientifically valid sensations and 2) knowing that relies on stories. These ways are very important for your growth pilgrimage on the Heartwood Path and for any other endeavor in your life.

Happiness and sustainability are reduced when our subjective stories do not accurately reflect our sensations of objective reality. Conversely, happiness and sustainability go up when our subjective stories accurately reflect not a separate reality but our sensations of natural beings.

The key teaching of this waypoint is to have you know that it is not a separate object that one is relating to when asked to find an attractive natural being, as you always will be asked to do at the start of each Heartwood Path Activity. To answer this call, you can pick an individual natural object such as a stone, a bird, or a tree. You can also choose to include in your chosen natural object the individual being and its surroundings. When choosing a natural being and its surroundings you are, in effect, choosing more of this compound object's Greater Self—the individual and its setting. Whether you pick a bush (an individual being) or a landscape (part of the Greater Self), the natural beings that you are asked to seek and find attractive are not isolated objects but are really aspects of the outer world that are fused with your own inner world impressions of them.

One is not doing a pure natural science when one does Heartwood Path Activities. You will not be asked, for example, to study things that are somehow separate from your impressions of them. Nor will you typically be asked to focus on the mental images or constructs formed solely within your mind.

We are, therefore, also not doing pure psychology here. We are doing eco-psychology in a way that keeps the natural being and one's impression of that natural being (be it a flower or a forest) fused. This constant combination of the outer world object and the inner world impression is a better reflection of how the world works.

For us on the Heartwood Path the natural being and our impression of it—are always fused together in what I call a "Natural Being Impression." As we shall see, this Natural Being Impression will work best for you when you give more specificity and power to it by making it what I call an "AttractiveNaturalBeingImpression." For reasons explained subsequently, guidance, healing, and information flow best when the being and your impression of it are deemed to be attractive.

For our purposes along the Heartwood Path, a natural object without our impression of it would be an incoherent jumble. Also, an impression without a natural object would be a self-absorbed mental fantasy, possibly even a mental mishmash.

The point here is to avoid thinking that things are just things and mental impressions are just inner world events. It is implausible that a natural object, somehow separate and independent of its surroundings and the one observing it, can offer perceptible guidance in the form of signal—a message that comes from the natural being and goes to the admiring perceiver of that being. Those who go down the Heartwood Path do not behave like Dr. Doolittle talking to the animals.

It is, however, plausible and accurate to have the fusion of a thing like a natural being and one's inseparable impressions of it provide what we are looking for in doing the HumaNatureConnect Activities at each Heartwood Path waypoint: important guidance, information, and healing. It is, furthermore, pointless to argue that nature cannot provide guidance. There is no coherent nature separate from our impressions of it. The guidance, the information, and the healing comes from the inseparable "being impression."

When one does the sort of activities that are dotted along the Heartwood Path, one's Individual Self puts a definite "spin" on the aspects of the natural being that is perceived. One colors the guidance that is received according to one's own fashion. Here's how and why this fashioning (this fabricating) is so important:

The How

Along the Heartwood Path, one applies one's own perspectives, memories, and psychological state of mind to fashion, make, tailor, or shape one's own guidance from nature. One begins this process by choosing natural beings (as you may have noticed, we don't like to call them objects) that are attractive. This attraction—determined by our own unique preferences and distinct sensibilities—is a critically important component that allows for the flow of benefits that stem from proceeding down the Heartwood Path.

The Why

Here's why regularly forming AttractiveNaturalBeingImpressions is so important:

1. We are working to overcome our nature disconnected way of thinking and behaving that has led us to dissatisfaction and environmental malaise. Dwelling on attractive natural beings puts us into a positive state of regard that sets in motion a receptivity to the life-affirming thoughts and actions.

2. By communing with an attractive natural being we open ourselves up fully to so-called individuals (natural beings) that we soon see are connected to the web-of-life (in natural settings and landscapes). We also quickly learn that the natural beings, the natural settings, the landscapes, and the web-of-life are all intelligent.

3. By following our attractions in nature, we naturally linger longer there. We are not repulsed. We are drawn by the attraction, which can be thought of as a sort of consent that enables us to glean the fullest amount of guidance, information, and healing.

4. By following your attractions you are able to become psychologically attuned to the same energy that attracted the Void to evoke the Big Bang (the flaring-forth of Creation), that attracts the Absolute to create each present moment, that attracts you to receive the sharing of the natural intelligence of the wholeness of nature, and to—simply put—live with the "vibes" that bring goodness, beauty, and truth into your life.

5. Once you set up patterns of connecting to attractive natural beings and pay attention to your natural senses (you have 54 and not just 6) you will bring goodness, truth, and beauty into your life (and into the lives of others) because you will have already created an AttractiveNaturalBeingImpression—that is already good (ethical, beneficial to all), already truthful (actual, not based

on fantasy), and beautiful (coming from your own intentions, which are appealing because they come from the attractiveness and uniqueness of you). Your AttractiveNaturalBeingImpression will not be inappropriate because it will be formed with the help of Nature which was *good* when it was created and remains so through time-tested care and helpfulness, because it will be *truthful* (based on actual physical presence rather than by your own mental creations which may be fraught with delusions, fantasy, and psychological defense mechanisms and because it will be *beautiful* (always coming from the eye of the beholder, whose intentions are beautiful even when the beholder's actions often are not).

6. You will be far more likely to continue to do the helpful activities along the Heartwood Path by regularly seeking out your attractions than you would if you were asked to go find something ugly in nature before each activity. If you have any doubts about the allure and positive influence of natural attractions simply remember a time when a beautiful setting induced positive thoughts and plans in yourself, or try to remember when perceiving an unattractive natural being led to positive thoughts, plans, or actions.

There is but one Greater Self. And amid this Greater Self are countless Individual Selves that form all the vital and important distinctions, all the variety, and all the endless possibilities that make the world so amazing. Do not live so much of your life indoors where your thoughts are colored by fantastical stories, where your thoughts make you devoted to acquiring more and caring less, and where you are isolated from the intelligence of Nature. You will need to establish AttractiveNaturalBeingImpressions to become the secular saint this series of courses is devoted to creating.

You do not need to form AttractiveNaturalBeingImpressions once you attempt to go beyond saintliness to sageness. That last step, where you give up pondering the world and instead turn to meditating on thoughts alone; is beyond the scope of this series of courses. No matter: very few people get to the psycho-spiritual stage of sageness. Very few people want to become a sage. By the end of this courses you may experience a temporary peak at sageness but, more importantly, you will by the end of this series of courses establish yourself on a permanent plateau of secular saintliness. You will be easily driven and prepared to help others, including Nature, without crashing.

Everything you may have read in the Heartwood Path books **Kosmos** and **Logos** was offered to prepare you to begin your forward pilgrimage towards happiness and sustainability. It is now time to proceed toward GladandGreen Junction, in earnest. For the reasons that will be made clear as you proceed, it will be both necessary and delightful to begin this first post-preparatory leg of the Heartwood Path with a good understanding of the individual self, especially your own.

This understanding will come not only from reading but also from doing. For this reason, we shall put you immediately into the "doing" mode and, at the same time, put more flesh to the topic of the individual self by having you jump right into the following important activity.

To Firm Up Your Individuality By Seeing Natural Beings As Parts
And As Wholes...

HumaNatureConnect Activity

Start-up Protocol

If this is not a day when you prefer to spend time in nature without an agenda, do the Heartwood Path Start-up Protocol found in the Appendix.

Finding Individual Or Collective Natural Beings

For this activity, form the habit of picking out natural beings within your view that exhibit their own unique "individual selves" such as a rock, a tree, or a flower and pick out (usually more expansive) natural beings within your view that exhibit their "More-Than-Individual-Selves--" their unique selves presented in a setting. Such More-Than-Individual-Selves will often be a forest, a beach, a scenic view, or a natural landscape. Can you see that individual beings are not really independent but only seem so when you allow your mind to hold an impression of them as individual objects? As you view the More-Than-Individual-Self, can you make your mind hold your view of a natural landscape as one attractive natural being? How about the whole world? Can you think of the earth as one living being?

Follow-up Protocol

For best results, write down your impressions of this activity in your journal using the Heartwood Path Follow-up Protocol found in the Appendix. Afterwards, consider sharing your interpretations with others.

Heartwood Path Axioms

Key Assertions From Waypoint 3.2

3.2.1.

Happiness and sustainability are reduced when our subjective stories do not accurately reflect our sensations of natural beings.

3.2.2.

Conversely, happiness and sustainability go up when our subjective stories accurately reflect not a separate reality but our sensations of objective reality.

3.2.3.

A natural object without our impression of it would be an incoherent jumble and an impression without a natural object would be a self-absorbed mental fantasy, possibly even a mental mishmash.

3.2.4.

Amid the Greater Self are countless individual selves that form all the vital and important distinctions, all the variety, and all the endless possibilities that make the world so amazing.

Nocturnal Pilgrimage 3.2

For best results, write down your impressions of each night's dreams in your journal using the Heartwood Path Dreaming Time Protocols found in the Appendix. Afterwards, consider sharing your Dream Tending with others.

As you lie in bed tonight, form the intention that you will awaken your feelings during your lucid dream, especially in that exact moment when you realize that you are awake in your dream. Do not just record what you see in your dreams. Pay as much attention to how you feel.

Continue moving down the Heartwood Path during your night-time slumbers. Dream, and look for clues in your dream that point to your sense of self, and particularly: to your self-confidence, to your ability to accept criticism, to your ability to set obtainable goals, to your willingness to take risks, to your strengths, to your ability to make decisions, to how you keep goals realistic, and to whether you feel empowered.

Often, certain animals show up repeatedly in your dreams. Pay attention to such Dream Characters, for they may be Animal Totems, the topic of the next waypoint.

3

Animal Totems

PAY ATTENTION TO YOUR ANIMAL SPIRIT GUIDES

An animal totem is a symbolic representation of an animal guide in the form of a crest, a totem pole, an emblem, a small figurine, or anything else that depicts the spirit guide for a tribe, clan, family, or individual. Your own animal guide instructs, protects, teaches, and reconnects you to your earth roots and the cycle of life. Some of the most important and powerful truth and knowledge that we can hold, the "medicine" from Animal Totems comes to you in both your dreams and your waking life.

Animal Totems lead us to our power. They deliver important life lessons. They help us to form both our crucial individuality and our important sense of oneness. They do these things only if we maintain a sense of reverence and a willingness to be helped.

As a reflection of the variety of our moods, situations, and earth conditions, we usually experience more than one totem animal in our lives. Except for the Lifelong Animal Totem and the Direction-specific Animal Totem team, which usually stays with you throughout your life, Animal Totems come and go, as needed. As one Totem leaves one's life, another steps in. These transitions occur most often during times of new tasks, new lessons, new events, and new directions.

Each and every person on earth has, or can have, Animal Totem Teams, made up of individual Totems, each having special "medicine." By "medicine" I mean the help the totem can deliver.

Animal Totems And Their Medicine

Here are some Animal Totems that work well for me.

- Alligator encourages you to develop new wisdom without being consumed by it.
- Antelope helps you end your procrastination.
- Badger helps you reach your objective.
- Bat helps you move forward while staying balanced in the present.
- Beaver helps you to develop your ingenuity and resolve.
- Bee helps you communicate effectively and stay in touch with your loved ones.
- Great Blue Heron helps you know who or what to follow.
- Canada Goose helps you honor your roots and honor those who have helped you.
- Cougar helps you with self-confidence and accomplishing your dreams.
- Jaguar helps you move on your plan.
- Cricket helps you stay positive.
- Groundhog helps you get to the root of the matter.
- Falcon helps you with research and planning.
- Lizard helps you with intuition and higher knowledge.
- Manatee helps you choose peace instead of struggle.
- Otter helps you remember that life can be fun with the right attitude.
- Owl helps you listen to your inner voice and to recognize deception.

- Dolphin reminds you to take time to play.
- Fox helps you to use seen and unseen resources.
- Panda helps you accept others for who they are and to expect the same for yourself.
- Raccoon helps you live for the moment.
- Redwing Blackbird helps you admit your true feelings to yourself.
- Seal helps you with creativity.
- Turtle helps you recognize abundance in the world.
- Whale helps you honor your Soul's purpose.
- Woodpecker helps you continue to hammer away at your project.
- Yorkshire Terrier helps you to accept whatever is and to laugh when you step on wet spots on the floor.

One can but need not imbue magical powers on your Animal Totems. If this helps, do it. If magic gets in your way, you can still benefit from your Animal Totems. The helpful correlations stem from the animal's typical behaviors. Whether you ascribe magical abilities to your Animal Totems, their offered "medicines" will be instructive, guiding, and healing. If mysticism is not your thing, think of the totems as psychological tools, useful to those who retain an open mind. By having a team of Animal Spirits at your disposal, rather than just one Lifelong Animal Totem, you will surround yourself with experienced advisors, skilled healers, diligent protectors, and like-minded fellow clan members.

Pre-established Totems

Some Animal Totems are already established for you. These include the Quarter Guardians, the totems for your Birth Clan, and your Direction-specific Animal Totem Team.

Quarter Guardians

Some animals are associated with the quarters (the four Elements) and can be called upon to activate the powers of the North, the East, the South, and the West. These powers come from the associated Elements (each quarter is composed of the Cardinal Direction stone and the next three Moon Stones moving clockwise around the Native American Medicine Wheel, which will be described in detail subsequently), and the Associated Cardinal Direction Animal Totem, which together bring forth the characteristics or states one can solicit to address a situation or solve a problem.

The North quarter affects and is affected by the Earth element, is pertinent to situations and problems having to do with riches, and has as Animal Totem Quarter Guardian the Buffalo.

The East quarter affects and is affected by the Air element, is pertinent to situations and problems having to do with desire and love, and has as its Quarter Guardian the Golden Eagle.

The South quarter affects and is affected by the Fire element, is pertinent to situations and problems having to do with liberty movement, dreaming, profoundness, and freedom, and has as its Quarter Guardian the Coyote.

The West quarter affects and is affected by the Water element, is pertinent to situations and problems having to do with softness and repose, and has as its Quarter Guardian the Grizzly Bear.

Clans

Butterfly Clan
If you were born between the Rest and Cleansing Moon (**Jan 20 to Feb 28**), the Corn Planting Moon (**May 21 to June 20**), or the Ducks Fly Moon (**Sep 23rd to Oct 23rd**), you are a member of the Butterfly

Clan. You are ruled by the element of Air. The Butterfly Clan is composed of people who live in the moment and tend to explore, wander, and look for what is new.

Condor (The Thunderbird) Clan

If you were born between the Budding Trees Moon **(Mar 21 to Apr 19)**, the Ripe Berries Moon, **(Jul 23 to Aug 22)**, or the Long Snows Moon **(Nov 22 to Dec 21)**, you are a member of the Thunderbird Clan. You are ruled by the element of Fire. Some members of the Thunderbird Clan seem to be people of paradox. At one moment they are warm and helpful, but they can suddenly turn into a dominating, hyperactive individual.

Frog Clan

If you were born between the Big Winds Moon **(Feb 19 to Mar 20)**, the Strong Sun Moon **(Jun 21 to Jul 22)**, or the Freeze Up Moon **(Oct 24 to Nov 21)**, you are a member of the Frog Clan. You are ruled by the element of Water.

Turtle Clan

If you were born between the Harvest Moon **(Aug 23 to Sep 22)**, the Frogs Return Moon **(April 20 to May 20)**, or the Earth Renewal Moon **(Dec 22 to Jan 19)**, you are a member of the Turtle Clan. You are ruled by the element of Earth. The Turtle Clan, the Clan of Earth, is filled with stable, practical, and grounded people with an appreciation of the Earth and its elemental energy.

Nine-member Direction-specific Animal Totem Team

As you proceed down the Heartwood Path or other pathways of growth, keep in mind the seven directions surrounding your physical body: East, South, West, North, Above, Below, and Within. The direction called Within exists inside of you, but also exists outside of you, since the entire universe is inside your awareness. The other two animals, which make up your nine totems are the ones which are walking at each side of you at all times, and which may possibly have been coming to you for years in your dreams.

Each of us have a totem animal associated with each of the nine directions. Spend some time learning the lessons of these directions. When *any* animal presents itself to you in some way that stands out in your mind, whether in a dream or while you are awake, study its Medicine—it's a message for you!

East

The animal in the East — Coyote—guides you to your greatest spiritual challenges and guards your path to illumination.

South

The animal in the South —Butterfly—protects the child within and reminds you when to be humble and when to trust, so that innocence will be balanced in your personality.

West

The animal in the West—Great Blue Heron—leads you to your personal truth and inner answers. It also shows you the path to your goals.

North

The North animal—Skunk— gives wise counsel and reminds you when to speak and when to listen. It also reminds you to be grateful for every blessing every day.

Above

The Above animal—Owl—is the guardian of the dreaming time and your personal access to the other dimensions.

Below

The Below animal—Turkey—teaches you about the inner World and how to stay grounded and on your path.

Within

The Within animal—Moose—teaches you how to find your heart's joy and how to be faithful to your personal truths.

Right Side

This animal—Eagle— protects your masculine side and teaches you that, no matter where you turn, you will have the courage and spirit of a warrior.

Left Side

This animal—Turtle— is the protector of your feminine side and teaches you that you must learn to receive abundance as well as to nurture yourself and others.

(Sams and Carson, *Medicine Cards*)

Chosen Animal Spirit Teams

Based on their medicine and your attraction to them, create a team of specially-tailored Animal Totems. Regularly call on them for assistance. This calling can be as simple as asking a question and going for a walk in nature, or as complicated as a full ritual to acknowledge a specific power animal. In either case, it is important to open yourself up to the natural world.

Remember to always show gratitude to a departing totem. Give both thanks and blessings to them when you become aware that their energy is moving away from you.

Healers

Many animals have unique resistance to certain diseases. Snakes that shed their old skin, for example, are symbols of transformation. Sharks, being largely cancer-free, are symbols of healing. Study the ways animals keep themselves healthy and align with their energy whenever you need to be healed physically or psychologically.

Advisors

Animal spirits are also great advisors and can be called on for help in particular situations. Whale, beaver, or any of those listed under the "Animal Totems And Their Medicine" section above can help you with quests, journeys, quandaries, situations, choices, decisions, and activities.

Protectors

Animal Spirits are also protectors, and can be called upon to give you extra energy for preventative purposes. You are well advised to pay attention to the Animal Spirits that appear in your life. Listen to their messages of warning. Some Animal Totems that have proven to be protective for me include Opossum, Owl, Dog, and Armadillo.

To Receive Guidance From Animal Totems...

HumaNatureConnect Activity

Start-up Protocol

If this is not a day when you prefer to spend time in nature without an agenda, do the Heartwood Path Start-up Protocol found in the Appendix.

Identifying Your Animal Totems, Both Life-long And Intermittent

When in the presence of your attractive natural being, look around the natural setting or scan your memories of animals, pick an animal that is "speaking" strongly to you (dominant in your awareness), that you feel drawn to, that keeps cropping up randomly in your life, or that you need to acknowledge. Doing so will assist your subconscious in being more open to the energy of the Animal Totem, allow messages and wisdom to flow to you from your Animal Totem more easily, and enable the energy of the Animal Totem to be welcome in your space.

If no obvious animal totem comes to mind, ask yourself the following questions (which cannot be answered wrongly and are best answered when you are intuitive and relaxed):

1. What animal, bird, or insect do you feel most drawn to?
2. When you go to a nature reserve, park, or zoo, what animal are you most interested in seeing?
3. What animal do you most often see (in nature and in your ordinary surroundings – contemplate any interaction, whether images, sounds, or the actual animal)?
4. What animal are you currently interested in learning more about?
5. What animal most frightens you, intrigues you, or makes you feel "out of your comfort zone"?
6. Have you ever been bitten, scratched, or attacked by an animal?
7. Do you ever have recurring dreams about a particular animal?
8. Are you drawn to figurines or pictures of a specific animal?
9. Are you the king of the jungle, like a lion (and 1.8 percent of human population)?j
10. Are you charming and clever, like a macaw (and 3.2 percent of human population)?
11. Are you strict and aggressive, like a wolf (and 8.7 percent of human population)?
12. Are you subtle and opportunistic, like a hyena (and 4.3 percent of human population)?

13. Are you loyal and affectionate, like a dog (and 2.5 percent of human population)?
14. Are you spontaneous and creative, like an orangutan (and 8.1 percent of human population)?
15. Are you gentle and caring, like an elephant (and 12.3 percent of human population)?
16. Are you fun and entertaining, like a dolphin (and 8.5 percent of human population)?
17. Are you a solitary hunter, like a tiger (and 2.1 percent of human population)?
18. Are you wise and calm, like an owl (and 3.3 percent of human population)?
19. Are you slow but tough, like a snapping turtle (and 11.6 percent of human population)?
20. Are you secretive and unpredictable, like a snake (and 5.4 percent of human population)?
21. Are you rare and fascinating, like a panda (and 1.5 percent of human population)?
22. Are you free spirited and kind, like an otter (and 4.4 percent of human population)?
23. Are you territorial and protective, like a rhinoceros (and 13.8 percent of human population)? Or
24. Are you harmless and sensitive, like a kitten (and 8.8 percent of human population)?

(Care2.com) & (myersbriggs.org)

If in answering these questions no Lifelong Animal Totem emerges, try the following:

1. Make a list of animals that have drawn your interest or have left a deep impression on you.
2. Keep a journal of the animals present in your dreams or that you encounter through the day for the next month.

3. Find a place where you can be alone to meditate and ask your Animal Spirits for assistance.

From the information and answers you assembled above, fill in the appropriate characteristics and Animal Questions in the blanks below:

Choose your Life-long Animal, if it had not already chosen you.

My Life-long Animal Totem is _____.

Choose your Task-oriented Animal Totem Team. Change it respectfully whenever you see fit.

My current Animal Totem Healer is _____.

My current Animal Totem Protector is_____.

My current Animal Totem Advisor is_____.

Follow-up Protocol

For best results, write down your impressions of this activity in your journal using the Heartwood Path Follow-up Protocol found in the Appendix. Afterwards, consider sharing your interpretations with others.

Heartwood Path Axioms

Key Assertions From Waypoint 3.3

3.3.1.

Pay attention to your Animal Spirit guides.

3.3.2.

The "medicine" from Animal Totems comes to you in both your dreams and your waking life.

3.3.3.

As a reflection of the variety of our moods, situations, and earth conditions, we usually experience more than one totem animal in our lives.

3.3.4.

If mysticism is not your thing, think of the totems as psychological tools, useful to those who retain an open mind.

Nocturnal Pilgrimage 3.3

For best results, write down your impressions of each night's dreams in your journal using the Heartwood Path Dreaming Time Protocols found in the Appendix. Afterwards, consider sharing your Dream Tending with others.

Now we come to the first of four discussions about making your intentions effective. You will know you have reached this topic when you see the following banner:

Make Your Dreams Come True

When striving to have a lucid dream do not just hope that it happens. Instead, upgrade you hopes, which are by nature relatively weak in power, to expectations, which are by nature relatively stronger in power. Expectations, repeated over and over, have great strength.

Saying, for example, "I hope to have a lucid dream tonight," is not as effective as repeating: "I expect to have a lucid dream tonight...I expect to have a lucid dream tonight..."

Think about what you learned about expectation and Animal Totems before you prepare for sleep. Retire early so you get a good night's sleep. Dream. Before getting out of bed in the morning, begin tending to your dreams, using our dream processing protocol. Before doing the next waypoint, remember:

Since Earth needs your attributes, lead.

Continue with your hoping but, when it really counts, switch over to expecting. With these two aspects of intension, you can achieve great things. You are making great strides. With your expectations and Animal Totem(s) in tow, move to the next waypoint: "Ways Of Knowing."

4

Ways Of Knowing

RIDE THE GREEN WAVE

To bring forth the most happiness while improving the world, be sure to do what I call "Riding the Green Wave" each time you do any of the following activities. We will be using a surfing analogy to summarize how this worthwhile endeavor is done.

It is surprising to most people that our senses are not limited to the five common ones learned in grade school. We actually share with nature fifty-four natural senses. By using these ways to register experience you not only learn more about the environment you also become more available to receive nature's guidance (which comes from your AttractiveNaturalBeingImpression, discussed in the previous waypoint).

We shall divide the natural senses into the ones that provide information by sensation and those that provide information by stories. We shall call the natural sensation mechanisms the "Blue Wave" Natural *Sensation* Senses" And we shall call the mechanisms used to tell stories the "Yellow Wave" Natural *Story* Senses.

From the standpoint of maintaining human happiness and a sustainable environment, our culture took a disastrous wrong turn when it focused so much on the "Yellow Wave" *story* senses, which include consciousness, reasoning, and literacy, and also down-played all the remaining fifty-one "Blue Wave" natural *sensation* senses (listed subsequently).

"Blue Wave" Natural Sensation Senses

- Sense of light and sight, including polarized light.
- Sense of seeing without eyes such as heliotropism or the sun sense of plants.
- Sense of color.
- Sense of moods and identities attached to colors.
- Sense of awareness of one's own visibility or invisibility and consequent camouflaging.
- Sensitivity to radiation other than visible light including radio waves, X rays, etc.
- Sense of temperature and temperature change.
- Sense of season including ability to insulate, hibernate and winter sleep.
- Electromagnetic sense and polarity which includes the ability to generate current (as in the nervous system and brain waves) or other energies.
- Hearing including resonance, vibrations, sonar and ultrasonic frequencies.
- Awareness of pressure, particularly underground, underwater, and to wind and air.
- Sensitivity to gravity.
- The sense of excretion for waste elimination and protection from enemies.
- Feel, particularly touch on the skin.
- Sense of weight, gravity and balance.
- Space or proximity sense.
- Coriolis sense or awareness of effects of the rotation of the Earth.

- Sense of motion, body movement sensations and sense of mobility.
- Smell with and beyond the nose.
- Taste with and beyond the tongue.
- Appetite or hunger for food, water and air.
- Hunting, killing or food obtaining urges.
- Humidity sense including thirst, evaporation control and the acumen to find water or evade a flood.
- Hormonal sense, as to pheromones and other chemical stimuli
- Pain, external and internal.
- Mental or spiritual distress.
- Sense of fear, dread of injury, death or attack.
  (previous three senses are attractions to *seek additional natural attractions* in order to support and strengthen well-being).
- Procreative urges including sex awareness, courting, love, mating, paternity and raising young.
- Sense of play, sport, humor, pleasure and laughter.
- Sense of physical place, navigation senses including detailed awareness of land and seascapes, of the positions of the sun, moon and stars.
- Sense of time.
- Sense of electromagnetic fields.
- Sense of weather changes.
- Sense of emotional place, of community, belonging, support, trust and thankfulness.
- Sense of self including friendship, companionship, and power.
- Domineering and territorial sense.
- Colonizing sense including compassion and receptive awareness of one's fellow creatures, sometimes to the degree of being absorbed into a superorganism.
- Horticultural sense and the ability to cultivate crops, as is done by ants that grow fungus., by fungus who farm algae, or birds that leave food to attract their prey.

- Sense of humility, appreciation, ethics.
- Senses of form and design.
- Intuition or subconscious deduction.
- Aesthetic sense, including creativity and appreciation of beauty, music, literature, form, design and drama.
- Psychic capacity such as foreknowledge, clairvoyance, clairaudience, psychokinesis, astral projection and possibly certain animal instincts and plant sensitivities.
- Sense of biological and astral time, awareness of past, present and future event.
- The capacity to hypnotize other creatures.
- Relaxation and sleep including dreaming, meditation, brain wave awareness.
- Sense of pupation including cocoon building and metamorphosis.
- Sense of excessive stress and capitulation.
- Sense of survival by joining a more established organism.
- Spiritual sense, including conscience, capacity for sublime love, ecstasy, a sense of sin, profound sorrow and sacrifice"
- Sense of homeostatic unity, of natural attraction aliveness as the singular essence-diversity attraction dance of all our other senses (NNIAAL).

(Cohen, website: http://www.ecopsych.com/insight53senses.html).

To help bring us (you, me, fellow eartHearts, and Society, in general) back on track towards a magnificent future, it is important to Ride the Green Wave by using not only "Yellow Wave" stories but also "Blue Wave" sensations.

As in surfing, you fall off the wave when you are not totally aware and when all of your faculties are not in balance. If you do not use your sensation senses you fall into the ocean but do not learn as much as possible in the process because you are not utilizing your full repertoire of ways of knowing. When you live to tell about your stories (of surfing or otherwise) you will see that they are based too much on fantasy or conjecture. If you are exposed to natural objects but do not use your story senses you have sensations but not some of the best ways to make them meaningful. And you cannot most easily and effectively tell others about your ride. The best Heartwood Path "surfing" happens when you combine (blue) sensations with (yellow) true stories and ride the green wave towards happiness and sustainability.

The "Green Wave," as described by Dr Michael Cohen (Project NatureConnect Website: http://www.ecopsych.com/journalaliveness.html and personal email June 8, 2016) and used along the Heartwood Path, leads to happiness because when a sense is satisfied with the consent of other senses the body produces hormones and enzymes that treat you to feelings of pleasure, satisfaction and joy. Ride the "Green Wave" when engaged at each waypoint.

The "Green Wave" leads to environmental sustainability because it develops and strengthens all the natural senses that enables you to love nature and use that love as motivation for actions that protect the natural environment. (Cohen, Personal Email June 8, 2016). By riding the "Green Wave" in each waypoint and always in your life, you are, purposefully or inadvertently, tipping a part of the world back into a state of sustainability.

Together, happiness and sustainability are hallmarks of the destination of the Heartwood Path—Gladandgreen Junction. "Ride the Green Wave" to get there by combining "Yellow Wave" Natural Story Senses with "Blue Wave" Natural Sensation Senses.

"Yellow Wave" Natural Story Senses

- Sense of mind and consciousness.
- Sense of reason, including memory and the capacity for logic and science.
- Language and articulation sense, used to express feelings and convey information in every medium from the bees' dance to human literature.

You will need to use more of your capabilities to make the best personal and environmental advances. Your ability to activate these oft-overlooked capacities needs to be carefully logged (as regular entries into your journal) so that you know you are using all of your innate tools for coming to know, so that you know that you are grasping the nature of the world, and so that you know you are living more fully. This logging in your journal will occur as "Ride The Green Wave" in the Follow-up Protocol repeated after each Heartwood Path Activity.

To fill-in the "I'm A Person Who..." line in the Follow-up Protocol after each Heartwood Path Activity you need to first make sure that you are registering impressions during each activity using any or all of the fifty-four natural senses. That way, after the activity, you can determine the validity of whether in each activity you are truly Riding the Green Wave by marking whether you understand and agree with each of the Validation Statements shown in the next activity.

When examining your acceptance of The Ten Green Wave Validation Statements, in your journal give yourself a plus sign ("+") whenever you understand and agree with all of the statements. If you do not understand or agree with all statements give yourself a minus sign ("-") in your journal. Anything less than 100% understanding and agreement (any minus sign ("-") means that you are not Riding the Green Wave and may wish to redo the activity and seek additional information and one-on-one guidance at www.heartwoodpath.com. It will be interesting to work through these statements before you start any of the activities and then once again at the end of all of the activities, as a way to measure changes in your self concept.

To validate whether you are successfully Riding the Green Wave, take the following three steps at each of the following Heartwood Path waypoints:

1. recall and prepare to use all of the natural senses as you engage in each activity (mixing Yellow Wave Natural Story Senses with Blue Wave Natural Sensations Senses);

2. as suggested in the Follow-up Protocol, determine the validity of whether in each activity you are Riding the Green Wave by determining your understanding and agreement with particular Green Wave Validation Statements (enumerated in the next paragraph); and

3. check your emerging self-concept by doing the "Nature Compared To Self" Activity described in the Introductory Experience.

Green Wave Validation Statements

(Start Doing Them Now)

Review these specific statements each time you do any of the activities for the remainder of this series of courses. Doing so will let you know whether you are on track or if you need to go back over previous activities. One hundred percent acceptance of the following Green Wave Validation Statements is necessary if you want the best chance of finding happiness in a sustainable environment:

1. It is true what I experienced in the Heartwood Path Huma-NatureConnect Activity.
2. Both myself and the natural attraction I experienced have at least some form of sensation and are, therefore alive.
3. Natural attraction is the essence of spirit, love, unity, and life.
4. There are ways of knowing that rely on scientifically valid sensations, there are ways of knowing that rely on stories, and happiness and sustainability are reduced when our subjective stories do not accurately reflect our AttractiveNaturalBeingImpressions;.
5. Humanity inherits fifty-four natural senses that enable us to register and relate reasonably to Nature's attractive aliveness and intelligence. **I used, or considered the use of, all of these senses**

while doing this Heartwood Path HumaNatureConnect Activity.

6. It is reasonable and intelligent to recognize that science is needed to clean up the mess made by believing that nature is an object to be exploited.

7. We suffer a wide range of disorders because, unreasonably, we live out of tune and balance with the purity of our Attractive-NaturalBeingImpressions. Without these impressions we habitually practice an artificial way of life whose nature-disconnected stories violate and injure the inherent natural wisdom that we share with the nature.

8. The whole of life deteriorates and we humans produce and suffer our discontents when our literate-story is inaccurate/imaginary/unreasonable and our consciousness is bonded to it and its nature-disconnected flaws.

9. HumaNatureConnect Activities improve our relationships by making space for NNIAAL (Now's Nameless, Intelligent, Alive, Attractive Love) to safely operate as we "Ride the Green Wave."

10. In any given moment we can come into balance and increase personal, social and environmental well-being by learning to empower our thinking and relationships through connecting with nature as we "Ride the Green Wave."

Review these statements each time you "Ride the Green Wave" in the Heartwood Path Activity Follow-up Protocol. When you understand and agree with all of these statements give yourself a big plus sign ("+") in your journal. Or, when you do not understand and agree with all of these statements give yourself a big minus sign ("-") in your journal.

To Logging Whether You Are "Riding The Green Wave"...

HumaNatureConnect Activity

Start-up Protocol

If this is not a day when you prefer to spend time in nature without an agenda, do the Heartwood Path Start-up Protocol found in the Appendix.

Becoming Proficient With The Natural Senses And Making Sure That You Are Riding The Green Wave

For this activity, review the list of fifty-four Natural Senses and, one by one, attempt to bring them into play as you visit an attractive natural object. Work to become proficient in as many senses as possible. To recall the list of Natural Senses, see the list provided earlier in this waypoint or purchase the list of natural senses to be carried in your wallet.

For the first of many times, determine whether you accept the Ten Green Wave Validation Statements (listed above). Do not be concerned if your acceptance does not come easily at first. You may need to visit several more waypoints before you can accept what it means to "Ride the Green Wave." Once you are consistently accepting all of the Validation Statements, you can either stop validating or use the validation process to keep yourself on track.

Follow-up Protocol

For best results, write down your impressions of this activity in your journal using the Heartwood Path Follow-up Protocol found in the Appendix. Afterwards, consider sharing your interpretations with others.

Heartwood Path Axioms

Key Assertions From Waypoint 3.4

3.4.1.

Attend to your natural senses.

3.4.2.

Balance literacy with sensation.

3.4.3.

AttractiveNaturalBeingImpressions stem disorders.

Nocturnal Pilgrimage 3.4

For best results, write down your impressions of each night's dreams in your journal using the Heartwood Path Dreaming Time Protocols found in the Appendix. Afterwards, consider sharing your Dream Tending with others.

By "Riding the Green Wave" and using the Dream Tending Protocol you are now better prepared for the challenges of your future. Make a real difference in the world. Have courage. Hold fast to good qualities. Protect Creation boldly. Restore your inner constitution. And return no evil for evil.

Doing something wrong as a way to correct something wrong is not the right approach. Sometimes we resort to an "eye for an eye"—a biblical way of saying that we resort to evil to fight what we see as evil. One way to make sure you don't resort to such unproductive methods, which only inevitably leaves us all blind, is to work on ridding yourself of unworkable ways to protect and improve yourself.

Make Your Dreams Come True

Use present tense wording to increase the effectiveness of your intentions, especially when making affirmations. If you want to bring forth a lucid dream, for example, do not say: "one of these nights, I'd like to have a lucid dream." Such a statement is future oriented. Likewise it is ineffective to use past tense wording, such as "I liked it when I consciously controlled what happened in my dream," A better approach to bring forth a lucid dream is to repeat an affirmation, using present tense wording: "I am lucid dreaming...I am lucid dreaming..." Use similar present tense affirmations to accomplish whatever your heart desires.

After "Riding the Green Wave," and with the value of present tense wording in mind, set an intention to have a lucid dream. Have a good nights sleep. Dream lucidly. Tend to your dreams, using the Dream Tending Protocol.

When you are ready, move to the next waypoint: "Defense Mechanisms." Doing so will help you learn that curbing certain inner world defense mechanisms (such as repression or intellectualization) can help anyone become more positive and connected in a good way to the world.

5

Defense Mechanisms

LEARN HOW YOU UNCONSCIOUSLY SPLIT OFF YOUR AWARENESS OF ENVIRONMENTAL PROBLEMS

Your job in this portion of the Heartwood Path is to look for ways you, like everyone else, fool yourself into doing dumb things while not feeling bad about doing them. There are numerous ways to fool yourself in this way, but we will consider the identification of ways that you psychologically allow yourself to do things that are harmful to the environment. This consideration is an important step in making necessary corrections in the way you and other Heartwood Path sojourners think and behave.

Sigmund Freud's object relations theory helps us to understand our impaired relationship with the environment. Like Copernicus and Darwin before him, Freud stopped most people from thinking of themselves as the center and pinnacle of the universe. Freud showed us that we are irrational and biologically determined. He thought that both nature and the inner psychological world are untamable and un-masterable and the best we can hope for are anxiety-based truces and compromises. He offers three principles relevant to our present work along the Heartwood Path:

1. behavior is largely a result of unconscious motivations (both the sexual pleasure and reproduction of Eros and the aggression, violence, and destruction of Thanatos);
2. conflict is universal, chronic, and inevitable;
3. to function effectively, we "split off our awareness of unwanted thoughts, feelings and wishes, and use defenses to disguise and contain them" (Winter and Koger, 2004, p. 30).

These defenses require psychic energy and are established in order to fool ourselves into thinking that we behave for rational or moral reasons, when, in reality, much of our behavior is propelled by subversive, selfish, and unacknowledged needs, wishes, fears, and impulses that are quite selfish and unacknowledged (Winter and Koger, 2004, p. 32). Each person has to divide up his or her psychic energy between the desires for pleasure (the Id), the mechanism that constrains impulses (the Ego), and the mechanism for moral principles (the Superego) (Winter and Koger, 2004, p. 33). With only so much energy to go around, Freud proposes that we defend ourselves from anxiety by "splitting" our awareness so that we can remain essentially unconscious about our instincts without entirely ignoring them. To this end, we build defense mechanisms that come in many forms, including engaging in:

1. rationalization (attractive but untrue explanations for our behavior);
2. intellectualization (abstract but impersonal explanations);
3. displacement (expressing our feelings to a different, less threatening audience as when we, for example, blame others for not recycling when we ourselves could make an even better contribution by curbing consumption);
4. suppression (consciously putting anxiety-provoking thoughts out-of-mind);

5. repression (similar to suppression but done unconsciously);
6. reaction formation (denying an impulse and giving intense energy to expressing in a holier-than-thou manner its opposite);
7. projection (perceiving in others what we fail to perceive in ourselves because it is easier to recognize weaknesses in others than it is to recognize weaknesses in ourselves);
8. sublimation (channeling unconscious anxiety into socially acceptable projects; and
9. denial (insisting that "anxiety-provoking material does not exist) (Winter and Koger, 2004, pp. 33-39).

Now that we have identified the means that you may be using to psychologically allow yourself to hurt the environment, do the following activity to begin the process of working out the remedies that are needed because of your defense systems.

To Ridding Yourself Of Unworkable Defense Mechanisms So You Can Pay Attention To Environmental Problems...

HumaNatureConnect Activity

Start-up Protocol
If this is not a day when you prefer to spend time in nature without an agenda, do the Heartwood Path Start-up Protocol found in the Appendix.

Ridding Yourself Of Defense Mechanisms

For this activity, become aware that you have some or all of the nine subconscious tendencies listed above (this is half of the work). Then, write down how, if at all, the tendencies exist in your life. Next, write down what actions or reactions you are now having regarding these tendencies. Lastly, write down what you want your actions or reactions to be next time. Consider what you can do to overcome any defense mechanisms you may be using as a way to split your awareness (to keep yourself from seeing the effects of your actions, for example) and, thereby, do things that are harmful to the environment.

Follow-up Protocol

For best results, write down your impressions of this activity in your journal using the Heartwood Path Follow-up Protocol found in the Appendix. Afterwards, consider sharing your interpretations with others.

Heartwood Path Axioms

Key Assertions From Waypoint 3.5

3.5.1.

Learn how you unconsciously split off your awareness of environmental problems.

3.5.2.

Defense mechanisms allow one to do dumb things and not feel bad.

3.5.3.

People defend themselves from anxiety in many ways, including: blaming others, putting bad thoughts out of mind, being holier-than thou, and denial.

Nocturnal Pilgrimage 3.5

For best results, write down your impressions of each night's dreams in your journal using the Heartwood Path Dreaming Time Protocols found in the Appendix. Afterwards, consider sharing your Dream Tending with others.

After identifying and rectifying your defense mechanisms, you may feel a bit disjointed because your old ways of relating in and to the world will be seen as less than ideal. The defense mechanisms pertinent to the world and your place in it tend to give you and other modern urban people the notion, popular in modern science, that the world is not alive. Since this notion will impede your progress to Gladandgreen Junction, ways have to be developed to rid yourself of pertinent defense mechanisms that hide your primal relationship with the living world. We also need to develop, or I ought to say redevelop, a worldview that "playfully and soulfully sees the world as alive and always dreaming" (Aizenstat, 2009, p. 144).

Having already practiced at ridding yourselves of defense mechanisms, it is time to concern yourself with the development of a worldview that counters your view of the world as anything but alive. Continue with this series of courses as you:

1. perceive the surrounding natural world as endowed with meaning, meaning whose significance is at once personal and galactic
2. work to develop the sense that the world is ensouled; and
3. perceive how the world communicates (often in dreams) and has purposes.

One has to both rid oneself of defense mechanisms that distort one's fullness of self and experience the waking reality and dreams of a living world or one will not be able to recover what is likely to be a fundamental More-Than-Individual aspect of oneself. One has to bring defense mechanisms to light while also turning to the dreams of the world in the dark. Do not let the brilliant glare of your rational thinking prevent you from gleaning the benefits of the instincts, emotions, imagination, intuition that lurk in the darkness as one dreams. "To be stuck in one mode of consciousness (waking consciousness), all the time" writes Aizenstadt, "is a kind of pathology, just as if night were to disappear and the world was left to burn under the unending glare of the sun" (2009, p. 148)

Halt your rational thinking for a spell. During the day, let the living presence of the world you behold communicate with you, and hold you. At night, sleep. Dream. Each morning, tend to your dreams before getting out of bed (see related Protocol). Then serve others, especially those called "undeserving" and those without a voice. Do not be one of those who support under-serving the so-called undeserving, for you will not be able to feel the joy of knowing that all people and all non-people are dear just because they are here.

Make Your Dreams Come True

Here's another thing to do to increase the effectiveness of your intention: clearly visualize what you want. If you cannot visualize it in your mind you will likely not see it in the world. Your vision needs to clearly be a picture of your desire coming to fruition. Practice seeing what you want in your mind's eye. Paint a vivid mental picture. Fuzziness detracts from the power of your desire. When you want to bring forth a lucid dream, for example, clearly picture yourself walking around in that dream, controlling what happens, and asking any Dream Characters who present themselves as the Natural Beings (perhaps the same ones that you encountered during recent HumaNatureConnect activities) for clarity and advice on how to get what you want, be it happiness, a beautiful and sustainable environment, or whatever. The importance of Dream Characters who come to you in your dreams as Natural Beings will be expanded upon in our upcoming discussions of what Aizenstat calls "Indigenous Images". The key for our purposes here is to repeatedly turn your intensions into clear pictures in your mind, and to regularly intend to have lucid dream encounters with Natural Beings.

After practicing visualizing over and over again, continue your pilgrimage by moving to the next waypoint, "Object Relations." After doing the next waypoint, you will be better prepared to go out into the world in peace.

6

Object Relations

CONSTRUCT YOUR SENSE OF SELF FROM YOUR INTERACTIONS WITH OTHERS

Doing so will help you understand your deepest attitudes about the environment. According to Object Relations Theory, we "construct our sense of self from our interactions with others, particularly the person who was our primary caregiver" (Winter and Koger, 2004, p. 43). If the caretaker fails to meet the basic needs of the child the child will "learn to build a false self in which the requirements of others are taken as his or her central being" (Winter and Koger, 2004, p. 44). This "false self" system explains much of the irrationality of our environmentally unsustainable actions. Without the development of an Actual Self one is likely to use external objects as a means of self-revealing expression. Writes Winter and Koger: "Adult character is built on an infantile pattern of neediness, and the accouterments of adult society function as symbolic expressions of those needs" (2004, p. 51). One buys cars and clothes, for example, to enhance status or to become employed in jobs that offer status but little or no deep satisfaction. We do not function in a healthy way if we do not have faith that our needs will be met in the future. If one has damaged trust because one's early primary caregiver gave inadequate attention or withdrew attention too early the result can be any of four neurotic reactions that are likely to impact environmental behavior:

1. A prolonged state of unmet needs can cause narcissism—the difficulty recognizing or respecting objects, beings, and people that do not offer to alleviate its needs (nature is, therefore, often unappreciated for its own complexity and beauty and appreciated only as a storehouse of resources). Having spent my early years in a loving home environment, for example, I was given the psychological luxury of wallowing in the beauty of nature near my home.

2. Narcissism or an early loss of a nurturing environment can lead to compulsion (wherein people buy excessive amounts of consumer goods as a temporary substitute for the loss of early nurturance). I do not feel the need to shop for recreation, an example of what happens when there is no early loss of a nurturing environment.

3. The sudden withdrawal of nurturance can lead to a sense of despair that is so strong it leads to the chronic sense of loss, helplessness, and grief that are some of the hallmarks of depression. Despite some attentiveness challenges exhibited by my direct parents (neither were involved in my life during the weekends), my paternal grandparents stepped in and, to the best of their considerable ability, prevented me from feeling any sudden withdrawal of nurturance. Their reliable care on weekends allowed me to avoid the helplessness, sense of loss, grief, and depression prevalent in many of the children of divorced parents.

4. Lack of trust can become paranoia, especially if one persistently feels threatened by nature (Winter and Koger, 2004, pp. 41-47). Having literally immersed myself in the swamps and forests along the Mississippi River as a child, partly as a way to avoid some dangers on the streets of my race-troubled neighborhood, I slowly, over many years, developed not only an appreciation of

nature but also a sense that it provides security and safety. The result was a nature-given sense of peace and trust that stunted any emergence of paranoia.

From this list the message is clear: Caregivers: give enough attention to your dependents to help them see nature as something of value beyond being a storehouse of goodies, give your attention long enough to keep your dependents from become compulsive consumers, hell-bent on gobbling up the environment; avoid sudden withdrawals of nurturance to stem the growing tide of depression; and enable your dependents to trust you so that they may not feel so threatened by others, including nature. Without a start in life with the help of effectively compassionate caregivers, people will not have the wherewithal to do the jobs they need to do, including working to make people happy and the environment sustainable.

Almost all the activities in this book ask the sojourner to use her awareness to seek out an attractive natural being and to use this being for guidance, healing, or information. This call to be in the midst of an attractive natural being is done for a very good reason. We have a deep need to be in the midst of "powerful, safe, solid and loving beings, especially those "who hold us physically in their arms and who also hold us emotionally in their hearts" (Cope, 1999, p.142). Since it is not always possible to spend time with caring therapists, loving parents or grandparents, and understanding lovers, we will in the activities of this book usually use a non-human attractive natural being or scene in their stead. Heinz Kohut describes the "need for merger with idealized self-objects." Being held and soothed has its transformative benefits, but, as we shall see, such acts of equanimity do not have to come from a human. Attractive natural objects (beings) and scenes can present to us much of the same thing that any good therapist, parent, or lover can bring forth in terms of spanning the therapeutic poles of both awareness and equanimity. Nature will be used to help us both see clearly (awareness) and to provide calm abiding (equanimity). We will present activities that provide self-object experiences aimed at helping us grow, not in purely mental, cold, and clinical ways but instead in ways that are emotional, warm, and earthy. We will be doing much self-soothing, even Greater Self-soothing.

The warm and helpful Teacher-Mother is everywhere in Nature. She is available to us most readily and profoundly where we find our attractions in Nature. In its infinite wisdom, Nature knows we need both poles: the awareness side of personal growth assistance and the equanimity side.

Part of Nature's intelligence is that it presents to us the benefits of both the Seer (which provides awareness) and the Mother (which provides equanimity). Anytime you see an animal being aware and anytime you see an animal being nurturing, you have an opportunity to learn very important lessons, for these (awareness and nurturing) are the two ways (polar sides) to be effective in your compassion to others. I say "polar sides" because Nature seems to know that it takes too much energy to stay on any one polar side, for eventually the pull in the other direction is too much to resist. There are examples in nature of animals being aware but not nurturing or nurturing but not aware, but these are hard to find because nature has brutal ways to eliminate those who linger too long on any one pole. The lesson is clear: be both a good seer and nurturing.

To The Dreams Of Natural Beings And The Landscape...

HumaNatureConnect Activity

Start-up Protocol

If this is not a day when you prefer to spend time in nature without an agenda, do the Heartwood Path Start-up Protocol found in the Appendix.

Dreaming While Awake

For this activity, review what you have experienced while awake for the last two weeks. Identify an odd experience that occurred during this period. When you take yourself back to this event you are experiencing a waking dream. Consider how you were inside a set of circumstances beyond your own doing. Determine what aspects of this experience are taking on a luminous quality. Notice how such recalling is similar to dreaming. Consider how the world itself is participating in your waking dream, how the world seems to be slowing or standing still, how your perception is more spatial and less linear. In your mind, look around you rather than straight ahead. Notice the dreamscape in your waking dream. Look for synchronicities, connections to a larger pattern, and what seems to intersect with each other in this larger pattern. Note what seems to happen at the same time. Look also for complementarities—what seems to like being with what. Look for how one entity complements another. Look for organizing principles. Write down in your journal how you feel about these synchronicities and complementarities. Write down what these synchronicities and complementaries tell you about your own being. Write down how you feel, if anything, about how dreamlike intelligence informs or complements some aspect of your own life.

Follow-up Protocol

For best results, write down your impressions of this activity in your journal using the Heartwood Path Follow-up Protocol found in the Appendix. Afterwards, consider sharing your interpretations with others.

Heartwood Path Axioms

Key Assertions From Waypoint 2.6

2.6.1.

If one has damaged trust because one's early primary caregiver gave inadequate attention or withdrew attention too early the result can be any of four neurotic reactions that are likely to impact environmental behavior.

2.6.2.

One constructs one's sense of self primarily from one's interactions with the person who was one's primary caregiver and if this caregiver fails to meet one's basic needs as a child one will build a "false self" in which the requirements of others forms one's individual sense of self.

2.6.3.

The "false self" system explains much of the irrationality of our environmentally unsustainable actions, for without the development of an Actual Self one is likely to use external objects as a means of self-revealing expression.

2.6.4.

Adult character is built on an infantile pattern of neediness, and the accouterments of adult society—cars, clothes, etc.—function as symbolic expressions of those needs and a way to enhance status or become employed in jobs that offer status but little or no deep satisfaction.

2.6.5.

Nature can be used to help us both see clearly (awareness) and to provide calm abiding (equanimity).

Nocturnal Pilgrimage 2.6

For best results, write down your impressions of each night's dreams in your journal using the Heartwood Path Dreaming Time Protocols found in the Appendix. Afterwards, consider sharing your Dream Tending with others.

The longer your nightmares stay hidden in your subconscious or unconscious, the more damage they'll do. You can deal with nightmares during the day by talking about them with your friends and family or by writing them down in your journal. Acknowledging them in your daily life is the first step to treating them. Let the sun fill in the darker shadows. You can also vanquish them at night while lucid. Our dreams might not be the first place our demons show up, but luckily they can be the last.

With this in mind, sleep. Dream. If necessary, vanquish your villainous Dream Images. Or, better yet, go toe-to-toe with your nightmares in the following ways: face them (trying to run will not work and could make things worse), know lucidly that you are safe, do not try to change the dream but rather change yourself, call upon dream allies to help you face your fears, face your fearful Dream Characters and ask: "What do you want?," "How can I help you?," and "What do you have to teach me?" When awake, tend to your dreams; which, among other things, means to make entries into your dream journal.

Once you store your impressions from your previous dreams in your journal, it is time to continue your wayfaring by moving to the next waypoint: "Frameworks." As you carry on, don't just do, also be. Be someone who notices and respects the nature found in the woods as well as the nature found in the heart. There is always time, when you step off the Heartwood Path, to imagine, plan, divide, subdue, and reshape. Establishing your supremacy over nature, over the material world, is not our chore here. Instead of being a complacent armchair marauder of the environment, leave your house for a spell and step into the world of nature with appropriate meekness.

7

Frameworks

REMEDY INNER WORLD CAUSES
OF OUTER WORLD TROUBLES

Until we become aware of the psychological reasons for our overconsumption, we humans will not be able to change our planet-rendering behaviors. Monitor not only your feelings, but also the ways in which you minimize and deny them. Without experiencing and expressing such feelings, part of our psyche arranges a defense of them, limiting greatly our abilities to find creative solutions (Winter and Koger, 2004, p. 49). Ultimately, our survival as a species rests on our ability to notice our own cognitive shortcuts and our own pathetic attempts to justify our actions and ward off discomforts (Winter and Koger, 2004, pp. 53-54).

To The Care Of A Worldly Essence...

HumaNatureConnect Activity

Start-up Protocol

If this is not a day when you prefer to spend time in nature without an agenda, do the Heartwood Path Start-up Protocol found in the Appendix.

Tending To The Psychoid

For this activity, put to use aspect of archetypes in your Dream Tending. Archetypes are universal primitive mental images that can show up in dreams. Archetypes are inherited from the earliest human ancestors and are believed to be present in the collective unconscious of humanity. Jung, who developed the concepts of archetypes in dream interpretation, puts forth that one type of archetype exists in the collective unconscious and another "independently in nature." He named . . . the external manifestation of an archetype, the 'psychoid.' So archetypes exist not only in the human brain; they also exist in the world around us" (Aizenstat, 2009, p. 164). The psychoid, or what Aizenstat calls "indigenous images," carry relevance that goes beyond the cultural or collective level. They are rooted in Nature. They are "powerful for personal growth and wellbeing. Because they are generated by the World's Dream, they are organic" (Aizenstat, 2009, p. 165). Like all other living things, Indigenous Images have the capacity to balance and self-regulate. They make these adjustments in response to our active awareness and communication with them. These capacities enable them to heal us on many levels. They show up in many guises and directly shape our personal evolution. "To connect with an Indigenous Image is to connect to Nature itself . . . touching the Indigenous Image will begin our return to wellbeing. On the other hand, if we become disconnected or alienated from our Indigenous Images, it can be catastrophic. When trying to stay in touch with your Indigenous Images make sure they are an expression of nature and not images from the media or commercial interests. Archetypes are usually heroic images that show up spontaneously in our dreams. As such, they do not need to be called or conjured up in any way.

To pull Indigenous Images back into your awareness look back over your dream journal for the last several weeks. Look for images in waking dreams and night dreams that seem out of the ordinary. Overlook images that seem like they may have been generated by the marketplace. To do so:

1. "look for images that are not obvious media images;
2. pay attention to the odd, deformed, aberrant, peculiar, even mutant-seeming images;
3. notice which images have a deeply 'resonant' quality different from the artificial 'charge' of commercial images;
4. pay particular attention to those images that originate in the natural world;
5. if the image is human-made or manufactured, look for those images that are artistic or that have a 'handmade' personality, a radiant, alive quality, different from those which seem mass-produced or artificial; and
6. allow your instincts to participate in the selection process.

Look for six or so Indigenous Images. Be sure to do so. Write them down. You will need to refer to this list in a future Activity. Write about each indigenous image in depth in your journal.

Follow-up Protocol

For best results, write down your impressions of this activity in your journal using the Heartwood Path Follow-up Protocol found in the Appendix. Afterwards, consider sharing your interpretations with others.

Heartwood Path Axioms

Key Assertions From Waypoint 3.7

3.7.1.

Remedy inner world causes of outer world troubles.

3.7.2.

Psychological reasons for overconsumption cause planet-rendering behaviors.

3.7.3.

Expressing the feelings that accompany depression, paranoia, compulsion, and narcissism promotes a sustainable environment and human happiness.

Nocturnal Pilgrimage 3.7

For best results, write down your impressions of each night's dreams in your journal using the Heartwood Path Dreaming Time Protocols found in the Appendix. Afterwards, consider sharing your Dream Tending with others.

Last night, before going to sleep, I was thinking about how riding a horse for those who do not give the horse its fair do, is like putting a conceptual being atop a dumb beast. I thought to myself how this image, fraught with the inaccuracies spawned during a few thousand years of horse-riding, has unfortunately today become the dominant metaphor by which we today live our lives. The man riding the domesticated horse creates the unfortunate notion of the brain over the body and the man over nature. This image is now being replaced with the even more destructive symbol of the man on the machine (big Ram Truck or Harley motorcycle).

Before you dream tonight, think of a revised symbol, one that puts us all into a better relationship with (rather than over) nature. Perhaps the visualization of a woman serenely soaking in a natural spring could replace the conception-dominated man on the horse or machine and lead us away from dominating nature and towards a future of pervasive sensation-filled nature experiences. Such images inspire the replacement of the matchless doer asserting his dominion over nature with a feminized approach that respects humaNature.

Continue tending to world dreams. When you are satisfied that you are making sufficient progress (even a tinge of headway will do, for now), move to the next waypoint: "Safe Places." The Dream Activity found there will lead you to becoming whole in dreams. Enjoy your next lucid dream!

8

Safe Places

ESTABLISH HOLDING ENVIRONMENTS

A challenge for those heading to Gladandgreen Junction is to experience defensive feelings without being overwhelmed by them. To avoid such emotional meltdowns, the experience and expression of such feelings is best conducted in the kinds of safe environments provided by attentive parents, and later in life by therapists, mentors, teachers, close friends, and loving partners. Such so-called "holding environments" (Koger and Winter, 2004, p. 49) are not only created by loving parents or supportive spouses. They can also be provided by attractive natural beings or natural environments. In all cases, holding environments offer any of the four kinds of endowments participants said they hoped for as we worked to develop the Life Adventures Outdoor Center in Belleville Illinois:

1. *A place for doing physical activities* of all kinds—fun activities that extend their skills, offer risks and challenges, but have adequate safety measures.

2. *A place for thinking*—a place for discovery, study, and learning; a place where the intellect can be stimulated; a place where participants can learn more about themselves and the world.

3. *A place for feeling*—a location full of color, beauty, and interest; a place that engenders a sense of pride and ownership; a place where participants can be small, vulnerable, caring, cared for, and appreciated.

4. *A place for being*—a location where participants can be themselves, where participants can be recognized for their abilities, be private if they choose, and have their choices accepted.

These are the kinds of opportunities eartHearts seek to provide in their groups (salons), in their temporary retreats, and in the inspired programs they hold at permanent destinations they seek to protect and/or develop. The four attributes of holding environments are the opportunities people can use to recollect their wholeness during the light of day. As we shall see, people can also uncover their wholeness during the day or night.

To Compassionate Action...

HumaNatureConnect Activity

Start-up Protocol

If this is not a day when you prefer to spend time in nature without an agenda, do the Heartwood Path Start-up Protocol found in the Appendix.

Observing The Impact Of Doing Random Acts Of Kindness

For this activity, come back from your time in nature and, without delay, do random acts of kindness and record how doing so makes you feel. Ideas for random acts of kindness include paying a fee or toll for someone in line behind you, giving flowers to passersby, giving your seat to someone standing, providing supplies or refreshments to schoolmates or workmates, improving the conditions for your chosen natural being without harming other beings (providing water during a drought, for example), and smiling and saying hello to someone you do not know.

Follow-up Protocol

For best results, write down your impressions of this activity in your journal using the Heartwood Path Follow-up Protocol found in the Appendix. Afterwards, consider sharing your interpretations with others.

Heartwood Path Axioms

Key Assertions From Waypoint 3.8

3.8.1.

The challenge is to experience defensive feelings without being overwhelmed by them.

3.8.2.

To avoid an emotional meltdown, the experience and expression of negative feelings is best conducted in the kinds of safe environments provided by attentive parents, and later in life by therapists, mentors, teachers, close friends, and loving partners.

3.8.3.

EartHearts create holding environments; that is, places where people can learn, feel, be physical, be themselves, and plan how to expand their kindness.

3.8.4.

Learn how to become aware that you are dreaming while you are dreaming and how to set the stage for a predetermined dream before bed.

Nocturnal Pilgrimage 3.8

For best results, write down your impressions of each night's dreams in your journal using the Heartwood Path Dreaming Time Protocols found in the Appendix. Afterwards, consider sharing your Dream Tending with others.

Sleep. Attend to your day dreaming. Examine your memories of your experiences with your chosen attractive natural beings. Use association, amplification, or animation, whichever you determine that gives you the most insight.

To proceed well, you will need to be able to distinguish lucid dreaming (which is controlling a dream once you are in it) from incubating a dream (which "allows you to set the stage for your dream before falling asleep). Putting these two together makes for some very productive sleeping. Both lucid dreams and incubating a dream will be covered more extensively later in this book.

When you get better at either lucid dreaming or incubating a dream you can work on making your dreams help you recover lost parts of your self. This will be done by looking over your dream journal entries to see if any of your dreams contain advice on how you can become happier and whole.

Give it a try now. Look in your dream journal for Dream Characters, often sad or injured people, who may be symbols of your emotional difficulties or repressed experiences. Look for Dream Images that match some aspect of your self. This can be done by affirming your intention to become whole. If you have lost your energy, for example, look for Dream Images with lots of energy and imagine absorbing it through the pores of your skin. If you are anxious, unite with a soothing waterfall while reminding yourself that its waters heal anxiety. "Use dreams to become mentally whole by reuniting with lost parts of yourself" (Tucillo, Zeizel & Peisel, 2013, pp. 200-204).

After tending to your dreams while still in bed, head outside for a calming tonic and creativity booster. Find a natural being or a natural landscape to steady your nerves. Use this time to coat your inherent susceptibilities in the soothing embrace of nature. In this way, you will be protected from the overstimulation, noise, smoke and stench of your work environment.

When ready, continue with this course by moving to the next waypoint: "Social Psych." In the next course you will learn some interesting things about the impact of others on one's environment-related behavior.

9

Social Psych.

LEARN HOW OUTER WORLD PERSONS AND INNER WORLD PSYCHIC PERSONALITIES AFFECT YOUR ACTIONS

Beyond inner world individual explanations, there are also aspects of social psychology that are pertinent to the topic of protecting the environment. Since I have more to say about social psychology in the Heartwood Path For Groups course, I will limit my presentation of the impact that others play in our environmental behaviors here to the following twelve points:

1. What we think and do arise from a mixture of socially determined beliefs, explanations, and rules.
2. Facts do not usually alter strongly held views, so focus on affecting what people believe.
3. Getting people to do the big thing (like attending an environmental meeting) is more likely if you first get them to do a small thing (like signing a petition), in part, because people seek to maintain their public image by appearing consistent.

4. Pro-environment attitudes are strongest amongst the well educated, the higher social classes, city-dwellers, the young, and women.

5. It may be nit-picking to say this, but environmentalists may want to reconsider their labeling of the environment as "Mother Earth" because this label implies that humans are the earth's children and are, therefore, not responsible for their own actions.

6. When attempting to influence behavior and to encourage the imitation of behavior, the social status of the presenter is as important or more important to the audience than the facts presented.

7. To influence the changing of another person's behavior, the activation of personal or social norms is more important than the presentation of information or pleas.

8. Feelings of moral responsibility have an influence on environmental behavior.

9. People who spend time in nature with significant others develop emotional bonds to the place they visit and are, therefore, more apt to seek to protect it.

10. The massive amounts of advertising people in developed countries are exposed to makes them feel deprived unless they consume, even though it seems to me that consumption does not deliver what is really important and even though in my experience people are not necessarily happier just because they own more things.

11. Practicing voluntary simplicity and green consumerism are antidotes to buying unnecessary goods that damage the planet. (Winter and Koger, 2004, pp 57-81).

12. Rather than thinking that our individual and collective problems are "solely or primarily a result of troubles within individual psyches," it will be more accurate and productive to . . ."understand that our psychological health relies profoundly on the . . . vitality of our natural environments" (Plotkin, 2013, p. 6).

The answer to how to heal and become whole does not come from suppressing symptoms. Rather, it comes from cultivating wholeness of Self. This cultivation requires a renewed relationship with the More-Than-Human or, said another way, the not-merely-human psyche which, when whole, contains a variety of inner world personality aspects described next.

Some of the key personalities that have an effect on your actions are not other humans. They are instead what eco-psychologist Bill Plotkin calls our four "multifaceted wild psyches" (2013, p. 2):

1. the "Sub-personalities"—the numerous "wounded and sometimes hidden fragments of our human psyches," (2013, p. 14)—including the so-called inner world Loyal Soldiers, the inner world Wounded Children, the inner world Escapists and Addicts, and the Shadow and Shadow Selves—and the four facets of the Self, the Psychic Personalities—the inner/outer world Nurturing Generative Adult, the inner/outer world Wild Indigenous One, the inner/outer world Innocent/Sage, and the inner/outer world Muse/Beloved;

2. the Spirit, (a.k.a. God, Mystery, and the nondual);

3. the Soul, which is our deepest individual identity; plus

4. the Ego, one's inner world aspect that seeks to control the everyday world of family, social, educational, economic, political, and ecological life.

We shall describe each of these Sub-personalities, the Ego, and More-Than-Individual aspects of the psyche (Spirit and Soul) here. We shall also provide an initial activity for how to nurture the first of the four categories of Sub-personalities. Activities for nurturing all the remaining Sub-personalities will be included later in this course. Activities for nurturing the four facets of the Self I call "Psychic Personalities," which have a more pronounced More-Than-Human aspect, will be included in the next Heartwood Path book—**Ecos**.

Each time I discuss the four facets of the Self or the four Sub-personalities I will described them as Plotkin does in his Nature Based Map of the Human Psyche (2013, pp. 22-23); that is, according to the cardinal directions—North, South, East, and West—and I will also be using my own Medicine Wheel of the Psyche of HumaNature (see the illustration that follows).

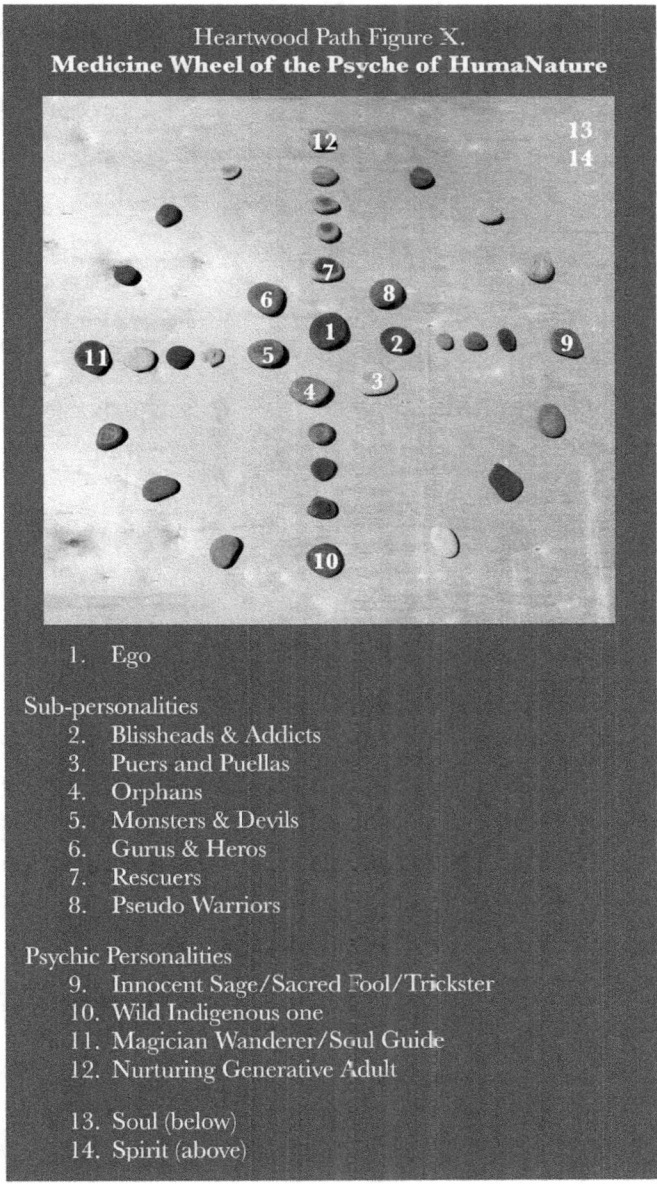

Heartwood Path Figure X.
Medicine Wheel of the Psyche of HumaNature

1. Ego

Sub-personalities
   2. Blissheads & Addicts
   3. Puers and Puellas
   4. Orphans
   5. Monsters & Devils
   6. Gurus & Heros
   7. Rescuers
   8. Pseudo Warriors

Psychic Personalities
   9. Innocent Sage/Sacred Fool/Trickster
   10. Wild Indigenous one
   11. Magician Wanderer/Soul Guide
   12. Nurturing Generative Adult

   13. Soul (below)
   14. Spirit (above)

In the Psyche of HumaNature illustration the Ego is represented by the Center Stone, the Sub-personalities are represented by the inner ring of stones, the three-stone lines represent what needs to be done to transition from reliance on immature personalities to mature Psychic Personalities (which are represented by the stones at the Cardinal

Directions of North, South, East, and West), and the three stones arcing between each Psychic Aspect represent the activities you can do with your mature inner world/outer world Psychic Personalities.

With all this advising and leading going on, some aspect of the mind has to be in charge, or at least attempt to be. That aspect will be addressed next.

The Ego

Number 1 on the Medicine Wheel of the Psyche of HumaNature is the aspect that typically wants to be in charge. Wanting to be in charge and doing a good job of it are two different things.

Before developing into a mature elder, one's Ego—one's seat of conscious self-awareness—is immature (undeveloped) and makes one understand oneself and act primarily as an agent for oneself. As a result, the More-Than-Individual-Self, the Soul, and Spirit, are not typically adequately experienced until later in life, if at all.

The Ego's all-too-common narrow view is why so many people seem to solely "look out for number one." With an immature Ego, there is very little sense of belonging to a human community or to an Earth community. One may talk of interdependence, but one does so mainly to look appropriate rather than to be appropriate. Despite its attempt to be an inner world despot, the Ego does not act alone.

The Sub-personalities

The all-too-common immature level of development, which in most people lasts well past the middle years, is a reason why humans give voice to substitutes for their more mature inner and outer world personalities (including inner world Archetypes and the Psychoid of the outer world). The maturity-resistant Ego and Plotkin's "Sub-personalities" may not give the best advice, but they do give us the advice we are capable of processing at our less-than-fully mature level of understanding. By basing our behaviors on the feelings and images given to us by our Sub-personalities we are protected from physical, psychological, and social injury. But, by listening too much to our Sub-personalities, one will contribute to the immaturity and pathology so evident in our mass culture.

This double-edged sword of dependence and protection comes from our early and lingering reliance on the following four categories of Sub-personalities, numbers 2-8 in the Medicine Wheel of the Psyche of HumaNature. With this summary, we shall now continue with a description of each type of Subpersonality.

Loyal Soldiers

Loyal Soldiers, which Plotkin places in the northern quadrant of the medicine wheel, act to keep us "safe by inciting us to act small . . . in order to secure a place of belonging in the world" (Plotkin, 2013, p. 19). In this category of Loyal Soldiers, we will focus on the Rescuers (# 7 on the Medicine Wheel graphic)—"who secure for us a safe place of belonging by prodding us into small social roles (including Caretakers, Enablers, and Codependents) that are useful to or enabling of others") and Pseudo Warriors (# 8 on the Medicine Wheel graphic), which appear to be successful, not in terms of being in service to the earth's unfolding (the goal of the Heartwood Path) but rather for the purpose of satisfying family pressures and for the purpose of meeting financial or social ambitions. As a result of these choices, often Loyal Soldiers induce us to suffer from emptiness and despair but they also manage to encourage us to avoid feeling guilty "for how (our) efforts plainly damage the world" (Plotkin, 2013, pp. 133-135). Ways to handle your Loyal Soldiers are presented in the next activity.

One of my dreaming time Loyal Soldiers appeared regularly to me in my youth. This dream image, usually an older peer, would prod me to work to overcome some wrong such as my dreams about a bulldozer flattening my forest playground. As the bulldozer approached one of my favorite trees I would grow in despair in my dream. The Pseudo Warrior, usually hiding behind another tree, would encourage me to somehow cause the bulldozer and its driver to drive off a cliff. This would cause me to celebrate and have no regard about the material damage or death of the driver. I had to tell this Loyal Soldier to go play in traffic when, later in life, I had to convince fellow dam fighters from destroying the equipment building the never-completed Meramec Dam. This strategy of remaining lawful gained much public support for our cause. The river continues to flow free.

Orphaned Wounded Children

Number 4 on this Medicine Wheel marks the spot for the Orphans. Note that these Sub-personalities—which may be conformists, victims, rebels, and princes and princesses—are located by Plotkin in the South quadrant of the wheel—the realm wherein the Sub-personalities help us to satisfy our needs through emotion-filled strategies, albeit immature ones.

If one is too much under the influence of the Orphans of the South, the common remedy—another immature one—is to pay more attention to the counterbalancing Sub-personalities; that is, the Loyal Soldiers of the North. Mentioning this shortsighted prescription does not mean, however, that one needs to run to the North each time one feels a tinge of emotion.

Be very wary when attempting to manage your emotions. "Emotionality is no more a sign of immaturity than steel-hearted imperturbability is a sign of maturity" writes Plotkin (2013, p 158).

> "Affective depression is, at root, the suppression of the South facet of the Self, the blockage of the wild, indigenous, emotive erotic, and fully embodied dimension of our human wholeness" (Plotkin, 2013, 160).

The recommended approach to excessive emotionality if one is immature (as most people at any age are) is to glean messages from the Loyal soldiers of the North. Seeking the wisdom from the opposite side of the Medicine Wheel will be a common approach throughout the next leg of the Heartwood Path. If you want better options and are mature enough to accept them, turn to the Psychic Personality of the South after you finish this book and begin the next part of the Heartwood Path.

And, if that doesn't do it for you, look to the mature Psychic Personality (the Wild Indigenous One) on the opposite side of the Medicine Wheel (in this case, The Nurturing Generative Adult).

Maturing is, in part, the process of recognizing, appreciating, and moving beyond all the immature Sub-personalities, which is why we are covering that topic in this book and leaving the deeper and wiser Psychic Personalities for the next course, when, if all goes well, you and the other participants will have an added measure of maturity and thus be prepared to consider whatever good direction is offered.

Included in the ranks of the Orphans are the fearful insiders, such as the Conformists; the fearful outsiders, the Victims; the angry outsiders, the Rebels; and the angry insiders, the Princes and Princesses. You may have experienced anyone or all of these when you were let down by a caregiver who was less than perfect in their caregiving. Being split off, or somehow tossed out of paradise, or suddenly separated and, therefore, needing to make independent decisions is how one tends to come face to face with one's inner world Orphan Wounded Children.

Each of these wounded, orphaned inner world "children" will provide you with a way to minimize your emotions, and thus protect you from them. This may be temporarily soothing, but it is extremely debilitating in the long run. Instead of moving away from your emotions (which could lead to depression), move more into them. Some assistance is provided in a later Activity, which is about overcoming one's preoccupation with the intellect (an example of how the opposite side of the medicine wheel—in this case the topic of the intellect—can be used to correct any imbalances—which, in this case, is the appropriate use of one's emotions). Later on, in the next book, the activity involving the Wild Indigenous One will be a huge help in this regard.

Personal Example:

How Curbing An Inner Wounded Child Helped To Stop A Nuclear
Power Plant

The one Orphaned Wounded Child that appeared most for me
before I told it to take a hike was the Rebel. This Dream Image,
usually in the form of an unruly teenage friend, would chide me for
not perpetually siding with the UnderDog. This Orphaned Wounded
Child Dream Image propelled me to march (in full counter-culture re-
galia) rebelliously against the Viet Nam war, to side vehemently with
minorities in discussions about environmental justice, and to play a
dirty trick or two on politicians, the Forest Service, the U.S. Army
Corps of Engineers, or other "authorities" hell bent on destroying some
place I loved. While I keep tabs on the whereabouts of this wandering
Loyal Soldier, and may use its advice again when pressed, I feel that
following its suggested methods blindly was—and is—not always the
mature response.

In 1976 I told this Wounded Child to take a short, not-too-
distanced, hike, and was, therefore, able to stand apart from my "hippi-
billy" friends, who wanted to oppose a proposed nuclear power plant
in Missouri by joining a multi-state effort to oppose nuclear power
due to safety concerns. I underwent considerable chiding and abuse
because I did not think that the safety issue, which I fully endorsed
personally, would win in the Sho-Me State. Eventually, I convinced
nuclear opponents all over the state to not take the rebellious, safety-
oriented approach to fighting nuclear power but to instead take a more
conservative means of stopping the power plant by making it illegal to
obtain a rate increase to build any utility facility before that facility was
on-line. I fully accepted that nuclear power plants were unsafe; but, because the voters all lived at the borders of Missouri and the power plant
was in the center of the state, I did not expect the voters—not known
to support causes that appeared radical or rebellious—to stop the plant
because of safety concerns. Had I followed the Rebel in my dreams

and virtually all of my environmentalist buddies, I would have been a follower instead of a leader. Of the dozen or so safety-oriented state referenda that year (1976), all failed at the polls. Unlike all of the other anti-nuclear referenda, the Missouri effort focused solely on making investors fund construction of any utility facility rather than raising construction-work-in progress funds from rate payers. Ours was the only ballot-measure that won, and by a land-slide. In retrospect, I am glad I had the gumption to tell my Rebellious Dream Character and long-haired allies (my own friends) to go march elsewhere. Taking the less rebellious approach made me look like I was "selling out," but it saved rate payers over a billion dollars and that nuke as never been built.

Addicts And Blissheads

While these images and feelings get us out of Dodge when the going gets rough, some of the methods of innerworld Addicts and Blissheads are dubious, at best. They often help us escape from reality through addition to food, shopping, impersonal sex, TV, gambling, work, drugs and drinking. The Addicts and Blissheads offer relief from pain and various doorways to ecstasy, but their positive effects are always temporary.

Some of their addictions, the ones that are very troubling to many of those who are following the Heartwood Path, are our culture's mad drives for technological progress at any cost, our individual penchants for over-consumption, and are our personal habits of discarding natural resources mindlessly. Such addictions cause us to live in a world of commodities rather the world of natural beings. We are consumers who are forgetting to be wholly human. Our addictions to economic progress makes us see the Gross National Product as the only measure of progress. Our Addicts and Escapists help us to value profits more than people, money over meaning, and nationalism over peace and justice.

When we become miserable following the addiction of "us over them," we turn to our Inner Blissheads in hopes of finding rapture and euphoria. Rather than true ecstasy, the Blissheads only offer restricted intimacy, inauthenticity, limited personal development, and a lack of participation in the world.

The adage that if we just think positively enough we will be fabulously wealthy, healthy and happy only works for those who are unconcerned about what such concentrations of goodies will have on other people and the planet. Such egocentric notions keep us immature and separated from our true emotions.

Whether our Sub-personalities are male Puers in the tradition of Peter Pan or female Puellas in the fashion of Tiger Lilly, our reliance on such inner world psychic aspects serves to protect us slightly from intolerable emotions and Ego-destroying perils. Despite these protections, rely on these immature Sub-personalities with caution. We cannot expect much more from these immature Sub-personalities than Spiritual Materialism and flights of fancy that keep us soaring away from any possibility of worthy spiritual practice. To escape the realities of our lives is to forsake our destinies. To be blurred by addictions keeps us from finding our fulfillment. Becoming too aerie-faerie keeps us from offering our greatest contributions to a world that presently needs much more from us than immature responses.

Personal Example:

How Curbing My Own Inner Blisshead Helped Me Find The Joy Of A Singular Relationship

My own inner world Blisshead would present herself to me alluringly in my dreams. Her own dream-time sexual availability made me feel, during the time of my life between my first love (1969-1973) and my marriage (1984-1997), that impersonal sexuality (more like serial, essentially always monogamous sexual relationships) was acceptable for a single man prior to the advent of HIV and AIDS. It was not until these epidemics that I had the personal wherewithal to tell my nighttime Siren that her adolescent advice was no longer sensible, fashionable, or safe. Putting plugs in my ears to her nighttime magnetic songs has enable me to, with two regrettable unplanned exceptions, be more enlivened by one good relationship (2000-present) than I was by adding up my conquests.

Fortunately, there are ways to deal effectively with our inner Addicts and Blissheads. In this regard, an activity at Waypoint 3.83, later in this book, will be most helpful.

The Shadow

The West side of the inner circle on the Medicine Wheel of the Psyche of HumaNature is home to an element of our psyches that is often unknown to us; namely, The Shadow. I do not include the Shadow as a psychic personality because it is more like a propensity not to be aware of aspects of oneself, including more that on psychic personality. The Shadow is a feeling, sometimes emerging as an inner world image of what we typically do not know about ourselves or, rarely what we do not like about ourselves. The Shadow is what is true about us that we do not know or admire. It is, therefore, a mostly hidden "personification" of mostly hidden or unwanted aspects of oneself. For this reason, the shame-producing Shadow is unmentioned and hides in the shadows of the representative sites on the above Medicine Wheel of the Psyche of HumaNature illustration. The "purpose of the Shadow is to protect us from enacting personal characteristics that, if expressed, might land us in big trouble with others or ourselves," writes Plotkin (2013, p. 208).

Personal Example:

How Curbing My Shadow Help Me Feel Like I Matter

Like all Shadows, mine shows up in my dreams and is always just out of sight whenever I try to boast about some accomplishment. Years ago, my Shadow, without me knowing it until I went to a clinical psychologist, made me feel, just under the radar of my own awareness, that I was a person who did not matter. I did not know that I was trying to overcome this subconscious sense of low self-worth (created, in part, by being separated from my own mother every weekend, beginning when I was six months old) by getting many degrees and by helping others to such an extent that, time after time, I hurt my own prosperity. It wasn't until I was called a "Mad Nurturer" by my therapist that the influence of my own Shadow was revealed. Now that I have been introduced to my Shadow I am able to let this inner world Sub-personality know that I do, after all, matter.

An exercise for how to properly deal with the aspect of yourself that is completely at odds with who you think you are is located at a waypoint later in this course.

To A Better Relationship With Your Immature Psyche...

HumaNatureConnect Activity

Start-up Protocol

If this is not a day when you prefer to spend time in nature without an agenda, do the Heartwood Path Start-up Protocol found in the Appendix.

Healing Your Relationship With Your Inner World Loyal Soldier

For this activity, begin the work of appropriately moving beyond the immature Sub-personalities, in this case, the Loyal Soldier (which, like all Sub-personalities, were helpful to you in your early stages of development but inevitably will hold you back from effective elderhood). With your attractive natural being by your side, evoke a sense of compassion by bringing fourth, to the best of your ability in this early section of the Heartwood Path, what you feel to be Spirit, Soul, Self, and Ego.

What is important here, as it will be often throughout the balance of the Heartwood Path, is to adopt a perspective that the ecological realm or the part of the universe that contains all sentient beings is primary while your own individuality is secondary. This will naturally evoke a greater sense of empathy and compassion for others, key elements in doing all of the Sub-personality Activities. From this vantage point, identify one of your Loyal Soldiers, a set of images and feelings, that you encountered in recent memory. Perhaps, for example, you were offered a new job and you decided not to take it because your Loyal Soldiers told you that taking the job will lead to embarrassment or disgrace. Name this Loyal Soldiers. Bring this Sub-personality vividly into your imagination. Thank this personality for keeping you safe by keeping you small. Out loud, tell your Loyal Soldier that you see how her survival strategy was helpful. Then offer your gratitude for how this advice kept you safe. Next, tell your Loyal Soldier that the War of Childhood Survival is about to end because soon you will have new strategies. Ask her to stay around in case she is needed during your ongoing pathway of personal development. Tell her that in the future you are going to evoke other inner and outer world resources. Tell her that you will soon be protecting yourself in a more effective way. Create a ceremony to honor your immature protector. Give her a full and honorable discharge. Ask her to remain vigilant, just in case.

Record in your journal what you did, how you felt, and what you learned. Continue on your pathway of growth. You will be doing another Sub-personality Activity soon.

Follow-up Protocol

For best results, write down your impressions of this activity in your journal using the Heartwood Path Follow-up Protocol found in the Appendix. Afterwards, consider sharing your interpretations with others.

Heartwood Path Axioms

Key Assertions From Waypoint 3.9

3.9.1.

Facts do not usually alter strongly held views, so focus most on having an impact on what people believe.

3.9.2.

When attempting to influence behavior and to encourage the imitation of behavior, the social status of the presenter is as important or more important to the audience than the facts presented.

3.9.3.

To influence the changing of another person's behavior, the activation of personal or social norms is more important than the presentation of information or pleas.

3.9.4.

Getting people to do the big thing (like attending an environmental meeting) is more likely if you first get them to do a small thing (like signing a petition) in part because people seek to maintain their public image by appearing consistent.

3.9.5.

Look over your detailed dream notes for emerging patterns, coincidences, synchronicities, odd characters or events, and

anything that may be used to put together, over time, some coherent guidance from a source much bigger than you know.

Nocturnal Pilgrimage 3.9

For best results, write down your impressions of each night's dreams in your journal using the Heartwood Path Dreaming Time Protocols found in the Appendix. Afterwards, consider sharing your Dream Tending with others.

Before starting another waypoint, keep sleeping, dreaming, and tending to your dreams—nighttime and daytime. Look over your dream journal for visitations of Indigenous Images. Make sure these images are natural and not imposed upon you by the media and advertisements. These Indigenous Images may not look anything like your chosen attractive beings. Tap into the World's Dream rather than your own dream alone. Remember that Dream Images shape shift. Look for signs and symbols that indicate that the Indigenous Images are the dreams of your chosen attractive natural beings, that they are unfamiliar natural beings, or that they are the world itself. Pay attention to the background scenery or the landscapes of the dreams, and not just the characters in the dreams. Keep detailed notes and look over them for emerging patterns, coincidences, synchronicities, odd characters or events, and anything that may be used to put together, over time, some coherent guidance from a source much bigger than you know.

After your Dream Tending and either before or after work, commune with nature as previously instructed and, in doing so, reduce any moroseness, irascibility, melancholy, or nervous excitability. After you feel that your immersion in nature has favorably improved your health, vigor, intellect, or level of happiness, in any small or large way, move to the next waypoint, "Inner Speech," and continue with the Heartwood Path course. Time in nature is a safe prescription for the ill-effects of one's screen-based, commodity-filled, narrowly-focused lifestyle. Persevere.

10

Inner Speech

LOWER YOUR AFFECT ON THE ENVIRONMENT BY TRACKING YOUR INTENTIONS

By looking at the Realm of Intention, one realizes that desires can be realized by focusing on positive inner speech. Holding on to the feeling that arises from the wish to be fulfilled and doing so despite all criticism or obstacles fulfills wishes. That really works. Here's what doesn't: focusing on what is missing in your life; complaining; limiting your thoughts and actions to what has always been rather than on what you intend to manifest; and using hate, anger, and condemnation rather than kindness and love.

To An Examination Of Your Eco-deliberateness...

HumaNatureConnect Activity

Start-up Protocol
If this is not a day when you prefer to spend time in nature without an agenda, do the Heartwood Path Start-up Protocol found in the Appendix.

Lowering Your Environmental Impact By Tracking Your Intentions

For this activity, track your intentions. Every action is preceded by an intention and every intention and action has a consequence in the environment, some more than others. You had an intention that caused you to pick the current natural being for this connection experience. Think about how you may need to change your direction, personality, and attitudes in ways that both make you happier and limit your impact on the environment. Use this activity to prepare the way to stretch towards a new way of being. Perhaps subconsciously or consciously you stretched towards your present chosen natural being because in some way it is a reflection of some intention you have or need to form. Often, one's intentions are hidden in the subconscious mind. To reveal these hidden gems, make a list of the attributes you like about your chosen natural being and then look over the list to see if there are patterns or correspondences in your list that suggest that you are intending (wanting) or need to intend (want) something that has previously been a low priority or beneath your awareness. In other words, since you may be picking the natural being because you subconsciously seek to emulate that being in some way, examine what it is about your chosen natural being that is lacking in yourself and what it is about your chosen natural being that you may like to develop in yourself. For example, if your chosen natural beings are blades of grass, leaves, water, or other flexible objects, you may be hiding from yourself your intention to be more changeable or lenient. The goal here is to look for attractive attributes that you share with your chosen natural being or you would like to have in common with your chosen being. Before and after you make your list of admired attributes think about aspects of your life and the life of the Greater Self that need to be repaired or changed. Highlight the attributes that will lower your environmental impact. All of your attributes will have some direct or indirect impact. In your journal, describe the relations between your attractive attributes and the nearby or chosen natural being or environment.

Follow-up Protocol

For best results, write down your impressions of this activity in your journal using the Heartwood Path Follow-up Protocol found in the Appendix. Afterwards, consider sharing your interpretations with others.

Heartwood Path Axioms

Key Assertions From Waypoint 3.10

3.10.1.

Desires can be realized by focusing on positive inner speech.

3.10.2.

To have your dreams fulfilled, hold on to the feeling that arises from your wish to be fulfilled and do so despite all criticism or obstacles.

3.10.3.

Focusing on what is missing in your life; complaining; limiting your thoughts to past actions rather than on what you intend to manifest; and using hate, anger, and condemnation rather than kindness and love, are sure ways to make sure your dreams are not fulfilled.

3.10.4.

Avoid condensing your nighttime dreams into only personal warnings or advice (dreams are far more than that).

Nocturnal Pilgrimage 3.10

For best results, write down your impressions of each night's dreams in your journal using the Heartwood Path Dreaming Time Protocols found in the Appendix. Afterwards, consider sharing your Dream Tending with others.

If you cannot interact with your presently occurring nighttime dreams or control them to some extent, then simply remember them by writing them down in your journal as soon as you wake up. During your recalling of your dreams you are day dreaming lucidly and can, therefore, more purposefully pull out more information about who is visiting and what intelligence is being brought forward. Do not condense your dreams into only personal warnings or advice. They are much bigger than that, and may have very little to do with your individual Self. Keep tending to your dreams. Without forcing it, eventually you will begin to develop guiding insights from your Dream Tending.

In between your dreams, feel free to visit previous or future Heartwood Path waypoints; but, unless you are strongly attracted to do otherwise, do your best to do all of the activities in order. Often the best lessons come in the most challenging activities.

After you do your Dream Tending in the morning, or after work tomorrow discover for your self the medicinal effect of communing with nature. Your time doing HumaNatureConnect activities or walking without an agenda in nature will provide a sort of tonic your brain can use to help you better cope with the ever-increasing complexities of your world. When ready, move to the next waypoint: "Added Vitality."

11

Added Vitality

RAISE YOUR ENERGY LEVEL

One needs to raise one's energy level so that one can become the light one seeks, the happiness one desires, or the change one needs. One raises one's energy level by being conscious of thoughts; by meditating; by eating mostly high-energy foods that are high in alkalinity, such as fruits, vegetables, and nuts; by refraining from alcohol and unnecessary drugs; by spending time outdoors; by listening to soothing music; by praying; by painting; by turning off the television; by maintaining self-respect; by making amends with adversaries; by showing gratitude; by viewing pleasing photographs or other works of art; by hanging out with positive people; by doing something kind for others without asking for anything in return; by affirming one's intentions; by forgiving; by listening to your heart rather than the opinions of others; and by placing a check on your Ego.

To More Energy...

HumaNatureConnect Activity

Start-up Protocol

If this is not a day when you prefer to spend time in nature without an agenda, do the Heartwood Path Start-up Protocol found in the Appendix.

Raising Your Energy Level

For this activity, raise your energy. To help with this activity, I refer you to a book by Jonny Bowden, PhD. C.N.S, entitled **The 150 Most Effective Ways to Boost Your Energy.** The following table, filled with ideas from Bowden's book, will help you plan out how to get more energy.

Ways To Boost Your Energy	Am I Boosting My Energy In These Ways And, If Not, What I Can Do To Put Each Idea Into Action, If At All
Eat protein at every meal for consistent energy.	
Eat the whole egg. Ordering egg white omelets and sandwiches rob you of the energy production capabilities of the yoke.	
Eat 40 percent carbohydrates, 30 percent protein, and 30 percent fat to stable and sustained energy.	
Eat low-glycemic-load foods such as apples, carrots, cashews, pears, and strawberries.	

Eat bee pollen, which is loaded with vitamins, minerals, enzymes, and amino acids.

Add more fiber to your diet to keep you regular.

Drink green drinks such as wheatgrass.

Eat the good fats in olive oil and egg yokes.

Cut out carbs from white sources such as white bread and sugar.

Do not add sugar or salt to your food. Learn what real food tastes like. Experiment with spices. Do not overdo fat-free foods (fat keeps you full longer). Read labels. Cut sugar cravings with a spoonful of powdered glutamine. Sweeten your food with lo-han (a Chinese fruit) or Xylitol.

Drink tea of any color.

Try the following energy boosters: Celery and almond butter, whey protein shakes, and hummus.

Drink Yerba Mate Tea which has caffeine and antioxidants.

Eat nuts.

Reboot your brain with a good breakfast.

Eat hot peppers, which have capsaicin and antioxidants.

Stop drinking diet soda. It raises blood pressure which drains energy. Many contain Aspartame which turns into formaldehyde in the body.

Stay hungry. It promotes energy.

Stay away from foods you are sensitive to and drain your energy. This means to eat more unprocessed foods, and depending on your sensitivities, possibly you may want to avoid sugar, soy, chocolate, citrus fruits, dairy products and wheat.

Stay away from energy drinks. They are loaded with sugar or Aspartame. Try purple fruit juices instead (not cocktails). Ingest less coffee than it takes to make you jittery or forces you to stay awake at night.

If you are going to eat grains, eat oatmeal, quinoa, and amaranth.

Eat more beans and lentils.

Put Maca in your smoothies.

Go to sleep an hour earlier.

Take a nap in the afternoon to increase performance.

Exercise early and often.

Clear your mind by writing down your worries and your To Do list and then put these notes away.

Enforce a prohibition on drinking alcohol excessively and before bed-time.

Stop smoking. Nicotine disrupts sleep.

Stay away from caffeine. It makes it hard to fall asleep.

Do not drink water before bedtime if doing so is disrupting your sleep.

Create a bedtime ritual.

Keep the bedroom off limits to work.

Do not sleep with the TV on.

Get up and do something if you cannot sleep.

Turn out lights and turn away the glowing alarm clock when you are trying to sleep. To help you wake up in the morning, try a dawn simulator that gradually turns up your lights.

Take inositol before bed.

Buy a better mattress and pillow.

Keep moving as much as possible during the day.

Do cross training mixed with running, walking, or biking.

Get some exercise daily.

Take Co-enzyme Q10, ENADA, D-Ribose, gingko, fish oil, a B-complex vitamin, probiotic-rich yogurt, and milk thistle with 80 % silymaran, and carnitine.

Drink a cleanse consisting of lemon juice, maple syrup, cayenne pepper mixed in heated water like tea.

Treat yourself to an infrared sauna which stimulates your pineal and pituitary glands and thus releases healthful hormones essential to your entire endocrine system. Additionally, it feels great, reduces stress, and thus increases your energy.

Detoxify your home by installing fans vented to the outdoors, lowering the humidity, cleaning drains, and maintaining dust-free floor and furniture.

Use home-made natural cleansers.

Breathe with your belly.

Practice Qi Gong.

Engage in aromatherapy.

Engage in ecotherapy outdoors, such as hiking in nature.

Listen to good energy-stimulating music. You will know it when you hear it.

Practice Yoga.

Check out Emotional Freedom Technique for emotional energy.

Get a massage, perhaps with reflexology.

Dance.

Take a day off.

Try acupuncture.

See a chiropractor, not a quackto-practor.

Improve your posture.

Get your Thyroid checked, your Estrogen checked, and/or your Testosterone checked.

Get some Sun, at least ten minutes worth a day. Do not overdo it. And try light therapy.

Take Vitamin D supplements.

Finish all "incompletes," stay active, organize your work spaces, de-clutter, process mail daily, recycle all non-essentials.

Sit on an ergonomic chair.

Have a powerful conversation.

Make a promise and tell the truth.

Answer these questions: What did I accomplish today? Why is accomplishing these tasks important? What further progress is war-ranted? And what further steps are needed?

Acknowledge someone daily.

Forgive.

Volunteer.

Exercise with a partner.

Do something creative.

Shift your attention to something alive, a plant, or an animal.

Apply Feng Shui to your living and working spaces.

Release negative feelings.

Take a cool shower.

Make a gratitude list.

Make peace with your Inner Critic.

Dress up. Change the colors of your wardrobe.

Perform a random act of kindness.

Have more sex and tasty sex, eating or playing with almonds, avocados, celery, chili peppers, chocolate, oysters, figs, and nutmeg.

Work with a life coach.

Change a negative habit.

Write down your goals.

Be in the moment. Practice it.

Stay connected.

Compose your own last lecture.

Activate your Third Chakra—the power center.

Follow-up Protocol

For best results, write down your impressions of this activity in your journal using the Heartwood Path Follow-up Protocol found in the Appendix. Afterwards, consider sharing your interpretations with others.

Heartwood Path Axioms

Key Assertions From Waypoint 3.11

3.11.1.

One needs to raise one's energy level so that one can become the light one seeks, the happiness one desires, or the change one needs.

3.11.2.

There are lots of things you can do to raise your energy level, including: meditate; eat mostly fruits, vegetables, and nuts; refrain from alcohol and unnecessary drugs; and spend time outdoors.

3.11.3.

When recalling nighttime dreams, focus most on an image that right off seems to point toward a nature-centered, ecological origin.

Nocturnal Pilgrimage 3.11

For best results, write down your impressions of each night's dreams in your journal using the Heartwood Path Dreaming Time Protocols found in the Appendix. Afterwards, consider sharing your Dream Tending with others.

In your present dream, or in your recollections of your dreams recorded in your journal, look for Indigenous Images and use these images to determine what intelligence is coming forward. Indigenous dreams will feel profoundly resonant, feel essential, and point toward a nature-centered origin. Make a list of Indigenous Images in your dreams.

When you are through assessing how you boost your energy and after you have made a list of Indigenous Images, do not just sit in front of some electronic screen. Instead, live for at least a brief moment as an outdoor animal, immersed in nature without a plan or go into nature more purposefully as you engage in the outdoor activity at the next waypoint of this course: "Self Importance."

12

Self Importance

KEEP YOUR EGO IN CHECK

The grip of the Ego causes feelings of self-importance and feelings of being offended by someone or something. Since many, if not most, of the problems of humankind are caused by unchecked Egos, it is vitally important to learn how to stop identifying with ideas of self-importance and with that which offends. One can become motivated to do these things by realizing that the notion of self-importance and being offended weakens one's Self and leads to unwise vulnerability.

The Ego wants you to win but you have to learn that you are much more than your winnings. The Ego wants you to be right but it is much better to be happy than it is to be right. The Ego wants you to be superior but it is much better to grow than it is to outdo others. The Ego wants you to have more but, as St. Francis of Assisi reminds us, "it is in giving that we receive." The Ego wants you to identify with your achievements but you are much more than your accomplishments. The Ego wants you to have a good reputation but the making of a good reputation is not your job. Let others bestow upon you whatever reputation they see fit.

Be a host to the Absolute. Do not be a hostage to your Ego.

To keep your Ego in check, keep your inner dialogue focused on what you want for all sentient beings rather than what you do not have for yourself; cast out doubt; tell your Ego that your Higher, More-Than-Individual-Self is in charge; observe obstacles as opportunities to exercise your unyielding intent; and do not allow negative circumstances to make you a victim. See setbacks as ways to learn.

To The Restraint Of Excessive Self-importance...

HumaNatureConnect Activity

Start-up Protocol

If this is not a day when you prefer to spend time in nature without an agenda, do the Heartwood Path Start-up Protocol found in the Appendix.

Keeping Your Ego In Check

For this activity, make a shift from being controlled by your Ego to being guided by your Greater Self that includes your Individual Self, your chosen attractive natural being, and all of Creation—both the Inner World and the Outer World. We will here be following a modified version of Barbara Marx Hubbard's ten steps to the universal self, as inspired by her book **Emergence: The Shift from Ego to Essence (2001).**

Step One: In your journal describe any previous examples of inner guidance you have received. What did your inner guidance tell you? What did it feel like? Then ask your chosen attractive natural being to give you the inner guidance you need for some important situation you are facing right now. Sit quietly. Offer appreciation before you return home. Sleep. When you become awake again, write down whatever comes to mind without any editing. Just let the words flow.

Step Two. In your journal, describe your Inner Guide. This guide is in the Realm of Interiority. It is a source of wisdom in your Inner Sanctuary. It may feel like the voice of God, the voice of Nature, the Voice of the Absolute Spirit, the voice of NNIAAL. It guides you all the time, but more effectively if you listen to it. You can call it your "Inner Guide," your "Inner Beloved," or your "Essential Self." Describe any experiences you have had with your Inner Guide/Essential Self." Note how, if at all, you can determine how it is encouraging you to transform from a local self focused on separation.

Step Three. Feel your Essential Self, it will span from your inner world to your outer world. Love it. Ask it to speak through your chosen attractive natural being to you as feelings, sensations, or perceived words. Ask: "Dear Beloved: What do you have to say to me today?" Do not expect clear English, or any other words as a response. Take the sensations, process them in your dreams, and then write in freeform in your journal. The Inner Guide "wants" its inner voice to be "heard." Listen. Sleep. Record.

Step Four. Ask your Inner Guide, which will be, among other things, the bearer of intelligent wisdom from your chosen attractive natural being and an emissary of Nature and the Absolute Spirit: "What do I **not** want to have happening in my life any more?" Note how the sensations, after dreamful sleep, become words that convince you that your Individual Self, your localized personal self, can no longer do all that you need to do in the world. Turn your life over to the higher power— your Greater Self, an indivisible cove in the ocean that is the Absolute Spirit. Your Greater Self is simply the Absolute Spirit, all of creation, and the enduring yet misconceived notion of the individual that has your name. This Greater Self is connected incorruptibly to The Source. Take a moral inventory and remove the veil of illusion that confuses you into thinking that you are separate from The Source, independent of Nature, or in any way (other than in our misconceived perceptions) self-arising and independent. You are interdependent: both individual and universal.

Step Five. Feel the bliss of union. Lift yourself up to see beyond your Individual Self. Note in your journal what this union feels like. Describe the Ecstasy. Write a poem of love as the Greater Self. Note any internal messages coming through your chosen attractive natural being, which is one outer world manifestation of your Inner Guide.

Step Six. Speak as your Inner Guide. Say, for example: "I am love." "I am wisdom." "I am courage." "I am patience." "I am surrender." "I am the Beloved." Offer the wisdom of your Inner Guide to others, once you have learned to give it to yourself.

Step Seven. Identify when your ego-controlled Individual Self causes you pain. Ask your Ego to speak of the nature of your problem. Give compassion to your Ego/Individual Self. This offering is good training for being an aspect of the Greater Self that leads.

Step Eight. Immediately after tending to last night's dreams, examine your thinking, looking particularly for separating or judgmental thoughts. Present whatever may be causing grief to your Individual Self to your More-Than-Individual-Self, your Universal Self—your self that Hubbard calls your "Essential Self" or your "Beloved Self." Mix in what we shall call the "Inner World Kettle of Emergence" the concerns of the Ego-dominated Individual Self with the perspective of the More-Than-Individual-Self. Consciously infuse separating feelings into the perspective of the Essential Self trading grief, agitation, anger, the urgency of time and other separating feelings with awe, love, joy, safety, beauty, and the ever-present Now. In so doing, you are becoming both fully human and fully divine. In this fusing, there is no destruction of the Individual Self. Instead, the individual self is like a devotee working in service of the Beloved More-Than-Individual-Self. Use the individual self to find what needs to be corrected in the parts of your life. Let your Beloved Self speak about solutions for you as a being embedded in the world as a More-Than-Individual, Essential, Sacred, Universal Self. The former are messages from the Ego, the latter are messages from the Beloved Self. Fill out your own Personal Record of Individual Problem statements and Messages from the Beloved in the Progress Chart below. In filling out this chart, do not expect rapid solutions. Sometimes it takes numerous messages before adequate solutions to problems emerge. Remember, the Individual Self is the Merely Human Self. Lastly, remember that what Hubbard calls the "Beloved Self" is the same thing as what we have been calling the "More-Than-Individual-Self," the "Greater Self," or the "Ecological Self."

Messages About Problems As Identified By The Ego-driven Individual Self	Messages About Solutions As Presented By The Divinely-driven Beloved Self

Step Nine. "As we shift our attention and identity to the Essential Self and experience the world outside from this inner vantage point, the outer action seems miraculously to re-pattern itself to a higher order, one that is more resonant with our inner values" (Hubbard, 2001, p. 121). Remove worries about getting things done. Instead, flow in your work. Write a description of what is being deferred or eliminated in your life. Express fully your desires for higher consciousness and greater freedom. Realize that you are your own force of creation.

Describe incidents in your life that illustrate the points mentioned in this waypoint.

Step Ten. Write in your journal the fruits of being guided, no longer primarily by your Ego, but by your Inner Guide, your Essential Self that is indivisible from the Greater Self, Nature, the Absolute Spirit, and the Source. Write down how these fruits can serve yourself **AND** others.

Follow-up Protocol

For best results, write down your impressions of this activity in your journal using the Heartwood Path Follow-up Protocol found in the Appendix. Afterwards, consider sharing your interpretations with others.

Heartwood Path Axioms

Key Assertions From Waypoint 3.12

3.12.1.

Since most of the problems of humankind are caused by unchecked Egos, it is vitally important to learn how to stop identifying with ideas of self-importance and with that which offends.

3.12.2.

Do not be a hostage of your Ego.

3.12.3.

The Ego wants you to win but you have to learn that you are much more than your winnings.

3.12.4.

The Ego wants you to be right but it is much better to be happy than it is to be right.

3.12.5.

The Ego wants you to have more but, as St. Francis of Assisi reminds us, "it is in giving that we receive."

Nocturnal Pilgrimage 3.12

For best results, write down your impressions of each night's dreams in your journal using the Heartwood Path Dreaming Time Protocols found in the Appendix. Afterwards, consider sharing your Dream Tending with others.

Look over the list of six or so Indigenous Images you made in your journal during the activity in Waypoint 3.7. Write some more about each image, providing as much detail as possible. Let the image reveal its unique qualities. Stay in the present. Make no associations. Stay away from meaning-making. Go with the image to its own depth. As you do so, pay attention to what is happening to you. Are you being connected through the image or the broader setting of the dream? What in the dream feels most natural? Wait for cognitive, intuitive, or somatic moments of surprise or remembrance. Write down what you believe to be the organic relationship between the dreamscapes and the Dream Characters.

Sometime during that portion of your day after Dream Tending, spend some time outdoors viewing scenes of nature. Doing so will create within you higher alpha wave amplitudes, which, like many prescribed drugs, increase the production of serotonin, which, in turn, increases nerve cell production and one's happiness (Selhub & Logan, 2012, p. 15). With more of this happiness chemical in your system, begin your next day's waypoint. Move to the next waypoint, "Exchange," take another step towards Gladandgreen Junction.

13

Exchange

GIVE OUT TO THE WORLD WHAT YOU SEEK TO ATTRACT TO YOURSELF

All of these inner world ponderings and suggestions are vital to the quest of eartHearts to improve the outer world environment and spread happiness. It is impossible to separate our selves from the universe except in our Ego-diminished thoughts. We live in an interconnected universe. All the improvements we make in our private inner worlds improve the outer world for everyone. So be the change you seek, heal yourself so you can heal others, and give forth what you seek to attract. You cannot attract fellow sojourners that are confident, generous, nonjudgmental, and kind while you are non-confident, selfish, judgmental, and mean.

One needs to raise one's energy to be more in line with the higher energy of the Source of humaNature. One person operating at a higher level of energy counterbalances many people operating at lower levels. I do not suggest that these higher-level people ought to draw attention to themselves because of their "specialness," nor are the leaders of the Heartwood Path looking to attract those willing to spend themselves for the cause of protecting humaNature. When we recruit eartHearts, we are not looking for immature people willing to die or harm themselves for a cause. We do, however, seek to help mature people live humbly for a cause while still taking time to perceive inner and outer beauty. We are not looking for so-called "free-riders"—a term explained the next in activity.

To Determine If You Are An Altruist, A Follower, Or A Free-rider...

HumaNatureConnect Activity

Start-up Protocol

If this is not a day when you prefer to spend time in nature without an agenda, do the Heartwood Path Start-up Protocol found in the Appendix.

Determining How You Arrive At Happiness

For this activity, determine if your happiness comes from altruism, from being a follower, or from being a so-called "free rider." We need to work to move many more people into the altruism camp. "And time is of the essence: to avoid crossing critical thresholds of environmental change, a transition toward a more sustainable mode of development . . . (will have to) be carried out between now and 2050," writes earth scientist Eric Lambin. For this shift to happen, most people will have to become altruistic.

Anyone who knows me well will tell you that I am a "free-rider" when it comes to popcorn and snow cone consumption, being perfectly content to eat more than a fair share of the fare at the fair no matter how unfair it is that I do not grow the corn or freeze the ice myself. I am a conditioned follower when it comes to prison rights. As evidence, I say prisoners ought to be treated fairly but do nothing when I hear they are not. When it comes to environmental rights, since I choose to eat grains rather than cows, since I choose to buy locally grown rather than foods from exotic places, and since I choose foods packaged to reduce environmental costs rather than foods packaged to sell more in the markets, you could say I'm an altruist. I'd tell you more about my altruism but I'm too selfish. I will say this: I know I don't have sun syndrome (the notion that everything under the sun revolves around me). And I'm not like a urologist who only thinks about number one. When it comes to sharing my movie popcorn, however, I guess I'm a little like a shrimp—a little shellfish.

Which do you consider yourself:

1. An altruist who is ready to change your "mode of consumption for ethical reasons and for the principle of responsibility vis a vis nature and future generations."
2. A follower or conditioned cooperator who will "follow the movement established by the majority and by opinion makers."
3. A free-rider who uses "up more than their fair share of resources and assumes less than their share of the associated costs. (Lambin, 2012, pp. 3-5).

Follow-up Protocol

For best results, write down your impressions of this activity in your journal using the Heartwood Path Follow-up Protocol found in the Appendix. Afterwards, consider sharing your interpretations with others.

Heartwood Path Axioms

Key Assertions From Waypoint 3.13

3.13.1.

We live in an interconnected universe wherein all the improvements we make in our private inner worlds improve the outer world for everyone.

3.13.2.

Be the change you seek, heal yourself so you can heal others, and give forth what you seek to attract.

3.13.3.

You cannot attract fellow sojourners that are confident, generous, nonjudgmental, and kind while you are non-confident, selfish, judgmental, and mean.

3.13.4.

One person operating at a higher level of energy counterbalances many people operating at lower levels.

3.13.5.

You are charged with not only interpreting the World's Dreams but also to take action on behalf of the World's Dreams.

Nocturnal Pilgrimage 3.13

For best results, write down your impressions of each night's dreams in your journal using the Heartwood Path Dreaming Time Protocols found in the Appendix. Afterwards, consider sharing your Dream Tending with others.

With this waypoint in mind, sleep and dream. In the next dream tending activity, imagine that the Dream Character or Dreamscape is a touchstone that connects you to your essential tendencies and instinctual wisdom. Determine if there is any way you will act differently now that you have connected to this image. How has, if at all, your tuning into the World Dream or your personal dream with Indigenous Images changed your relationship to the environment, to your community, to your dreams, and to yourself? Since one's own dreams can arise from the World's Dream, one can "perhaps glimpse what the world itself desires. Knowing this, we can then act in the world, on behalf of the world" (Aizenstat, 2009, p. 172). You will know you are witnessing the World's Dream when you ask "Who is visiting now?" and "What is going on here?" and when the answers come from creatures and inanimate beings. Now your job expands. You are charged with not only interpreting the World's Dreams but also with taking action on behalf of the World's Dreams. "When we directly confront what the World's Dream is telling us, we respond from the strength and resources found in our dreaming body-mind . . . (It) is imperative that we declare our responsibility to one another, as well as to the World's Dream that unites and informs us all" (Aizenstat, 2009, p. 176). Work to determine what your dreams are pushing you to do. As you witness or recall the dream, work to determine what restoration, acknowledgment, or action your Dream Characters seek. Also, in your journal, write down how the suffering in the world affects your mental and emotional health, if at all. Make a list of the things that you can do to respond to any of the calls to action embedded in your World Dreams.

After you are through with today's Dream Tending, look to your inner world and the outer world for signs that you are suffering from stress. At the slightest sign of anxiety, go outside and immerse yourself in nature. It will act as a sort of visual valium. But, unlike Valium pills, there will not be unwanted side-effects. Instead, you will experience a more positive mental outlook. Pretty nature pictures such as those found in nature documentaries or on the Heartwood Path website will have a similar effect, but to a lesser degree (Selhub & Logan, 2012, p. 16).

You are making great progress. When ready, move to the next waypoint, "Heady," to take the next step down the Heartwood Path.

14

Heady

OVERCOME THE PREOCCUPATION WITH THE INTELLECT

To really perceive the beauty of the outer world one needs serenity in the inner world. While some of this serenity comes from the mental realm inside one's mind, a bigger portion comes from the theological realm of the Spirit within one's inner world.

Determining the source of one's inner world serenity—that is, whether it comes from one's own personal thoughts or from sources that are ecological or spiritual—may be a mystery for you at this point. Some of the descriptions that follow—explanations about your inner world images and thoughts plus discussions of the Soul that spans both inner/outer and lower/higher realms of existence—will help you find appropriate and important sources of serenity.

Your Soul is your own cove in the ocean of the Spirit. To come to know the realm of the Soul, one needs to overcome the preoccupation with the intellect. Think of your Soul as a vast and unending experience. It enables the largest conversation you can have with the world.

Know that there is no distance between one's personality and one's Soul. Since the Soul has no way to manifest itself in the world, it needs the Ego to be made real. The "Ego is long on know-how and short on know-why; the opposite is true of the Soul" (Plotkin, 2013, p. 25).

Accept that the traditional scientific method could cause one to feel lost in an impersonal world. Feel that one's connection to the larger realities of life is rooted in a deep love that is permanent and not diminished by the temporary maladies of the physical world such as pain, fear, and frustration.

Know that it will be difficult, but not impossible, to determine the difference between thoughts and spiritual guidance. True guidance from the spiritual realm does not interfere with free will, nor does it express anything that is judgmental, critical, or selfish.

Such lower forms of expression are inspired instead by one's "Sub-personalities." Getting past such negative and immature forms of assistance—help that may come from the what may be an orphaned, wounded, immature, inner world Sub-personality—will help you find good a good source of serenity and overcome any preoccupation with the Intellect. This worthy endeavor is the topic of the next activity.

To Heal Your Inner World Immature Helpers...

HumaNatureConnect Activity

Start-up Protocol

If this is not a day when you prefer to spend time in nature without an agenda, do the Heartwood Path Start-up Protocol found in the Appendix.

Healing Your Relationship With Your Inner World Immature Helpers

On this activity, develop new strategies for dealing with emotions. Arenas in which you can practice to become more mature in your emotions include: discovering your genuine values and feelings, assessing your authentic social roles where your emotions are put to the test, learning ways to protect yourself from the immature criticisms and rejections of others, honing your negotiation skills, developing skills that are community building, and becoming more self-reliant. In all of these arenas, use the following four steps for moving deeper into your emotions, for legitimizing them, and for making yourself more comfortable with them, as identified by Bill Plotkin (2013, p. 170):

1. Identify the emotions of you or someone else's Wounded Children (are they angry, hurt, guilty, ashamed, sad, sacred, jealous, envious, hopeless?).
2. Determine what happened to elicit the emotion.
3. Mention how it makes total sense how the Wounded Children are feeling.
4. Determine what these emotions say about yourself or the other emotional party.

Write down in your journal what you learned about the emotion under consideration and what you learned by the emotional person and/or yourself. Continue your pathway to Gladandgreen Junction. The next Sub-personality Activity will be encountered at Waypoint 3.83).

Follow-up Protocol

For best results, write down your impressions of this activity in your journal using the Heartwood Path Follow-up Protocol found in the Appendix. Afterwards, consider sharing your interpretations with others.

Heartwood Path Axioms

Key Assertions From Waypoint 3.14

3.14.1.

Your Soul is your own cove in the ocean of the Spirit.

3.14.2.

To come to know the realm of the Soul, one needs to stop being preoccupied with the rational mind (stop relying too much on the intellect).

3.14.3.

Know that there is no distance between one's personality and one's vast and unending experience we call one's "Soul."

3.14.4.

True guidance from the spiritual realm does not interfere with free will, nor does it express anything that is judgmental, critical, selfish, or negative.

Nocturnal Pilgrimage 3.14

For best results, write down your impressions of each night's dreams in your journal using the Heartwood Path Dreaming Time Protocols found in the Appendix. Afterwards, consider sharing your Dream Tending with others.

Day and night, you are experiencing a slow conversion of yourself into a person with extraordinary integrity. Your spiritual maturity continues, waypoint-by-waypoint, dream-tending session-by dream-tending session.

Before jumping ahead to the next waypoint, look through your dream journal, which now has many dreams recorded, and pick out a dream with several Dream Characters. Draw a picture of the dream-scape from your dream, complete with the Dream Figures. Place this drawing in the Sun and notice how the Sun lights up your picture. Then take five steps back, experience the dream picture as part of the larger landscape that includes the things in the surrounding area, see how the sun lights both the images in the picture and everything in the landscape, notice how the images in the dream (picture) animate and begin to interact with the things in the landscape. Continue watching for some time. Notice how eventually there is no separation between the dream picture and the outside landscape. It has all becomes one Whole Worldscape. Repeat this same exercise at night but this time experience how at night, it is even more possible to experience the world's dreaming. By doing these little activities can you conjure up that all creation is the world dreaming itself into existence, moment by moment? Write down your impressions of this activity in your journal. With this and the previous waypoint in mind as you head off to sleep, dream and tend to your dreams.

After tending to your dreams, go into nature, commune with it as previously instructed, and notice how doing so lowers your heart rate and raises your creativity. When ready to continue, move to the next waypoint: "Trail Blazer."

15

Trail Blazer

CHART A PATH TO
INDIVIDUALITY AND ONENESS

Most humans have already chosen the road to instant gratification. While this highway of the Ego often eases short-term pain, what is gained in materialism is often lost in long-term suffering. We as a species need to blaze a new course that is based on the awareness of both individuality and oneness.

To become whole again requires one to break the hard shell of one's Ego and thus develop beyond one's lower nature to higher realms of consciousness. With wider perceptions and access to the higher realms of consciousness one can have better thoughts and, thus, a better life.

I know someone who perceives things almost solely from where she is right now and, from where she is at the moment, things are usually bad somehow. Things are unpleasant for her now because of a neglectful and abusive husband. It seems that she can only see a horizon where her life will get worse because of her reduced finances after her impending divorce. It is as if, metaphorically speaking, she can only see from her back porch, across her lawn, to the edge of the marsh, and the whole span is, for her, worrisome. She needs to look at life beyond the yard, beyond the present domestic situation. She needs to see in the marsh beyond the edge of the grass the serenity and safety she will experience after her separation; in the ocean beyond the edge of the marsh her new life living close to her grown children, where she will live after her divorce; and in the sky beyond the edge of the ocean her freedom and opportunities for fun, romance, and growth after the dust settles.

The author of **Sight and Sensibility: the Ecopsychology of Perception**, Laura Sewall, writes that the...

> "edge is where one thing becomes the next. The edge is also shared, although it seems to belong to the one thing more than the other, to the mountain more than the sky, the self more than the other. We tend to see the edge as the property of the figure we are attending to. But any edge also delineates the ground—the background, the negative space, or the unattended form. It marks what is on the other side of our attention, of our current reality, signifying that the world is more" (Sewall, 1999, p. 135).

Look from where you are to the edge, and beyond. Alter the way you perceive things and the things you perceive will be altered. The way to find higher realms of consciousness begins by surrendering your relatively "little mind" to the relatively "Big Mind" of Spirit. Then, determine how to use your innate and developed talents plus your desire to best serve others. Remain blissfully deaf to the reality-check repercussions that the Egos of others give to you as a way to keep you from wondering into the uncharted inner world terrain where greatness can be found. Remember that the Egos of your friends may not want to you get ahead of them in this way.

Ignore what others tell you about your purpose. Listen instead to your own heart. It and the universe always work on your behalf. Then, model the work of others who have known their purpose but also keep your own individuality. Be thankful for the opportunity to live purposefully. Live happily on purpose. Living this way requires that you write down your purpose, that you be the peace you seek, that from time to time you start over without regrets, and that you practice for-giveness. Experience what you intend before it shows up in the Realm of Exteriority. In a prayer-like message to yourself, say: "I am spiritu-ally developed." If you are not where you want to be in your spiritual development, say it is so as if it were so. You are not lying. You are re-orienting your perspective. Doing so often casts away anxiety, despair, depression, and stress. It also clears the way to find connection to your Source. To boost the positive results of these prayer-like messages, find silence (it is the Voice of The Absolute Spirit), meditate, and pray. Live in a state of appreciation. Uplift others. Focus more on being inspired and inspiring than on being informed and informing. Know that you are a success, do not hoard or become attached to what comes to you materially in life, and further your practice of forgiveness by doing the following activity:

To A Raid On Defeatism...

HumaNatureConnect Activity

Start-up Protocol

If this is not a day when you prefer to spend time in nature with-out an agenda, do the Heartwood Path Start-up Protocol found in the Appendix.

Coping By Dispelling Pessimistic Thoughts

For this activity, assume the essence of your chosen natural being, and, as it, remind yourself of a time when you were forgiven. Re-member how the forgiveness was communicated to you. How did the forgiveness feel? What was your response? How, if at all, did forgiv-ing someone else be being forgiven by someone else dispel pessimistic thoughts?

Follow-up Protocol

For best results, write down your impressions of this activity in your journal using the Heartwood Path Follow-up Protocol found in the Appendix. Afterwards, consider sharing your interpretations with others.

Heartwood Path Axioms

Key Assertions From Waypoint 3.15

3.15.1.

What is gained in materialism is lost in long-term suffering.

3.15.2.

Look from where you are to the edge, and beyond.

3.15.3.

Focus more on being inspired and inspiring than on being informed and informing.

3.15.4.

Rather than listening to what others tell you about your purpose, listen instead to your own heart.

3.15.5.

Model the work of others who have known their purpose but also keep your own individuality.

Nocturnal Pilgrimage 3.15

For best results, write down your impressions of each night's dreams in your journal using the Heartwood Path Dreaming Time Protocols found in the Appendix. Afterwards, consider sharing your Dream Tending with others.

One cannot expect much from affirmations if they consist of words without much feeling. Feel your desires earnestly and they will come true. For practice, use both present tense words and strong feelings as you intend to have a lucid dream. At the moment you realize that you are awake in your dream, catalogue your elevated feelings right at the "A-Ha" moment. Resolve to repeat such wonderful feelings by living a life full of frequent realizations, both day and night. Let the realizations bring you the feelings and let the prospects of having the feelings encourage you to set up opportunities for the realizations.

When you are done with today's Dream Tending you are encouraged to refresh yourself in nature. Any natural landscape will do. Forests, for example, have a tranquilizing influence on the mind, especially when the mind is worn down by mental efforts. If you like, use your time in a forest to re-enforce your individuality by shedding pessimistic thoughts (which lead to feelings of separation) and by paying more attention to your feelings (which, when done honestly, leads to greater bonding).

When ready, continue your pilgrimage down the Heartwood Path by moving to the next waypoint: "Contentment." There, you will learn how to heighten your satisfaction by doing good deeds for others.

16

Contentment

FIND YOUR DEEP SATISFACTION

You are a success, you feel good, and you are spiritually developed not because the world is right. The world is right because you feel good, you are a success, and you are spiritually developed.

Environmentalists and other social activists find satisfaction for themselves by doing good works for others. EartHearts, conversely, do good works for others by finding satisfaction for themselves.

Like all of creation, one has a natural destiny to evolve to higher stages of development. To reach these stages one needs to overcome one's Ego. For this transformation to occur, one needs to learn how to live in the moment, surrender to the belief in an unseen natural order and higher power; and balance Ego/man/technology with Soul/God/Nature.

To Determine Your Source Of Motivation...

HumaNatureConnect Activity

Start-up Protocol

If this is not a day when you prefer to spend time in nature without an agenda, do the Heartwood Path Start-up Protocol found in the Appendix.

Determining What Motivates You

For this activity, determine if:

1. You seek to ensure your happiness by reducing your impact on the environment. For a person to fall into this community, one has to establish a strong relationship between the environment and the individual's well-being: to become happier, one (has to) protect the environment (Lambin, 2012, p. 7).
2. You are motivated by fear. This classification will not be a good basis to determine the future stance of environmental campaigns. "The rhetoric of fear, which warns of a collapse of our civilization unless we abandon our current way of life, engenders denial among skeptics, cynicism among nihilists, despair among pessimists, and rejection by optimists" (Lambin, 2012, p. 7).
3. You are motivated by seeking environmental protection for the purpose of protecting nature—a source of happiness for you. If "a less degraded natural environment will make us happier, we would then enter into a virtuous, mutually reinforcing cycle of conservation of nature and an increase in personal happiness" (Lambin, 2012, p. 7).

Which statement from above—1, 2, or 3—most reflects what motivates you to happiness?

Follow-up Protocol

For best results, write down your impressions of this activity in your journal using the Heartwood Path Follow-up Protocol found in

the Appendix. Afterwards, consider sharing your interpretations with others.

Heartwood Path Axioms

Key Assertions From Waypoint 3.16

3.16.1.

The world is right because you feel good, you are a success, and you are spiritually developed.

3.16.2.

Environmentalists and other social activists find satisfaction for themselves by doing good works for others.

3.16.3.

EartHearts do good works for others by finding satisfaction for themselves.

3.16.4.

To evolve to higher stages of development one needs to learn how to live in the moment, surrender to the belief in an unseen natural order and higher power, and balance Ego/man/technology with Soul/God/Nature.

Nocturnal Pilgrimage 3.16

For best results, write down your impressions of each night's dreams in your journal using the Heartwood Path Dreaming Time

Protocols found in the Appendix. Afterwards, consider sharing your Dream Tending with others.

You already know that each time you incubate a certain dream with your intention you need to use present-tense affirmations, apply strong feelings, visualize what you want clearly, and convert weak hope into strong expectation. As you lie down to incubate a dream tonight, add one more element to your normal process of making your dreams come true. That element is dominance of thought right before falling asleep. Your thoughts, expectations, feelings, and visualizations need to be solely about the object of your desire; which in our present case, is to have a lucid dream that brings you into the nocturnal presence of Dream Characters that are Indigenous Images or the image of familiar attractive Natural Beings. If there is a certain Dream Character you want to summon into your lucid dream, make this desire your dominant thought immediately before falling asleep. Let any other competing thoughts pass. Concentrate on your singular intention up to the point of falling asleep and your desire will produce exactly what you want in your dream. Once the desire is in your lucid dream, you can make modifications, seek advice, plotting strategies, and do what it takes to set the stage for the manifestation of your desires.

When many of these desires are about developing yourself so that you can better help others, your happiness will become abundant, abiding, and authentic. This Triple-A happiness will occur in a stronger and faster way if the "other" that you are helping includes, not just people like you, not just people you serve professionally, and not just your family, but also all other sentient beings.

Persevere in your Dream Tending. There are vast riches in your dreams that will be most helpful in your life. After tending to your most recent dreams, go to a forest to make yourself available for a possible transcendent experience; that is, an unforgettable moment of extraordinary happiness and attunement to aspects of the Greater Self that are typically considered outside of the Individual Self. When your moment of focus is centered beyond your own individuality, and it feels very important, you are likely having a transcendent experience. These are peak experiences that propel you towards greater depth of character. Foster them and welcome them. They are a chief benefit of the kinds of outdoor experiences encouraged as you proceed through this course of learning. When ready, recommence your daytime advance down the Heartwood Path by moving to the next waypoint: "Inventiveness Bands."

17

Inventiveness Bands

GO THROUGH THE STAGES OF INNER CREATIVITY

To effectively work towards environmental sustainability by working on one's self—the premise of the Heartwood Path—one will have to undergo some inner world developmental stages so that one will have the requisite creativity. In going through these stages one may become impatient and quite doing the necessary inner work because one may not realize that the results come in stages. Knowing the order of these stages, however, will help one continue to the necessary level of development. To reach GladandGreen Junction, where your deep happiness meets the deep need for environmental sustainability be sure to transcend from the domination of the Ego to the freedom of the Spirit. This wonderful leap in your inner world development will not really occur until you reach the third stage, as described below.

In one's efforts to shift from Ego to Spirit one will go through four stages for the development of inner creativity:

1. a period of learning, Ego-development, and spiritual initiation;
2. a period of identifying with the Ego and enjoying the bittersweet fruits of the world;

3. a period of looking inward and cultivating the awakening of the extended self-identity beyond Ego; and

4. a period leading to a transcendence of all duality and all the various drives (often referred to as the period of "liberation").

Of all these stages, the third developmental stage is most critical to the success of eartHearts.

You can notice when you are achieving the necessary level of development when you begin to see the unfolding of the various attributes associated with cultivating and awakening your extended self beyond the Ego. This awakening, which is required for passage to our destination of deep gladness and sustainability, unfolds the third developmental stage as four successive bands. Knowing where you are in your inner world development helps you look for and recognize the next level. Nothing breeds success like success. Once you have achieved the next level of development, you will likely become motivated to move to yet another higher level. Here's how you can recognize the various bands of the Third Stage in your inner world advance into creativity:

1. In the psychic/mystical band you will likely still be too motivated by personal desires to shift decisively to truly expanded identity but you will most likely have non-local psychic and mystical experiences that enlarge their vision of the world and their role in it.

2. In the transpersonal band "otherness" is discovered and the joys of discovery and service begin to enhance motivation. This may be as far up the developmental "ladder" as you choose to go, which is fine. You can become a non-secular saint at this level.

3. In the spiritual band, which few people have been known to achieve, life is lived in an ease-without-effort way, themes of the collected unconsciousness are explored extensively, and actions are appropriate to events. At this stage, you are likely to become an exceptional non-secular saint.

4. In the Atman band, cosmic consciousness is achieved—separateness vanishes as the subject, self, and consciousness become one. Getting this far makes you a sage, an extraordinary accomplishment. The Atman band is not required to reach Gladandgreen Junction.

To Happiness...

HumaNatureConnect Activity

Start-up Protocol

If this is not a day when you prefer to spend time in nature without an agenda, do the Heartwood Path Start-up Protocol found in the Appendix.

Understanding And Ranking Your Sources Of Happiness

Learn about and rank your sources of happiness. In his book, **An Ecology of Happiness**, Eric Lambin presents the five sources of happiness. After reviewing these sources, give a ranking (on a zero to one hundred scale) of where you think your happiness comes from. The total of all of these numbers ought to equal 100. It will be interesting to see if, after you finish this course, the amount of happiness you get from each of these sources changes.

1. Personal situation: health, affective life, leisure, work, mobility. Rank_____.
2. A feeling of security: the fear of criminality, conflicts, wars. Rank_____.

3. The social environment: belonging to a network of relation-ships, feeling of confidence, availability of help in case of need. Rank_____.
4. The institutional environment: freedom, political involvement, the proper functioning of the judicial system. Rank_____.
5. The natural environment: exposure to noise and air pollution, access to preserved natural spaces, the feeling of being connected to nature (Lambin, 2012, p. 8). Rank_____.

Follow-up Protocol

For best results, write down your impressions of this activity in your journal using the Heartwood Path Follow-up Protocol found in the Appendix. Afterwards, consider sharing your interpretations with others.

Heartwood Path Axioms

Key Assertions From Waypoint 3.17

3.17.1.

In one's efforts to shift from Ego to Spirit one will go through four stages for the development of inner creativity: 1) a period of learning, Ego-development, and spiritual initiation; 2) a period of identifying with the Ego and enjoying the bittersweet fruits of the world; 3) a period of looking inward and cultivating the awakening of the extended self-identity beyond Ego; and 4) a period leading to a transcendence of all duality and all the various drives (often referred to as the period of "liberation").

3.17.2.

Of all these stages, the period of looking inward and cultivating the awakening of the extended self-identity beyond Ego is most critical to the success of eartHearts.

3.17.3.

The period of looking inward and cultivating the awakening of the extended self-identity beyond Ego unfolds in four successive bands but only the first two are typically achieved by eartHearts: 1) in the psychic/mystical band people are still too motivated by personal desires to shift decisively to truly expanded identity but they do have non-local psychic and mystical experiences that enlarge their vision of the world and their role in it; 2) in the transpersonal band, "otherness" is discovered and the joys of discovery and service begin to enhance motivation.

Nocturnal Pilgrimage 3.17

For best results, write down your impressions of each night's dreams in your journal using the Heartwood Path Dreaming Time Protocols found in the Appendix. Afterwards, consider sharing your Dream Tending with others.

Stephen Aizenstat, Ph.D reports that "maintaining a healthy relationship with our dream life (is) integral to physical health" (2009, p. 189). Later we will demonstrate how to use dreams for healing. For now, however, keep practicing tending to your dreams as previously described.

After dream tending, or before you go to sleep, practice what is called "Shinrin-yoku." This practice, started in Japan, involves a sort of bathing, showering, or basking in a forest. Whether you today prefer to wander agenda-free in a forest or go there to conduct the next HumaNatureConnectActivity, Shinrin-yoku will be both helpful and healthful. Shinrin-yoku involves much more than a simple walk through the woods. Shinrin-yoku practitioners use all of their senses to take in the forest atmosphere. Beginning now, when you go to a forest (or any natural landscape), bathe your mind and body in the greenery. Doing so will lower your level of the toxic stress hormone cortisol (Selhub & Logan, 2012, pp. 18-19).

When you are ready, continue your sojourn, and do so knowing that you are also making progress during the nighttime as you sleep and dream. Move to the next waypoint, "Imagination Prompts," to continue your spiritual advancement on the road to Gladandgreen Junction.

18

Imagination Prompts

EMPLOY CREATIVITY-PRODUCING BEHAVIORS

While all the above stages of inner development affect one's creativity, it is not necessary to reach advanced stages of inner development to demonstrate some form of creativity. To increase creativity, certain creativity-producing behaviors can be employed at any level of inner development. These behaviors include: altering, arranging, designing, combining, paraphrasing, generalizing, modifying, questioning, rearranging, reconstructing, regrouping, renaming, restating, reordering, revising, rewriting, varying, valuing, simplifying, and synthesizing. Many times people open themselves to the possibilities of greatness merely by adopting such creative behaviors or by forcing themselves to think in ways that are not part of their normal mental habits.

Before one can preserve anything in the external world, one needs to preserve and enhance access to the freedom and creativity one finds in the inner world. One needs to be able to look at existence not only as an "it," but also as a "we." This can be done both by going through the stages of inner creativity (as described in the previous section) or by doing some of the things listed in the previous paragraph.

To A Log Of Your Support For The Heartwood Path Premise…

HumaNatureConnect Activity

Start-up Protocol

If this is not a day when you prefer to spend time in nature with-out an agenda, do the Heartwood Path Start-up Protocol found in the Appendix.

Recording Your Impressions Regarding Statements That Reflect The Thesis Of The Heartwood Path Course

For this activity, record in your journal your impressions on the following quotes, both from Eric Lambin:

Humans "have an interest in preserving nature, because our happi-ness depends greatly on the natural environment" (2012, p. 9).

And

"Sheltered in our cities, secure in our cars on our paved roads or in our heated and air-conditioned houses, we are detached from what is at the heart of humanity: our biological roots, which plunge deep into the natural world; our psychic relationship with the diversity of life forms; an anchoring in the beautiful landscapes; and a fraternity with the animal world" (2012, p. 11).

Follow-up Protocol

For best results, write down your impressions of this activity in your journal using the Heartwood Path Follow-up Protocol found in

the Appendix. Afterwards, consider sharing your interpretations with others.

Heartwood Path Axioms

Key Assertions From Waypoint 3.18

3.18.1.

While all the stages of inner development affect one's creativity, it is not necessary to reach advanced stages of inner development to demonstrate some form of creativity.

3.18.2.

Creativity-expanding behaviors include: altering, arranging, designing, combining, paraphrasing, generalizing, modifying, questioning, rearranging, reconstructing, regrouping, renaming, restating, reordering, revising, rewriting, varying, valuing, simplifying, and synthesizing.

3.18.3.

Before one can preserve anything in the external world, one needs to preserve and enhance access to the freedom and creativity one finds in the inner world.

3.18.4.

One needs to be able to look at existence not only as an "it," but also as a "we."

3.18.5.

Humans seek to preserve nature because our happiness depends greatly on the natural environment, because we have a deep psychological relationship with the diversity of life forms, and because we seek to repair the spirit of fraternity we had with the natural world which was torn apart when we began to live our lives mostly indoors.

Nocturnal Pilgrimage 3.18

For best results, write down your impressions of each night's dreams in your journal using the Heartwood Path Dreaming Time Protocols found in the Appendix. Afterwards, consider sharing your Dream Tending with others.

One aspect of dreams seems to astonish even Dr. Aizenstat: "Dream Images have inherent healing properties" (2009, p. 189). Build up your medicine chest of dreams by continuing to make entries in your dream journal. How to use dreams to improve your health will be addressed subsequently.

For now, move to the next waypoint: "Bridge To Oneness." When the activity at the next waypoint instructs you to go outside to a natural being or a natural landscape, know that studies of 500 participants who engaged in the forest bathing of shinrin-yoku (conducted by Chiba University, Center for Environment, Health and Field Services) show that spending time in a forest setting reduces depressive symptoms, psychological stress, and hostility while at the same time improves sleep, vigor, and feelings of liveliness (Selhub & Logan, 2012, p. 19). Be sure to keep going to the next waypoint. It will carry you one step further towards happiness and health.

19

Bridge To Oneness

MERGE MENTALLY WITH THE EXTERNAL WORLD

The psychological action (force) helpful for this merger is transpersonal therapy, which combines the approaches of Western psychology (helping people integrate the Ego so they can better handle life's practical realities) with the approach of Eastern psychology (helping people find serenity, receive and express compassion, and experience oneness). Transpersonal therapy is accomplished usually in two stages:

First, clients learn to identify inner thoughts and feelings, develop Ego strength, raise self-esteem, and release negative patterns of self-invalidation—thus becoming more responsible for their lives.

Second, after "getting themselves together," clients confront questions about the meaning and purpose of existence. At this stage, clients engaged in transpersonal therapy often have built a psychological bridge between the Ego and the divine. This bridge allows them to have more capacity for compassion, love, and wisdom. The clients feel a sense of oneness with all of existence. It is the development of this sense, and using it for the good of others, that is the chief purpose of the Heartwood Path.

To Put the Architecture Of The Soul To Good Use...

HumaNatureConnect Activity

Start-up Protocol

If this is not a day when you prefer to spend time in nature without an agenda, do the Heartwood Path Start-up Protocol found in the Appendix.

Merging Mentally With The External World

For this activity, apply the various zones of one's psyche to the chore of merging mentally with the external world. In the table that follows are descriptions of the various zones of the human psyche. Next to each description (inspired by Albert J. Lachance's chapter "The Architecture of the Soul: Sacred Process Ecopsychology" in the book **The Greening of Faith: God, the Environment, and the Good Life,** edited by John E. Carrol, Paul Brockelman, and Mary Westfall) write down what you have done, what you are doing, and/or what you plan to do to employ each zone of the psyche during your journey down the Heartwood Path or, more generally, in your life. Be sure to describe how each level of cognitive functioning helps you to perceive increasingly the wholeness of Creation. List personal experiences, ideas, and plans regarding how each zone has been, is, or will be employed in the quest of fulfilling your goals as an eartHeart (person who helps others be happy and, thereby, improves the health of the planet).

The Architecture Of The Soul (Zones Of The Psyche)	Previous, Present, And/or Planned Uses Of Each Zone Of The Psyche In My Efforts To Become Happy, Make Others Happy, And Improve The Health Of The Planet
Consciousness–Cognition. The seat of thought. Moving in one's consciousness beyond the mental construct of the nation-state to species consciousness, continent-consciousness, and planet-consciousness.	
Consciousness–Affectivity. Feelings. Sensitivity to all life.	
Consciousness–Instinct. The possession of beliefs as the truth of one's experience. Spontaneous experiences of reality. Feeling the agony of the nonhuman world and responding to these feelings. Being emotionally motivated to get involved ecologically.	
Subconsciousness–Personal. Buried memories. Secret pleasures. Things that are too big to deal with. Migraines, addictions, neurotic symptoms, escapism, and half-remembered shames.	

Subconsciousness–Familial. Weeping about one's parents.

Subconsciousness–Cultural. The springing forth from holy books. Reinventing the human at the species level. Hearing the music of nature. Shamanism.

Preconsciousness–The Primal. Leaving the innocence of the Garden and allowing the world to heal.

Preconsciousness–Mammalian. The pain and madness of not knowing who we really are. Knowing that to destroy the earth is to destroy us.

Preconsciousness–Biogenetic. Concern for non-mammals. Making the link between us and the Earth, the Sun, and all life forms. Knowing that the destruction of the ecological fabric will make us go mad and then disappear.

Preconsciousness–Geogenetic. Knowing that life emerged from the wisdom of the Earth. Being one with the psyche of the universe. Losing any linkages is to diminish ourselves.

Preconsciousness–Cosmogenetic.
Immanence. Being embedded in
the cosmos. We are the Cosmos
thinking.

Preconsciousness–The Cosmogenetic. Transcendence. The
Source. A psychology that includes
the client, the therapist, family,
culture, animals, plants, Earth,
Cosmos, and the Absolute Spirit.
Adept at affective therapy. Adept
spiritually in at least one tradition
and respectful towards all others.
Being an environmental activist.
Helping to awaken the person to
her connection to the Source, to
truth, and to vitality.

Follow-up Protocol

For best results, write down your impressions of this activity in
your journal using the Heartwood Path Follow-up Protocol found in
the Appendix. Afterwards, consider sharing your interpretations with
others.

Heartwood Path Axioms

Key Assertions From Waypoint 3.19

3.19.1.

Transpersonal therapy helps one merge mentally with the external world.

3.19.2.

In transpersonal therapy clients first become more responsible for their lives and develop increased personal freedom and self-determination by learning to identify inner thoughts and feelings, develop Ego strength, raise self-esteem, and release negative patterns of self-invalidation; and then they get themselves together by confronting questions about the meaning and purpose of existence.

3.19.3.

Answering questions about the meaning and purpose of existence tends to blur the boundaries of the Ego, allowing clients to transcend the separate self and encounter the transpersonal Self.

3.19.4.

Through transpersonal therapy, clients build a psychological bridge between the Ego and the divine; increase their capacity for compassion, love and wisdom; and increase their sense of oneness with all of existence.

3.19.5.

It is the development of the sense of oneness and using it for the good of other people and the Earth that is the chief purpose of the Heartwood Path.

Nocturnal Pilgrimage 3.19

For best results, write down your impressions of each night's dreams in your journal using the Heartwood Path Dreaming Time Protocols found in the Appendix. Afterwards, consider sharing your Dream Tending with others.

Be thankful for the knowledge you have been given about becoming lucid in your dreams. If you have not had a lucid dream yet, perhaps you have not shown enough gratitude. Before your next attempt at lucid dreaming, give thanks for having a lucid dream in advance. Prior gratitude is a key that opens the door to lucid dreaming, just as it is a tool to use in other aspects of life.

After tending to dreams, you are ready to seek pleasure and happiness outdoors. Perhaps the following information will help you to decide where to go. Research has demonstrated that pleasure and happiness goes up as people visit forested areas and the bigger and denser the forest the better—up to a point. If the trees are too tightly packed, as they are in many of our younger, second-growth forests (those that sprang up after the massive clear-cutting at the turn of the last century), the "natural" landscape becomes foreboding. To minimize any sense of fear in a forest, seek out timberlands where the trees are spaced further apart (as they are in virgin forests) or go to forests with lots of natural openings.

To continue, move to the next waypoint: "Many Minds." You are on your way to the happiness and environmental sustainability that are the key features of Gladandgreen Junction.

20

Many Minds

**USE THE HEARTWOOD PATH
PRINCIPLES OF PERSONAL
DEVELOPMENT TO DEVELOP YOUR
MULTIPLE INTELLIGENCES**

One's intellect is not fixed at birth. Intelligence can be developed. A person's overall intelligence, however, cannot be measured accurately by a typical IQ test because such tests only measure a person's mathematical and verbal reasoning skills. We all have multiple intelligences: logical/mathematical; verbal/linguistic; spatial/mechanical; musical—music is sensual and spiritual nourishment; bodily/kinesthetic; interpersonal/social; and intrapersonal/self-knowledge. Work to develop each of them.

Sometimes I wonder if, by having so many ways of thinking, our multiple intelligences lead us to gather that odd and unneeded collection of stuff most of us deal with only when changing homes. I, for example once had a ton of books to occupy my linguistic mind, an ever-disappearing collection of tools for my mechanical mind, a huge collection of drums for my musical mind, and various balls, bats, canoes, and bikes for my bodily mind. I got rid of essentially all of my possessions in 2022. Did the results of my acquisitiveness really reflect my intelligence? Does my long-overdo purging show an emergence of proper thinking? Besides thinking about all your "priceless heirlooms" and assorted junk, engage in the follow activity to test your feelings about your possible planet-burdening tendency to over-acquire.

To An Accounting Of Your Feelings About Having Excess Stuff...

HumaNatureConnect Activity

Start-up Protocol

If this is not a day when you prefer to spend time in nature without an agenda, do the Heartwood Path Start-up Protocol found in the Appendix.

Recording Your Impressions About Materialism

For this activity, delve deep within regarding your own personal response to what Eric Lambin calls "the screen of material artifacts" (Lambin, 2012, p. 12).

" . . . beyond a threshold of basic material comfort, money does not buy happiness" (Lambin, 2012, p. 12).

"The relentless pursuit of an accumulation of material goods leaves very little time to devote oneself to that which truly creates happiness" (Lambin, 2012, p. 12).

In your journal record your impressions of these two quotes and describe what you think about the role of materialism in your quest for happiness?

Follow-up Protocol

For best results, write down your impressions of this activity in your journal using the Heartwood Path Follow-up Protocol found in the Appendix. Afterwards, consider sharing your interpretations with others.

Heartwood Path Axioms

Key Assertions From Waypoint 3.20

3.20.1.

One's intellect is not fixed at birth but can be developed.

3.20.2.

A person's overall intelligence cannot be measured accurately by a typical IQ test because such tests only measure a person's mathematical and verbal reasoning skills.

3.20.3.

Work to develop all of your multiple intelligences: logical/ mathematical; verbal/ linguistic; spatial /mechanical; musical —music is sensual and spiritual nourishment; bodily/ kines- thetic; interpersonal/social; and intrapersonal/ self- knowledge.

3.20.4.

Devote your intellect to more than acquiring things.

Nocturnal Pilgrimage 3.20

For best results, write down your impressions of each night's dreams in your journal using the Heartwood Path Dreaming Time Protocols found in the Appendix. Afterwards, consider sharing your Dream Tending with others.

Dreams "function as imaginal medicines that can be used in the treatment of physical disease symptoms . . . as an adjunct to regular medical treatment" (Aizenstat, 2009, p. 189). We will show you how to work with dreams in this way later. For now, stick with tending to your dreams everyday.

By beginning each HumaNatureConnect Activity with an immersion in nature, you are, day and night, both building up your medicine chest for healing and moving towards Triple-A Happiness. Compared with twenty minutes in an urban setting, twenty minutes of walking in a forest ...induces a greater state of relaxation. More specifically, those who bathe their senses in a forest for twenty minutes have reduced levels of hemoglobin in their pre-frontal cortexes. Hemoglobin goes up during the anticipation of a threat (stress) and after periods of intense mental and physical work. Decreased levels of hemoglobin indicates that the brain is taking a much needed and helpful rest while in a forest. We will later discuss how this timeout is valuable. We will present information that shows the restorative impact of nature on one's cognitive abilities.

When you are ready, move on to the next waypoint, "Perpetual Education." We are no where near the end of showing you the benefits of doing HumaNatureConnect Activities.

21

Perpetual Education

CULTIVATE INSATIABLE CURIOSITY AND CONTINUOUS, LIFELONG LEARNING

To do so, cultivate freedom of thought and expand your perspective by looking at things from a variety of unusual and extreme perspectives. Take time off for reflection. Keep a journal. Take time for observation. Read a lot. Learn from children. Remain open-minded. Learn a foreign language. Solicit feed back from others you admire. Make a list of one hundred questions that you deem significant. Start by listing ten such questions.

To The Elements Of Happiness And Economic Stability...

HumaNatureConnect Activity

Start-up Protocol

If this is not a day when you prefer to spend time in nature without an agenda, do the Heartwood Path Start-up Protocol found in the Appendix.

Pinpointing The Factors That Underlie Both A Happy Society And A Sustainable Economy

For this activity, write down your impressions of the each of the following three statements.

1. Two factors make up a happy society and a sustainable economy: 1) a good educational system and 2) values that are less focused on economic and physical security and more concerned the pursuit of the quality of life, (Lambin, 2012, p. 17).
2. A "profound relationship with natural things is a source of ... self-realization and of happiness . . . " (Lambin, 2012, p. 20).
3. There are "nine possible dimensions to the biophilic (life-loving) tendency of humans . . ." (Lambin, 2012, p. 21). These nine dimensions are:

   1. Utilitarian. "Nature is of material value to humans . . ."

   2. Naturalistic. "A simple, direct contact with nature in different forms (landscapes, animals, flowers . . .) leads to mental and physical satisfaction . . ."

   3. Ecological-Scientific. Nature is a source of learning.

   4. Aesthetic. Nature is full of attractive beings.

   5. Symbolic. "The diversity of nature suggest notions of category and differentiation, central to the structuring of language . . ."

   6. Humanistic. "The humanistic experience of the natural world is characterized by a strong effect on the individual elements of nature . . ."

7. Moralistic. In certain circumstances, people have moral responsibility, vis-a-vis nature.

8. Dominative. Humans dominate nature but recent history shows us that this mastery often degrades nature.

9. Negativistic. An over-reaction to dangers in the natural world often leads to the extermination of animal populations . . ." (Lambin, 2012, pp. 21-23).

Write in your journal your impressions of the first two statements plus the previously listed nine dimensions and your reactions to them.

Follow-up Protocol

For best results, write down your impressions of this activity in your journal using the Heartwood Path Follow-up Protocol found in the Appendix. Afterwards, consider sharing your interpretations with others.

Heartwood Path Axioms

Key Assertions From Waypoint 3.21

3.21.1.

Cultivate freedom of thought and expand your perspective by looking at things from a variety of unusual and extreme perspectives and by reading a lot.

3.21.2.

Take time off, solicit feed back from others you admire and keep a journal of your impressions.

3.21.3.

Make a list of one hundred questions that you deem significant, none of which having anything to do with how to gain non-essential material objects.

Nocturnal Pilgrimage 3.21

For best results, write down your impressions of each night's dreams in your journal using the Heartwood Path Dreaming Time Protocols found in the Appendix. Afterwards, consider sharing your Dream Tending with others.

It will not do you any good to learn how to initiate a lucid dream if, as soon as it starts, you lose it. For that reason, and to avoid over-whelming you, let us give you one technique to try here (in case you are already initiating but losing your lucid dreams), saving the others for later (when, after practicing you may be ready to initiate **and** sustain your lucid dreams).

First Stabilization Technique For Lucid Dreaming

Use the following technique soon as you begin your lucid dream as a way to keep it going:

Refrain from celebrating that you are having a lucid dream until it is over. Upon its initiation, stay calm. Only after you are relaxed do you begin to consciously explore the dream landscape.

After tending to your dreams and receiving the following motivational information, you are ready to continue down the Heartwood Path to the next waypoint. At this waypoint, you will be encouraged to go outside to commune with nature. A trip through a city does not typically lower urinary stress hormones. That does happen, how-ever, with couple of hours or more in a natural setting. Researchers at Nippon Medical School have demonstrated that such exposure can have long-lasting positive impacts on immune markers (beneficial bio-logical regulators of the immune system which help to fight diseases). They found, for example, that either a day trip or a couple hours daily over three days in a forest setting while practicing shinron-yoku (taking in the forest atmosphere during a leisurely walk) markedly increases the number of so-called natural killer cells, increases the activity of antiviral cells, and increases the amount of intracellular anti-cancer proteins. These increases last for about a full week after the forest immersion (Selhub & Logan, 2012, p.21).

With the information you just received in this Nocturnal Pilgrim-age as an incentive, move to the next waypoint: "Perpetual Nature." Go out there and improve your immune markers!

22

Perpetual Nature

TEST KNOWLEDGE THROUGH EXPERIENCE, PERSISTENCE, AND WILLINGNESS TO LEARN FROM MISTAKES

Put more emphasis on experience—the heart of wisdom—than on theory. Go straight to Nature for information and inspiration. Question conventional wisdom and authority. Persevere in the face of obstacles, even in the face of so-called "mistakes" made accidentally or deliberately. Such mistakes can be formative.

To put the wisdom of this part of the Heartwood Path to use, do the following activity.

To Benefit From Important Life-altering Incidents...

HumaNatureConnect Activity

Start-up Protocol

If this is not a day when you prefer to spend time in nature without an agenda, do the Heartwood Path Start-up Protocol found in the Appendix.

Making Journal Entries Regarding Formative Experiences

For this activity, list the formative experiences of your life. If you are having difficulty, assume the essence of a natural being that has been with you for your whole life such as the sky, a local river, or a rock formation and, as it, list the formative experiences of your life. Write a sentence about what you learned from these experiences. Write another sentence on how you can apply what you learned from this activity in your own life today. List at least ten of your most significant heartfelt beliefs. Describe how the media, friends, books, friends, and your own experiences in and out of nature influence what you believe.

Follow-up Protocol

For best results, write down your impressions of this activity in your journal using the Heartwood Path Follow-up Protocol found in the Appendix. Afterwards, consider sharing your interpretations with others.

Heartwood Path Axioms

Key Assertions From Waypoint 3.22

3.22.1.

Put more emphasis on experience—the heart of wisdom—than on theory.

3.22.2.

Go straight to Nature for information and inspiration.

3.22.3.

Question conventional wisdom and authority.

3.22.4.

Persevere in the face of obstacles, even in the face of so-called "mistakes."

3.22.5.

Mistakes can be formative.

Nocturnal Pilgrimage 3.22

For best results, write down your impressions of each night's dreams in your journal using the Heartwood Path Dreaming Time Protocols found in the Appendix. Afterwards, consider sharing your Dream Tending with others.

Do not get your dreams mixed up with your memory of your dream. You and everyone else dream every night but you may only remember a few dreams or even a few fragments of dreams.

Do not discount your dreams as unreal. Like your day time experiences such as your HumaNatureConnect Activities, your dreams are real experiences. Just as you walk through a natural area searching for an attractive Natural Being, explore your lucid dreams looking for the Psychoid or Dream Characters in the image of your familiar attractive Natural Beings.

Whether walking through an outdoor natural area or an inner world lucid dream, focus on what is vivid and pristine. Either way the brain operates the same way. It only registers "separate but equal" if you impose such outdated notions upon it. Dropping the "separate" part is a big lesson along the Heartwood Path. You will begin to see and appreciate the seamless fabric that binds your dream time world to your waking time world when you begin to focus on the impressions you form in each world rather than on the characters or objects that often appear to be distinct from each other and yourself.

After tending to your dreams, improve your immune functioning by going out into nature. After a good dose of Vitamin N (the tonic of Nature), you are ready to continue to the next learning station. To take your next step down the Heartwood Path, move to the next waypoint: "Sense-ational Fun."

23

Sense-ational Fun

REFINE YOUR SENSES AS A MEANS TO ENLIVEN EXPERIENCE

To continue down this leg of the Heartwood Path is to experience sense-ational fun. Each sense contributes to the richness of one's experience of life:

Smell. When one's olfactory nerves detect something—i.e. during a float trip, sex, or eating—they trigger the cerebral cortex and send messages straight to the limbic system (which is a network of structures in the brain involved in memory and emotions).

Touch. Your skin is really the only thing that stands—not very effectively—between you and the environment, between your own body with that which is considered the environment. The significance of touch is more than skin deep. Touch is the first sense that develops in the womb, it helps build social relationships, it can be used to heal or abuse, it stimulates brain growth and helps one cope, it brings forth psychological closeness, it helps the one doing the touching and the one being touched, it can establish or break boundaries, and it helps us survive and live well.

Hearing. Sounds, unlike visual colors and tasty foods, do not blend well inside us. We want to sort them out. Perhaps this is a defense mechanism: to make sure the sound of swishing prairie grasses does not also contain the purr of a lion, for example. Along with protecting us, sounds convey a wide range of emotions. The sound of one's mantra utterances provides a link between Interiority and Exteriority. The sound of mantric utterances encapsulates how one feels and thinks. Words may carry to the Exterior the thoughts and feelings one has on the Interior. These words are limited by the nature of the humans that produced them. We will be focusing most on how the mantric sounds (not the words) convey feelings and spiritual revelations and not so much on the concepts that the linguistic translations of the sounds present to our Ego-driven, concept-producing minds.

Seeing. Seventy percent of the body's sense receptors are in the eyes. Therefore, it is mainly through the eyes that one contacts and understands the Realm of Exteriority.

Our senses reach far beyond us. They are an extension of the chain that connects us to other people and to the environment as a whole. They bridge the personal and the impersonal, the individual with the universe.

The senses and the Soul cure each other. They are mutually healing. They each solve the problem of not awakening to the other. The senses and the Soul preserve each other.

Treat yourself to a variety of sensual treats—different smells, different textures, different visual patterns, and different foods. Consider using a blindfold and try to distinguish what you are experiencing without the use of your eyes.

You can also enliven your experiences by looking for curiosities and patterns as you seek attractive natural beings for the activities of this course. To facilitate this enlivening, return to the following activity throughout your pilgrimage down the Heartwood Path.

To Spot Patterns And Curiosities In The Great Outdoors...

HumaNatureConnect Activity

Start-up Protocol

If this is not a day when you prefer to spend time in nature without an agenda, do the Heartwood Path Start-up Protocol found in the Appendix.

Enlivening Your Experiences

In this activity, look for and check off patterns and curiosities in nature. You do not have to find all the patterns listed below at once. Come back to this activity whenever you feel like varying the types of connection beings. Doing so may help you find new attractive natural beings for your HumanNature Connect Activities and teach you how to diversify what you observe in nature. To avoid naming or having to identify the beings in this activity you can simply write down where you can return to the being for future connection experiences. For pictures of what the beings look like, go to the **Nature Handbook** by Ernest H. Williams, Jr. (2005).

1. Look for the most showy flowers, such as wild passionflower or fairy slipper orchid. Among my favorite showy flowers are:

   _____.

2. Look for ray or disk flowers such as dandelions or fleabane. Among my favorite ray or disk flowers are:

   _____.

3. Look for the most inconspicuous flowers such as sagebrush, maple or smooth brome grass. Among my favorite inconspicuous flowers are: _____.

4. Notice the timing of flowers in a meadow, probably an adaptation to avoid competition. Write out the sequencing of flowers during the growing season.

   _____.

5. Look for early blooming forest wildflowers such as Dutchman's breeches and bloodroot. Among my favorite forest flower are:

_____.

6. Look for winged seeds such as red maple, cottonwood, and milkweed. Among my favorite winged seeded plants are:

_____.

7. Look for burs or stickseeds such as burdock or sand-bur. I am attracted to the following burs and stickseeds:

_____.

8. Look for fleshy fruits such as honeysuckle, holly, and rasp-berry. I am attracted to the following fleshy fruited plants:

_____.

9. Look for stored nuts such as the acorns of oaks or the nuts of hickory trees. I am attracted to the following stored nuts:

_____.

10. Look for ballistic seeds (those that throw their seed) such as or-ange jewelweed (also known as Touch-Me-Nots) and wild gera-nium. I am attracted to the following plants that practice ballistic seeding: _____.

11. Look for seeds that can bury themselves through a twisting action such as seed heads and needle grass. I am attracted to the following twisting seeds: _____.

12. Look for a forest that is mostly deciduous and one that is mostly evergreen. I am attracted the following de-ciduous forests: _____. and the following evergreen forests:

_____.

13. Look for a very broad tree and a very tall tree: I am attracting the following broad trees: _____. and the follow-ing tall trees _____.

14. Look for a very old tree. I am attracted to the following old trees:

_____.

15. Look at trees with different types of bark, such as smooth-bark beeches, the furrowed bark black locusts, shag bark hickories, and peeling bark birches. I am attracted to the bark of the following trees: _____.

16. Look for trees with flaring trunks (buttresses) near the ground such as bald cypress and American beeches. I am attracted to the following trees with buttresses: _____.

17. Look for different shaped leaves such as the toothed leaves of beeches, the palmately-lobed leaves of the sugar maple, the compound leaves of ash trees, and mitten or variable shaped leaves of sassafras trees. I am attracted to the leaves on the following trees: _____.

18. Look for shade trees. I am attracted to the following shade trees: _____.

19. Look for trees that retain their leaves in the winter such as the red oak. I am attracted to the following leaf-retaining trees: _____.

20. Pay attention to how long the pine trees in your area hold their needles (some last two years, others for decades) Notice how pine trees have large woody female pine cones and small pale male cones at the tips of the branches. Notice also the variety of pine cones, big and small, open and closed. I am attracted to the following pine trees: _____.

21. Look for plants with hairy leaves, such as the blazing star, common mullein, and New England aster. My favorite hairy-leafed plant is: _____.

22. Watch out for spines, thorns, and prickles, such as those on cacti, roses, and locust trees. I am attracted to the following thorny plants: _____.

23. Look for plants with resins and waxes such as pine trees, junipers, and blue spruces. I am attracted to the following plants with resins or waxes: _____.

24. Look for plants with swellings on their stems called "galls,"which are "active growth responses of plants to the presence of insect eggs and larvae" (Williams, 2005, p. 49).

25. Look for leaf mines. Blotches or serpentine trails within a leaf reveal the presence of leaf-mining larval insects. Mines are pale in color because the leaf mines have consumed the leaf tissue. Leaf mines are made by the larvae of tiny moths, flies, beetles . . I am attracted to the following leaf mine patterns I have witnessed:

_____.

26. Look for spirals on plants such as giant sunflowers. I am attracted to the following plants showing the results of the Fibonacci Sequence and the golden ration in the spirals they exhibit:

_____.

27. Look for lenticels (raised dots, ovals and lines) that contribute to a rough texture to the uniform surfaces of plants with otherwise smooth bark, such as cherry trees, pear trees, and paper birch trees. I am attracted to the patterns made by lenticels on the following trees: _____.

28. Look for carnivorous plants such as the purple pitcher plant, the round-leaved sundew, and the Venus flytrap. I am attracted to the following flesh-eating plants:

_____.

29. Look for parasitic plants such as the white paintbrush, the clustered broomrape, larkspur, and Indian pipe. I am attracted to the following parasitic plants:

_____.

30. Look for solar-tracking flowers such as little sunflowers and subalpine buttercups. I am attracted to the following solar-tracking flowers: _____.

31. Look for animals with iridescence such as the shells of abalones, or the bark-gnawing beetle. My favorite iridescent animals are:

_____.

32. Look for animals with bioluminescence such as fireflies and glow worms.

33. Look for animals with camouflage or cryptic coloration such as the tulip-tree beauty moth and the pika (a small mammal).

34. Look for animals such as the octopus, the catfish, the yellow perch, and the sanderling with countershading (dark tops and light bottoms), adaptions that makes the animals less visible to predators. I am attracted to the following animals with counter-shading: _____.

35. Look for animals with disruptive coloration that is useful in hiding from predators, such as the spots on your white-tailed deer and the color blotches on copperhead snakes. I am attracted to the following animals with disruptive coloration:

_____.

36. Look for animals with eye spot (four-eye butterfly-fish) or false head colorations (spicebush swallowtail)—both used to confuse predators. I am attracted to the fol-lowing animals with false head or eye spot colorations:

_____.

37. Look for animals such as skunks with warning colorations. I am attracted to the following animals with warning colorations:

_____.

38. Look for animals with disguise colorations such as the greater angle-wing katydid or treehoppers. I am at-tracted to the following animals with disguise colorations:

_____.

39. Look for the smallest mammal, the largest mammal, the small-est bird, the largest bird, and the smallest reptile and the largest reptile you can find. Which of these do I find most attractive?

_____.

40. Look for animals that shiver, pant, or visit salt licks. Which of these do I find most attractive?

_____.

41. Look for animals with hard solid antlers (deer, elk, moose) hard hollow horns (mountain goat and big horn

sheep). Which of these do I find most attractive?

_____.

42. Look for animals with misleading displays such as a kill-deer (which feigns injury to lure predators away from its nest) and skunks and eastern hognose snakes (which both play dead). Which of these do I find most attractive?

_____.

43. Look for birds with various bills and beaks and birds with various wing shapes and tail shapes. Which of these do I find most attractive? _____.

44. Notice how male birds are often more brightly colored than the females of their species (especially cardinals, wood ducks and painted buntings). Which of these do I find most attractive?

_____.

45. Notice which baby birds are helpless at birth (robins, for example) and which baby birds are immediately capable of feeding for itself (snowy plovers, for example). Which of these do I find most attractive? _____.

46. Notice the various calls of birds. Which of these do I find most attractive? _____.

47. Notice which birds get mobbed (hawks, for example) and which birds do the mobbing of other birds (crows, for example). Which of these do I find most attractive?

_____.

48. Notice which birds soar (hawks, for example), which first fly in V formation (Canada geese, for example), and which birds fly in large flocks (snow geese, for example). Which of these do I find most attractive? _____.

49. Notice which kind of butterflies form puddle clubs when they feed (swallowtails and white admiral butterflies, for example). Which of these do I find most attractive?

_____.

50. Look for insect nymphs, larvae, inch worms, spun silken cocoons, naked larvae chrysalids, or insects that shed their

exoskeletons (cicadas and stoneflies), and caterpillar webs, ant-hills, and wasp nests. Which of these do I find most attractive?

_____.

51. Look for soil tubes such as those made by moles. Which of these do I find most attractive?

_____.

52. Look for fall leaf colors, regrowth after fires, bark galleries (tunnels under the bark of trees caused by bark beetles, bark rubs caused by deer as part of the mating ritual and trees marked by beavers, bears, and bison. Which of these do I find most attractive? _____.

53. Look for holes on trees caused by woodpeckers and sapsuckers. Which of these do I find most attractive?

_____.

54. Look for forest shelf fungi, grass runways, bubble masses (such as those formed by spittle bugs), fairy rings (the visible above ground reproductive structures—"mushrooms"—of the unseen below ground fugal filaments that grow outward in all directions), and the variety of spider web patterns. Which of these do I find most attractive? _____.

55. Along the coasts, look for the intertidal life zones (from the high zone rich in barnacles to the low zone rich in a form of algae known as "kelp"), look for the variability in the tide pools (as a result of salinity, temperature, and sun exposure), look for sand dune zones, look for life in the sand, and look for marsh zones and salt pan depressions. Which of these do I find attractive?

_____.

Follow-up Protocol

For best results, write down your impressions of this activity in your journal using the Heartwood Path Follow-up Protocol found in the Appendix. Afterwards, consider sharing your interpretations with others.

Heartwood Path Axioms

Key Assertions From Waypoint 3.23

3.23.1.

Being an extension of the chain that connects us to other people and the environment, our senses reach far beyond us.

3.23.2.

The senses bridge the personal and the impersonal, the individual with the universal.

3.23.3.

Each sense preserves each other sense by solving the problem of not awakening to the other.

3.23.4.

You can enliven your experiences by looking for curiosities and patterns as you seek attractive natural beings.

Nocturnal Pilgrimage 3.23

For best results, write down your impressions of each night's dreams in your journal using the Heartwood Path Dreaming Time Protocols found in the Appendix. Afterwards, consider sharing your Dream Tending with others.

When you become conscious within your dream do not just be passively aware from one vantage point. It is best to move around in the dream landscape. And here is where it really gets fun. I like to move around in my dreams by swimming in the air. Some may conjure up magical doors or create time machines. Since everything is an illusion, do what you want to move through your dream world simply by using your intention. Happy travels!

After completing your next dream tending session, go on a search for evergreen trees. They are known to produce phytoncides. These natural chemicals improve the activity of one's frontline immune defenders, particularly when they are released into moist air and then breathed in (Selhub & Logan, 2012, pp. 21.22). Breathing in phytoncides is yet another reason to get out into the forest.

When ready, move to the next waypoint: "Clutch Mystery." Prepare to hug unpredictability as you take your next step to Gladandgreen Junction.

24

Clutch Mystery

BE WILLING TO EMBRACE THE UNKNOWN, AMBIGUITY, PARADOX, AND UNCERTAINTY

The embrace of the unknown, ambiguity, paradox and uncertainty means risking making mistakes—a peril that is often worth the gamble because it can open the door to wonder. Courageous spiritual searchers go on an adventure that never ends. Along the way they find risk, wildness, play, quiet, and grace. They will not get far unless they are brave enough to interrupt and ask embarrassing, uncomfortable, dangerous, and so-called "inappropriate" questions. By asking and answering rather than shunning such questions they embrace uncertainty—an important and significant step needed as a precursor to throwing out doubt.

Do what is foolish sometimes. Take measured risks. Doing so builds aliveness, passion, enthusiasm for whatever truly matters to you, and the kind of terror that attracts only the few but has the power to transform. Do not worry. Ask for help. Play like a child. Make it a point to take breaks from work to reflect and incubate ideas. Observe the Sabbath. Take a true vacation at least once per year. Risk failure. To put the wisdom of this section to work for yourself, do the following activity.

To The Acceptance Of Uncertainty, Vagueness, Contradiction, And Unpredictability...

HumaNatureConnect Activity

Start-up Protocol

If this is not a day when you prefer to spend time in nature without an agenda, do the Heartwood Path Start-up Protocol found in the Appendix.

Embracing The Unknown, Ambiguity, Paradox, And Uncertainty

For this activity, embrace uncertainty. Assume the essence of your natural being, and, as it, use the greater objectivity and broader perspective this assuming provides to you as you face your uncertain future. Ponder how not knowing can be enlivening, how good signs lead to complacency, how hopelessness leads to giving up, and how if the future is undecided there is room for one to "play a role in influencing what will happen" (Macy and Johnstone, 2012, p. 230). This influencing begins with one's intentionality—the choice-making that is the bridge between one's history and one's future. An intention is a preference for the kind of world one wants. Such a world is evoked through intention plus persistence. Write down in your journal how your history, your intention, your uncertainty, and your persistence together mold the kind of world you want.

Follow-up Protocol

For best results, write down your impressions of this activity in your journal using the Heartwood Path Follow-up Protocol found in the Appendix. Afterwards, consider sharing your interpretations with others.

Heartwood Path Axioms

Key Assertions From Waypoint 3.24

3.24.1.

The embrace of the unknown, ambiguity, paradox and uncertainty means that you may be opening the door to wonder.

3.24.2.

Take measured risks and secure a safety net.

3.24.3.

Make it a point to take breaks from work to reflect and to incubate ideas.

Nocturnal Pilgrimage 3.24

For best results, write down your impressions of each night's dreams in your journal using the Heartwood Path Dreaming Time Protocols found in the Appendix. Afterwards, consider sharing your Dream Tending with others.

You are the creator of your own dream world. Just take whatever is in your mind's eye and, with intention, place it into your lucid dream. Expect something to happen and it will. Create good images in you dreams with enough intention and you will have the confidence and clarity to create them in the real world.

After your usual dream tending session, head outside. If you absolutely cannot get immersed in a natural place, at least look out a window at a natural being as you do the next activity. Did you know that patients in a hospital with rooms that afforded natural scenes do better than patients with views of bricks and other unnatural objects? (Selhub & Logan, 2012, pp. 22-23). Be sure do get your daily view of wildness. It will do you good.

When ready, move to the next waypoint, entitled the "Complete Mind," to resume your pilgrimage down the Heartwood Path. You will learn how to make better decisions.

25

Complete Mind

DEVELOP WHOLE BRAIN THINKING

Develop whole brain thinking—both intuitive and rational—by developing ideas through mind mapping. This is a great alternative to organizing thoughts through the restrictive and stifling process of making outlines. Mind maps are graphic representations of a person's or a group's ideas. Mind maps adequately represents graphically in the Realm of Exteriority what is going on in the Realm of Interiority. Mind maps are charts of what individuals and groups are thinking for the purpose of planning. To put the wisdom of this section of the Heartwood Path to work for you, do the following activity.

To Chart Your Intelligence...

HumaNatureConnect Activity

Start-up Protocol

If this is not a day when you prefer to spend time in nature without an agenda, do the Heartwood Path Start-up Protocol found in the Appendix.

Experimenting With Mind Mapping

For this activity, experiment with mind mapping. If you are having difficulty, assume the essence of your attractive natural being and, as it, begin your mind map by placing a symbol or topic at the center of the page inside a circle. Write down (print, not cursive) key words around this central image and connect them with lines, one keyword per line. The lines are to radiate out from the center. Do not edit the words at this point. Use color to highlight important points. Look for themes, connecting them with arrows or colors. Take off any irrelevant words. Make redrafts for further clarification. Stop when the information presented is sufficient for the task at hand. Your first mind map can be about all the mind maps you need to make to improve your life or the lives of others. Set a goal of having twenty mind map topics radiating from the center.

Follow-up Protocol

For best results, write down your impressions of this activity in your journal using the Heartwood Path Follow-up Protocol found in the Appendix. Afterwards, consider sharing your interpretations with others.

Heartwood Path Axioms

Key Assertions From Waypoint 3.25

3.25.1.

Develop whole brain thinking—both intuitive and rational— by developing ideas through mind mapping.

3.25.2.

Mind mapping is a great alternative to organizing thoughts through the restrictive and stifling process of making outlines.

3.25.3

Begin your mind map by placing a symbol or topic at the center of the page inside a circle, then write down (print, not cursive) key words around this central image and connect them with lines, one keyword per line.

3.25.4

As your mind map takes shape, look for themes, connecting them with the use of arrows or colors.

Nocturnal Pilgrimage 3.25

For best results, write down your impressions of each night's dreams in your journal using the Heartwood Path Dreaming Time Protocols found in the Appendix. Afterwards, consider sharing your Dream Tending with others.

Pay attention to your Dream Characters. Some are intelligent. Some aren't. Some are wise. Some aren't. But they can all offer you some level of advice. Be nice to them.

If, after tending to the dreams of a night's rest, you absolutely cannot go outside to commune with nature for the next activity, and if you do not have a view of nature from your room, commune with a house plant. According to Selhub & Logan (2012, p. 23), a few potted plants can have an influence on stress and the maintenance of health. Selhub and Logan also report that inmates in a jail with views of nature spent less time in the infirmary (2012, p. 23). Use these reports to motivate yourself to spend time with a natural being, as instructed in the next activity.

Once you complete tending to your dreams from the previous night, move to the next waypoint, entitled "Financial Triumph." You are making progress on your pilgrimage towards Gladandgreen Junction.

26

Financial Triumph

DETERMINE YOUR MOST LIKELY AVENUE TO FINANCIAL SUCCESS

Financial success is most likely when three factors are present:

1. passion, doing what you really love to do;
2. expertise, doing what you can do better than anyone else in your area; and
3. an economic engine, doing something that can bring in adequate financing.

Check on your likelihood for finding success by engaging in the following activity.

To Triumph, Fervor, And Competence...

HumaNatureConnect Activity

Start-up Protocol

If this is not a day when you prefer to spend time in nature without an agenda, do the Heartwood Path Start-up Protocol found in the
Appendix.

Finding Success With Your Passion And Expertise

For this activity, as illustrated in Figure 4, draw three large inter-
secting circles, one on the left, one overlapping but on the right, and a
third overlapping the other two but in the middle and slightly below.
In the non-overlapping portion of the upper left circle write what you
are most passionate about (focus here on vocations and "advocations").
In the non-overlapping portion of the circle to the right of the previous
circle write down what you are skilled to do that nobody else in your
area can do better than you. In the portion of the third circle, which
is overlapping the other two circles and is below the other two circles,
write in the non-overlapping portion an occupation you have that
drives your economic engine (provides the most amount of revenue).
The middle space of the Venn diagram, where all three circles overlap represents your passion, your expertise, and your economic engine.
This Venn diagram demonstrates that your best chance for finding
financial success occurs where your passion, your unique and superior
expertise, and your economic engine overlap. Think what that would
be for you and write it down.

Figure 4: Venn Diagram for Finding Financial Success

Follow-up Protocol

For best results, write down your impressions of this activity in your journal using the Heartwood Path Follow-up Protocol found in the Appendix. Afterwards, consider sharing your interpretations with others.

Heartwood Path Axioms

Key Assertions From Waypoint 3.26

3.26.1.

Financial success is most likely when three factors are present: 1) passion, 2) expertise, and 3) an economic engine (something that can bring in adequate financing).

3.26.2.

Your best chance for finding financial success occurs where your passion, your unique and superior expertise, and your economic engine overlap.

Nocturnal Pilgrimage 3.26

For best results, write down your impressions of each night's dreams in your journal using the Heartwood Path Dreaming Time Protocols found in the Appendix. Afterwards, consider sharing your Dream Tending with others.

Dream interpretation ought not replace regular medical treatment by a physician. The health-producing aspect of dream tending ought to be regarded as a complement to standard medical treatment. Keep improving your Dream Tending skills between each Heartwood Path waypoint. Doing so will help you better understand the teachings; help you receive guidance; and, eventually, improve your health.

To motivate yourself to commune with nature for the next activity consider that Norwegian researchers have proven that having a plant near a work station reduces the risk of sick leave significantly (Selhub & Logan, 2012, p 24). When ready to continue, move to the next waypoint: "Ideal You Ahead." The Heartwood Path is leading you to happiness and health, one waypoint, one HumaNatureConnect Activity, and one tended dream at a time.

27

Ideal You Ahead

GET TO KNOW YOUR FUTURE CORE SELF

Here you are challenged to move beyond the limits you may have set for your life purpose. Abundant possibilities exist beyond what you now think are "realistic options."

Your "Future Core Self" is the one you are becoming as you progress down the Heartwood Path to your own place of fulfillment. Your Future Core Self is your Higher Self that can rise above the influences of your own Inner Critic or others who provide negative influences in your life. For now, break your pattern of adapting and accommodating. Break away from any possible limiting views you may be harboring. Discover your evolved Self. This is the one you will be when you no longer care about the judgments and opinions of others. Some of the best advice you can receive can come from your Future Core Self. To obtain such advice, have an imaginary conversation with your Future Core Self, as described in the following activity.

To The Best You...

HumaNatureConnect Activity

Start-up Protocol

If this is not a day when you prefer to spend time in nature without an agenda, do the Heartwood Path Start-up Protocol found in the Appendix.

Obtaining Advice From Your Future Core Self

For this activity, obtain advice from your Future Core Self. Begin by closing your eyes and focusing on your breath. Create in your mind a time machine that can transport you five, ten, or twenty years into the future. Allow this machine to transport you to your ideal future environment—a place where your Future Core Self vacations, lives, or works. Imagine finding two chairs there, greeting your Future Core Self, and sitting down for a meaningful conversation. Pause for a moment to scan the scene. Bring all the details of this place, including your Future Core Self, into your consciousness. Now is your chance to ask your Future Core Self anything you like. Perhaps you may want to know what your next step is to move forward. Pause and listen to the answer. Perhaps you may be interested in what your Future Self remembers most about the last twenty years. Pause and listen to the answer. Perhaps you need to know what you need to be most aware of as you make your journey from where you are to where your Future Self is. Pause and listen to the answer. You may receive a name from your Future Core Self. Note what name you receive. You may discover that there is no spouse twenty years from now. Do not be alarmed. This is not a psychic prediction. Try again. This exercise can call you forward into your life. Consider at some point asking your Future Core Self what brings him/her joy, excitement, contentment, or a sense of accomplishment.

If, during any of the ponderings that you are encouraged to do along the Heartwood Path, you do not know an answer, ask yourself what your Future Core Self would say. Ask yourself what is the bridge between you and your Future Core Self. Listen to stories told by your Future Self. Ask for your Future Core Self's list of, for you, future New Year's resolutions. Ask what would be your Future Core Self's agenda for the day. Check the advice of your Inner Critic against the advice of your Future Core Self.

Follow-up Protocol

For best results, write down your impressions of this activity in your journal using the Heartwood Path Follow-up Protocol found in the Appendix. Afterwards, consider sharing your interpretations with others.

Heartwood Path Axioms

Key Assertions From Waypoint 3.27

3.27.1.

Abundant possibilities exist beyond what you now think are "realistic options."

3.27.2.

Discover your evolved Self—one you will be when you no longer care about the judgments and opinions of others.

3.27.3.

Some of the best advice you can receive can come when you have an imaginary conversation with your Future Core Self.

Nocturnal Pilgrimage 3.27

For best results, write down your impressions of each night's dreams in your journal using the Heartwood Path Dreaming Time Protocols found in the Appendix. Afterwards, consider sharing your Dream Tending with others.

Here's the kind of intelligent dream-oriented message you might expect to receive during your conversation with your ideal Future Core Self:

"During my lifetime, much of which is still in your future, I received many benefits from my dreams. I started my life only becoming aware of my dreams as vague, sporadic, and fleeting recollections. Using dream incubation techniques, I started to become conscious that I was dreaming while still sleeping. Then, I was able to direct the action of my dreams and control what happened. My life really began to take off after I was able to change the content of my dreams. That's when my nocturnal pilgrimages, as you call them, really began to pay off. By controlling the dreams in the ways you suggest, I was able to become the ideal Future Core Self you see before you. All because my dreams—your dreams—came true!

As soon as I started having lucid dreams, I began having control over my dreaming time adventures. The benefits were enormous. I used my daring dreams to boost my self-confidence. As a result, my development soared. While having lucid dreams I faced my various fears. In this way, I learned to make the most of situations. With this confidence, I was able to convert scary dreaming time Characters into trusted allies. I dreamt that I was healthier and I became healthier. As my unconscious appeared to me in my dreams, I developed creative ways to solve problems. Now, I only have a distant memory of the financial problem you grapple with daily. By listening to how I used lucid dreaming you will have a clear path to follow. Just let me know how I can help. Be assured, you can see by looking at me that an ideal future lies ahead."

After having a conversation with your ideal Future Core Self, sleep. Wake up in your dream. Tend to your dreams.

If you are having trouble having lucid dreams, maybe the problem is you are having a problem falling asleep. Perhaps if you adopt a calming routine before going to bed you will be able to sleep more readily and then control your dreams.

After waking, go into nature for another boost you can use in the next activity. More ideas for how to sleep better follow in the next few waypoints.

Motivate yourself to commune with a natural being by knowing that the Journal of the Japanese Society for Horticultural Science reports that putting potted plants in a classroom for four months significantly reduced visits to the infirmary compared to similar students without visible plants (Selhub & Logan, 2012, p. 24). With your ideal Future Core Self foremost in your mind, resume your pilgrimage. Move to the next waypoint: "Cosmic Consciousness." Enjoy the road to Gladand-green Junction.

28

Cosmic Consciousness

MOVE THROUGH THE TRANSCENDENT STAGES OF THE MIND

This particular Heartwood Path book is about your individual self. As we will see, your individual self is an integral part of the universe.

The Black Plague shook Fourteenth Century Europeans free of their dogmatic thinking and allowed the Renaissance to flourish. In the same way, let the past fifty years of unprecedented resource liberation and environmental destruction shake you to the recognition that it is you and billions more like you that need to change if the world is to be a better place.

Beginning at birth, humans undergo changes that take place in four transcendent stages of the Mind (each preceding stage includes the former stage(s):

1. the Preceptual Mind, the mind made up of precepts (which means sensory impressions);
2. the Receptual Mind, the mind of both sensory impressions and simple consciousness (there is no self-consciousness yet);

3. the Conceptual Mind, the mind of precepts, recepts, and concepts (self-consciousness begins with concepts); and

4. the Intuitive Mind, the mind of precepts, recepts, concepts and intuition.

Just as animals use their intuition to stay alive, hone yours to thrive. Ways to heighten your intuitive abilities are provided in the subsequent exercises that awaken your Sixth Chakra (especially in the section entitled "Kindle Your Inner Fire").

In the Intuitive Mind, sensation, simple consciousness, and self-consciousness are crowned with cosmic consciousness. This last stage does not occur fully in everyone at will. It occurs as a gift. Through the kinds of exercises presented in this course, you can make yourself more prone for cosmic consciousness to occur.

While described in this series of courses, cosmic consciousness is not required for admission to Gladandgreen Junction. There is plenty of other work to do that will also leave you happy in a sustainable environment. Most of this work occurs in the inner world. The growth of the human intellect occurs when the mind fuses precepts, recepts and concepts together in a kettle of morality.

The achievement of cosmic consciousness, while not mandatory, is certainly very helpful for pilgrims en route to Gladandgreen Junction. Cosmic Consciousness, described by Whitman as "ineffable light," shows the universe to be immaterial, spiritual, and alive. The occurrence of cosmic consciousness requires one to transcend mental agitation, quiet the mind, and sensitize one's body to all sensations. Through this development process of transcendence, in which one ends up excellent and magnificent, one is prepared for the ultimately moral job of working to preserve the environment. This preparation also makes one capable of accepting one's own infinite, eternal, loving connection to all: the Soul.

To Happiness And Well-being...

HumaNatureConnect Activity

Start-up Protocol

If this is not a day when you prefer to spend time in nature without an agenda, do the Heartwood Path Start-up Protocol found in the Appendix.

Responding To Statements About The Relationship Between Happiness (Well-being) And Protected Nature

For this activity, make contact with your own responses to the following statements:

"Climb the mountains and get their good tidings. Nature's peace will flow into you as sunshine flows into trees. The winds will blow their own freshness into you, and their storms their energy, while cares will drop off like autumn leaves" —John Muir (Lambin, 2012, p. 23).

Research "in environmental psychology proves that being in contact with nature, or contemplating it, either in reality or in an image, has a beneficial effect on one's well-being" (Lambin, 2012, p. 25).

"Inciting fear vis-a-vis future environmental conflicts leads to a decrease in a sense of security, and therefore of happiness" (Lambin, 2012, p. 122).

Follow-up Protocol

For best results, write down your impressions of this activity in your journal using the Heartwood Path Follow-up Protocol found in the Appendix. Afterwards, consider sharing your interpretations with others.

Heartwood Path Axioms

Key Assertions From Waypoint 3.28

3.28.1.

Just as animals use their intuition to stay alive, hone yours to thrive.

3.28.2.

In the Intuitive Mind, sensation, simple consciousness, and self-consciousness are crowned with cosmic consciousness.

3.28.3.

While cosmic consciousness occurs as a gift, the kinds of exercises presented in this book will make you more prone for it to occur.

Nocturnal Pilgrimage 3.28

For best results, write down your impressions of each night's dreams in your journal using the Heartwood Path Dreaming Time Protocols found in the Appendix. Afterwards, consider sharing your Dream Tending with others.

Spooky Dream Characters remind me of children who resort to bad behaviors because disciplinary attention is better than no attention. To make your frightening Dream Characters more helpful pay attention to them. Wave a white flag. Ask them who they are and what you can do for them. Be kind. They may return the favor by bringing re-pressed aspects of your subconscious to your attention. When you heal a nightmarish Dream Character, you gain the confidence to correct a real world problem.

As you read the text and do the activities at the Heartwood Path waypoints during the day (and as you sleep and dream during the night) you are making consistent progress towards finding happiness, personal health, and environmental health. This progress is occurring, in part, because you are lowering your stress by spending more time communing consciously with nature. You are not alone in this positive result. One study demonstrated that those who lived with a three kilometer radius of a high amount of green space were less likely to experience negative stress (Selhub & Logan, 2012, pp. 24-25).

With Selhub and Logan's information as motivation, keep going. Move to the next station along the path to Gladandgreen Junction. It is entitled "Cove Of The Spirit." There, you will learn about attune-ment, spiritual development, getting rid of negativity, and conscious breathing.

29

Cove Of The Spirit

CONNECT WITH ONE'S OWN SOUL

The Heartwood Path leads through numerous portals to the Soul. These portals include attunement (described in the next waypoint), spiritual development, getting rid of negativity, and active conscious breathing (discussed later in this course). The experience of going through any one of these passageways is unmistakably a feeling of being permeated by love. Once one sets out to encounter one's Soul, personal desires for pleasure become subordinate to a new purpose in life—that of establishing deep loving relationships with others to find the vitality and direction needed to do right actions persistently.

The Heartwood Path leads to some transitions in one's thinking and values. These transitions are precursors to connecting with one's Soul in profound ways. By undergoing these transitions, your thinking will become less dominated by over-rationality. Instead, it will become more intuitive. Your tendency to analyze will eventually give way to more synthesis; by which I mean that you will reduce your amount of "reductionist" thinking and begin to think holistically and ecologically. Nonlinear thinking (that is, thinking of diverse analogies) will begin to replace linear thinking (thinking along narrow but rational tracks). Concerning your feelings, be prepared to feel more prone to conservation rather than expansion, more prone to cooperation rather than competition, more prone to quality rather than quantity, and more prone to partnership rather than dominance.

The form of attention that hides your Soul most effectively is negative thought. Such thoughts will always come but they need not be nurtured. Dwelling on them makes you a victim. Be a victor instead by replacing negative thoughts with positive thoughts. The Soul is always positive; your negative thoughts come not from your Soul but from your own mind. Encountering your Soul is important to eartHearts because it is through the Soul that one is connected to all living things, to the Earth, and to the Absolute (God)—the spirit world's Big Kahuna.

This oceanic feeling of connectedness feels very good, creates deep vitality, and provides a positive direction to one's purpose in life. Like shooting a tube while surfing, passing through a portal to one's Soul involves some skillful maneuvering. Yet, this doing is not a forceful striving on an angry sea. The voyage to oneness is more like surfing on a gentle wave that swells higher and higher, giving the wave rider a vantage point that expands her awareness.

Getting rid of negativity is the first step to reaching your Soul. Negativity often arises from the feelings of unworthiness, rejection, sadness, and depression (a kind of intensification of sadness, multiplied by self-preoccupation, losing yourself in your negative feelings, loneliness, and anger).

To The Resolution Of Alternatives...

HumaNatureConnect Activity

Start-up Protocol

If this is not a day when you prefer to spend time in nature without an agenda, do the Heartwood Path Start-up Protocol found in the Appendix.

Reconciling Choices

For this activity, reconcile the following five choices for the future regarding the "quest for happiness with the preservation of the integrity of nature:

Choice # 1. The Choice Between The Promotion Of A Materialistic System Of Values And The Quest For A More Authentic And Sustainable Happiness.

"Either we fill our houses with objects and gadgets . . . (or) we adopt a less materialistic system of values, which not only makes us happier in the long term but also would have a smaller ecological imprint (Lambin, 2012, pp. 155-156).

Choice # 2. The Choice Between An Urban Culture Within Which Lifestyles Are Shaped By Artifacts and Built Environments That Are Substituted For Nature And Cultivating Our Biophilic Tendencies And Increasing Opportunities For Them To Be Expressed.

"Nature also offers enough possibilities so that everyone can find in it that which creates his or her own personal form of happiness" (Lambin, 2012, p. 156).

Choice # 3. The Choice Between Positive And Negative Interactions With Animals.

" . . . we can see animals as living beings, certainly different from our species, but who deserve respect, who have rights, and with whom we can establish a mutually beneficial modus vivendi (a peaceful way of living) (Lambin, 2012, pp. 156).

Choice # 4. The Choice Between A System of Globalization That Benefits the Elite and A System of Globalization That Is Beneficial To Everyone.

" . . . globalization can be a vector of economic and cultural poverty . . . or of human progress respectful of the diversity of cultures and ecosystems" (Lambin, 2012, pp. 156-157).

Choice # 5. The Choice Between An Egocentric Attitude And An Altruistic Attitude.

"Short-term egocentricism degrades nature and thus kills individual happiness . . . By contrast, developing a sense of the Other—poor populations, future generations, the animal world, and even nature, is a good investment in human happiness" (Lambin, 2012, pp. 156-157).

In your journal, write down your impressions of each of the five choices above.

Follow-up Protocol

For best results, write down your impressions of this activity in your journal using the Heartwood Path Follow-up Protocol found in the Appendix. Afterwards, consider sharing your interpretations with others.

Heartwood Path Axioms

Key Assertions From Waypoint 3.29

3.29.1.

Attunement is a process of inner work that needs to be done day after day to release oneself from the limited perceptions of ordinary reality and to expand conscious awareness to include the experience of the spiritual realities of life.

3.29.2.

Portals to the Soul include attunement, spiritual development, getting rid of negativity, and active conscious breathing.

3.29.3.

The experience of going through any one of the Portals to the Soul is unmistakably a feeling of being permeated by love.

3.29.4.

The Soul is always positive; your negative thoughts come not from your Soul but from your own mind.

3.29.5.

Encountering the Soul is important to eartHearts because it is through the Soul that one is connected to the Absolute Spirit, connected to all living things, connected to the Earth, and enabled to make the best positive choices.

Nocturnal Pilgrimage 3.29

For best results, write down your impressions of each night's dreams in your journal using the Heartwood Path Dreaming Time Protocols found in the Appendix. Afterwards, consider sharing your Dream Tending with others.

Do something to help you relax. Read. Take a hot shower. Or light incense. Going through a soothing end of day ritual will help you sleep. Dream lucidly. Write down your impressions of your dreams in your journal.

As you continue to travel day and night to Gladandgreen Junction, you are growing spiritually. This is precisely what you need for your own uncommon happiness and what the world needs for environmental sustainability. You may also be overcoming life stressors such as major losses, financial problems, relationship problems, or legal issues. Again, in these instances, you are not alone. Having ample amounts of greenspace within three-kilometers of the homes of people with similar stressors has been known to reduce health complaints compared to those with low amounts of greenspace (Selhub & Logan, 2012, p 25). Use this information as a stimulus to take the next important step—moving to the next waypoint: "Spiritual Acclimation."

30

Spiritual Acclimation

SEEK ATTUNEMENT

Attunement is a process of inner work that needs to be done day after day to release oneself from the limited perceptions of ordinary reality and to expand conscious awareness to include the experience of the spiritual realities of life. This inner work will open one up to guidance from the Soul.

As a being in your present human form, it is often difficult to determine with certainty whether it is your Soul or your own thoughts that is giving you guidance. If the guidance one experiences is critical, judgmental, selfish, fearful or negative, the message definitely arises from someone else or one's own personality. If the message is about harmony, order, creativity, or love and if the message is presented with kindness, understanding, love, and encouragement, the message may be coming from the Soul or it may simply be coming from one's intuition—that inner faculty that allows one to know more about life than one can consciously perceive in the physical world. Talk with a safe and trusted friend if you are unsure about the source of your guidance.

Attunement is the making of a portal to the Soul that requires confidence in one's own ability to make an inner opening—a blank space in the psyche where one can place a newly refined level of sensitivity.

This "blankness" is created by temporarily disengaging from one's own fascination with the physical world. In the place of this blankness you will eventually accept many "affordances" from the spiritual realm, including: an expanded awareness of the magnificence of life; an inner power you can use to balance the strong influences of the outer physical world; and an ability to project yourself in your imagination beyond your present experience of yourself as a human being.

The experience of attunement is usually temporary but never insignificant. During this More-Than-Individual experience of your Self you will experience:

1. Greater Self-confidence, strength, power, and increased creativity;
2. wonderful feeling of belonging that is based upon an enlightened awareness of new bonds of love that you are continually weaving with the loved ones in your life, and
3. a deep sense of joy and fulfillment as you express yourself with greater freedom.

To bring these experiences into your life do the following activity.

To The Components Of Contemplation...

HumaNatureConnect Activity

Start-up Protocol

If this is not a day when you prefer to spend time in nature without an agenda, do the Heartwood Path Start-up Protocol found in the Appendix.

Using The Elements Of Meditation

For this activity, experience the elements of attunement meditation in seven steps:

Step One: Relax and Notice Your Breathing: Sit comfortably, close your eyes and take a few deep breaths. Relax your body. Say to yourself inwardly "I now release all tension in my thoughts, emotions, and body. My body is now relaxing more and more. I am now entering a deep, calm state of relaxation. I feel completely relaxed and peaceful." As you speak, notice your breathing but do not adjust or control it.

Step Two: Letting Go of Physical Reality. Direct your inner awareness away from your thoughts. Let your attention gently float away from your thoughts. Imagine that you are beginning to slowly float upward above the Earth. You are feeling yourself leaving behind all burdens as you float away from all physical reality.

Step Three: Creating Loving Harmony: Accept but ignore any distracting thoughts that arise. Pay attention to your imagination and direct it into alignment with your intuitive capacity for loving harmony. Initiate this by imagining a setting that inspires a feeling of loving harmony in you. Imagine that the powerful intuitive capacity that lives within you is coming forward into the moment. Inwardly feel that you are intuitively aligning with your own deep inner wisdom. Use your imagination to place yourself fully into your harmonious inner landscape. Enter that landscape and begin to live within it with great abandonment and joy. Turn your attention to the force that unites all beings in all realms of existence-the force of love. Be aware that a divine energy of love permeates all of life. Bring your imagination and creativity together in your beautiful inner landscape. Begin to imagine that you are surrounded by loving souls who share the wonder of existence with you. Feel surrounded by beloved ones of an exalted nature and become joined to them by the energy of love.

Step Four: Sense Your Soul. Imagine your Soul surrounding you lovingly. Give yourself to the feelings that arise from your Soul's energy. Open the spiritual intuition through which you can sense your soul. Know that your soul is present and that it loves you.

Step Five: Experience Your Soul More Deeply. Create a real and current feeling of love for a person in your life or generate a similar feeling of self-love. In your imagination, give of yourself without straining or forcing. Imagine how precious you are to your Soul. Feel your Soul's love deeply.

Step Six: Give Yourself to Your Soul. Allow everything to slip away from your awareness. In this moment begin to project yourself beyond your circle of familiarity. Prepare your blank mind for newness by having no ideas about what is coming. Become calm, poised, expectant, and trusting. Resist the temptation to imagine where your Soul will take you. Know that if you think and do nothing your Soul will deepen your attunement. Begin to feel your gentle and soft Soul moving close to you. Allow your Soul to give you new, clear, and profound perceptions. Rejoice as you release yourself into the love and wisdom of your Soul, into goodness and the love of all life.

Step Seven: Return To Your Personal Life. Let go of the expanded awareness that you have created during your attunement period. Gently and slowly move back toward your strong feeling of yourself. Gradually release your expanded awareness. Turn your attention to your physical body. Notice any sensations present in various parts of your body. Turn your attention to your outer physical surroundings. Feel yourself comfortably contained in your physical surroundings.

Think about your daily affairs. Slowly open your eyes. Sit until you regain your equilibrium. Then slowly and joyfully resume your daily activities.

Follow-up Protocol

For best results, write down your impressions of this activity in your journal using the Heartwood Path Follow-up Protocol found in the Appendix. Afterwards, consider sharing your interpretations with others.

Heartwood Path Axioms

Key Assertions From Waypoint 3.30

3.30.1.

Attunement is a portal to the Soul that requires confidence in one's own ability to make an inner opening—a blank space in the psyche where one can place a newly refined level of sensitivity.

3.30.2.

The blank space in the psyche needed to create a Portal to the Soul is created by temporarily disengaging from one's own fascination with the physical world; and, in the place of this blankness is the acceptance of many "affordances" from the spiritual realm, including: an expanded awareness of the magnificence of life; an inner power you can use to balance the strong influences of the outer physical world; and an ability to project yourself in your imagination beyond your present experience of yourself as a human being.

3.30.3.

During this More-Than-Individual experience of your Self you will experience: greater self-confidence, strength, power, and increased creativity; a wonderful feeling of belonging that is based upon an enlightened awareness of new bonds of love that you are continually weaving with the loved ones in your life, and a deep sense of joy and fulfillment as you express yourself with greater freedom.

Nocturnal Pilgrimage 3.30

For best results, write down your impressions of each night's dreams in your journal using the Heartwood Path Dreaming Time Protocols found in the Appendix. Afterwards, consider sharing your Dream Tending with others.

If you are still having difficulties falling asleep add another component to your end of day ritual. Strive to go to sleep at the same time every day.

Tend to your dream before learning how to ascend, branch by branch up the beanstalk of spiritual growth. This topic is covered at the next waypoint.

After reading about the Beanstalk of Spiritual Development be sure to do the activity in nature. Doing so will help to demonstrate your deepest roots in nature. You will find that you remain irrevocably linked with the whole of the world. Don't be like the 11,000 adults in Denmark who lived more than a half mile from forests, parks, beaches and lakes were 42 percent more likely to report high stress and score badly on general health, mental health, and bodily pain evaluations (Selhub & Logan, 2012, p.25).

Move to the next waypoint, "The Beanstalk And The Tree," to begin your ascent towards greater depth and integrity. There, you will learn how going through developmental steps having to do with duty, wants, finding peace, intuition, meeting desires, miracle-making, and ultimate unity help you to become a secular saint.

31

The Beanstalk And The Tree

CLIMB YOUR WAY TO SPIRITUAL MATURITY

Each person undergoes spiritual development, a long climb towards fulfillment. How far you go in this development becomes your spiritual formation.

We all begin at a level where we gain fulfillment through fight or flight responses involving family, community, a sense of belonging, and material comforts. Most of us add to this level of develop reactive responses that are attempts at fulfillment through success, power, influence, status and other ways to satisfy our egos. Some of us may hold on to the flight or flight responses and the reactive responses but temper them with restful awareness responses that have to do with finding fulfillment through peace, centeredness, self-acceptance, and inner silence. Thinking that what amounted to Branch Three was the highest plateau, I remained at this level for over thirty years. It wasn't until I began to find fulfillment through insight, tolerance, and forgiveness that I saw glimpses of my higher potential. Such peak experiences sometimes come through unpleasantness. I am recalling a conversation

I had during my Thirties wherein I was informed of the difference between sympathy and empathy (as I was told, sympathy is getting someone a drink of water; empathy is sharing in the feelings of being thirsty —well, excuuuuussse me!). Apparently, since I did not know what empathy was, I had not yet reached the fourth level of spiritual development. I certainly did not know that there was three more possible stages. This portion of the Heartwood Path is a metaphorical climb up seven distinct branches of spiritual development on something similar to Jack's beanstalk in the popular children's fable (See Figure 5.).

While there is nothing someone can do to guarantee that one will move to a certain level of development, what follows gives you a very good map for the course of your spiritual development (the Beanstalk of Spiritual Development) and what psycho-spiritual work one will need to do to move to each stage of growth (working on overcoming certain dilemmas identified shortly).

BEAN STALK
OF SPIRTUAL
DEVELOPMENT

7. INFINITE KNOWLEDGE

6. VISIONARY

UNITY WITH GOD

MIRACLE MAKER

5. CREATIVE

4. INTUITIVE

MEET DESIRES

INNER KNOWLEDGE

3. RESTFUL AWARENESS

PEACE

2. REACTIONARY

GET WHAT YOU WANT

1. SURVIVAL

FIGHT OR FLIGHT

ART WORK DONE BY THERESA GRANT

Figure 5: The Beanstalk of Spiritual Development

The Beanstalk of Spiritual Development is a fitting metaphor because, like Jack who climbed from his backyard to the clouds, we move,
step-by-step, from the tribulations of our earthly existence to God's
Heaven or the Realm of The Absolute Spirit. In our beanstalk model

of spiritual development each person's step up from one branch to another breaks the boundaries of the previous level.

The Beanstalk of Spiritual Develop is inspired by Dr. Deepak Chopra's rungs of spiritual development as described in his excellent book, **How to Know God** (2000). In honor of the way Chopra wrote his book, we shall in this section often use the Judeo-Christian term for The Absolute Spirit: "God."

Writes Chopra, "God is another name for infinite intelligence " (1999, p. 16). As we make achievements in our lives and as we grow spiritually, we come to know, little by little, more of God, more of infinite intelligence.

Branch One

At the first level, life becomes fulfilling through family, community, material comforts, and a sense of belonging. Hiding the onset of deeper spiritual beliefs, one is likely to an atheist, a cynic, or a failed seeker. Life is experienced as full of danger, threat, and struggles for survival. The chief way one responds to life is through fight-or-flight reactions. One's fall-back emotion is anxiety. One's identity is tied to the physical body and the physical environment. God is seen as The Protector. One holds onto this stage of separation by saying, in effect, "I am in such separation that I sense deep fear inside."

Branch Two

At the second level, life become fulfilling through success, influence, power, status, and various ways to satisfy the Ego. Hiding from deeper spiritual beliefs, one is likely likely to be a leader who is and achiever but also a skeptic. Key life experiences have to do with striving, competition, and power. One's fall-back emotion is anger and obstinacy. The main way one responds is reactive. One's identity is tied to one's Ego and personality. God is seen as The Almighty One begins to lose this stage of separation by say, in effect "I don't feel so separate, I am gaining a sense of power."

Branch Three

At the third level, life becomes fulfilling through peace, centeredness, self-acceptance, and inner silence. As a thinker and dreamer, life becomes peaceful and calm. There is time for reflection. The tell-tale way one responds is through restful awareness (like when you are quietly visiting a natural being at the beginning of each waypoint along the Heartwood Path). One's identity becomes a silent witness. God is seen as Peace. One begins to move from this stage of separation when one begins to say, in effect: "Something larger than me is drawing near, I feel much more peaceful."

Branch Four

At the fourth level, which may not be known to some younger Heartwood Path participants, life becomes fulfilling through insight, empathy, forgiveness, and tolerance. One's fall-back emotion is a healthy detachment. As an idealist and a liberator, one is nonjudgmental and defies normal expectations. Being insightful, understanding, and forgiving come to the forefront. The main way one responds is through intuition. One becomes a co-creator with God. God, who is seen as The Redeemer. One may be on the verge of the next level when one begins to say, in effect, "I am beginning to intuit the Nature of God."

Branch Five

At the fifth level, life becomes fulfilling through inspiration, expanded creativity in art and science, and unlimited discovery. As an artist, adventurer, and explorer, one has a tendency to be emotionally resilient and sensitive. Aspirations, creative outlets, and discovery are the notable ways life is experienced. The dominant way the few who achieve this level of spiritual development responds is through creativity. Enlightenment illuminates one's identity. In this light, God is seen as The Creator. A sign that one may be ready to move to the next level occurs when one begins to say, in effect: "My actions and thoughts are drawing on God's force field and we together are creating the future."

Branch Six

At the sixth level, which marks the enduring destination or outcome of the Heartwood Path, life becomes fulfilling through reverence, compassion and universal love. One's tell-tale experiences at this level have to do with reverence, and compassion. One's fall-back emotion is love. As a prophet and redeemer, one humbly sees the depths of any person or situation. The main way the visionary ones at this lofty level respond is through devoted service. God is seen through Miracles. You will know that you are approaching the end of the Heartwood Path when you begin to say, in effect: "God and I are almost together now."

Branch Seven

This level of spiritual development for those who follow the Heartwood Path is typically only experienced as temporary peak experiences, just long enough to achieve a momentary but profound glimpse of wholeness and unity with the divine—that is, with God or the Absolute. Unbounded unity is the experience that tells the pilgrim on a spiritual development path that one is, at least, peaking over the threshold of this level. One's indicative responses are of sacredness. One's fall-back emotion is compassion. One merges with the source of all. Oneself and God are unified as Pure Being. Your tell-tale sign that you have achieved the last level of spiritual development may come as a fleeting impression that there is no difference between you and God.

To Begin The Work Of Determining Your Level Of Spiritual Development...

HumaNatureConnect Activity

Start-up Protocol

If this is not a day when you prefer to spend time in nature without an agenda, do the Heartwood Path Start-up Protocol found in the Appendix.

Determining Your Level Of Spiritual Development

For this activity, in what ever fashion you like, answer the following questions. Do not worry if you seem puzzled by these questions at this time. Some helpful guidance follows, beginning in the next Nocturnal Pilgrimage section.

It is always a treat to see what you are learning. You will be given directions in more elaborate ways of answering the following eight questions in the following seven waypoints. It will be interesting to compare the answers you give here, prior to tutoring, to the post-tutoring statements you give concerning topics related to each question in the next few waypoints.

1. Who am I?
2. How do I fit in?
3. What is the nature of good and evil?
4. How do I find God?
5. What is my life challenge?
6. What is my greatest strength?
7. What is my biggest hurdle?
8. What is my greatest temptation? (Chopra, 2000, pp. 51-179).

Follow-up Protocol

For best results, write down your impressions of this activity in your journal using the Heartwood Path Follow-up Protocol found in the Appendix. Afterwards, consider sharing your interpretations with others.

Heartwood Path Axioms

Key Assertions From Waypoint 3.31

3.31.1.

Attunement is a portal to the Soul that requires confidence in one's own ability to make an inner opening—a blank space in the psyche where one can place a newly refined level of sensitivity.

3.31.2.

The blank space in the psyche needed to create a Portal to the Soul is created by temporarily disengaging from one's own fascination with the physical world; and, in the place of this blankness is the acceptance of many "affordances" from the spiritual realm, including: an expanded awareness of the magnificence of life; an inner power you can use to balance the strong influences of the outer physical world; and an ability to project yourself in your imagination beyond your present experience of yourself as a human being.

3.31.3.

During this More-Than-Individual experience of your Self you will experience: Greater Self-confidence, strength, power, and increased creativity; a wonderful feeling of belonging that is based upon an enlightened awareness of new bonds of love that you are continually weaving with the loved ones in your life,

and a deep sense of joy and fulfillment as you express yourself
with greater freedom.

Nocturnal Pilgrimage 3.31

For best results, write down your impressions of each night's
dreams in your journal using the Heartwood Path Dreaming Time
Protocols found in the Appendix. Afterwards, consider sharing your
Dream Tending with others.

Sleep, dream, and tend to your dream before learning how to
ascend, branch by branch up the ladder of spiritual growth. This topic
is covered at the next waypoint.

But before you go there and begin your next daytime activity,
understand how to use the Tree of Life in your nocturnal reveries.

Put The Tree Of Life To Good Use

Tree Of Life

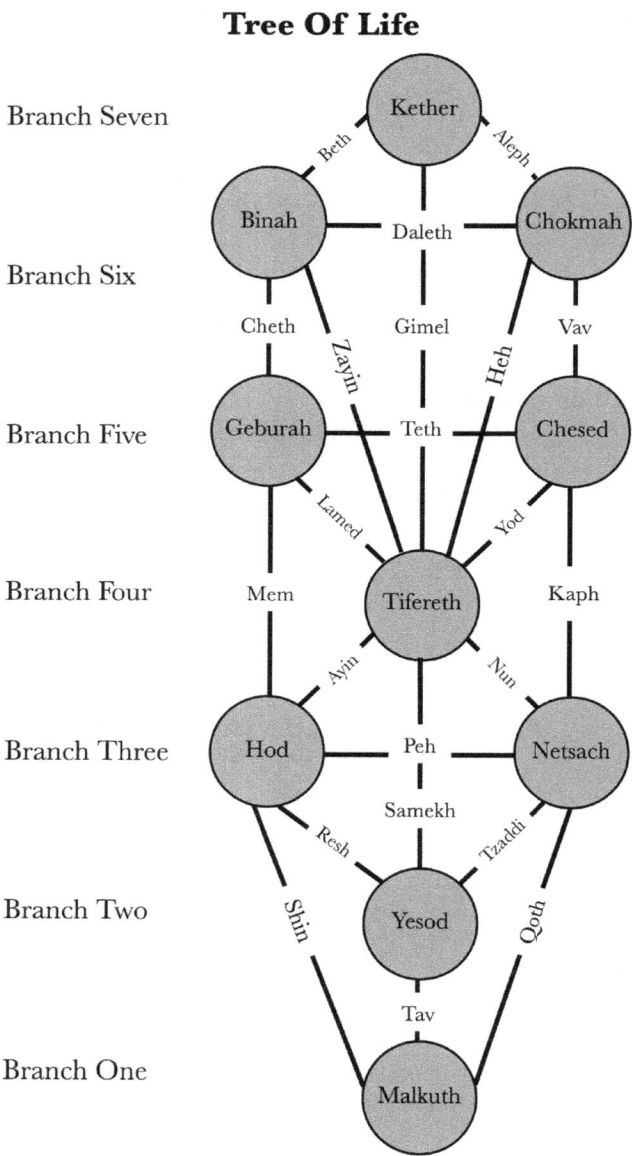

Branch Seven

Branch Six

Branch Five

Branch Four

Branch Three

Branch Two

Branch One

In the next seven Nocturnal Pilgrimages we will present correspondences between dreams and the various stops and pathways of the Kabbalist's Tree of Life, shown above. We do this because certain dreams
tend to be indicators of one's spiritual development, not perfectly, but

at least enough so that one can monitor one's development through one's dreams.

We will be stating what your dreams may be indicating. We say "may" because you may have a different interpretation. By linking one's dreams to the various locations in the Tree of Life we are not claiming (or denying) anything magical, just as we are not claiming nor denying anything magical about Native American Medicine Wheel, the Hindu Sri Yanta, or any other forms of sacred geometry allayed along the Heartwood Path. At the least, the associations that are presented here, which come largely from Jonathan Sharp's book **Divining Your Dreams,** are included here just to get the participant's minds working on possible interpretations. Feel free to take the dream interpretations submitted in the following tables with a grain of salt. The interpretations are certainly not presented here as a way to condense the meaning of your dreams down to any set explanation. Do not impoverish the meaning of your dreams by attempting to prematurely interpret their meaning. Often, hasty interpretations deplete the real world by replacing it, or aspects of it, into a duplicate, shadow world of "meanings." Instead of merely relying on hastily made duplicates that are made of premature interpretations, favor the experiencing of what is before you. Do not make your dream tending only a process of solving riddles or problems. Instead, make your dreams and your dream tending mysteries to be experienced. In dream tending as in living your daytime life, favor experiencing being alive over pigeon-holing your life into the tunnel vision of problem-solving. That way your life and your dreams will have resonance with your innermost being and outer world reality. Having said this, I do feel that the interpretations in the following seven tables are worthy food for thought. They may help you find certain solutions. Just be sure not to let them squelch out the rapture of being alive. **You and your dreams will always be more than your constructed definitions or conclusions.**

For this reason, always will your "known self" be a fiction. Rather than minimizing yourself into a capsulated "known self," seek instead to center yourself in the realm of the present. You cannot be both a fiction and an actual presence. Choose to be present.

We will, in the last Heartwood Path book, present an integral, non-interpretive way to make sense of one's dreams. This integral approach, which includes the Dream Tending methods presented by Dr. Aizenstat, will be most helpful in using your dreams to glean guidance from your nature connect activities or any other aspect of your life. But, for now, use the following dream associations as a footing, as a way to begin your own process of tending to your dreams. These associations will provide a useful component, rather than a "be all, end all," to your overall dream tending approach.

Now for a few words about the Kabbalist's Tree of Life. The circles you see on the Tree of Life represent universal forces. Note that there are levels (some horizontal and some diagonal) which I have associated to our Branches of the Beanstalk of Spiritual Growth. The forces that form the right column have to do with action and wisdom. The forces on the left have to do with receptive intelligence and understanding. At the top of the Tree of Life is Kether, the highest level of spiritual development. Below it are Binah, which represents understanding, and Chokmah, which represents wisdom. The Sephorot I have associated with Branch Five include Chesed, which represents mercy, and Geburah, which represents strength. I associate Tiffereth, which represents beauty, with the Fourth Branch of Spiritual Development. Branch Three is correlated with both Hod, which represents glory and Netsach, which represents victory. Yesod, which I correlated with Branch Two, stands for foundation. For the First Branch, I place Malkuth, which represents kingdom. In these associations, one may notice some further correlations with the seven chakras. In the interest of moving ahead, I will hold on this discussion; but it will be included in the Heartwood Path book called **Eros**. Between the various Sephorot are twenty-two pathways. As you dream, it will likely help you tend to your dreams by noting which of these pathways Jonathan Sharp associates with your dream characters. As you continue to commune with nature it is reasonable to assume that, more and more, natural beings will be present in your dreams. In the tables presented here, you can see how Sharp associates some of the natural beings in your dreams with the various Tree of Life Sephorot, which represent the forces previously mentioned, and the pathways between the Sephorot, which represent various life situations, as follows:

1. Tav, serving consciousness, administrative intelligence, power/servitude;
2. Ayin, natural consciousness, renovating intelligence, mirth;
3. Qoth, perpetual consciousness, corporeal intelligence, sleep;
4. Mem, eternal consciousness, the garden of pleasure, stable intelligence, water;
5. Samekh, exciting consciousness, temperance, tentative intelligence, anger;
6. Tzaddi, corporeal consciousness, constituting intelligence, imagination;
7. Lamed, consciousness of will, faithful intelligence, work;
8. Nun, faithfulness consciousness, imaginative intelligence, movement;
9. Resh, consciousness of trial, collecting intelligence, fertility or barrenness;
10. Yod, consciousness of disposition, the foundation of beauty, willful intelligence, sexual love;
11. Peh, consciousness of the desired-which-fulfills, exciting intelligence, grace/indignation;
12. Aleph, perfect consciousness, the plan of the primordial, scintillating intelligence, air;
13. Teth, scintillating consciousness, spiritual intelligence, taste;
14. Kaph, consciousness of the house of influence, conciliating intelligence, riches/poverty;
15. Daleth, luminous consciousness, illuminating intelligence, peace/war;
16. Cheth, pure consciousness, influencing intelligence, speech;
17. Shin, imaginative consciousness, perpetual intelligence, fire;

18. Gimel, transparent consciousness, uniting intelligence, wisdom/folly;
19. Zayin, mediating consciousness, disposing intelligence, smell;
20. Heh, illuminating consciousness, natural intelligence, sight;
21. Vav, root consciousness, triumphal intelligence, hearing; hearing; and
22. Beth, overflowing consciousness, transparent intelligence, life/death (Clark) & (Byzant Kabbalah) & (Copenhagen Qabalah).

As you dream about natural beings, use Sharp's associations as a beginning point in your attempts to make some sense of your nighttime reveries (especially if nothing seems to come to mind initially). Rather than diminish your dreams into absolute, static, single, concrete interpretations, take Sharp's interesting and telling associations as helpful starting points for your own ongoing dream tending. By starting with an association of your dream to the various stations in the Tree of Life you will have worthwhile food for thought. Always, however, feel free to accept or reject any predetermined meaning for your dreams. The significance of your dreams are yours alone. The pre-established meanings of others cannot reflect your own unique perspectives and situations. That said, you may be tapping into dreams of the earth, which could have more universal meanings, as displayed in the following tables. For these reasons, the informed and time-tested associations in the following tables will give you a significant way to initiate your dream tending. Be sure to use the associations as a jump-start rather than a stopping place. The associations are presented as suggestions and not as final answers, which is why the tables are titled with the words "**Possible** Meaning" and "**Suggested** . . . Actions." Use these helpful and thought-provoking tables, but do not live by them alone.

Answer Key Questions For Each Branch Of Spiritual Development

In a directed way in each of the activities that follow, you will have a chance to answer pointed questions for each of the branches of spiritual development. Attempting to answer these question will help you determine which branch on the Beanstalk of Spiritual Development best represents your current spiritual formation. If the job of answering the questions at one level seems boringly obvious, you are likely to be on a higher branch. If you cannot answer the questions on a level or have no idea what the question is about, you are likely to be on a lower branch. If the questions I have included for a particular branch seem particularly pertinent to your life right now, that is likely to be your current "place" on the Beanstalk of Spiritual Development. By looking over all of the questions, you will be able to anticipate what comes next. Knowing what comes next may quicken your assent up the Beanstalk of Spiritual Development, but not as much as living fully on the preceding branch. Resist the temptation to push yourself up the Beanstalk prematurely. There is no need to rush and certainly it is not wise, nor even possible, to skip branches. Live your life fully by carefully absorbing the lessons at each branch. Most people will remain for the duration of their lives on the lower branches. This is to be expected and not a cause for concern. There are no preferred branches. Like emotions, one's level of spiritual development are not to be judged. One's level of spiritual development and one's emotions are not to be favored nor condemned; any level, like any emotion, is outside of the prerogative of what ought to be judged. Each is to be accepted merely because it exists. Judgements about anyone's position on the Beanstalk are, therefore, inappropriate. Don't make such assessments; and, if you do, keep them to yourself. It is better to be honestly functioning on a lower branch than it is to pretend to be on an upper level. Let other's speculate about your position on the Beanstalk. It is as socially unacceptable to openly state your level of spiritual development as it is to go around talking about your net worth. Let your own actions speak for themselves. Your responses to life situations will offer clues about your place on the Beanstalk. Openly boasting or complaining about your place on the Beanstalk is blowing your own horn to a lousy tune.

By avoiding actions that are unnecessary or unproductive one can move up the Beanstalk of Spiritual Development without wasting too much time. While transcendence (carrying all previous developmental levels up with you as you move to a new level) is never guaranteed, knowing specifically what one has to do to move up to the next branch makes spiritual development faster and easier. Having said this, it is important to remember not to try to short circuit the process by turning it into a race. In this section on the Beanstalk of Spiritual Development, it is extremely likely (and acceptable) that you will be ready to move to the next waypoint before you have achieved what it takes to stand firmly on its higher branches. If this is the case, read on anyway. Do so for fact-finding purposes only. Just as there is nothing wrong with remaining on a lower level, so too is there nothing wrong with finding out what may come next for you. Discover what to look for at each branch. You may very well have to engage in waypoints way down the Heartwood Path before you begin to actually transcend to higher branches on the Beanstalk of Spiritual Develop. Your continued development, whether you remain on a single branch or move up to higher branches, is a purpose for this series of books. If you *are* undergoing spiritual transformations as you take this course, take the time to savor the changes in your mental processing, view, and actions. Disregard anyone's judgments as your spiritual development stalls or as you proceed from branch to branch. To help you know what to look for as you learn about adding depth to one's character, take note of the step-by-step benchmarks in the process of moving up the Beanstalk of Spiritual Development.

With these preparatory remarks about the Beanstalk of Spiritual Development and the Tree of Life, you are now well prepared to move to (or learn more about) the next waypoint: "Branch One." You are making good headway towards the fortuitous junction of gladness and greenness.

32

Branch One

SOLIDIFY YOURSELF ON THE FIRST BRANCH OF THE BEANSTALK OF SPIRITUAL DEVELOPMENT

This is the branch with the shallowest depth—the level of spiritual development where people exhibit the fight or flight response that expands their consciousness sufficiently to reveal the Supreme Being as God the Protector. Those who rest on the first branch are bounded by guilt, duty, and victimization. Faith—a good teacher, especially in the absence of fact—is, for those at this branch, a matter of survival. God, it is believed, can destroy a devotee if he or she does not pray to Him. Those who rest on Branch One are bounded by anxiety, insecurity and dependency. People on Branch One feel vulnerable to the vast expanse of Nature, which, they feel, God sometimes uses to punish them for wrongdoing. People on Branch One focus most on survival—survival at any cost.

The Dilemma Of Branch One

The predicament that needs to be transcended before those on Branch One can move on to Branch Two begins with the feeling of being afraid of losing the acceptance of others in their family, tribe, or social group. People on Branch One believe that those who are closest to them offer physical and psychological protection. But protection that goes too far is tyranny. To disobey God's wishes, social customs, or laws is seen by those on Branch One as committing a wrongful act.

Only when personal integrity is seen as being more important than being accepted will the devotee be able to stand on the next higher branch. The onset of this shift to a deeper level of spiritual growth is marked by three things:

1. the beginning of the feeling that asking God to protect you is like asking the perpetrator of a criminal act to protect you (since God both protects and punishes);
2. asking the question "Why did God make such a world of suffering?" and
3. being tired of existing in a state of dependency, vulnerability and insecurity.

When a person begins attempting to solve the dilemma of Branch One with any or all the above stated psychological events, that person is ready to step up to Branch Two.

To Fulfillment Through Family, Community, A Sense Of Belonging, And Material Comforts...

HumaNatureConnect Activity

Start-up Protocol

If this is not a day when you prefer to spend time in nature without an agenda, do the Heartwood Path Start-up Protocol found in the Appendix.

Standing Solidly On The First Branch Of Spiritual Development

For this activity, take another stab at the eight determining spiritual development questions, this time with some pertinent direction. Given what you learned about the nature of the first stage of spiritual development, answer the following questions:

1. For the "Who am I?" question, describe ways that you are a survivor.
2. For the "How do I fit?" question, describe ways that you cope.
3. For the "What is the Nature of good and evil?" question, talk about how you relate to goodness (specifically, safety, comfort, food, shelter, and family) and evilness (specifically, physical threats and abandonment).
4. For the "How do I find God?" question, describe how you do so with fear and/or loving devotion.
5. For the "What is my life challenge?" question, describe your challenge to survive, challenge to protect, and challenge to maintain.
6. For the "What is my greatest strength?" question, focus of describing your courage.
7. For the "What is my biggest hurdle?" question, focus on any issues of abandonment and any fear of loss. And
8. For the "What is my greatest temptation?" question, describe how tyranny impacts your life.

Follow-up Protocol

For best results, write down your impressions of this activity in your journal using the Heartwood Path Follow-up Protocol found in the Appendix. Afterwards, consider sharing your interpretations with others.

Heartwood Path Axioms

Key Assertions From Waypoint 3.32

3.32.1.

Climb the Beanstalk of Spiritual Development.

3.32.2.

The Soul has do with relationship—how a person or thing relates to others.

3.32.3.

The Beanstalk of Spiritual Development includes the following themes for each of its branches: duty, obtaining wants; finding peace, intuition; meeting desires; miracle-making; and ultimate unity.

3.32.4.

The Beanstalk of Spiritual Development illustrates one of the processes used along the Heartwood Path to become a secular saint.

Nocturnal Pilgrimage 3.32

For best results, write down your impressions of each night's dreams in your journal using the Heartwood Path Dreaming Time Protocols found in the Appendix. Afterwards, consider sharing your Dream Tending with others.

Look over the table below. Set an intention to dream about any of the topics listed in the first column.. Consider how such dreams are anchoring you on each associated branch or how such dreams are indicators of your accomplishment of a branch on the Beanstalk Of Spiritual Development. You may not be good at evoking certain dreams yet. If this is the case, you may want to read about all the dreams and that way you can process a wider variety of potential natural-being oriented dreams.

Dream Subjects Related To Branch One	Path Of Wisdom Locations Associated With Dream	Possible Meaning Of Dreams And Their Tree Of Life Associations	Suggested Dream-inspired Developmental Actions
Autumn	Tav (Between Malchut and Yesod/ Between Branches One and Two).	Moving from the comforts of the material world to the uncertainties of the spiritual world. Connecting to feelings of suffering and melancholy. The positive completion of a phase of your life.	Seek out like-minded individuals who have more experience. Look for the positive in the distressing.

Cats	Sefirah of Malkut.	One has a materialistic outlook, behave in a self-interested way, self-absorption, focused on bettering one's material status rather than on one's spiritual state.	After being driven by the Absolute through the occurrence of an initiatory spiritual experience, open the door to inner development.
Insect	Tree of Life Sephorah of Malkut. Branch One.	Beginning of the struggle for higher knowledge. The start of the commitment to the Great Work. Understanding that, while physical items perish, the Soul lives on.	Develop your sense of wonder. Walk in a natural landscape and notice how even the smallest and lowliest beings are wonderfully constructed.
Fog	Tree of Life Pathway Qoph, between the Sephorahs of Netsach and Malkut.	Uncertain about direction, worries about losing one's way, successfully picking a route.	Put your considerable spiritual energy into drumming or chanting.

Forest	Tree of Life Sephorah of Malkut. Branch One.	Gloom and wild freedom.	Talk to someone capable of listening to you about your fears.
Honey	Tree of Life Pathway Shin, joining Hod with Malkut.	One's sweet relationship with the Divine.	Access the spiritual energy within you by practicing tai chi, or Kundalini yoga.
Leaves	Tree of Life Pathway of Tav, between Yesod and Malkut. Branch One.	Wisdom is falling from the Tree of Life, resulting in the initiation of personal profound development.	Take ample time to watch carefully and relate natural beings to a spiritual view of the world
Nest	Tree of Life Pathway of Qoph, between Malkut and Netsach. Transitioning beyond Branch One, leaping to Branch Three.	The desire to return to a protected state or an earlier branch of one's spiritual formation. No feelings of evidence of a higher power.	Continue your inner journey. Face fears of finding doubt and challenges to your beliefs. Look for ways to connect with a higher power. Look for the promise of the existence of the macrocosmic force.

Planet	Tree of Life Sephorah of Malkut. Branch One.	Thinking of the Earth spinning its way through the universe is humbling. One can see the realm of the physical in its proper context, as a sort of launching pad into the realm of the spiritual. One may feel uncertain about the prospect of leaving the certainties of the physical plane.	Make a conscious commitment to the Great Work.
Quartz	Tree of Life Sephorah of Malkut. Branch One.	One is beginning to comprehend that the world is more than just physical.	Reconsider the nature of the physical world. Look for the presence of the Absolute.

| Rain | Tree of Life Sefi-rah of Malkut. | A source of life and abundance. A symbol of divine grace. An initial sensing of the presence of the Absolute. | To return home to your spiritual source, renew your energy, trust the physical world, tend a garden, experience the wonder of the natural world. Your relationship with plants will be a mirror of the Absolutes relationship with you and a preparation for your participation in the Great Work. |

| Sex | Tree of Life Sefirah of Malkut. | The potential to create a new and complete being. Associations with the material world. A new conception of the spiritual nature of the universe. Bringing new creation to the universe may be painful, but it will result in important new conceptions. | Have sex responsibly. Use Tantric and other methods to bring a spiritual component to your lovemaking. |
| Shark | Tree of Life Pathway of Qoth, between Malkuth and Netsach. Moving from Branch One to Branch Three. | Fear of a dead and unfeeling universe, fear of a cold and inevitable death. Defensiveness about the spiritual quest. | Study and practice meditation. |

| Wildness | Tree of Life Pathway of Shin, between Malkuth and Netsach. Moving from Branch One to Branch Three. | Spiritual beings have both a need for order and a need for wildness. | Include compassion and empathy in your spiritual quest. |

When ready, move to the next waypoint: "Branch Two."

33

Branch Two

CLIMB TO THE SECOND BRANCH ON THE BEANSTALK OF SPIRITUAL DEVELOPMENT

This level of spiritual development is where people exhibit the reactionary response that expands their consciousness sufficiently to reveal the Supreme Being as God the Almighty. For those on Branch Two, faith is a matter of getting what you want. People on the second branch believe God is powerful and dangerous. They succumb to power, which is seen as irresistible. They believe that God rules by laws and governance rather than by acts of Nature (as was believed in Branch One). People on the Second Branch of Spiritual Development frequently seek to fulfill Ego demands. They follow the dictum "More for me" and live in a world of competition and ambition. They seek to satisfy the Ego without looking bad in the omniscient eyes of God. They find satisfaction in being a skilled worker. They begin to set up rules for self-governance. Lastly, they seek to have perfect bodies, perfect families, and perfect careers (sometimes to the point of killing spontaneity).

The Dilemma Of Branch Two

The predicament that needs to be transcended before those on Branch Two can move on to Branch Three begins with the feeling that too much consideration of "I," "me," and "mine" leaves a person feeling empty inside. Additional and related aspects of this dilemma include believing that power, the outward symbols of power, and possessions lead to a lack of meaning. People with this dilemma begin to wonder why one's own hard work is not paying off.

Only when one's own external pleasures lead to guilt will the devotee be able to enter the next level. The onset of this shift to a deeper level of spiritual growth is marked by the rejection of the addiction to money, the rejection of physical pleasure for its own sake, and the rejection of other desires of the Ego; the questioning of laws; and the desire to turn inward to break the spell of cravings.

When a person begins attempting to solve the dilemma of Branch Two with any or all the above stated psychological events, that person is ready to step up to Branch Three.

To Fulfillment Through Success, Power, Influence, Status, And Other Ego-gratifications…

HumaNatureConnect Activity

Start-up Protocol

If this is not a day when you prefer to spend time in nature without an agenda, do the Heartwood Path Start-up Protocol found in the Appendix.

Standing Solidly On The Second Branch Of Spiritual Development

For this activity, take another stab at the eight determining spiritual development questions, made pertinent to the present discussion.

Given what you learned about the nature of the second stage of spiritual development, answer the following questions:

1. For the "Who am I?" question, describe your ego and personality.
2. For the "How do I fit?" question, describe ways that you seek to win.
3. For the "What is the Nature of good and evil?" question, discuss whether you are good at getting what you want and how, if at all, evil is an obstacle in your pathway toward your goals.
4. For the "How do I find God?" question, discuss the role of obedience and awe in your life.
5. For the "What is my life challenge?" question, describe your greatest achievement.
6. For the "What is my greatest strength?" question, describe what you brought to bear to achieve your accomplishments.
7. For the "What is my biggest hurdle?" question, discuss the impact of guilt and victimization in your life. And
8. For the "What is my greatest temptation?" question, describe whether you have any addictions.

Follow-up Protocol

For best results, write down your impressions of this activity in your journal using the Heartwood Path Follow-up Protocol found in the Appendix. Afterwards, consider sharing your interpretations with others.

Heartwood Path Axioms

Key Assertions From Waypoint 3.33

3.33.1.

Climb to the second branch of the Beanstalk of Spiritual Development.

3.33.2.

Make your life better by fulfilling yourself through success, influence, power, status, and various ways to satisfy the Ego.

3.33.3.

People on the Second Branch of Spiritual Development frequently seek to fulfill Ego demands through competition, ambition, being a skilled worker and setting up rules for self-governance.

3.33.4.

The predicament that needs to be transcended before those on Branch Two can move on to Branch Three begins with the feeling that too much consideration of "I," "me," and "mine" leaves a person feeling empty inside.

Nocturnal Pilgrimage 3.33

For best results, write down your impressions of each night's dreams in your journal using the Heartwood Path Dreaming Time Protocols found in the Appendix. Afterwards, consider sharing your Dream Tending with others.

Look over the next table and consider the associations as food for thought for your own dream tending.

Dream Subjects Related To Branch Two	Path Of Wisdom Locations Associated With Dream	Possible Meaning Of Dreams And Their Tree Of Life Associations	Suggested Dream-inspired Developmental Actions
Eggs	Tree of Life Sephorah of Yesod.	One's foundation, the promises that lie within oneself, being reborn as a spiritual being, at once both interconnected and unique.	Be dogged in your persistence, sticking to a definite plan.
Evening	Tree of Life Pathway of Resh, between Hod and Yesod. Branch Two.	One's level of insight is progressing. One senses that the Divine is being encouraging and protective.	Focus on your intuitive sensitivity. Avoid harsh lessons, favoring instead warm and calm sources of learning. Calm yourself by lying on your back and breathing in an out deeply, completely, and calmly.

Mosquito	Tree of Life Pathway of Samech, between the Sephorahs of Yesod and Tifereth. Branch Two and Branch Three.	Represents an obstacle to one's inner progress, encourages retreat, and shows a lack of balance. One is likely to be overly reliant on the Absolute.	Work on standing alone confidently in order to continue your progress.
Springtime	Tree of Life Pathway of Resh, between the Sephorahs of Yesod and Hod. Moving from Branch Two to Branch Three.	Represents optimism, hope, and benevolence.	Awaken the divine spark within you. Continue to work on your spiritual development.

When ready, move to the next waypoint: "Branch Three."

34

Branch Three

CLIMB TO THE THIRD BRANCH ON THE BEANSTALK OF SPIRITUAL DEVELOPMENT

This level of spiritual development is where people exhibit the restful awareness response that expands their consciousness sufficiently to reveal the Supreme Being as the God of Peace. Faith, for those on Branch Three, is a matter of peace.

Those who rest on Branch Three are bounded by karma, introversion, and lack of power. One knows one has a lack of leverage when one has to tell people one has power.

The Dilemma Of Branch Three

The predicament that needs to be transcended before those on Branch Three can move on to Branch Four begins with the feeling that integrity (even unpopular aspects of one's self) is more important than being accepted. Sometimes a person feels the need to express one's differences. Sometimes being true to one's self makes one shunned in society.

When a person begins attempting to solve the dilemma of having the sort of personal integrity that makes one at risk of being unfashionable, unhip, or unwelcome and, therefore, potentially ostracized by members of one's culture, that person is ready to step up to Branch Four.

To Fulfillment Through Peace, Centeredness, Self-acceptance, And Inner Silence...

HumaNatureConnect Activity

Start-up Protocol

If this is not a day when you prefer to spend time in nature without an agenda, do the Heartwood Path Start-up Protocol found in the Appendix.

Standing Solidly On The Third Branch Of Spiritual Development

For this activity, take another stab at the eight determining spiritual development questions, with some direction to make them pertinent to the present discussion. Given what you learned about the nature of the third stage of spiritual development, answer the following questions:

1. For the "Who am I?" question, describe your role as a silent witness.
2. For the "How do I fit?" question, describe how you remain centered in yourself.
3. For the "What is the Nature of good and evil?" question, discuss the role of clarity, inner calmness, contact with self, inner turmoil, and chaos in your life.
4. For the "How do I find God?" question, discuss whether you engage in meditation or silent contemplation.
5. For the "What is my life challenge?" question, describe how, if at all, you can be both engaged and detached at the same time.

6. For the "What is my greatest strength?" question, describe the role of autonomy in your life.
7. For the "What is my biggest hurdle?" question, discuss the impact of fatalism in your life. And
8. For the "What is my greatest temptation?" question, describe the impact of introversion in your life.

Follow-up Protocol

For best results, write down your impressions of this activity in your journal using the Heartwood Path Follow-up Protocol found in the Appendix. Afterwards, consider sharing your interpretations with others.

Heartwood Path Axioms

Key Assertions From Waypoint 3.34

3.34.1.

Climb to the third branch of the Beanstalk of Spiritual Development.

3.34.2.

On the third branch of the Beanstalk of Spiritual Development, life becomes fulfilling through peace, centeredness, self-acceptance, and inner silence.

3.34.3.

The tell-tale way one responds while on the third branch of the Beanstalk of Spiritual Development is through restful awareness.

3.34.4.

One begins to move from third branch of the Beanstalk of Spiritual Development when one begins to say, in effect: "Something larger than me is drawing near, I feel much more peaceful."

Nocturnal Pilgrimage 3.34

For best results, write down your impressions of each night's dreams in your journal using the Heartwood Path Dreaming Time Protocols found in the Appendix. Afterwards, consider sharing your Dream Tending with others.

Look over the next table and consider the associations as food for thought for your own dream tending.

Dream Subjects Related To Branch Three	Path Of Wisdom Locations Associated With Dream	Possible Meaning Of Dreams And Their Tree Of Life Associations	Suggested Dream-inspired Developmental Actions

Bear	Tree of Life Pathway of Peh (Between Hod and Netsach, Between Branches Three and Four).	Conflicting views of one's emotions and one's logical outlook make resolution difficult.	Overcome opposition, stop ignoring any problem, rise above.
Bird	Tree of Life Sephorah of Tiferet, Branch Four.	One is beginning to become united with one's Higher Self and, therefore, one is gaining a birdlike unfettered liberation.	Find the freedoms that become available when one is committed to the Great Work. Genuinely appreciate the wonders of nature.
Cliffs	Tree of Life Pathway of Peh (Between Hod and Netsach, Between Branches Three and Four).	The need to calm down to avoid falling over metaphorical cliff.	Practice yoga to find calmness.

Feather	Tree of Life Sephorah Netzach. Branch Three.	The need to work through strong emotions and find harmony and balance.	Put yourself in the place of those who are bothering you. See things from the perspective of others.
Flowers	Tree of Life Sephorah Netzach. Branch Three.	Indicates a yearning for union with the Divine and an appreciation of unconditional love.	Be watchful of false experiences of revelation. Spend a great deal of loving energy on a work of art that reflects your sense of the Divine.
Fruit	Tree of Life Sephorah of Hod. Branch Three.	Knowledge, Goodness, and Evilness. The verge of a significant spiritual experience. Expulsion occurs not due to knowledge but in failure to trust in the Divine.	Trust in the benevolence of the Divine. Read voraciously from a variety of sources and on a wide range of topics.

Garden	Tree of Life Pathway of Nun, joining Sephorahs Tifereth and Netsach. Branch Three.	The impact of beauty on one's life. The desire for protection. A crossroads. The beginning of a deepening of faith. The leap from melancholia to joy.	Spend at least a half hour per day meditating quietly. Find a regular rhythm to your breathing. Find the power of the Divine without any fear.
Goats	Tree of Life Pathway of Ayin, between Tiferth and Hod. Moving from Branch Three to Branch Four.	One feels dynamic, unlike docile sheep. The responsibility for finding one's own truth. Excessive self direction.	Overcome feeling the need to protect yourself from the directions of the Divine by meditating regularly.
Horse	Tree of Life Pathway of Ayin, between Tiferth and Hod. Moving from Branch Three to Branch Four.	Like dreams of a goat, one is dealing with finding one's own truth. Strength of will. One's considerable energy may be lacking direction.	Set aside space in your home for spiritual activity.

Hurricane	Tree of Life Pathway of Nun, joining Sephorahs Tifereth and Netsach. Branch Three.	Eye of Hurricane depicts calm, unmoving center of Divine Energy surrounded by intense forces of daily life. Finding spiritual revelation through sorrow.	Talk to those close to you about your feelings.
Ice	Tree of Life Sephirah of Hod. Branch Three.	One is about to refocus one's thinking about the world. One needs more order in one's life.	Try a range of relaxation therapies.
Plants	Tree of Life Pathway of Mem, between Sephorahs Hod and Gevurah. Leaping from Branch Branch Three to Branch Five.	The value of being unobtrusive, still, and resilient. Teaches a lesson about how attachment is the source of all sorrow.	Personify persistence as you replace desires and attachment with compassion and altruism.

| River | Tree of Life Pathway of Mem, between Sephorahs Gevurah and Binah. Leaping from Branch Branch Three to Branch Five. | Relates to one's emotional state. | Make significant changes in your emotional responses, especially as you help others. Grow emotionally by helping others. Use your inner strength as you use your own ways of seeing and the perspectives of others. |
| Rose | Tree of Life Pathway of Kaph, between Sephorahs Netsach and Chesed. Moving from Branch Three to Branch Four. | One is both spiritually beautiful, honest, and loyal to others and to your efforts with the Great Work. | Continue to focus on your inner development. The reward will be your unity with the Absolute. |

Sand	Tree of Life Pathway of Nun, between Netsach and Tifereth. Moving from Branch Three to Branch Four.	Not only sand on a beautiful beach but also sand in an inhospitable desert. Being trapped in a soulless world. Represents the uninspiring nature of the totally secular life.	Face yourself honestly, bear through the sorrow that accompanies most spiritual paths, call for protection from the Absolute, face yourself openly and honestly.
Sheep	Tree of Life Pathway of Kaph, between Sephorahs Netsach and Chesed. Moving from Branch Three to Branch Four.	Trustworthiness, practicality, peacefulness, a passive outlook.	Approach the Great Work at your own pace but do so with sincerity.

Spider	Tree of Life Pathway of Ayin, between Tiferth and Hod. Moving from Branch Three to Branch Four.	Represents one's desire to gain access to the Absolute. Represents the dual need to create a complex web of understanding for the purpose of spiritual development and the need to protect one's individuality.	Face the dread of having the feelings that you can no longer relate to those who do not share your spiritual perspective.
Torrent	Tree of Life Pathway of Nun, between Netsach and Tifereth. Moving from Branch Three to Branch Four.	Represents the feeling of being overwhelmed and being tested. It leads to the deepening of resolve.	Although you will have to how your own row, share your spiritual development experiences and concerns with others.

Valley	Tree of Life Pathway of Kaph, between Sephorahs Netsach and Chesed. Moving from Branch Three to Branch Four.	Represents a period of intense sorrow but do not despair for your despondency will end as you move to higher branches of spiritual development.	Move through this temporary phase of your spiritual path by keeping a positive outlook towards higher levels of spiritual development.
Water	Tree of Life Pathway of Mem, between Hod on Branch Three and Geburah on Branch Four.	Desire to return to the protection of the womb, a demonstration that the dreamer is compassionate and altruistic.	Pay attention to your emotional state as you continue to be compassionate towards others.
Wind	Tree of Life Sephorah of Hod. Branch Three.	Wind is a symbol of impending change in one's life.	Accept the changes that will come as you gradually understand more of the Great Mystery associated with your spiritual path.

Woman	Tree of Life Pathway of Mem, between Hod on Branch Three and Geburah on Branch Four.	Represents the need to be humble before the divine.	Muster a great deal of energy to deal with the demands of spiritual growth.

When ready, move to the next waypoint: "Branch Four."

35

Branch Four

CLIMB TO THE FOURTH BRANCH ON THE BEANSTALK OF SPIRITUAL DEVELOPMENT

This level of spiritual development is where people exhibit the intuitive response and see God as the Redeemer. On Branch Four faith is a matter of inner knowledge that upholds the devotee. Those who rest on Branch Four are bounded by hidden secrets, past conditioning, and Ego needs.

The Dilemma Of Branch Four

The predicament that has to be transcended before one can move on to Branch Five begins with the question "How can I manifest my own desires?"

To Fulfillment Through Insight, Empathy, Tolerance, And Forgiveness...

HumaNatureConnect Activity

Start-up Protocol

If this is not a day when you prefer to spend time in nature without an agenda, do the Heartwood Path Start-up Protocol found in the Appendix.

Standing Solidly On The Fourth Branch Of Spiritual Development

For this activity, take another stab at the eight determining spiritual development questions, with some direction to make them pertinent to the fourth stage of spiritual development. Given what you learned about the nature of the fourth stage, answer the following questions:

1. For the "Who am I?" question, describe the knower within you.
2. For the "How do I fit?" question, describe ways that you seek understanding.
3. For the "What is the Nature of good and evil?" question, discuss your relationship to the truth, blindness, and denying the truth.
4. For the "How do I find God?" question, discuss the role of self-acceptance in your life.
5. For the "What is my life challenge?" question, describe whether you are able to go beyond duality.
6. For the "What is my greatest strength? question, describe how you brought insight to bear during the achievement of your accomplishments.
7. For the "What is my biggest hurdle?" question, discuss the impact of delusion in your life. And
8. For the "What is my greatest temptation?" question, describe an example in your life of being deceived or how you deceived someone else.

Follow-up Protocol

For best results, write down your impressions of this activity in your journal using the Heartwood Path Follow-up Protocol found in the Appendix. Afterwards, consider sharing your interpretations with others.

Heartwood Path Axioms

Key Assertions From Waypoint 3.35

3.35.1.

Climb to the fourth branch on the Beanstalk of Spiritual Development.

3.35.2.

On the fourth branch of the Beanstalk of Spiritual Development life becomes fulfilling through insight, empathy, forgiveness, and tolerance.

3.35.3.

The main way one responds while on the fourth branch of the Beanstalk of Spiritual Development is through intuition.

3.35.4.

One may be on the verge of moving to the fifth branch of the Beanstalk of Spiritual Development when one begins to say, in effect, "I am beginning to intuit the Nature of God."

Nocturnal Pilgrimage 3.35

For best results, write down your impressions of each night's dreams in your journal using the Heartwood Path Dreaming Time Protocols found in the Appendix. Afterwards, consider sharing your Dream Tending with others.

Look over the next table and consider the associations as food for thought for your own dream tending.

Dream Subjects Related To Branch Four	Path Of Wisdom Locations Associated With Dream	Possible Meaning Of Dreams And Their Tree Of Life Associations	Suggested Dream-inspired Developmental Actions

Hawk	Tree of Life Sefirah of Tiferth. Branch Four.	All forms of mysticism. The maintenance of control.	Practice regular meditation, make regular journal entries. Balance your energy through self-purification in preparation for communion with the Divine (Fire), a careful consideration and adjustment of the resources you consume (Earth), your relationship with your community (Air), and your creative expression (Water).
Island	Tree of Life Pathway Ayin, between Tifereth and Hod. Branch Four.	One may be wanting more solitude as one decides between great spiritual understanding and misanthropy with empty pride.	As a way to avoid pride and a setback, listen to your intuition.

Locust	Tree of Life Pathway of Lamed, between Givurah and Tifereth. Branch Four.	The removal of things that threaten your development. A harsh force driving you to a higher state of consciousness. The need to remove irritants and trivial distractions.	Seek mutual support with others engaged in improving the spiritual quality of their lives.
Mountain	Tree of Life Pathway of Heh, between Tifereth and Hokhmah. Spans the gulf between Branch Four and Branch Six.	Recognizes spiritual achievement. One is on a pathway leading to a splendorous point of view. One is becoming worthy of the status of a hero.	Struggle some more to fully commune with the Absolute.
Oak Tree	Tree of Life Pathway of Heh, between Tifereth and Hokhmah. Spans the gulf between Branch Four and Branch Six.	Steeped in mystical associations. Indicates exceptional spiritual insight.	Struggle to uncover hidden spiritual truths.

Ocean	Tree of Life Pathway of Yod, between Tifereth and Chesed.	Relates to the fiery and active aspects of one's Soul. Represents the metaphorical womb of life. One is embodying the creative force of the Absolute as one engages in the Great Work. One is capable of both action and stillness.	Create an interval of both action and reflection. Engage, and reflect.
Thorn	Three of Life Pathway Zayin. Moving from Tiffereth to Binah.	Some sort of block is preventing the dreamer from moving forward on her spiritual request.	Discard that which is unhelpful.

When ready, move to the next waypoint: "Branch Five."

36

Branch Five

The branch marks the level of spiritual development where people exhibit the creative response and see God as The Creator. Here, faith is a matter of God meeting all desires.

There is a telltale prayer that shows that a devotee is spiritually developed at the level of Branch Five. That prayer is . . . "God, make me worthy of your faith."

The Dilemma Of Branch Five

When a person begins attempting to solve this predicament related to self- absorption, grandiosity, and playing God, that person is ready to step up to Branch Six. But before jumping ahead, anchor yourself more firmly on Branch Five by doing the following activity.

To Fulfillment Through Inspiration, Expanded Creativity In Art Or Science, And Unlimited Discovery...

HumaNatureConnect Activity

Start-up Protocol

If this is not a day when you prefer to spend time in nature without an agenda, do the Heartwood Path Start-up Protocol found in the Appendix.

Standing Solidly On The Fifth Branch Of Spiritual Development

For this activity, take another stab at the eight determining spiritual development questions, as before with some pertinent direction. Given what you learned about the nature of the fifth stage of spiritual development, answer the following questions:

1. For the "Who am I?" question, describe in what ways, if at all, you are a co-creator with God.
2. For the "How do I fit?" question, describe ways that you use your intentions.
3. For the "What is the Nature of good and evil?" question, discuss how in your life goodness stems from being in a state of higher consciousness and evil stems from being in a state of lower consciousness.
4. For the "How do I find God?" question, discuss the role of inspiration in your life.
5. For the "What is my life challenge?" question, describe ways that you align yourself with the creator.
6. For the "What is my greatest strength?" question, write down examples of the use of your imagination in your life.
7. For the "What is my biggest hurdle?" question, discuss the impact of self-importance in your life. And
8. For the "What is my greatest temptation?" question, describe whether you believe that the self is all that can be known to exist,

that only your mind is real, or that all objects in the Realm of Exteriority are but images that depend on you for their existence.

Follow-up Protocol

For best results, write down your impressions of this activity in your journal using the Heartwood Path Follow-up Protocol found in the Appendix. Afterwards, consider sharing your interpretations with others.

Heartwood Path Axioms

Key Assertions From Waypoint 3.36

3.36.1.

Climb to the fifth branch on the Beanstalk of Spiritual Development.

3.36.2.

At the fifth branch on the Beanstalk of Spiritual Development, life becomes fulfilling through inspiration, expanded creativity in art and science, and unlimited discovery.

3.36.3.

The dominant way the few who make it to the fifth branch on the Beanstalk of Spiritual Development respond to life situations is through creativity.

3.36.4.

A sign that one may be ready to move beyond the fifth branch on the Beanstalk of Spiritual Development occurs when one begins to say, in effect: "My actions and thoughts are drawing on God's force field and we together are creating the future."

Nocturnal Pilgrimage 3.36

For best results, write down your impressions of each night's dreams in your journal using the Heartwood Path Dreaming Time Protocols found in the Appendix. Afterwards, consider sharing your Dream Tending with others.

Look over the next table and consider the associations as food for thought for your own dream tending.

Dream Subjects Related To Branch Five	Path Of Wisdom Locations Associated With Dream	Possible Meaning Of Dreams And Their Tree Of Life Associations	Suggested Dream-inspired Developmental Actions
Desert	Tree of Life non-Sefirah of Daat, a metaphorical destination where there is no evidence of the divine.	The value of faith.	Seek the secret of non-duality. Once found, one will be led to the benevolence of the divine. Balance gentle protection with forceful action.

Dogs	Tree of Life Pathway of Zayin, between Binah and Tifereth, Branch Five.	Knowledge of your spiritual home will lead you through hardships, especially when one employs dog-like loyalty.	Perform a relaxation ritual each morning to help you get through hard times. In this ritual, lie down, breathe slow and steady, visualize a golden ball of light moving slowly over your whole body, its warmth removing worries.
Doves	Tree of Life Pathway of Tav, between Chokmah and Chesed. Branch Five.	The long and arduous search for peace.	Even on your unique quest, find ways to help and protect those around you. Look into charity work.
Eagles	Tree of Life Pathway of Kaph, between Chesed and Netsach. Branch Five.	A promising show that you have developed spiritual knowledge regarding morality.	Concern yourself with practical activity that benefits others.

Insect	Tree of Life Sefirah of Geburah, Branch Five.	The inevitability of destruction and decay of all forms of life, essential to provide the raw material for new life. Separating the serious seeker from the merely curious.	Increase your ability to see through the veils of illusion by reading the works of Aleister Crowley and Eliphas Levi.
Jungle	Tree of Life Sefirah of Gevurah. Branch Five.	Death is as fundamental to the nature of the Divine as is life. Death clears the way for new life to emerge. New perspectives will change the way you see the world.	Value new lessons and be prudent and aware of danger.
Lion	Tree of Life Pathway of Teth, between Sephorahs Gevurah and Chesed. Branch Five.	Benevolence, strength, and justice. Inner focus.	Remain amiable and not dismissive as you await a glimpse of the Absolute.

Quicksand	Tree of Life Pathway of Check, bwtween Sephorahs Gevurah and Binah. Leaving Branch Five, entering Branch Six.	Represents the feeling that one is loosing direction or control. One may be experiencing a stagnation in one's spiritual formation.	Overcome being satisfied with what you are used to.
Rats	Tree of Life Pathway of Chieth, between Gevurah and Binah. Moving from Branch Five to Branch Six.	A metaphor for whatever may be disrupting your spiritual development. A call to protect your soul from negative influences.	Overcome cynicism and doubt about the validity of your spiritual quest.
Sky	Tree of Life Pathway of Tav, between Hokhmah and Chesed. Branch Five.	Indicates a developed spiritual knowledge, particularly of the Four Elements of Air, Water, Fire and Earth.	At all times, assume a reflective and contemplative approach while engaging in spiritual matters.

Storm	Tree of Life Sefirah of Gevorah. Branch Five.	Represents the raw power of nature and the divine. Indicates the one is contemplating the place of violence and chaos in the world. Indicates that one is on the verge of a power spiritual experience.	Apply yourself diligently to your spiritual studies and practices.
Trees	Tree of Life Pathway of Tav, between Hokhmah and Chesed. Branch Five.	A positive dream. Tree roots represent the spiritual side of life. Dream indicates that one is half wedded to the material world (the roots) and half wedded to the spiritual realm (the branches).	Remain committed to your spiritual quest.

Vulture	Tree of Life Sefi-rah of Gevurah. Branch Five.	The necessity of mortality, the inevitability of decay, and the eventual break-down of all living things.	Know that even in death the pro-tective force of the Absolute is still with you.
Whirlpool	Tree of Life Pathway of Heh, between Tifer-eth and Binah, Pathway Five.	The awesome power of the divine.	Do not let the intense power of the dream vision cause you any concern.

When ready, move to the next waypoint: "Branch Six."

37

Branch Six

CLIMB TO THE SIXTH BRANCH ON THE BEANSTALK OF SPIRITUAL DEVELOPMENT

This level of spiritual development is where people exhibit the visionary response and see God as the Miracle Maker. Faith for the person on Branch Six is a matter of moving mountains.

The Dilemma Of Branch Six

Those who rest on the sixth branch face the dilemma of being bounded by thought, the personal Ego, and old habits. Of all the levels, Branch Six is the one the Heartwood Path is charted towards.

It is the main branch of development for play, the vibration of wholeness, miracles, awareness that one is the light of the world, healing touch, grace, the reconciliation of good and evil, and nirvana.

To Fulfillment Through Reverence, Compassion, Devoted Service, And Universal Love...

HumaNatureConnect Activity

Start-up Protocol

If this is not a day when you prefer to spend time in nature without an agenda, do the Heartwood Path Start-up Protocol found in the Appendix.

Standing Solidly On The Sixth Branch Of Spiritual Development

For this activity, take another stab at the eight determining spiritual development questions, made pertinent to the present discussion. Given what you learned about the nature of the sixth stage of spiritual development, answer the following questions:

1. For the "Who am I?" question, discuss the notion that you are enlightened awareness?
2. For the "How do I fit?" question, describe the role of love in your life.
3. For the "What is the Nature of good and evil?" question, discuss whether you believe that good and evil are cosmic forces.
4. For the "How do I find God?" question, discuss the role of grace (divinely given talent or blessing) in your life.
5. For the "What is my life challenge?" question, describe the role of liberation in your life.
6. For the "What is my greatest strength?" question, write down ways that you express your holiness, if at all.
7. For the "What is my biggest hurdle?" question, discuss the impact of false idealism and the private nature of your relationship with God in your life. And
8. For the "What is my greatest temptation?" question, describe the role of martyrdom in your life, specifically in ways that you are

seeking to prove your holiness to God. When you stop seeing the distinction between you and God, you are ready to stand on the Seventh and Final Branch of Spiritual Development.

Follow-up Protocol

For best results, write down your impressions of this activity in your journal using the Heartwood Path Follow-up Protocol found in the Appendix. Afterwards, consider sharing your interpretations with others.

Heartwood Path Axioms

Key Assertions From Waypoint 3.37

3.37.1.

Climb to the sixth branch on the Beanstalk Of Spiritual Development.

3.37.2.

Life on the sixth branch of the Beanstalk of Spiritual Development becomes fulfilling through reverence, compassion and universal love.

3.37.3.

The main way the visionary ones at the sixth branch of the Beanstalk of Spiritual Development respond to life situations is through devoted service.

3.37.4.

One is approaching the end of the Heartwood Path when one begins to say, in effect: "God and I are almost together now."

Nocturnal Pilgrimage 3.37

For best results, write down your impressions of each night's dreams in your journal using the Heartwood Path Dreaming Time Protocols found in the Appendix. Afterwards, consider sharing your Dream Tending with others.

Look over the next table and consider the associations as food for thought for your own dream tending.

Dream Subjects Related To Branch Six	Path Of Wisdom Locations Associated With Dream	Possible Meaning Of Dreams And Their Tree Of Life Associations	Suggested Dream-inspired Developmental Actions
Earth (Soil)	Tree of Life Pathway of Tav, between the Sepherahs of Hokhmah and Chesed. Branch Six.	Awareness of inappropriate means of escapism, ways to overcome the hollowness of modern life.	Learn to stand alone, despite the opinions of others.

Emeralds	Tree of Life Pathway of Daleth, between Sepherahs, Hokhmah and Binah, Branch Six.	Connecting Wisdom with Understanding.	Pass on the benefits of your experience to others. Help others to see a glimpse of the divine.
Lamb	Tree of Life Pathway of Zayin, between Tifereth and Binah. Branch Six.	One is both endowed with free will and in relationship with the Divine. As such, you are both humble and meek, helpful qualities for those on a spiritual journey.	Prepare for the long struggle between Branch Four and Branch Six. Seek practical as well as inner consequences. Engage is some form of contemplative physical exercise such as yoga.

Love	Tree of Life Sefirah of Hokhmah. Branch Seven.	A very positive dream. One is moving towards a communion with the Absolute. Fosters awareness of both individual uniqueness and unity. Indicates a great deal of creativity that can be used for the benefit of your community.	Find out which groups in your community need assistance. Set up a volunteer team to help people and the environment.
Sea	Tree of Life Sephorah of Binah, the Great Mother, one of the three Supernal Sephorot. Branch Six.	Indicates emotional sensitivity, support and guidance, compassion and altruism.	Continue to support and guide others according to the will of the Absolute and, in doing so, receive spiritual support and increase your spiritual understanding.

Waterfall	Tree of Life Sephorah of Binah, the Great Mother, one of the three Supernal Sephorot. Branch Six.	Exposure to a beautiful force that is both beautiful and powerful.	Seek universal understanding but, since humans are not capable of such totality of empathy, work towards this goal only as a worthy aspiration. Emulating the capacity for absolute understanding is enough.
Weed	Tree of Life Pathway of Zayin, between Tifereth and Binah. Branch Six.	One has to make an individual decision about the merits of any idea.	Remove aspects of your life that exert negative influences.

Very few people are ever ready to move to Branch Seven. You may, especially if you know what to look for, have a brief so-called "peak experience" of the conditions that mark Branch Seven. Even these temporary peaks at oneness will have a profound and powerful impact on your perspective and actions.

When ready, move to the next waypoint: "Branch Seven."

38

Branch Seven

CLIMB TO THE SEVENTH BRANCH ON THE BEANSTALK OF SPIRITUAL DEVELOPMENT

This level of spiritual development is where people exhibit the infinite intelligence response and see God as the God of Pure Being. On Branch Seven, faith is a matter of unity with God.

The Dilemma Of Branch Seven

Those who rest on the top branch are faced with the dilemma of being bounded by nothing. One returns to the source.

Being an eartHeart and becoming a saint are long journeys. There is no short cut, no fast way to get a halo.

The previously described Beanstalk of Spiritual Development is a good way to visualize the work that is needed to be done to add layers of depth to one's spiritual development. It is a good guide for how to become a saint, particularly for the vast majority of people who subscribe to the religious or mythic way of thinking and speaking. It is a very good method of moving one's development from a perspective dominated by Ego to a deeper perspective wherein Theo is more pronounced. It describes a, more or less, linear route towards the perception of the boundless eternal mystery that animates and transcends all: the Mystery variously referred to as "Spirit," "God," "the Absolute," "the Anima Mundi," "Allah," or "Buddha Nature."

What is needed for our purposes here is a developmental model that is about both ascent to Spirit and descent to Soul—one that, in other words, also describes, through the symbol of a rolling circle or wheel, how to grow by coming into better connection with one's "ultimate place in the world" (Plotkin, 2008, p. 43). By "place" I not only mean geographical *location* (as in, "I live in the place called the Middle Mississippi Forested Hills Natural Region") but also *niche* (as in "it is not my place to tell a nuclear engineer how to do his job"). "Place," as I am using it here, has to do with role or purpose.

The Soul has to do with relationship—how a person or thing relates to others (as in, "its place in the great scheme of things"). The Soul has to do with uniqueness—its distinct but not separate place in the web of life.

While nothing said at this waypoint guarantees that if you do some specific practice you will end up on a particular branch of spiritual development, for me, just knowing how to recognize the branches and what dilemmas had to be overcome psycho-spiritually to arrive at the next higher branch helped me to move to higher stages of development. Without this knowledge, I may still be happily in my long-held, familiar state of restful awareness and peace at the Third Branch, thinking that being a concerned environmentalist is the culmination of spiritual growth when, in reality, it is only about half way up the Beanstalk.

To Fulfillment Through Wholeness And Unity With The Divine...

HumaNatureConnect Activity

Start-up Protocol

If this is not a day when you prefer to spend time in nature without an agenda, do the Heartwood Path Start-up Protocol found in the Appendix.

Standing Solidly On The Seventh Branch Of Spiritual Development

For this activity, take another stab at the eight determining spiritual development questions, again with some pertinent direction. Given what you learned about the nature of the seventh stage of spiritual development, answer the following questions:

1. For the "Who am I?" question, describe how you are the Source.
2. For the "How do I fit?" question, describe how you are the realization of what you always have been, unchanged more than changed, no longer projecting versions of reality that are inadequate.
3. For the "What is the Nature of good and evil?" question, discuss how in your life good is the union of opposites and evil no longer exists.
4. For the "How do I find God? question, discuss the role of transcendence in your life.
5. For the "What is my life challenge?" question, describe ways that you seek to be yourself.
6. For the "What is my greatest strength? question, describe how unity works in your life.
7. For the "What is my biggest hurdle?" question, describe how duality works in your life. And
8. For the "What is my greatest temptation? question, describe how you live without temptation.

Follow-up Protocol

For best results, write down your impressions of this activity in your journal using the Heartwood Path Follow-up Protocol found in the Appendix. Afterwards, consider sharing your interpretations with others.

Heartwood Path Axioms

Key Assertions From Waypoint 3.38

3.38.1.

Climb to the seventh branch of the Beanstalk of Spiritual Development.

3.38.2.

The seventh branch of Beanstalk of Spiritual Development is typically only experienced as temporary peak experiences, just long enough to achieve a momentary but profound glimpse of wholeness and unity with the divine.

3.38.3.

Unbounded unity is the experience that tells the pilgrim on a spiritual development path that one is, at least, peaking over the threshold of the highest stage. When one is on the seventh branch of the Beanstalk of Spiritual Development one's indicative responses are of sacredness and one's fall-back emotion is compassion.

3.38.4.

The tell-tale sign that one has achieved the last level of spiritual development may come as a fleeting impression that there is no difference between you and God.

Nocturnal Pilgrimage 3.38

For best results, write down your impressions of each night's dreams in your journal using the Heartwood Path Dreaming Time Protocols found in the Appendix. Afterwards, consider sharing your Dream Tending with others.

Look over the next table and consider the associations as food for thought for your own dream tending.

Dream Subjects Related To Branch Seven	Path Of Wisdom Locations Associated With Dream	Possible Meaning Of Dreams And Their Tree Of Life Associations	Suggested Dream-inspired Developmental Actions
Camel	Tree of life Pathway of Gimel, directly into Keter—the Crown—from Tifereth.	Last stage of your spiritual quest. A breath away from unity with the divine.	Maintain a rigorous schedule of meditation and prayer.

Music	Tree of Life Pathway of Aleph, between Hokhmah and Keter. One of three pathways to the top of the Tree of Life.	A celebration of Life and the Absolute The rules of music demonstrate the divinity in music. One is beginning to tune into the underlying formulas that define demonstrate the presence of the Absolute. The joy of being so close to the divine makes the pilgrim less concerned about mundane anxieties.	Take on the mantle of the priesthood. Encourage others to understand and revel in the unlimited love of the Absolute.
Weather	Tree of Life Pathway Aleph, between Chokmah and Kether. Branch Seven.	One can never second-guess the divine. Despite ample preparations, one is always in the hands of higher forces. Much will always remain hidden.	Be optimistic that you will be able to see a portion of the Great Mystery.

Think about your climb up the Beanstalk of Spiritual Development before you prepare for sleep. Then dream and, upon waking, tend to your dream.

After your dream tending ritual, you are ready to continue down the Heartwood Path. Be sure to go into nature to do the next activity as a way to more fully associate yourself with the deeper realities of who you are and what you need in life. Regularly attending to nature rekindles your access to beauty, inspiration, meaning, and the sustenance you receive from the natural world.

Take notice of the wildness that is around you by doing the Huma-NatureConnect Activities in a natural landscape, if only for your own health. Researchers in The Netherlands, after examining the records of 195 families, report that the annual prevalence of 15 of the top 24 diseases were lowest among the families with the most greenspace close to their homes (within a half-mile or so) (Selhub & Logan, 2012, p. 26).

When ready, move to the next waypoint: "Position Of The Psyche."

39

Position Of The Psyche

LIVE IN YOUR SOUL PLACE AND FUNCTION ACCORDING TO YOUR SOUL PURPOSE

The Soul, being simultaneously a place, a niche, and a function, is not, as most people tend to articulate, a ghostly thing within that one possesses. You are in a place—the location that is your Soul, and you provide a function—the task of your Soul. That place and function are not inside you. You are located in your Soul place and you do the tasks associated with your Soul purpose. When someone lives a life they can truly call their own, that soul-full life—hardly ethereal or unreal—is visible, public, and typically full of values, interests, and abilities.

When someone is living without a firm connection to their Soul they are out of their minds and out of place. They are unable to have a large conversation with the world. They cannot unfold their own richest story. I am not referring to their life's history but to their own meaningful fable or truth-filled myth that puts them into a deep relationship with the world's core structure—its hidden blueprint, which is, more or less, the same thing as Rupert Sheldrake's "morphic field," or David Bohm's "implicate order," or Buckminister Fuller's "pattern integrity" or Robert Johnson's "primal pattern" or Thomas Berry's "primary, organizing, sustaining, guiding principle of a living being" (Plotkin, 2008, p. 52).

To Happiness In A Healthy World...

HumaNatureConnect Activity

Start-up Protocol

If this is not a day when you prefer to spend time in nature without an agenda, do the Heartwood Path Start-up Protocol found in the Appendix.

Procuring Happiness Through Environmental Health

For this activity, respond to the following statement:

"A positive perception of nature and its benefits promotes the adoption of behaviors that are in accord with sustainable development. Indeed, respect for the environment is based on an affective connection with nature, and thus contributes to human happiness" (Lambin, 2012, p. 160).

In your response to this quote, you may want to include a personal example of how you connect with nature in a way that increases your happiness.

Follow-up Protocol

For best results, write down your impressions of this activity in your journal using the Heartwood Path Follow-up Protocol found in the Appendix. Afterwards, consider sharing your interpretations with others.

Heartwood Path Axioms

Key Assertions From Waypoint 3.39

3.39.1.

Live in your Soul Place and function according to your Soul Purpose.

3.39.2.

Rather than a ghost within, the Soul is simultaneously a place, a niche, and a function.

Nocturnal Pilgrimage 3.39

For best results, write down your impressions of each night's dreams in your journal using the Heartwood Path Dreaming Time Protocols found in the Appendix. Afterwards, consider sharing your Dream Tending with others.

Understanding and identifying one's Soul Place is an important step in one's life of self-inquiry and self-understanding. Along with one's Soul Place, dreaming is an integral part of who we are. I say "integral" to indicate that making sense of who one is requires looking at various dimensions of one's life, from cellular to global. At whatever level your dreams seem to be addressing, work to be present with them, always looking for references about the growing tip of your own developing being, about ways to know yourself better, about clues to overcome self-limitations, and about divided or un-connected aspects of the whole. With this advice in mind, sleep, dream, and tend to your dreams.

When you are ready, proceed to the next waypoint: "Soul Initiation."

40

Soul Initiation

MAKE YOUR EGO AN AGENT OF YOUR SOUL

Virtually everyone's Ego, if left unchecked, drives one to distraction. It will lead one away from what really matters in an endless quest to be first and to have the most stuff. Making the Ego an agent of the Soul removes this distraction from better personal qualities. Making the Ego an agent of the Soul fosters and lays bare something that is vital to one's personal growth, personal happiness, and environmental sustainability. This uncovering reveals one's true calling. It reveals "The source of your deepest personal fulfillment and of your greatest service to others" (Plotkin, 2008, p. 54).

The Ego is the source of self-importance. Comparatively, the "Soul" is one's ultimate place and that position is both distinctively yours and ultimately the world's (in a similar way that a whirlpool is distinct from the river but still a part of the river). One's Soul can be said to be one's unique ultimate location and function within the world. Connecting with one's Soul, while instinctual for other animals, is not guaranteed in humans, largely because, for most of us, our Soul seems to be communicating from two different and hard-to-access locations—1) buried in our psyches and 2) lost in nature. It takes wandering to find your true place, and, without forcing a destination upon you, the Heartwood Path offers tools to use for this search wherever that may lead you. You will know when you find your Soul, your true place, because it will be a "place" where you cannot be hired or fired, a "place" that, wherever it is, you are always "home." Writes Plotkin: "Before soul initiation, wherever you go, there you are. After soul initiation, wherever you go, *Here* you are" (2008, p. 55).

This discussion of making your Ego an agent of your Soul and Plotkin's words are reminiscent of the these lyrics of a song by Nahko Bear & Medicine for the People:

"What is the purpose

and would you believe it?

Would you believe it if you knew

what you were for and

how you became so in form?"

(Onecommunityglobal.org)

The Heartwood Path is not about, as Nahko says, "how you became so in form." Nor is it about changing one's Soul. It is rather about Ego development and, more specifically, helping participants alter their Egos in a way that it becomes an agent for the Soul.

Although the Ego—sometimes fearful of losing its dominant role in one's life—may attempt to stall personal development, it, nevertheless, has an important role. While the Soul "knows what the ego might find fulfilling in life," only "the ego knows how to manifest in the world the Soul's desires" (Plotkin, 2008, p. 58). That is why we need both; but, to keep the Ego from encouraging us to find self-esteem through endless striving and acquiring, the Ego ought to be an agent of the Soul. One way to begin to temper the Ego by the Soul is to become very relaxed. A way to find this relaxation is the purpose of the next activity.

To Begin Sabotaging Long Standing Patterns...

HumaNatureConnect Activity

Start-up Protocol

If this is not a day when you prefer to spend time in nature without an agenda, do the Heartwood Path Start-up Protocol found in the Appendix.

Listening To Your Heart Rhythm

For this activity, shift from willful doing to the spacious energy of Being. Begin this "*practice*," which means "leading over or beyond," by simply lying on your back, preferably in a quiet spot outdoors, until you can hear or feel your heartbeat. Count up to sixty heartbeats before you sit up. Focus on the wholeness of your sensitivity by consciously pacifying your masculine doing aspect. It will take considerable relaxation to hear or feel your heartbeats clearly. Note how a quiet mind depends on a quiet body. Write down your impressions of this activity in your journal.

Follow-up Protocol

For best results, write down your impressions of this activity in your journal using the Heartwood Path Follow-up Protocol found in the Appendix. Afterwards, consider sharing your interpretations with others.

Heartwood Path Axioms

Key Assertions From Waypoint 3.40

3.40.1.

Make your Ego an agent of your Soul.

3.40.2.

Virtually everyone's Ego, if left unchecked, drives one to distraction.

3.40.3.

The Ego is the source of self-importance.

3.40.4.

One way to begin to temper the Ego by the Soul is to become very relaxed.

Nocturnal Pilgrimage 3.40

For best results, write down your impressions of each night's dreams in your journal using the Heartwood Path Dreaming Time Protocols found in the Appendix. Afterwards, consider sharing your Dream Tending with others.

Sleep. Dream. Tend to your dreams. Engage in imaginary dialogue with your Dream Characters and talk to others about your dreams as a way to cultivate the skill of developing multiple perspectives—that of the "selves" of others and that of the culture as a whole. Focus these discussions on gaining a greater awareness of the roles you enact culturally.

When you are ready to continue making progress, move to the next waypoint: "World's Soul."

41

World's Soul

ACHIEVE KNOWLEDGE OF THE TOTEMIC SELF

While the Soul is one's potential, this capability does not mean that one will automatically and effortlessly succeed in finding one's destiny. This search, an unconscious act in most youth, begins before adulthood and, because the looking is risky and, particularly in early attempts, prone to failure, success is more likely when the Soul search is aided by one or more eco-centric elders.

Note that I say "eco-centric elders" rather than "adults." The latter can offer good advice because, being adults, they have already achieved some knowledge of their own Soul. For those seeking to become eco-centric elders themselves or more ecologically-centered adults, working with an eco-centric life coach is more productive. That is because rather than just achieving some knowledge of their own Soul, eco-centric life coaches take it an important step farther: they achieve knowledge of the world's Soul. By following a course such as the Heartwood Path, people become eco-centric elders by helping others embody their Soul and by "supporting the human-Earth system in the evolution of *its* Soul" (Plotkin, 2008, p. 56).

The world's Soul is evident to us humans because our "species always had a kinship with the Other—with a greater-than-human world. This form of kinship—which is what is meant by our Totemic Self— allowed us to become and to flourish as humans. We need to get back in touch with the Other, our Totemic Self, and this will require a cultural shift from an egocentric, mechanized view to an theo-centric ecological view. The current dominant world view is, among other things, stultifying. Says Albert Einstein: "Our task (has to) be to free ourselves from this prison by widening the circles of compassion to embrace all living creatures and the whole of nature in it beauty" (Kahn & Hasbach, 2012, p. 23). Similarly, author Joanna Macy says: "I consider that this shift [to an emphasis on our capacity to identify with the larger collective of all beings] is essential to our survival at this point in history . . . We are gradually discovering that we are our world" (Kahn & Hasbach, 2012, pp. 2-5). Wilderness "experiences foster 'the sense that we are each unique and individual and, at the same time, part of the larger whole' and 'trigger the sense that the world is enchanted" (Kahn & Hasbach, 2012, pp. 2-5). That is just the beginning, for Kahn and Hasbach see the kind of work to be done in this book series, namely expanding the self to include the natural environment, to be a solution to the big problems we face. "We suggest that the solution for world problems—and a viable and entirely possible cultural evolution on our planet—involves a reintegration of parts of our earlier totemic selves, our Neolithic selves, and our modern sensibilities" (Kahn & Hasbach, 2012, p. 12). How do we free ourselves from this Egocentric prison, identify with the larger collective of all beings, and reintegrate parts of our selves?

Certainly a part of the answer is to promote more place-based learning, learning that has as its foundation a local place. Placeless, abstract learning alone will be "insufficient to foster deep bonds with place or even an affective sense of place" (Kahn & Hasbach, 2012, p.40). The places for this learning can be anywhere from "hearth to the entire universe, but the world is typically used to convey an intermediate geographic understanding of the earthly region we inhabit . . ." (Kahn & Hasbach, 2012, p. 41). The Heartwood Path fosters the reinvigoration of our Totemic Self, our More-Than-Individual-Self, our Ecological Self, a self that allows one to achieve uncommon happiness.

Kahn, Ruckert and Hasbach propose "a new agenda for the field of ecopsychology. It is to generate a nature language—a way of speaking about patterns of interactions between humans and nature, their wide range of instantiations (which provide tangible examples of abstract concepts) and the deeply meaningful and often joyous feelings that they engender" (Kahn & Hasbach, 2012, p. 57). Through this book, I encourage you to get out into nature and to help create the "nature language" through your processing of about thirty specially numbered activities—called "Touchstone" Activities—that are scattered through-out the balance of this book. In your responses for these numbered "instantiations," we are looking to find "the deepest meanings of rela-tionships, relationships between 'mind' and Nature" (Kahn & Hasbach, 2012, p. 56). There could be an infinite number of instantiations—mo-ments for participants to react to, but we here shall present the thirty or so identified by Kohn, Ruckert and Hasbach. Their instantiations are aimed at helping participants get back into the habit that made humans the incredible species it is. "Paul Shepard (1996) argued that the "human species emerged enacting, dreaming, and thinking about wild animals and that through such interactions they help to make us who we are" (Kahn & Hasbach, 2012, p.p. 60). These instantiations—which will be patterns of behavior such as building shelter, harnessing natural forces, and having encounters with animals—can be perverse (which will produce psychological ill health and a normative judge-ment against it), domestic (which will do no harm but will not inspire either, or wild (which will produce the most intricately sensorial and inspirational meanings).

To Continue To Sabotage Long Standing Patterns By Joining The Essential Fluidity Of The Present...

HumaNatureConnect Activity

Start-up Protocol

If this is not a day when you prefer to spend time in nature without an agenda, do the Heartwood Path Start-up Protocol found in the Appendix.

Awakening Your Capacity For Relationship

For this activity, stand in nature and imagine yourself as kelp, a seaweed plant. Imagine your feet rooted in the seabed and the rest of your body floating upwards toward the surface of the ocean. The bulk of your body is buoyed by the sea around you. Allow your body to yield and sway to the merest current. One direction at a time, imagine the current coming from the back of you, in front of you, from your right side, and then from your left side. Pay attention to where in your body you feel tightness as you sway. Once felt, see if you can move in a way that releases this tightness to the fluidity of the sea currents.

Follow-up Protocol

For best results, write down your impressions of this activity in your journal using the Heartwood Path Follow-up Protocol found in the Appendix. Afterwards, consider sharing your interpretations with others.

Heartwood Path Axioms

Key Assertions From Waypoint 3.41

3.41.1.

The Soul, being simultaneously a place, a niche, and a function, is not, as most people tend to articulate, a ghostly thing within that one possesses.

3.41.2.

We need to get back in touch with the Other, our Totemic Self, and this will require a cultural shift from an Egocentric, mechanized view to an theo-centric ecological view.

3.41.3.

The Heartwood Path fosters the reinvigoration of our Totemic Self, our More-Than-Individual-Self, our Ecological Self, a self that allows one to achieve uncommon happiness.

3.41.4.

The instantiations found along the Heartwood Path—which will be patterns of behavior such as building a shelter, harnessing natural forces, and having encounters with animals—can be perverse (which will produce psychological ill health and a normative judgement against it), domestic (which will do no harm but will not inspire either, or wild (which will produce the most intricately sensorial and inspirational meanings).

Nocturnal Pilgrimage 3.41

For best results, write down your impressions of each night's dreams in your journal using the Heartwood Path Dreaming Time Protocols found in the Appendix. Afterwards, consider sharing your Dream Tending with others.

"Using Dream Images as medicines," writes Aizenstat, "works because the body is always dreaming" (2009, p. 189). Our subconscious mind registers the distress signals from bodily ailments and "represents them as images in our dreams" (2009, p. 190). Use your dream journal to record your health-producing dreams.

Each time you stop at another waypoint and tend to another dream as you continue down the Heartwood Path you are one step closer to that extraordinary place (sense of purpose) we call "Gladandgreen Junction." Get closer by moving to the next waypoint: "Talk Of The World." In doing each of the outdoor activities that follow you will discover that it is difficult to stay stressed out after communing with nature.

42

Talk Of The World

BE THE UNIVERSE'S MEANS OF SELF-EXPRESSION

It is through humans that the universe is made capable of knowing and admiring itself. This privilege of being the universe's conscious means of self-knowledge, self-appreciation, and self-expression is not taken lightly by those who purposefully seek out attractions in nature.

Given the magnitude of the job of being the universe's conscious knowers, appreciators, and expressers, elders will need to be prepared to help others mature more completely—that is, to grow to come closer to a psycho-spiritual totality that includes savoring nature, saving nature, and singing praises of nature. Whether one seeks to begin by savoring nature (appreciating its attractions), by singing praises of nature (casually in conversations with others or artistically through painting, photography, or writing), or by saving nature (showing gratitude toward nature by interceding on its behalf) the resulting advances in psycho-spiritual development rarely goes easily or smoothly, particularly if one attempts to mature without the assistance of an ecologically-minded, eco-centric elder or life coach.

That is precisely why we need so many of them. One per city would be a good minimum. At least one per loving couple would be better.

Nonhumans know their Soul, their function, and their place— things many humans never learn. To learn what non-humans know in this regard is a purpose of this book, a purpose fulfilled through Dr. Cohen's (Natural Systems Thinking Process) methodology, which will become evident to you as you continue down the Heartwood Path.

I am speaking of the work it takes to find one's *complete* conscious self, meaning the self-known aspects of one's individual self and one's Ecological Self. These aspects are Spirit, Ego, and Soul. The following activity, the first of many of our Touchstones Activities, will help one find that helpful interaction between humans and nature.

To The First Of Many Touchstones of People-Nature Interfacing...

HumaNatureConnect Activity

Start-up Protocol

If this is not a day when you prefer to spend time in nature without an agenda, do the Heartwood Path Start-up Protocol found in the Appendix.

Generating Patterns Of Human-Nature Interaction # 1:

Sitting By Fire

For this activity, carefully build a fire near your attractive natural being. You could be sitting by a video screen showing a flickering image of a fireplace (a perverse interaction pattern) or sitting by a fireplace in a family room (a domestic interaction pattern). By choosing to build a fire in a natural setting (a wild interaction) you are doing something that will have a positive psychological effect on you. In your journal, write down what meaning you derived from this wild interaction pattern; what joy, if any, it produced; how, if at all, it built within you a bond between your mind and nature; and how, if at all, the wild version of this interaction pattern was better for you than the perverse or domestic instantiation of the same interaction pattern; and how not being allowed to participate in this sort of wild interaction pattern—building a fire in a natural setting—would make you feel? How does interacting in this way in the presence of your attractive natural being make you feel? How would it feel to have this interaction without the presence of your attractive natural being? In writing down these responses you will be adding to our collective nature language, so important to rekindling the bond between humans and nature. Look over your impressions and think about them as you fall asleep tonight before dreaming.

Follow-up Protocol

For best results, write down your impressions of this activity in your journal using the Heartwood Path Follow-up Protocol found in the Appendix. Afterwards, consider sharing your interpretations with others.

Heartwood Path Axioms

Key Assertions From Waypoint 3.42

3.42.1.

It is through humans that the universe is made capable of knowing itself.

3.42.2.

The Eco-centric elders developed along the Heartwood Path will need to be prepared to help others mature more com-

pletely—that is, to grow to come closer to a psycho-spiritual totality that includes both savoring nature and saving nature.

3.42.3.

Whether one seeks to begin by *savoring* nature (appreciating its attractions) or by *saving* nature (showing gratitude toward nature by interceding on its behalf) the resulting advances in psycho-spiritual development rarely goes easily or smoothly, particularly if one attempts to mature without the assistance of an ecologically-minded, eco-centric elder or life coach.

3.42.4.

Nonhumans know their Soul, their function, and their place— things many humans never learn.

3.42.5.

Advances in psycho-spiritual development rarely goes easily or smoothly, particularly if one attempts to mature without the assistance of an ecologically-minded, eco-centric elder or life coach.

Nocturnal Pilgrimage 3.42

For best results, write down your impressions of each night's dreams in your journal using the Heartwood Path Dreaming Time Protocols found in the Appendix. Afterwards, consider sharing your Dream Tending with others.

Dreams may be images from repressed yearnings, mythical figures representing universal symbols, landscapes reaching out for our understanding, or living psychic beings seeking recognition and an audience for their intelligent messages. Tend to these Dream Images overtime and you will experience different worlds.

After tending to your dreams, continue to the next waypoint: "The Spheres." Once there, be sure to do the activity outdoors as a way to continue to develop a more sober respect for the extraordinary manifestations of nature. Seek out the wisdom embedded in Mother Nature and you will likely find yourself in a state of reverence in Her presence.

43

The Spheres

EXPERIENCE THE UPPER WORLD, THE MIDDLE WORLD, AND THE UNDER WORLD

The Spirit comes more into one's consciousness as one transcends or moves up the branches of the Beanstalk of Spiritual Development after considerable prayer, after meditation, after contemplation, or after yoga. The results of such transcendence in the realm Plotkin calls the "Upperworld" (2008, p. 59) are numerous:

1. a sense of unity,
2. non-duality,
3. grace,
4. bliss,
5. enlightenment, and, when one achieves the highest levels, and
6. a dis-identification from all attachments, including personal and cultural beliefs, goals, and desires.

The Ego comes more into one's consciousness in one's every day-time life—the waking time when one differentiates the Self as one interacts with family members, community members, workmates, and playmates. The results of such differentiation in the realm Plotkin calls the "Middleworld" (2008, p. 59) are the healing of emotional wounds; the development of physical grace; the creation of personal bonds; greater empathy, imagination, authenticity, and intimacy; enhanced emotional expressiveness; and improved feeling, thinking, sensing and intuition.

The Soul comes more into one's consciousness in the nighttime dream world. Here, one deepens or ripens one's Self as one confronts in the realm Plotkin calls the "Underworld" (2008, p. 59). The Underworld is confronted through dreamwork but also through deep imagery journeys, nature communication, drumming, symbolic artwork, and Soul-oriented poetry. In these ways, the Underworld helps to spawn greater individuality and the discovery of one's ultimate place in the world.

Whether it is "Upperworld" transcendence, "Middleworld" differentiation, or "Lowerworld" ripening, such soulwork is vitally important to eartHearts. It is all about finding one's place or purpose in the world.

The place—the "Here" that is a person's calling—is "granted and revealed by nature" (Plotkin, 2008, p. 61). This is one reason why eartHearts need Plotkin's wheel and not just the Beanstalk of Spiritual Development inspired by Deepak Chopra.

To The Second Of Many Touchstones Of People-Nature Interfacing...

HumaNatureConnect Activity

Start-up Protocol

If this is not a day when you prefer to spend time in nature without an agenda, do the Heartwood Path Start-up Protocol found in the Appendix.

Generating Patterns Of Human-Nature Interaction # 2:

Sleeping Under The Night Sky

For this activity, sleep under the night sky near an attractive natural being. You could be sleeping in a closed-up, heated or air-conditioned house with an image of the sky in a framed picture high up on your bedroom wall (a perverse interaction pattern) or sleeping in a tent in your backyard (a domestic interaction pattern). By choosing instead to sleep directly under the night sky near an attractive natural being (a wild interaction) you are doing something that has a more positive psychological effect on you. In your journal, write down what meaning you would derived from this wild interaction pattern (sleeping near an attractive natural being outside under the stars); what joy, if any, it produced; how, if at all, it built within you a bond between your mind and nature; and how, if at all, the wild version of this interaction pattern was better for you than an imaged or remembered perverse or domestic instantiation of the same interaction pattern; and how not being allowed to participate in this sort of wild interaction pattern— sleeping near an attractive natural being under the night sky—would make you feel? How does interacting in this way in the presence of your attractive natural being make you feel? How would it feel to have this interaction without the presence of your attractive natural being? In writing down these responses you will be adding to our collective nature language, so important to rekindling the bond between humans and nature. After your journaling about your night's sleep outside, look over your impressions and think about them as you fall asleep tonight (indoors or outdoors) before dreaming.

Follow-up Protocol

For best results, write down your impressions of this activity in your journal using the Heartwood Path Follow-up Protocol found in

the Appendix. Afterwards, consider sharing your interpretations with others.

Heartwood Path Axioms

Key Assertions From Waypoint 3.43

3.43.1.

The Spirit comes more into one's consciousness as one transcends or moves up the branches of the Beanstalk of Spiritual Development after considerable prayer, after meditation, after contemplation, or after yoga.

3.43.2.

The Ego comes more into one's consciousness in one's everyday life—especially during the waking time when one differentiates the Self as one interacts with family members, community members, workmates, and playmates.

3.43.3.

The Soul comes more into one's consciousness as one attains— through dreamwork but also through deep imagery journeys, nature communication, drumming, symbolic artwork, and Soul-oriented poetry—greater individuality and the discovery of one's ultimate place in the world.

3.43.4.

The place that is a person's calling is given and discovered by connecting with nature.

Nocturnal Pilgrimage 3.43

For best results, write down your impressions of each night's dreams in your journal using the Heartwood Path Dreaming Time Protocols found in the Appendix. Afterwards, consider sharing your Dream Tending with others.

The nighttime complement to connecting with attractive natural beings in the daytime is tending to Indigenous Images (discussed previously) after dreaming. Tending to these messengers—both natural beings and Indigenous Images—helps to guide you to your own spiritual maturity.

Take the next step towards becoming an eco-centric elder by moving to the next waypoint: "Up And Around." Once there, do the activity outdoors in nature as a way to find your deepest satisfactions, your biggest fulfillments, and your best source of meaning.

44

Up And Around

MOVE UP THE "BEANSTALK" AND AROUND THE "WHEEL"

EartHearts seek to make the meeting of Eco-Soul-centric elders a more common event, indeed a regular part of life. When this happens, the work of such eco-centric elders will mean that those who relate to only a small part of life—such as one's possessions or one's job—will no longer be the only option.

With the clear alternative of the mindset of an eco-centric elder, thinking of oneself as merely a worker or a consumer will be seen as a pathological aberration. Other unhealthy forms of self identification have to do with class stratification; power differentials; and the exploitation of women, children, the poor, and nature.

Moving up to higher branches on the Beanstalk of Spiritual Development means that a person is going through a process of transcendence. While that is certainly a necessary series of steps towards becoming an eco-centric elder, it is not the only way one will need to go.

Along with spiritual transcendence, an eco-centric elder will need to have a mature ego, one that "understands the occasional necessity of surrendering to or being defeated by a force greater than itself . . ." (Plotkin, 2008, p. 59). This overcoming of the Ego is fraught with difficulty, one reason why those who are seeking a complete self are not and never will be perfect. They will still at times have confusion, make mistakes, and cause tragedies. They will remain challenged and troubled, even as they seek wholeness.

Despite their human frailties, eco-centric elders will offer more-than-typical help to others. As we will see in Ethos, they will attain and deserve their uncommon respect because, instead of just, symbolically speaking, moving up the Beanstalk of Spiritual Development they will, metaphorically speaking, also go with the flow around a quadrated circle.

Briefly speaking, this flow is the process of maturity as one transitions from birth to death. It will be described as a wheel because many of the qualities of one's younger years—playfulness, for example —return in one's older years.

Just as one can scramble blindly and slowly or more consciously and rapidly up the Beanstalk of Spiritual Development one can also either muddle around the circle of life or, knowing what stages come next and what hindrances have to be overcome, move more consciously, more swiftly, and more effectively to future stations on the wheel of life. Attempting to skip a Beanstalk Branch or a section of the wheel of life is pointless and counterproductive. Neither can be done successfully.

While one's age plays a significant role in one's development, in knowing what comes next and what has to be done to move up the "Beanstalk" or around the "Wheel," one can expedite all passages successfully and without undue delay. The Heartwood Path will help with both ways of looking at your development—both up and around.

The details of the Wheel Of Life were presented in the first course: "**Kosmos**." The main point of the present waypoint is that successful eco-centric development requires too kinds of map-reading: one that represents the process of moving up to one's own potential—whatever that may be without any malice towards lower levels of development— and the other—the Wheel Of Life—which is a map to "elderhood." In using these maps remember that it is pointless to attempt to skip a branch of development and a quadrant of the Wheel. Do not, for example attempt to skip ahead to being an elder without properly processing childhood and young adulthood. Before we describe this wheel of Eco-Soul-centric development, there are many other topics that need to be addressed, beginning in the next waypoint with the topics of "flow" itself.

To The Third Of Many Touchstones Of People-Nature Interfacing...

HumaNatureConnect Activity

Start-up Protocol

If this is not a day when you prefer to spend time in nature without an agenda, do the Heartwood Path Start-up Protocol found in the Appendix.

Generating Patterns Of Human-Nature Interaction # 3:

Recognition By The Nonhuman Other

For this activity, prepare to be recognized by an animal near your attractive natural being. You could be trying to get the attention of a monkey in a zoo (a perverse interaction pattern) or you could be calling your dog to dinner (a domestic interaction pattern). By choosing instead to swim with the manatees or other attractive aquatic beings (a wild interaction) you are doing something that has a more positive psychological effect on you. In your journal, write down what meaning you derived from this wild interaction pattern (swimming with a natural attractive being); what joy, if any, it produced; how, if at all, it built within you a bond between your mind and nature; and how, if at all, the wild version of this interaction pattern was better for you than the perverse or domestic instantiation of the same interaction pattern; and how not being allowed to participate in this sort of wild interaction pattern—swimming with an attractive natural being—would make you feel? How does swimming in the presence of your attractive natural being make you feel? How would it feel to swim without the presence of your attractive natural being? In writing down these responses you will be adding to our collective nature language, so important to rekindling the bond between humans and nature. Look over your impressions and think about them as you fall asleep—possibly outdoors—tonight before dreaming.

Follow-up Protocol

For best results, write down your impressions of this activity in your journal using the Heartwood Path Follow-up Protocol found in the Appendix. Afterwards, consider sharing your interpretations with others.

Heartwood Path Axioms

Key Assertions From Waypoint 3.44

3.44.1.

EartHearts seek to make the meeting of Eco-Soul-centric elders a more common event, indeed a regular part of life.

3.44.2.

With the clear alternative of the mindset of an Eco-Soul elder, thinking of oneself as primarily a worker or a consumer will be seen as a pathological aberration, as will class stratification; power differentials; and the exploitation of women, children, the poor, and nature.

3.44.3.

Eco-centric elders will attain and deserve uncommon respect because instead of just, symbolically speaking, moving up and down the Beanstalk of Spiritual Development they will, metaphorically speaking, also go with the flow around a quad-rated wheel of eco-centric development.

Nocturnal Pilgrimage 3.44

For best results, write down your impressions of each night's dreams in your journal using the Heartwood Path Dreaming Time Protocols found in the Appendix. Afterwards, consider sharing your Dream Tending with others.

You learned about staying calm as a dream stabilization technique at Waypoint 3.21. Now, after more practicing with lucid dreaming initiation, it is time to make sure you can hold on to your nocturnal lucidity. Here's another tip, useful for when you want to keep a dream from fading. Simultaneously interact with Dream Characters while also remembering that you are dreaming. The Bible, while not talking about lucid dreaming, offers the most poignant words for what I mean here: "Be in the world, but not of it." In East St. Louis as a child, I would also say something that is also applicable: "Keep one foot in, and one foot out."

Besides being a good thing to think while attempting to stabilize a lucid dream, "keep one foot in, and one foot out" is what I said right before entering my familiar wet sanctuary as a kid. Every complete immersion in a nearby swamp—which I did to find peace, information, and safety—began with a single, tentative step, during which I would say: "put one foot in." I would also say, partly to keep myself from thinking that I was weird by spending my days beyond the riparian zone, "keep one foot out," which, to me, meant to stay "normal" by avoiding becoming the "Swamp Thing." After a typical day of swimming with snakes, amphibians, turtles, and frogs, I thought I could reestablish my membership in the human race merely by making sure I could change back into dry clothes after steeping myself in nearby, shady, chest-deep, ancient water-filled oxbows (abandoned river channels) or prehistoric borrow pits (created over a thousand years ago to build the largest pyramid in North America). Oddly, it worked; or, at least, I thought it did. Saying "one foot in, one foot out," at least stabilized my dream of deceiving others about my peculiar wet immersions.

You are doing a great job moving down the Heartwood Path on your journey to Gladandgreen Junction. You have gleaned a lot of information. And, there are many treasures ahead.

Each step is a part of your conversion from separation to integrity. Enjoy your pilgrimage more by doing the activities in nature. Doing so will lead to both profound insights into your complex problems and an overwhelming feeling of peacefulness.

When ready, move to the next waypoint, entitled "Roll." There, you will learn the value of moving to the flow of the implicit order of the universe.

45

Roll

GO WITH THE FLOW

There is an interconnectedness of all things, a pattern that connects. There is a subtle perfection and order to the world, an "implicit order" of the universe (which eastern practitioners call "wu Wei"). Getting into the flow of this order, by generally not forcing things, is the art of right living. Living in this way is not easily understood by the intellect alone; and understanding wu Wei requires the kind of attunement with the Soul described above.

To The Fourth Of Many Touchstones Of People-Nature Interfacing...

HumaNatureConnect Activity

Start-up Protocol
If this is not a day when you prefer to spend time in nature without an agenda, do the Heartwood Path Start-up Protocol found in the Appendix.

Generating Patterns Of Human-Nature Interaction # 4:

Interacting With The Periodicity Of Nature

For this activity, interact with a sunrise, a sunset, or any other periodicity of nature (displays of a change of season, for example) after you feel connected to your chosen attractive natural being. You could think about growing tomatoes in a hydroponic greenhouse (a perverse interaction pattern) or you could think about planting a garden in your backyard (a domestic interaction pattern). By choosing to picking wild blackberries at the edge of a forest at sunrise (a wild interaction) you would be doing something that has a more positive psychological effect on you. In your journal, write down what meaning you derived from this wild interaction pattern; what joy, if any, your experience of watching the rising or setting of the sun produced; how, if at all, the experience built within you a bond between your mind and nature; and how, if at all, the wild version of this interaction pattern was better for you than the perverse or domestic instantiation of the same interaction pattern; and how not being allowed to participate in this sort of wild interaction pattern—watching a sunrise or sunset—would make you feel? How does interacting in this way in the presence of your attractive natural being make you feel? How would it feel to have this interaction without the presence of your attractive natural being? In writing down these responses you will be adding to our collective nature language, so important to rekindling the bond between humans and nature. Look over your impressions and think about them as you fall asleep tonight before dreaming.

Follow-up Protocol

For best results, write down your impressions of this activity in your journal using the Heartwood Path Follow-up Protocol found in the Appendix. Afterwards, consider sharing your interpretations with others.

Heartwood Path Axioms

Key Assertions From Waypoint 3.45

3.45.1.

There is an interconnectedness of all things, a pattern that connects.

3.45.2.

There is a subtle perfection and order to the world, an "implicit order" of the universe known as "wu Wei."

3.45.3.

Getting into the flow of the implicit order, by generally not forcing things, is the art of right living.

3.45.4.

Living in harmony with the implicit order is not easily understood by the intellect alone; and understanding "wu Wei" requires an attunement with the Soul.

Nocturnal Pilgrimage 3.45

For best results, write down your impressions of each night's dreams in your journal using the Heartwood Path Dreaming Time Protocols found in the Appendix. Afterwards, consider sharing your Dream Tending with others.

You have already learned about keeping calm, spinning, engaging the senses, and not getting too wrapped up in any nocturnal event as ways to stabilize the lucid dream. There are more ways. Use the the following recommended stabilization tip whenever your lucid dreams start to go out of focus. Be in command. If your dream starts to fade yell "clarity!" Yelling "Stabilize! or "more lucidity" also works.

With the information from this waypoint in mind, prepare for sleep. Relax as a way to induce sleeping and dreaming. Do something soothing. Head to bed at your regular time. If such things do not help you to fall asleep, add to your customary end of day ritual making your private slumber space dark, comfortable, safe, calm, and quiet. Sleep well.

After tending to your dreams, resume your daytime sojourn down the Heartwood Path. Go into nature to help you recall your full-fledged membership in the natural order. Doing so will also help you to overcome being merely an individual in search of self-centered personal contentment.

Your step by step conversion into a state of spiritual maturity continues each time you visit a new Heartwood Path waypoint. For this reason, move to the next waypoint: "Pull." There, you will learn how to bring more into your life.

46

Pull

USE THE "DRAW LAW"

When one falls into tune with the universe (attunement), as described in a previous waypoint, it becomes readily apparent that a precise and powerful universal law affects everything and everyone. This law controls the pattern that connects. Since it controls the way everything is drawn together, I prefer to call it "the Draw Law." According to this tenet, thoughts and things of a like nature are attracted to one another. One rhythm, for example, will entrain with another and one musical note will resonate with a like note because matching frequencies are drawn to one another.

Thoughts too have their own frequencies. So, under the influence of the Draw Law, whatever goes on in one's mind is pulled into manifestation in a way that matches the thoughts. Each person is like a powerful magnet. Each thought attracts like thoughts, both within oneself and within others. When one limits one's thoughts to what one wants the most, the Draw Law pulls what one wants most into one's life.

One receives mixed results when one has scattered thoughts. Negative thoughts (having a certain frequency) become negative things (of a matching frequency); and, in a like manner, positive thoughts become positive things. In this way, one's thoughts become the cause and one's life becomes the effect.

Since you are always thinking you are always creating. Whatever you think about the most will become your life. For these reasons it is important to change the way one thinks to keep the music of one's thoughts uncomplicated, clear, and positive.

Before one learns to control one's scattered thinking, one spends much time thinking about what one does not want. The frequency of thinking about what one does not want is the same frequency as the things one does want. The Draw Law does not compute negation. It does not recognize the negatives in one's thinking. So, thinking that one does not want to be fat, for example, makes one fat. Thinking that one does not want a polluted environment tends to manifest a polluted environment. The law responds to the subject of one's thinking and not one's desires about the subject. The answer to this dilemma is to limit one's thoughts and then make sure these thoughts are positive. Think, for example, about being thin rather than not wanting to be fat, or about a clean environment rather than not wanting a polluted environment.

At this point along the Heartwood Path we come to a fork in the road: the hard, paved road to the left can only be driven on with the help of the human Ego; conversely, the soft, organic trail to the right requires less technology to traverse, but it requires the help of a spiritual connection to Nature. Following the road to the left (towards pollution, greed, an Ego gratification) often leads to miasms (pervasive influences that tend to deplete, corrupt, decay, or even kill). Despite these ill-effects, many people still risk following the left road. When they do, they are usually rewarded with increased material possessions and other Ego-driven benefits, at least in the short term.

These rewards come at a high cost, particularly in the areas of nutrition, immunity, and health. For the long run, the road to the left is clearly the wrong way. The right way is the path that leads to better nutrition for the natural body, enrichment for the natural mind, and fulfillment for the natural spirit. One can choose to follow the right path—the wu Wei. Optimal flow is achieved, in part, by balancing within one's life both active and quiet elements. The following exercise will help set you on a good course.

To An Examination Of Thrusting And Acceptance In Your Life...

HumaNatureConnect Activity

Start-up Protocol

If this is not a day when you prefer to spend time in nature without an agenda, do the Heartwood Path Start-up Protocol found in the Appendix.

Renewing Yourself Through The Yin And Yang In Your Life

For this activity, describe what is quiet yin in your life. Describe how, if at all, you renew yourself after spending time around busy people and noise? Describe how, if at all, you bring greater active yang into your life after you spend long hours quietly bringing passive yin into your life. Do you force yourself to be quiet or active? What can you do to allow for a more relaxed balance of both yin and yang in your life?

Follow-up Protocol

For best results, write down your impressions of this activity in your journal using the Heartwood Path Follow-up Protocol found in the Appendix. Afterwards, consider sharing your interpretations with others.

Heartwood Path Axioms

Key Assertions From Waypoint 3.46

3.46.1.

A precise and powerful universal law, the Draw Law, affects everything and everyone and controls the pattern that connects.

3.46.2.

Thoughts and things of a like nature are attracted to one another.

3.46.3.

Under the influence of the Draw Law, whatever goes on in one's mind is pulled into manifestation in a way that matches the thoughts.

3.46.4.

One receives mixed results when one has scattered thoughts.

3.46.5.

When one limits one's thoughts to what one wants the most, the Draw Law pulls what one wants most into one's life.

Nocturnal Pilgrimage 3.46

For best results, write down your impressions of each night's dreams in your journal using the Heartwood Path Dreaming Time

Protocols found in the Appendix. Afterwards, consider sharing your Dream Tending with others.

Keep heading on your way down the Heartwood Path, both day and night. During the day, pause regularly in nature to prepare yourself for each new HumaNatureConnect Activity. As you pause in nature you will likely acquire a complete perspective on life plus the kind of wisdom only a sincere seeker can unearth.

Your vigilance in doing the outdoor activities may also help you live longer. When comparing mortality rates to percentage of forest cover, the Nippon Medical School discovered that, after controlling for smoking and socioeconomic factors, the higher the forest coverage the lower the incidents of cancers (Selhub & Logan, 2012, p. 26).

Both day and night, prepare for lucid dreaming by heeding my Great Grandma Boswell's stern admonition: no alcohol, marijuana, coffee, or tobacco. Each of these substances have a different side-effect, such as increasing deep sleep or suppressing the state of REM. These side effects are not conducive to dreaming.

Without using the substances forbidden by Kate Boswell, move to the next waypoint: "Sole And Melded." There, you will be reminded that the less your Ego does, the more Nature will do through you. You will also be presented with another human-nature interface: immersing yourself in water. As we all know, without alcohol, marijuana, coffee, or tobacco, the following activity will be dull and boring; but at least you will have a better chance of living and dreaming for another day.

47

Sole And Melded

LEARN TO BE AND LEARN TO BECOME

One thinks a positive world into being not by wishful thinking or through random flights of imagination. Specific steps for using the Draw Law will be covered subsequently.

Before one can fruitfully and ethically jump into action one needs to learn to be. This requires one to both individuate—that is, to anchor one's uniqueness (the topic of this Heartwood Path course) and to integrate one's individual self into the world (the topic of the next Heartwood Path course).

Going with the flow that is wu Wei—the implicit order—is usually an act diametrically opposed to the human Ego; and, the less your Ego does, the more Nature will do through you.

To The Fifth Of Many Touchstones Of People-Nature Interfacing...

HumaNatureConnect Activity

Start-up Protocol

If this is not a day when you prefer to spend time in nature without an agenda, do the Heartwood Path Start-up Protocol found in the Appendix.

Generating Patterns Of Human-Nature Interaction # 5:

Immersing Yourself In Water

For this activity, think about or actually immerse your body in water after you feel connected to your chosen attractive natural being. In doing this interaction pattern, you could think about swimming in a crowded, chlorinated, concrete public wave pool (a perverse interaction pattern) or you could think about swimming in a backyard pool (a domestic interaction pattern). By choosing to swim in the ocean, a natural stream, or a lake (a wild interaction) you are doing something that has a more positive psychological effect on you.

In your journal, write down what meaning you derived from this wild interaction pattern; what joy, if any, swimming in a natural body of water produced; how, if at all, your experience built within you a bond between your mind and nature; and how, if at all, the wild version of this interaction pattern was better for you than the perverse or domestic instantiation of the same interaction pattern; and how not being allowed to participate in this sort of wild interaction pattern— swimming in a natural body of water—would make you feel? How does interacting in this way in the presence of your attractive natural being make you feel? How would it feel to have this interaction without the presence of your attractive natural being? In writing down these responses you will be adding to our collective nature language, so important to rekindling the bond between humans and nature. Look over your impressions and think about them as you fall asleep tonight before dreaming.

Follow-up Protocol

For best results, write down your impressions of this activity in your journal using the Heartwood Path Follow-up Protocol found in the Appendix. Afterwards, consider sharing your interpretations with others.

Heartwood Path Axioms

Key Assertions From Waypoint 3.47

3.47.1.

Before one can fruitfully and ethically jump into action one needs to both individuate (anchor one's uniqueness) and integrate one's individual self into the world.

3.47.2.

Going with the flow that is wu Wei—the implicit order-—is usually an act diametrically opposed to the human Ego; and, the less your Ego does, the more Nature will do through you.

Nocturnal Pilgrimage 3.47

For best results, write down your impressions of each night's dreams in your journal using the Heartwood Path Dreaming Time Protocols found in the Appendix. Afterwards, consider sharing your Dream Tending with others.

Continue your journey down the Heartwood Path at night by dreaming. After you awaken from your sleep, resume your waking time pilgrimage by tending to your dreams.

When ready, move to the next waypoint: "Evoking." As usual, you will be presented with an activity that begins by instructing you to commune with nature. This approach is included in this book, in part, as a way to end any likely near-amnesia you may be experiencing regarding your nature-based origins. To do well along the Heartwood Path, and to do well in life, one needs to bring down the walls of separation that isolate oneself from the world of other life forms—the world that sustains and supports life.

As a further incentive to get outside to commune with nature, as you are instructed to do continually along the Heartwood Path, take heed: a study in Florida, looking at five years of data on stroke mortality found that large amounts of greenspace (nature) offered significant protection (Selhub & Logan, 2012, p. 26). Get some Vitamin N today.

48

Evoking

VISUALIZE

Visualization is a twofold process: 1) introspection of images as they are presented randomly to the mind and 2) purposeful stimulation of visual images through imagination. Either way, Heartwood Path pilgrims are encouraged to focus on visual images that concern expansion and contraction. All created things expand and eventually contract repeatedly. Examples of this pulsation can be seen in many ways, including: the sun, stars, galaxies, life forms, the act of respiration, and the sexual act. Along with expansion and contraction, another recommended topic for the last stage of one's spiritual development is the visualization of emptiness. Everything can be visualized as being mostly empty; empty of matter and substance, mostly consisting of unoccupied blankness. Examples of this visualization include the human body that, when magnified greatly, is seen as full of empty space; and the universe that, when viewed through a telescope, is seen as an empty expanse.

Here is why expansion, contraction, and emptiness is so important to those who follow the Heartwood Path or other pathways to enlightenment. When one adds introspection to the visualization of expansion, contraction, and emptiness a mental conclusion eventually emerges that is crucial: in empty space there is consciousness and bliss.

It is this bliss, this great happiness, this amazing joy that constitutes the uncommon happiness that so wonderfully supports those who work for sustainability. By focusing on the expansion, contraction and emptiness of all things—from you yourself to the universe—the beneficial sense of oneness will naturally grow. Tapping into this oneness of the universe is beneficial because it allows one to replenish the body, the mind, and Spirit in ways never before imagined. As one focuses on the breathing—just one good way to feel the results—the expansion and contraction of the lungs and the emptiness—the awareness of the felt sense at the beginning and ending of each breath of a mental state containing little or no concepts clears out the mental objects that block our blissful connection to the whole. This emptiness—this awareness— is always there but usually forgotten in the hubbub of daily life. This bliss makes all the work of going down the Heartwood Path, and all the effort of being alive, worth the exertion. There may be bliss of fragrance, bliss of sight, bliss of touch, and so on. These forms of bliss are impermanent and not what we are looking for in this waypoint, although they can be a good intermediate way to enlightenment. We are here foreshadowing what will be found at a latter point along the Heartwood Path, when one feels the compulsion to take a peak at the conditions of sageness, the marriage of bliss and emptiness. This coupling is important, for bliss without emptiness is little more than indulgent sensuality.

Compassion and joy mark the latter stages in one's possible development. These positive emotions support one's saintly endeavors as an enduring eartHeart. But if one wants to take it a step further, and we will do so along the Heartwood Path in at least temporary peaks, then mediation without form—emptiness—will be required. For now, however, just know that brief peaks at emptiness are important and coming, but focus mostly on the various topics and activities having to do with mediation on form—its impermanence, its contractions, and its expansions (which lead to saintliness).

To The Sixth Of Many Touchstones Of People-Nature Interfacing...

HumaNatureConnect Activity

Start-up Protocol

If this is not a day when you prefer to spend time in nature without an agenda, do the Heartwood Path Start-up Protocol found in the Appendix.

Generating Patterns Of Human-Nature Interaction # 6:

Moving Away From Human Settlement And Return

For this activity, move yourself away from human settlement and return after you feel connected to your chosen attractive natural being. In doing this interaction pattern, you could think about having the virtual experience by watching a television show (a perverse interaction pattern) or you could think about taking a day hike through a regional park (a domestic interaction pattern). By choosing instead to think about embarking or, better yet, actually embark on a three day vision quest in a remote wilderness area (a wild interaction) you are doing something that has a more positive psychological effect on you.

In your journal, write down what meaning you would derive from this wild interaction pattern; what joy, if any, it would produce; how, if at all, it would build within you a bond between your mind and nature; and how, if at all, the wild version of this interaction pattern would be better for you than the perverse or domestic instantiation of the same interaction pattern; and how not being allowed to participate in this sort of wild interaction pattern—embarking on a vision quest in nature—would make you feel? How does interacting in this way in the presence of your attractive natural being make you feel? How would it feel to have this interaction without the presence of your attractive natural being? Not knowing what to say to this question is a hint that you may not be spending enough time in the presence of natural beings for these activities. One can speak best of what one is missing after the loss, real or imagined, takes place. What needs to be said is similar to what would be said if you could not go to a party with your lover, or to a movie with a friend, or to church with your family. There would probably be a sense of missing the company of your partner, of feeling that the experience would be complete or fruitful if experienced with a loved one. The experience may seem shallow or dull without the company of an attractive being. You may also sense that the meaning of the experience is lowered without the give and take of feelings, vibes, or words that can only be experienced when in the company of another being. The fun of the event may be diminished without someone to share it with. Expressing how you would feel if you could not be with someone adds to the chances that you will be more diligent in seeking out shared experiences in the future. In writing down these responses, you will be adding to our collective nature language, so important to rekindling the bond between humans and nature. Look over your impressions and think about them as you fall asleep tonight before dreaming.

Follow-up Protocol

For best results, write down your impressions of this activity in your journal using the Heartwood Path Follow-up Protocol found in the Appendix. Afterwards, consider sharing your interpretations with others.

Heartwood Path Axioms

Key Assertions From Waypoint 3.48

3.48.1.

Visualization is a twofold process: 1) introspection of images as they are presented randomly to the mind and 2) purposeful stimulation of visual images through imagination.

3.48.2.

Pilgrims along the Heartwood Path are encouraged to focus on visual images that concern expansion and contraction.

3.48.3.

All created things expand and eventually contract repeatedly.

3.48.4.

When one adds introspection to the visualization of expansion, contraction, and emptiness a mental conclusion eventually emerges that is crucial: in empty space there is consciousness and bliss.

3.48.5.

By focusing on the expansion, contraction and emptiness of all things-from you yourself to the universe—the sense of oneness will naturally grow.

Nocturnal Pilgrimage 3.48

For best results, write down your impressions of each night's dreams in your journal using the Heartwood Path Dreaming Time Protocols found in the Appendix. Afterwards, consider sharing your Dream Tending with others.

After dreaming, wake up slowly. Nothing will kill the memory of your dreams faster than waking up too rapidly.

Set a slow pace by restricting your movements as much as possible upon walking. Only after a motionless period of dream reflection, begin to tend to your dreams.

After you are done making journal entries, resume your waking travels down the Heartwood Path by moving to the next waypoint: "Familiarity." Once you are at the next waypoint, be sure to do the activity in nature. In doing so, it will be helpful if you ponder how you fit into the scheme of things. Such communing with nature is a surefire way to motivate you to reduce your destructive impact on the earth. It is also a very good way to increase your chances of living longer. Selhub and Logan report on studies in Shanghai and Scotland that support this claim (2012, p. 26).

49

Familiarity

KNOW YOURSELF

One's self-image determines how one acts. It affects one's ability to be satisfied, educated, creative, happy, and organized. One's self-image has four components:

1. movement—temporal and spatial changes in breathing, eating, speaking, blood circulation, and digestion;
2. sensation—the five senses plus the kinesthetic sense which allows us to be aware of pain, orientation in space, the passage of time, and rhythm;
3. feeling—joy, grief, anger, self-respect, inferiority, sensitivity, and emotions; and
4. thought—imagining, classifying things, recognition of right from wrong, recognizing rules, and all functions of the intellect.

One needs to be self-aware before one can work on self-development. Once one is self-aware one can develop a proper balance of feeling, senses, thought and movement. Without this balance, a person will be limited in his or her ability to create, discover, change, and know. We need to balance the concepts of the cranial brain with the feelings of the enteric brain. We need to sometimes sit still and use our fifty-plus natural senses (described in an earlier course) and, at other times, experience feelings that can only come from movement. Movement without feelings is nothing more than transportation. Feelings without movement is limiting, often too conceptual, and promotes both physical and emotional lethargy. Movement raises one's energy to levels where a greater variety of feelings can be tapped.

The process of self-awareness is made more fruitful by answering of a set of questions, as is done in the following activity:

To Self-knowledge...

HumaNatureConnect Activity

Start-up Protocol

If this is not a day when you prefer to spend time in nature without an agenda, do the Heartwood Path Start-up Protocol found in the Appendix.

Becoming Self-aware

For this activity, work on becoming more self-aware by answering the following questions:

1. Where do you prefer to focus your attention?
2. In what ways are you attuned to the external environment?
3. In what ways are you sociable and expressive?
4. In what ways are you drawn to the inner world?
5. In what ways are you private and contained?
6. How do you take in information and find out about things?
7. Do you focus on what is real, actual, and concrete; or do you focus on possibilities, abstractions, and the theoretical?
8. How do you make decisions?

9. Are you analytical, tough minded, and reasonable; or are you sympathetic, tenderhearted, and compassionate?
10. How do you orient yourself to the outer world—to externality?
11. Are you scheduled, organized, methodical, and prefer closure; or are you spontaneous, open-ended, flexible, and like things open to change?

By answering the kinds of questions found in the previous activity you will understand better how your mind functions. You will be able to identify potential problem areas in your personality. You will be able to check communication patterns. By knowing the answers to the previous questions, your reactions can be anticipated, and tasks not suitable to yourself can be better allocated to people with preferences and skills best suited to the job.

Follow-up Protocol

For best results, write down your impressions of this activity in your journal using the Heartwood Path Follow-up Protocol found in the Appendix. Afterwards, consider sharing your interpretations with others.

Heartwood Path Axioms

Key Assertions From Waypoint 3.49

3.49.1.

Know yourself.

3.49.2.

To control the mind, control the breath.

3.49.3.

For eartHearts, it simply will not be enough to allow the eyes to take them into the world; they need to learn to truly use the ears so that the world can come into them.

Nocturnal Pilgrimage 3.49

For best results, write down your impressions of each night's dreams in your journal using the Heartwood Path Dreaming Time Protocols found in the Appendix. Afterwards, consider sharing your Dream Tending with others.

Prepare yourself for a good night of dreamful sleep. Wake up and tend to your dreams before you get out of bed.

Think about how the sustainability of the planet is not solely about recycling and doing the other things that make you a good "green" citizen. The sustainability of the planet is ultimately about perpetuating an intimate relationship with nature. Research shows that to truly care about being "green" one has to have meaningful exposure to nature. (Selhub & Logan, 2012, p 3). For this reason, before moving to the next waypoint, "Active Breathing," go outside and find the significance, value, and expressiveness of nature.

Along with knowing yourself, other key instructions as you continue to prepare yourself for love include conscious breathing, mindfulness, stress reduction, and the importance of hearing and making music. These are the topics of the next five related waypoints.

50

Active Breathing

UNDERSTAND THE VALUE OF ACTIVE CONSCIOUS BREATHING

The moment one's umbilical cord is cut, that human being becomes a human breather. One inhales and exhales day and night, usually unconsciously. In doing so, one converts cosmic Chi energy—the life force also known as "Prana" in yoga—into the physical form of one's body. When a person breathes consciously and actively a process of opening up occurs. It is this process that vitalizes the body and connects one to the universe. Through a certain method of active breathing you can become charged up with prana. More than just the physical air that goes in and out of one's lungs, prana keeps up the activities of the mind and body, maintains equilibrium, and guards against imbalance and disorder throughout the universe. It is a real current, measurable on today's sophisticated devices.

When one breathes, air moves in and out of the physical body. Along with this current of air, prana enters the body and runs through ethereal but well-marked channels called "nadis." These channels are a vital part of the nonphysical, subtle body that is the counterpart to the physical body and is composed of, among other things, both chakras and nadis.

Active conscious breathing also forms a bridge from one's body to one's mind. To control the mind, control the breath. The bridge of the breath reconciles one's body and mind, making the feeling of oneness of body and mind possible. This feeling of oneness is at once illuminating, peaceful, and calming. These benefits can be enhanced through conscious, active breathing.

To breathe consciously is to "inspire" which means "to breathe in" and to "cause, guide, communicate, or motivate as by divine or supernatural influence." This dual meaning is telling, and the power of breathing is most obvious when one consciously inhales and exhales more deeply than usual, without any pause between inhaling and exhaling, and does so consciously over an extended period of time.

Such purposeful breathing will usually bring forth a tingling sensation that can lead to ecstatic joy. Under certain circumstances purposeful breathing can send waves of sexual pleasure throughout the whole body. Moreover, the deep relaxation that also occurs through conscious breathing may be accompanied by powerful insights, visions, or a feeling of oneness with the universe (Unio Mystica).

Conscious deep breathing can be a reminder that one is inseparable from the wholeness of the universe. When one inhales one accepts energy from the universe. When one exhales one releases energy to the universe. Inhaling strongly demonstrates and fortifies one's will. Exhaling completely demonstrates and fortifies one's ability to surrender. Experience wholeness by becoming a "human breathing!"

For the purposes of the Heartwood Path, a "human breathing" is a human being who has mastered the following five types of breathing: 1) the *cleansing breath* to prepare the muscles for exertion, reduce minor nervous tension, and focus mental attention; 2) the *sighing breath* to release pent up emotions and enhance pleasurable feelings; 3) the *charging breath* to build excitement and relax while in a state of increased pleasurable stimulation; 4) the *active breath* to improve physiological function, reduce blood pressure and pulse rate, and postpone fatigue; and 5) the *Fullness of Success* breath to aid with mindfulness and meditation.

These breathing rhythms occur with each of the Three Intensities of Pleasure. First Intensity Pleasures are those that help you relax. The spontaneous corresponding breathing rhythm is the long exhale. Second Intensity Pleasures are those that make you relaxed but also alert and energetic. The spontaneous corresponding breathing rhythm is slow and deep, with some deep sighs. Third Intensity Pleasures are those that cause enthusiasm and excitement. The corresponding breathing rhythm is quickened and sometimes heavy.

You will learn how to do various breathing techniques in a moment. But first, it will be motivating to learn what each breathing style can do for you.

The cleansing breath facilitates First Intensity Pleasures. It also exercises the respiratory muscles; increases the elasticity of the lungs; awakens and relaxes the torso; massages the muscles of the throat, shoulders, chest, back abdomen, rib cage, pelvis, and internal organs; and removes carbon dioxide from the lungs and makes more room for oxygen, which causes a feeling of lightness on many levels.

The sighing breath facilitates Second Intensity Pleasures. It also helps you let go; get in touch with your emotions; increase sexual arousal; and surrender sexually.

The charging breath facilitates Third Intensity Pleasures. It also helps you build energy, charge your bio-electrical system, intensify the feeling of vitality, and learn to enjoy the feeling of floating and/or the sensation of energy streaming through your body.

The active breath facilitates Second Intensity Pleasures. It also helps you feel more connected to the universe.

Fullness of Success breathing facilitates First and Second Intensity Pleasures in heights prana. Fullness of Success breathing is critical to the success of eartHearts because prana is the master of the mind. As prana is the master of one's thinking, the master of prana is sound.

The sound made during Fullness of Success breathing is critical to the success of the practice. The sound gives the mind something upon which to focus. The act of listening to the breath refines the breath and quiets the mind. Since one needs to focus one's attention even to make the Fullness of Success sound, one's mind will already be there with each breath.

Have you ever noticed how your breathing becomes shallow when you are under stress? This behavior is the result of the intimate relationship between the mind and the breath. When the mind is excited, the breath is irregular; and when the mind is lethargic, the breath is often labored.

The combination of conscious breathing (discussed here) and mindfulness (discussed in the next waypoint) can be both inspiring and healing. But, before moving on to mindfulness, we need to first demonstrate how to allow some prana into all the tight, closed-down, or injured areas of the body through various forms of conscious breathing. This demonstration occurs in the following activity:

To Purposeful Respiration...

HumaNatureConnect Activity

Start-up Protocol

If this is not a day when you prefer to spend time in nature without an agenda, do the Heartwood Path Start-up Protocol found in the Appendix.

Breathing Consciously

For this activity, engage in various forms of conscious breathing:

The Cleansing Breath. To do the cleansing breath, make yourself comfortable while sitting in an upright position and do the following: Place both feet on the ground. Keep your head straight and your chin parallel to the floor. Inhale slowly and fully through the nose. Feel how your chest lifts as you inhale completely. When you cannot inhale anymore, pucker your lips softly and blow out all of your air in a steady stream. Suck your abdomen in slightly as you push out the last bit of your air. Keep exhaling as much as much as you can until the inhale happens spontaneously. Make your exhalations twice as long as your inhalations. As you continue breathing in the manner described above, feel the muscle in your torso moving like a bellows. Become aware to all sensations of tension or tightness. Imagine that this tension is a smoggy haze that can be removed with each exhale. Puff your cheeks as you blow out tensions. After four or five cleansing breaths, notice how tensions are removed and how much more aware you are of your body.

The Sighing Breath. To engage in the Sighing Breath, do the following: take a deep sigh in and out with your mouth open. Relax your throat as you sigh. Feel your upper back become more expansive as you inhale. As you exhale say "hah" as if you were cleaning a pair of glasses. After your first "hah," take three deep breaths in a row. Do not worry if you are yawning a lot as this is just your body's way to achieve the proper oxygen/carbon dioxide balance. If you become lightheaded, close your mouth and breath through your nose and enjoy the floating sensation until it subsides.

The Charging Breath. To practice this breathing rhythm, do the following: through your open mouth suck in as much air as possible all the way into your chest. Let out the air all at once in a big rapid "hah." If you desire, repeat five times. Notice any feelings of lightheadedness, extra energy, and hyper-alertness.

Active Breathing. This breathing technique is done solely through the nose. Sit upright. As you breathe, put the bulk of your attention on the exhale and forget about the inhale. Close your mouth. Put your palms on your lower belly. Exhale and press on the lower rib cage down and back while simultaneously contracting the belly back toward the spine and lifting it up onto the thoracic cavity. Push as much of the air out of your lungs as you possibly can. Hold for a second, then let go. Repeat several times. When you "let go" and relax the belly and ribs, the in-breath will get sucked in all by itself. Through practice, the act of paying attention to the breath will become more natural. This breathing technique has been proven to improve physiological function, reduce blood pressure and pulse rate, and postpone fatigue.

The Fullness of Success Breath. The basic premise of this technique is to control the flow of air. Consciously narrowing the passageway of the throat through which the air is moving by making a kind of hiss similar to the sound made when we whisper. But, unlike a whisper, in Fullness of Success breathing the mouth is closed. To learn Fullness of Success breathing, it is permissible to begin by whispering an "ahhh" or "urrr" sound with the mouth open on exhalation. Completely empty the lungs with the sound. Then inhale by whispering the "ahhh" or "urrr" sound. Completely fill the lungs with the inhale. Then do it with the mouth closed. The sound will be similar to whispering with your mouth closed. By listening to the sound of the breath, especially when the breath is following a regular pattern or rhythm, the mind is less likely to wander, the Fullness of Success breathing can be maintained, and you will be better prepared for practicing mindfulness and meditation.

Follow-up Protocol

For best results, write down your impressions of this activity in your journal using the Heartwood Path Follow-up Protocol found in the Appendix. Afterwards, consider sharing your interpretations with others.

Heartwood Path Axioms

Key Assertions From Waypoint 3.50

3.50.1.

Understand the value of conscious breathing.

3.50.2.

The moment one's umbilical cord is cut, that human being becomes a "human breather."

3.50.3.

Through a certain method of active breathing you can become charged up with pranic energy.

3.50.4.

To control the mind, control the breath.

3.50.5.

The bridge of the breath reconciles one's body and mind, making possible the illuminating, peaceful, and calming feeling of oneness of body and mind.

Nocturnal Pilgrimage 3.50

For best results, write down your impressions of each night's dreams in your journal using the Heartwood Path Dreaming Time Protocols found in the Appendix. Afterwards, consider sharing your Dream Tending with others.

Prepare for sleep. Dream and tend to your dreams the next morning. Do not skip ahead down the Heartwood Path without spending some time in nature.

Research shows that exposure to nature lowers blood pressure and reduces levels of the stress hormone cortisol. As you linger in nature, practice your breathing. If you find that you are not devoting enough time to active, conscious breathing, read the next section and try the next practice often. Then begin a regular program of active, conscious breathing and mindfulness. The combination can be both inspiring and healing.

When you have done enough conscious breathing in nature, continue on your journey to gladness and environmental sustainability by moving to the next waypoint: "Practice Mindfulness." Rejoice in finding a free and non-pharmaceutical way to lower your blood pressure and stress.

51

Practice Mindfulness

BE HERE, NOW

Mindfulness is useful for everyone, particularly those who find it difficult for some reason to practice conscious breathing or meditation. The harried pace of our workaday world makes it difficult to find time for sitting still for a long time while mentally following the in and out flow of your breath. Being mindful does not require that you sit on a floor (neither does meditation). You can be mindful sitting in a chair or, as I prefer, lying down with my back straight and my head not on a pillow (pillows tend to constrict the flow of energy to the head).

Mindfulness means simply being aware of the present. It is a superb way to bring back a mind that has become—through work, family, or other pressures—too dispersed. It concentrates your attention. Best of all, mindfulness allows you to be aware that you are living the moments of your life.

The present is the only time one has to live. One needs to learn from the past, and it is wise to plan for the future. Forgetting to live in the present, however, is giving up actually living one's life!

Practice being aware of the present moment in everything you do. Removing the distinction between subject and object and seeing all things with compassion will be easier when you set aside time for meditation. If you find it difficult now to meditate while remaining still, try it while walking alone in a serene setting.

To This Place At This Moment...

HumaNatureConnect Activity

Start-up Protocol

If this is not a day when you prefer to spend time in nature without an agenda, do the Heartwood Path Start-up Protocol found in the Appendix.

Noticing The Here And Now

For this activity, gain awareness of the immediate moment and of the "now" of content and structure. Doing so requires focus and concentration—two critical skills to learn for self-growth. Remaining in present awareness is a taxing discipline that usually can be maintained at first only for short periods. The activity consists of stating what you are at this moment aware of. To keep you in the present, begin each sentence with "Now I . . ." First focus on the external world. Let your eyes roam about the outdoor scene, settling on objects (beings) at random. State specifically what you see. What smells and tastes do you experience? What do you hear? Now close your eyes and turn to your body sensations. Start with the big toe on one foot. Sense the inside of it, then the skin around it, then the space between it and the neighboring toe. Repeat this for every part of the body. Lastly, tune in to your emotions. What are you feeling in the gut? Your emotions may be all over the place. Let them take you where they will.

Follow-up Protocol

For best results, write down your impressions of this activity in your journal using the Heartwood Path Follow-up Protocol found in

the Appendix. Afterwards, consider sharing your interpretations with others.

Heartwood Path Axioms

Key Assertions From Waypoint 3.51

3.51.1.

Be here, now.

3.51.2.

Mindfulness is a superb way to bring back a mind that has become—through work, family, or other pressures—too dispersed.

3.51.3.

The present is the only time one has to live.

3.51.4.

If you find it difficult now to meditate while remaining still, try it while walking alone in a serene setting.

Nocturnal Pilgrimage 3.51

For best results, write down your impressions of each night's dreams in your journal using the Heartwood Path Dreaming Time Protocols found in the Appendix. Afterwards, consider sharing your Dream Tending with others.

After finishing the previous activity and after sleeping, it is time to remember your dreams. Few people will be able to recall their dreams in their entirety. For this reason, it is perfectly acceptable to remember and jot down only the fragments of your dreams.

After writing in your journal you may again be faced with a decision about whether to go outside to commune with nature. To help you decide to get back out there again, consider that exposure to nature is responsible for activating that part of the nervous system—the para-sympathetic branch—that works to calm you down (Selhub & Logan, 2012, p. 3).

When ready, continue with your efforts to become glad and green—that is, happy in a beautiful and sustainable environment. Move to the next waypoint: "Mental Tonic." It will help you to reduce stress.

52

Mental Tonic

REDUCE STRESS

Stress, often viewed only negatively, is best defined as the way the body responds to any demand. This response is nonspecific; meaning, for example, that one can break out in a sweat regardless of the stressor —be it a kiss, a game of checkers, an attacking lion, or a broken finger.

Pleasant stress, desired stress, or curative stress from exercise all cause low levels of uncertainty. This type of "good stress" is called "eustress."

Unpleasant stress, such as that which occurs from trying to meet an impossible deadline, is the result of frustration—the cumulative effect of the many difficulties and annoyances of everyday living. Such unwanted stress is called "distress."

The body's mechanism for handling stress has three stages (each not totally distinct, more like a spectrum): alarm, resistance, and exhaustion. These stages are taxing. The most effective intervention for stress reduction is the clarification of values and goals; followed in order of effectiveness by high performance nutrition with vitamin and mineral supplements, effective relaxation; self-affirming communication; and exercise.

The top ranking stress reducer—goals and values clarification—is explainable in three ways:

1. It promotes inner peace, self-acceptance, and balance.
2. Having a clear sense of priorities helps one use stress energy efficiently; and
3. It helps one deal with a high degree of uncertainty.

For those suffering from stress, the solution is clear: the first priority is to make a priority list. The second priority is to eat properly. The third priority is to relax effectively. The fourth priority is the use of self-affirming communication skills. The fifth priority is exercise.

To The Reduction Of Tension...

HumaNatureConnect Activity

Start-up Protocol

If this is not a day when you prefer to spend time in nature without an agenda, do the Heartwood Path Start-up Protocol found in the Appendix.

Reducing Stress

For this activity, practice living life more fully. This activity will help you become joyfully mindful. Ask the questions that follow to your chosen natural object but do not expect to be able to answer the questions immediately. Just ask for permission to ponder these questions on site in nature; immerse yourself in the qualities of the natural being and its natural surroundings; use one or more of your natural senses; think of your chosen being as an emissary carrying the wisdom of nature to you after granting you its consent to have this connection experience by remaining attractive; resonate with the underlying tone or rhythm you feel in your heart as you sit, stand, or lie next to your chosen natural being; allow the questions to be processed (answered) in the natural realm of your unconscious mind overnight; after a night's sleep, return to this activity, and write out your answers. Doing so allows the intelligence of nature to silently (or perhaps in your dreams) work its magic on you so that you can then write out answers that are not too mental, piously heady, or tainted by fluctuating social pressures or willy-nilly moods. For the following set of activities, inspired by a book by Jacquelyn Ferguson (2010), do each part, one at a time.

Part One: Scan each part of your body, one at a time, to see if you are holding any stress anywhere. If so, let that part of your body write in your journal what it needs to relieve its stress.

Part Two: Make a list of complaints. Write down who you complain to, when you are most likely to complain, why you choose a particular person to complain to, what you may be avoiding by doing nothing about your grievance, what is gained by doing nothing, and three alternative responses to your grievance other than complaining.

Part Three: Pick one of your complaints and exaggerate to the point of ridiculousness. Then consider what a comedian would say about your grievance.

Part Four: Answer the following: "As I lie on my deathbed I wish I had done more_____."

List three things that you which you had done to make you smile.

List three things that you wish you had done to touch your heart.

List two activities that you previously enjoyed but have since stopped doing.

List what would you like to do simply for fun?

Part Five: Determine what volunteer work you would like to do and write it down.

Part Six: What would you like to do to help yourself get more sleep (i.e.. exercise; avoid large meals; nicotine or alcohol near bedtime; meditation; maintain a sleep schedule even on weekends; and make journal entries about your worries before bedtime)?

Part Seven: List three things for which you are thankful.

Follow-up Protocol

For best results, write down your impressions of this activity in your journal using the Heartwood Path Follow-up Protocol found in the Appendix. Afterwards, consider sharing your interpretations with others.

Heartwood Path Axioms

Key Assertions From Waypoint 3.52

3.52.1.

Reduce stress.

3.52.2.

Stress, often viewed only negatively, is best defined as the way the body responds to any demand.

3.52.3.

The body's mechanism for handling stress has three taxing stages : alarm, resistance, and exhaustion.

3.52.4.

Make a priority list as a way to reduce stress.

Nocturnal Pilgrimage 3.52

For best results, write down your impressions of each night's dreams in your journal using the Heartwood Path Dreaming Time Protocols found in the Appendix. Afterwards, consider sharing your Dream Tending with others.

It stands to reason that it is better to bring your whole self to the solving of real world problems than it is to attempt to make corrections when you yourself are not fully present. Bringing wholeness to your Self, therefore, may be the best reason to engage in lucid dreaming. Look for and befriend the lost parts of yourself revealed in your dreams and you will receive real world benefits beyond your imagination. This is especially true if you supplement your dream tending with doing HumaNatureConnect Activities.

Let us say that after sleeping, dreaming, and tending to your dreams you simply cannot on some days get yourself out into nature. While not as good as communing with nature as we have been doing in each previous waypoint, here are some ways to, at least, get some benefits from nature without leaving the confines of your indoor spaces: keep living plants in your house and office, use essential oils derived from nature, spend more time with your pet, practice indoor gardening, and follow a Mediterranean, raw, living, organic, or whole foods diet.

When you are ready, power down your gadgetry and go outside. Resume your journey to Gladandgreen Junction after you do many of things mentioned in this waypoint to reduce stress and improve your health. After consuming your "Vitamin N" (the tonic of nature) one way or another, continue your learning at the next waypoint: "Sound's Helpful." Prepare to be moved by what you hear.

53

Sound's Helpful

PAY MORE ATTENTION TO WHAT YOU HEAR

Listening to sound can be deeply moving. This effect of sound on a person is due largely to the fact that our bodies are mostly water—an excellent conductor of sound. Because of the liquid nature of our tissues, the effect of listening to sound is like a deep massage of each microscopic part of the body. With such a pervasive effect, it is highly recommended that one pay conscious attention to the nature of the sounds bathing the body.

For eartHearts, it simply will not be enough to allow the eyes to take them into the world; they need to learn to truly use the ears so that the world can come into them. The eye is directed outward and only perceives the external surface of things while the ear allows one to get closer the heart of things.

There is an elaborate journey from sounding to resonating—from the making of a sonic vibration to the perceiving of the auditory energy. Along this elaborate journey, sound provides a connection between the source of the sound and the perceiver of the sound, sound changes form, sound moves between the Realms of Exteriority and Interiority, and sound begins as a vibration of matter and ends as a vibration with meaning. It is because of this amazing journey that I can say again. . . "Hearing makes matter...matter."

It is very difficult to see the oneness of the universe not only because everything is too large and too far away for the eyes to perceive but also because the very act of seeing creates a separation between the seer and the seen. This separation is a precondition for judgment, criticism, the creation of perceived distance, and remoteness. Bring something close to your eye and it becomes blurred. Touch it to your eye and the eye stops functioning. We can see from these examples that sight is not a good way to perceive oneness. Sight is good for perceiving the surfaces of differentiated parts, but hearing reveals that beneath all surfaces is a mightier hidden harmony.

If hearing were taken more seriously by individuals and society at large, the result would be an overall intensification of receptivity, gentleness, understanding, discretion, openness, and tolerance.

To A Main Form Of Attentiveness...

HumaNatureConnect Activity

Start-up Protocol

If this is not a day when you prefer to spend time in nature without an agenda, do the Heartwood Path Start-up Protocol found in the Appendix.

Listening

For this activity, use your natural sense of hearing—including resonance, vibrations, sonar and ultrasonic frequencies—to develop your abilities to open yourself up to the invisible world of audible vibrations. As you remain with your chosen natural attractive being, bring your attention to the sounds you hear. Really listen to a particular sound.

Explore every sensation of that one sound. Then, pay attention to all the sounds near yourself and your chosen being. Notice how some are faint and some are loud. Notice how they are coming to you from various directions. Count how many different sounds you can hear. Next, rather than picking out individual sounds, listen to all the sounds as if you are listening to an orchestra playing a beautiful song. Relax and enjoy the performance. Pick out one sound again. Attempt to determine if that sound is occurring out in the environment, in your own ears, or in your own brain. Picture the events that are causing the sound waves to move toward you. Think about the mechanical vibrations the sound is causing in the tissue of your ears, how the sound is becoming neuro-electric impulses, and how the sound is triggering associations in your mind. Think of the miracle of this sound and your listening to it.

Follow-up Protocol

For best results, write down your impressions of this activity in your journal using the Heartwood Path Follow-up Protocol found in the Appendix. Afterwards, consider sharing your interpretations with others.

Heartwood Path Axioms

Key Assertions From Waypoint 3.53

3.53.1.

Pay more attention to what you hear.

3.53.2.

Listening to sound can be deeply moving.

3.53.3.

Due to the liquid nature of our tissues, the effect of listening to sound is like a deep massage of each microscopic part of the body.

3.53.4.

The eye is directed outward and only perceives the external surface of things while the ear allows one to get closer the heart of things.

3.53.5.

Since sound begins as a vibration of matter and ends as a vibration with meaning, hearing makes matter matter.

Nocturnal Pilgrimage 3.53

For best results, write down your impressions of each night's dreams in your journal using the Heartwood Path Dreaming Time Protocols found in the Appendix. Afterwards, consider sharing your Dream Tending with others.

Prepare for a nice, dream-filled night's sleep. Do your dream tending before you leave your bed in the morning.

Countless ages of direct contact with nature has left us humans with a preference for certain landscapes: places where the tress are present but not too densely packed, vistas (originally for predator surveillance), fresh water, and a rich diversity of animals and plants (Selhub & Logan, 2012, p.9). You may more easily find your natural attractions if you head to such places.

After dream tending and nature communing, move to the next Heartwood Path place of learning. The next waypoint, "Tuneful," will conclude our current discussion of five ways to get to know yourself:

1) conscious breathing, 2) mindfulness, 3) stress reduction, the 4) importance of hearing and 5) music as a tool.

54

Tuneful

REGARD MUSIC AS A CRITICALLY IMPORTANT TOOL

Music is a pattern of vibratory motions. These vibrations are repetitions of the rhythms, relationships, proportions, and harmonies that exist throughout the natural and man-made world. No language is more universal.

Through the ever-moving, forward-moving, and constantly shifting patterns of music, one can easily slide in and out of mental focus. This mental flux prompts original thinking, encourages deeper understanding of the world—both consciously and unconsciously—and leads one's imagination to go to specific places or subjects.

To The Incantation Of A Favorite Tune...

HumaNatureConnect Activity

Start-up Protocol

If this is not a day when you prefer to spend time in nature without an agenda, do the Heartwood Path Start-up Protocol found in the Appendix.

Singing A Cherished Song

For this activity, use your natural sense of hearing including resonance, vibrations, sonar and ultrasonic frequencies as you sing your favorite song. Stand up next to your chosen natural being and sing your favorite or most familiar song. Belt out this song. Then take a moment to reflect. Now imagine that you are about to perform the best rendition of this song in the history of musical performances. Sing the song again, with confidence and gusto. Hold nothing back. Imagine that your audience loves your performance of this song.

Follow-up Protocol

For best results, write down your impressions of this activity in your journal using the Heartwood Path Follow-up Protocol found in the Appendix. Afterwards, consider sharing your interpretations with others.

Heartwood Path Axioms

Key Assertions From Waypoint 3.54

3.54.1.

Regard music as a critically important tool.

3.54.2.

Music is a pattern of vibratory motions.

3.54.3.

Musical vibrations are repetitions of the rhythms, relationships, proportions, and harmonies that exist throughout the natural and man-made world.

3.54.4.

No language is more universal than music.

Nocturnal Pilgrimage 3.54

For best results, write down your impressions of each night's dreams in your journal using the Heartwood Path Dreaming Time Protocols found in the Appendix. Afterwards, consider sharing your Dream Tending with others.

Consider your dreams to be messages from your physical body. View the figures, actions, and feelings in dreams as commentary about your physical condition. Continue practicing tending you your dreams before you begin your next Heartwood Path waypoint.

When ready, move to the next waypoint: "Samadhi." Once there, learn to achieve a meditative state of oneness that leads to profound degrees of intuition.

55

Samadhi

ENTER INTO A PROFOUND STATE OF CONTEMPLATION

Through Samadhi, the meditative state of oneness, one can attain profound degrees of intuition. One's own individual consciousness blends with a consciousness that is universal (mostly external to the individual). Although Samadhi may last less than a minute, its effects will be lodged in your memory track. Being the "awareness of the eye of God" or the direct perception of the "all-seeing eye of life" Samadhi offers a profoundly positive transformation.

After Samadhi, you may become less irritable, less fearful, less harsh, and less restricted. These benefits can last a lifetime. Your criterion for measuring success in Samadhi is your new heightened degree of serenity, wisdom, and compassion. You will become a secular saint, or—with heroic repeated practice— a sage.

To reach higher levels of meditation, one needs to practice. Samadhi is attained in subtle steps, and only rarely does one achieve Samadhi in one full sweep. There is a simple secret for attaining Samadhi: in everything you do—while working, eating, playing, making love, or meditating—understand the terms "consciousness" and "awareness" and consider the think about the following statements:

"I am the self-existent one."

"I am self-awareness itself."

In the former sentence, the "I" usually refers to the Absolute, or, if you prefer, to God. The Absolute, including the Christian God, has inherent existence, "aseity," no other source. God, or the Absolute, does not arise from any other being or cause. This independence is the nature of the Absolute. We humans also exist according to our own nature, which, unlike the Absolute (or God), includes our mortality. The Absolute's approval of us (attraction to us) and our nature is evidenced through peace, joy, free will, and grace. Receiving these grants is a sign of our ultimate significance, gifts that we as a species will need to work on to accept and preserve.

Each one of us may not be the Absolute, but we can, with some effort, achieve universal consciousness and thereby make wise determinations. The Heartwood Path is not meant to explain, in the ultimate sense, the source of one's existence, other than to say that at least one key step in our unfolding was through nature on the third planet from the Sun.

We will leave it to others to prohibit or condone one's ideas and statements about one's ultimate Source. We will instead focus most on the latter of the two sentences presented previously. We will condone the notion that you are *self-awareness itself.*

As a person you cannot be said to exist in your own right. Nevertheless, you can and do construct a concept of Self in your imagination which, depending on how you construct it, will or will not be bound by space and time.

The objects of observation, including your Self, are not what they appear to be. You are not, for example, just a fearful person nor are you just a positive do-gooder.

You are the Highest Self, yet it takes getting rid of wrong ideas to experience it. This Higher Self is your ultimate teacher. You experience your Highest Self when yoga works the Inner Self—the seat of your inspiration and imagination—on the Outer Self—the controller of the body and breath.

All "perceivables" are transient and unreal in the sense that they are fluid and based on one's interpretations. One is not an object in Consciousness. One is the source of Consciousness. One is the Witness of Consciousness. One is pure shapeless Awareness. When there is a Self, self-awareness is the Witness.

There is no such thing as a permanently separate person. Awareness, matter, and mind are one reality, both moveable and immovable, with inertia, energy, and harmony.

There are subtle differences between Consciousness and Awareness, yet often writers swap the terms. Knowing more about these terms will help you get more out of the outdoor activities at each course waypoint.

Consciousness is the field of experience, including thoughts, feelings, body sensations, the environment, and other conscious happenings. Awareness, by contrast, is the knowing that knows, the way we make something real, and the knowledge that something exists somewhere.

Awareness, arising out of consciousness, is the state or ability to perceive. Consciousness is the state of being aware, which, I suppose, is why the words are often used interchangeably. For the moment let's focus on "consciousness."

There are two modes of consciousness: the person and the Witness. The person resists, desires, fears, and lives in unrest. The person—born of the earthly mother—says "I am this, I am that." In contrast, the Witness—the self-existent one—is unaffected by pleasure and pain, and lives unruffled by the comings and goings of events. The Witness simply says "I am." The Witness is not a person but a point of consciousness without dimension.

Just as you are both individual and collective and just as you have both inner and outer world dimensions, you are not just a person. You are also the Witness. As a person, you think what you experience exists. So it does. As the Witness, you are timeless, bodiless awareness that imagines experiences. When fully present, what you as the Witness perceives in each moment does not exist as a separate reality. It is imagined. You interpret the world and it becomes what you imagine it to be.

It is the person that is skeptical about the plausibility of objects (natural beings) offering guidance to people. It is the Witness that makes no such distinction between the person and the object; and, so, there is no need to solve the argument about whether in the Huma-NatureConnect Activities it is the separate object communicating with the independent person or just the person's imagination running wild. The Witness has knowledge that it is all just Awareness anyway. For these reasons, it will be much easier to receive guidance from nature if you bring the Witness along on your outdoor activities. When you act as the Witness you rise in your consciousness as Awareness Itself. As such, there is no need to determine if objects can communicate with people. Both the object and the person is nothing other than Awareness Itself—indistinguishable from objects, nature, attractive beings, and so forth—using the imagination as it always does anyway. When that imagination comes as guidance from nature, heed the advice. It will be time-tested, helpful, insightful, and full of more depth than you will be capable of generating as an individual (which is, in truth, a false or Incomplete Self).

For greater success, carry these thoughts with you during the following eight steps to Samadhi:

1. Guidelines for universal morality, social contracts mostly having to do with abstention (described in the previous Heartwood Path book).
2. Personal practices that include observance (respect, deference, an act done to fulfill or respect morality, or an act done for ceremonial reasons), and vows (all described in the previous Heartwood Path book).

3. Physical postures to give focus to the body, all aimed at helping the practitioner abide and stay in the exercise (described in the previous Heartwood Path course).

4. Breathing exercises to give focus to the mind, aimed at controlling the Life Force.

5. Sensory control, turning inward to give focus to the senses, as if one is shutting off the wi-fi on the computer-brain. The benefit of doing so will be self-mastery. Since you have participated in the previous activities of this course you are already working on sense withdrawal and turning inward.

6. Concentration by cultivating perceptual awareness, bringing your mind to a single focus.

7. Devotion, meditation on a single concept, meditation on a single person, meditation on a single place, meditation on the Divine, and—most often in our instance—meditation on one's awareness of a single attractive natural being.

8. Samadhi, union with the Divine (bodymindgreen.com). Once you successfully take the previous seven steps you are prepared to reach Samadhi. This exalted state is subdivided into Savikalpa Samadhi and Nirvikalpa Samadhi. This distinction is important to pilgrims along the Heartwood Path because it is Savikalpa and not necessarily Nirvikalpa Samadhi that is so necessary for their later endeavors as eartHearts. Here's how to move towards each of the types of Samadhi (we are eliminating Dharma Megha Samadhi from our discussion because it cannot be obtained through desire, it comes as a gift, and it removes the practitioner from time and space):

1. Savikalpa Samadhi—contemplation with form—progresses in the following steps:

    a. the direct perception of the form of an object without thought or conversation,

b. the direct perception of the form of an object accompanied by lights, knowledge, astral (mental) sounds and causal (blissful) sounds,

c. the direct perception of the form of an object along with reflections of ideas but no thoughts,

d. the direct perception of the form of an object without the sounds, lights, and knowledge found in the previous steps (wakefulness, sense withdrawal, concentration ceases),

e. the withdrawal of all objective realities having to do with the exterior form of matter and the beginning of the process of penetrating into matter, and

f. the attainment of bliss and the beginning of God-consciousness.

2. Nirvikalpa Samadhi—contemplation without form (achieved by very few individuals) progresses in the following steps:

a. the discerning vision without any interruption between the universe and the Self;

b. the renunciation of all worldly objects;

c. liberation involution (envelopment), emancipation, becoming one with all life; and

d. God-consciousness or the experience of eternal, compassionate, unselfish love.

The achievement of Samadhi requires three procedures:

1. the stilling of your being,

2. turning inward, and

3. the recognition that you can change your life.

To put the wisdom of this section of the Heartwood Path to work for you, do the following activity.

To Sensory Control, The Cultivation Of Perceptual Awareness, Devotion To The Absolute, And Samadhi...

HumaNatureConnect Activity

Start-up Protocol

If this is not a day when you prefer to spend time in nature without an agenda, do the Heartwood Path Start-up Protocol found in the Appendix.

Attaining Universal Consciousness

For this activity, we will continue and complete the steps began in **Logos**, the second book in the Heartwood Path series. If you faithfully did the first three steps towards Samadhi found there (the external disciplines called "yamas," the internal disciplines called "niyamas," and the postures called "asanas"), you have already made your personal and social contracts and you have already mastered yoga poses aimed at helping you stay longer in a state of awareness or contemplation with your chosen, attractive natural beings. Before you continue with the remaining steps towards Samadhi, it will be helpful to find a way to slow down and deepen the breath so that your body rhythm will produce the physical and spiritual well-being that invites the onset of Samadhi.

That way is the chanting of the sound "Om." The resonance produced through such chanting provides an inner massage, it alters brain waves to frequencies that produce expanded creativity, it evokes a state of relaxation, it lowers blood pressure, it dissipates muscle tension, and it slows the heart rate.

Enter fully into the sound. Close your eyes and repeat "Ooommm-m-m-m. . . . Ooommm-m-m-m . . .Ooommm-m-m-m . . . Make the sound gentle and slow but full and strong. Allow the sound to quiet and still the body. Repeat the sound until you draw yourself into your inner world. Concentrate your mind on this sound. It is the sound of the fullness of the universe. Allow bliss to break free as the sound pushes your Ego aside. In your mind, become the sound (if you cannot imagine how to do this say in your mind that you are the sound and create the feeling in your mind that this is true). Next, move visualized light up your chakra system. Perceive yourself as light and your seven chakras (described in the previous Heartwood Path book, in a waypoint entitled "Transformers"), as spiraling vortexes of light. Without mentally "looking" at these chakras of light, place your consciousness inside the first chakra at the base of the spine. Visualize a stronger light that moves slowly up your chakra system aligned along your spinal column. Allow this light to accumulate and emanate from within each chakra— all the way up, step by step, to the seventh or crown chakra at the top of the skull. Repeat this upward bathing of light five to 100 times. The light energy will follow your consciousness. Notice how the light becomes increasingly subtle as it ascends from chakra to chakra. As the light ascends, you gradually become more centered within, you become more aware of the divinity within you, and you become more open to joy, bliss, and ecstasy.

Now that you have been exposed to external disciplines, internal disciplines, postures, the topic of chanting "Om," and everything that was said about anchoring your individuality (so you do not lose yourself as you psychologically merge with the universe) you are ready to complete the remaining five steps leading to Samadhi.

To get to the fourth limb or step towards Samadhi, called "Pranayama," one has to learn to control the breath as a way to control the Life Force. The following practice will help you reduce your fight-or flight tendency and replace it with the relaxed response so important to the attainment of universal consciousness: start by counting your breath. For ten times count to four for the inhalation's and count to four for the exhalations. In doing so you will have a greater understanding of the origin of your negative beliefs. As a way to help induce healing, write down in your journal what you plan to do about these beliefs.

To get on the fifth limb on your ascent to Samadhi, called "Pratyahara," one has to withdraw from sensory nourishment. Doing so will change your reality as you squelch all the sensory inputs (the clutter of sensations) that tend to prevent you from entering into a heightened sense of awareness. The main job on this limb is to tune out all the static that prevents you from connecting without distraction to your own mind. Try the following actions to withdraw from the senses:

1. do not call friends and family for one week;
2. turn off the lights for one night;
3. keep the television turned off for one night; and
4. turn inside to your mind as you sit outside, blindfold, with cotton up your nose, and plugs inserted in your ears.

Write in your journal how you feel to turn to yourself as you pay little or no attention to sensory inputs.

To get to the sixth limb in your progress towards Samadhi, called "dhyana," you have to concentrate your newly uncluttered mind. The task here is to free yourself from the past and and to concentrate on the present. To focus the mind:

1. every time your mind wanders, return your focus to your breathing;
2. as you focus on a single person, concept, place, or thing say to yourself: "I am content with what I have."
3. be in wonder as you focus on the randomness of your free-roaming thoughts.

In your journal, write down your impressions about doing these three tasks. State how, if at all, your attempts to concentrate your mind have made you more empathetic, compassionate, connected, and aware.

When the process of concentrating the mind become an effortless flow between the mind and the object, you have arrived on the seventh step leading to samadhi, called "dhyana."

When you get to the eighth and final limb, called "Samadhi," you enter into a state of "non-duality;" that is, you perceive that the self and the world are one and the same. This state results in a sense of boundless peace, a detachment from time, freedom from suffering, a profound sense of well-being, and the sense that saving the environment is saving one's Self. Having done what needs to be done to prepare the way for your awakening into the state of Samadhi, you will know you are there when:

1. the experience of a separate "I" disappears;
2. love is all there is, the product of a benevolent universe; and
3. one is happy in one's endeavors to preserve the beauty of nature and to make the environment sustainable.

Follow-up Protocol

For best results, write down your impressions of this activity in your journal using the Heartwood Path Follow-up Protocol found in the Appendix. Afterwards, consider sharing your interpretations with others.

Heartwood Path Axioms

Key Assertions From Waypoint 3.55

3.55.1.

Through Samadhi, the meditative state of oneness, one can attain profound degrees of intuition.

3.55.2.

There are important precursors to the meditative state of oneness wakefulness, sense withdrawal, concentration, meditation, and mind-enstasis (becoming super-conscious of your own uncluttered mind in its pure unformed state).

3.55.3.

Samadhi comes in two varieties: 1) Savikalpa Samadhi—contemplation of form, which leads to becoming a secular saint, driven easily to do for others and 2) Nirvikalpa Samadhi —contemplation on no form (achieved by very few individuals), which leads to becoming a sage.

3.55.4.

Those who follow the Heartwood Path focus most on Savikalpa Samadhi.

Nocturnal Pilgrimage 3.55

For best results, write down your impressions of each night's dreams in your journal using the Heartwood Path Dreaming Time Protocols found in the Appendix. Afterwards, consider sharing your Dream Tending with others.

Aizenstat informs us that dreams "sometimes tell of disease formation long before the occurrence of tangible physical systems, particular in severe afflictions that take a long time to develop such as cancer or heart disease." Aizenstat's statement is reason enough to continue tending to your dreams.

After adding another dream to your dream journal, continue your daytime advancement down the Heartwood Path by moving to the next waypoint: "Elation." Good spirits await, especially if you become strongly attracted to the beauty of a natural being or landscape as you may do in the next activity.

56

Elation

SEEK TRIPLE-A HAPPINESS: ABUNDANT, AUTHENTIC, AND ABIDING

Be a person who causes happiness wherever you go. Do not be that person who causes happiness when you go.

Bring contributions rather than calamities to all of your endeavors and you will prepare the ground for the growing of happiness. Whether your seeds of happiness will grow seems to many to be a mystery; but, as we shall see in this waypoint, there are ways to bring abundant, authentic, and abiding happiness into your life and into the lives of others once you know the nature of gladness itself.

Some say happiness is like a feral cat. There is a popular perception that one cannot call one's happiness and expect it to come. For many, happiness seems to come when not summoned. Despite these perceptions, there are ways to increase your happiness.

We each do have a fixed range of happiness, just as we have a fixed range for weight. Fortunately, while we do have a predetermined range of happiness, lasting happiness within our predestined range is possible. We can, despite widely held beliefs to the contrary, be authentically happy.

One can alter one's state of happiness by changing both the external and internal circumstances of one's life. The next two steps down the Heartwood Path—the next two paragraphs—explain how:

To live in the uppermost portion of your own capacity or range of happiness by changing the external circumstances of your life, you have a number of options, including: you can live in a wealthy democracy, you can get and remain married (proven to be true but perhaps not causal), you can avoid negative events and negative emotion, you can create a rich social network, and you can practice a religion. If your sole purpose is to become happier, do not bother making more money after you are moderately financially comfortable, do not work to stay healthy, and do not bother getting numerous advanced degrees. Wealth, health, and accomplishments may be beneficial for other reasons, but they are not proven to be causes of abundant, authentic, abiding happiness.

With real effort you can also improve your happiness by working on the following internal circumstances: concerning your past, be satisfied, prideful, and serene; concerning the future, build within yourself hope, faith, optimism, and trust; and concerning the present, seek out joy, ecstasy, enjoyment and—most importantly—flow. Flow is doing exactly what you want to do, doing it well, never wanting it to end, endeavoring without high emotions, and going into action with the sense that the self vanishes and time stops. Discussed earlier at the waypoint entitled "Roll," flow is being completely psychologically absorbed in an activity for its own sake. According to Mihaly Csikszentmihalyi, there are ten factors that accompany the experience of flow (all the following components are not necessary):

1. Challenging goals that are attainable.
2. Focused attention.
3. The activity is rewarding intrinsically.
4. There is a loss of self-consciousness as the activity spawns feelings of serenity.
5. One loses track of time.
6. There is immediate feedback.

7. One is skillful enough for the challenge, which is felt to be doable.
8. One feels control over the situation and outcome.
9. There is a lack of awareness of physical needs.
10. There is complete focus on the activity itself. (Csik-szentmihalyi. http://psychology.about.com/od/PositivePsychology/a/flow.htm)

Finding moments of flow are better stepping stones towards happiness than are the stumbling block of excessive worry about wealth, health, and accomplishments. Flow is a much better happiness-producer than being guilty about your past or than being worried about your future.

The future and the past have minor effects on the present. Neither determines it. Do not be bitter about your past or unaware of your present or passive about your future. Anger about the past shortens your life, unawareness of the present causes you to miss your life, and passivity about the future cause you to get less out of your life. Anger, unawareness, and passivity, therefore, all lead to the unfortunate rationing of your consciousness.

You cannot remove the memory of unhappy days gone by, but you can lessen their sting by being grateful and by forgiving the hurtful people of your past. Reducing the stings of the past often requires one to remember the hurts objectively; to empathize with wrongdoers (looking through the eyes of the wrongdoer for reasons for the misdeed); to forgive persons for the wrongdoing, to rise above the wrongdoing, to commit to forgive publicly (such as making a sign visible to others), and to holding on to forgiveness. By forgiving in this way you are not erasing the thoughts of the wrongdoing, but you are taking the important step of changing your reactions to the memories.

To prepare for the future, use optimism and hope as a fulcrum against things that go wrong. This brings us to a key assertion along the Heartwood Path:

situations are not permanent

nor do they usually have a pervasive effect your life.

Permanence is about time. Pervasiveness is about space. Sometimes problems can be long lasting and cut across a number of aspects of one's life. Other times, problems can be short-lived and affect only narrow aspects of one's life. It helps to bolster one's optimism by believing what is true: most bad effects are temporary and causes of good events have long-lived consequences.

It helps to know that bad events have specific, less pervasive causes and effects—they affect a narrow part of one's life. It also helps to know that good events have general, more pervasive, and universal causes and effects—they come from pervasive goodness and affect a larger part of one's life. In short,

if it is bad, think about it as temporary and specific;

if it is good, think about it as long lasting and universal.

This will set you on the threshold of abundant, authentic, abiding happiness.

Happiness in the present moment stems from both pleasures—temporary, immediate sensory thrills, delights, and comforts that require very little thinking but lead to positive emotions—and gratifications—longer term inner world events that engage one fully, immerse one in the kind of absorption that seems to stop time, and result from skills matching challenges. Base your life more on gratifications than you do on bodily pleasures, which tend to lead to habituation and short-lived happiness.

Rapture, bliss, hilarity, elation, and excitement are higher pleasures that lead to more enduring happiness than do the bodily pleasures. Still, higher pleasures lead to less enduring happiness than do the gratifications. Both bodily pleasures and higher pleasures have external stimuli that result in positive emotions but these emotions often have sudden endings and sometimes lead to the lingering aftermath of craving.

Still, it's a good idea to have as much pleasure as you can as long as it is experienced in reasonable amounts, spread out over time, or comes as the result of a surprise. Otherwise, addictions often are the result.

To Happiness That Is Abundant, Authentic, And Abiding...

HumaNatureConnect Activity

Start-up Protocol

If this is not a day when you prefer to spend time in nature without an agenda, do the Heartwood Path Start-up Protocol found in the Appendix.

Seeking Triple-A Happiness

For this activity, take significant strides towards that place called GladandGreen Junction, in this instance, working on the "Glad" part. The statements you will be asked to respond to in the following activity are inspired by Dr. Anthony J. Castro's book **Creating Space For Happiness: The Secret of Giving Room.** (2009).

Putting The "Glad" In Gladand-green Junction	My Impressions
Guilt keeps one from experiencing a fulfilling live. In the space at right, describe and feelings of guilt you may be harboring. Bringing these difficulties into the light is the first step in getting them out of the way of your own happiness.	

Sometimes one prevents oneself from feeling happy because of the feeling that no one is, or ever has been, in one's corner. It may be difficult for you to lean on someone for help. In the space at right, write down who is in your corner, who you would like to be in your corner, and what you will need to do to solicit and maintain the support you need. " ... life is so much more enjoyable when you have someone on your side and in your corner, sharing this magnificent experience called life" (Castro, 2009, p. 115).

It creates happiness when you give others the room to grow. Who in your life needs a good listener? What can you do to allow someone in your life to grow?

Follow-up Protocol

For best results, write down your impressions of this activity in your journal using the Heartwood Path Follow-up Protocol found in the Appendix. Afterwards, consider sharing your interpretations with others.

Heartwood Path Axioms

Key Assertions From Waypoint 3.56

3.56.1.

Be a person who causes happiness wherever you go, not that person who causes happiness when you go.

3.56.2.

Bring contributions rather than calamities to all of your endeavors and you will prepare the ground for the growing of happiness.

3.56.3.

The following truism will set you on the threshold of abundant, authentic, abiding happiness: if it is bad, think about it as temporary and specific; if it is good, think about it as long lasting and universal.

3.56.4.

Rapture, bliss, hilarity, elation and excitement are higher pleasures that lead to more enduring happiness than do the bodily pleasures.

3.56.5.

Both bodily pleasures and higher pleasures have external stimuli that result in positive emotions but these emotions often have sudden endings and sometimes lead to the lingering aftermath of craving.

Nocturnal Pilgrimage 3.56

For best results, write down your impressions of each night's dreams in your journal using the Heartwood Path Dreaming Time Protocols found in the Appendix. Afterwards, consider sharing your Dream Tending with others.

At various waypoints earlier in this course we have mentioned incubating a dream. This practice is important because it allows you to decide what you are going to dream about before going to sleep. It is different from lucid dreaming, which allows you to control your dream once you are in it. Right now, before you go to sleep, try out these dream incubation techniques:

1. Write down your intention for tonight's dream. Make it clear and specific. Doing so will send a stronger message to your subconscious.
2. Turn your written intention in a graphic intention. Draw a picture of what you want to dream about tonight.
3. Reinforce your intention by engaging in a supportive ritual. Examples include: putting your intention under your pillow, taking a ceremonial bath, or putting your drawing in some sacred spot.

With your intentions fortified, sleep and dream.

After tending to your dream, fortify your motivation to do next activity outdoors with the following information:

1. The mortality rates of those with low income but high levels of greenery near their homes compared favorably with those with higher income levels.
2. Greenspace as an independent variable is capable of saving thousands of lives in lower income populations.
3. Living in areas with high levels of greenery greatly increase the likelihood of its residents being physically active.

4. Greenspace creates opportunities for greater social connectivity and physical activity.
5. Merely having a view of nature or being in it for brief periods reduces the stress hormone cascade and improves the immune system (Selhub & Logan, 2012, p. 27).

Go to a natural place and do the next activity. Be sure to take notes. When ready, continue on your way down the Heartwood Path by moving to the next learning station: "Pleasures Vs. Gratifications." When you do the activity found at this waypoint, notice how being with an attractive being outdoors improves your mood.

57

Pleasures Vs. Gratifications

ENHANCE YOUR PLEASURES BUT DWELL IN YOUR GRATIFICATIONS

Pleasures can be enhanced in two ways:

1. Savoring—in the form of focusing on congratulations, thankfulness, marveling in the wonder of the moment, and luxuriating; and
2. Mindfulness—the focusing of the mind solely on present events —that allows one to see the present moment anew and to make stale moments fresh. Mindfulness can be heightened through meditation.

Gratifications and the resulting exhilarating state of flow builds psychological capital that can be used later in life. Those who dwell in pleasure typically have more fun but those who dwell in the gratifications typically achieve more and have later lives that are more successful.

More striving for gratifications and less pursuit of pleasure is a large part of the antidote needed to overcome the epidemic of depression.

What is more pleasurable and gratifying than hearing your own name? Your name is intimately linked with your sense of Self. Saying it out loud will cause the sound to reach deeply into your psyche. This chanting of your name will trigger a lifetime of associations. Try it.

To The Intonation Of One's Moniker...

HumaNatureConnect Activity

Start-up Protocol

If this is not a day when you prefer to spend time in nature without an agenda, do the Heartwood Path Start-up Protocol found in the Appendix.

Chanting Your Name

For this activity, use your natural sense of hearing including resonance, vibrations, sonar and ultrasonic frequencies as you chant your name. When you do, use one note or make up a melody. Chant one note per syllable or release a string of notes for each syllable. Chant with fervor and you will be sending your unique sound into the vastness of the universe. After chanting loudly, chant softly. Then whisper your name. Be playful and humorous. Think of the sound of your voice as a deep bell, calling your Soul into full embodiment.

Follow-up Protocol

For best results, write down your impressions of this activity in your journal using the Heartwood Path Follow-up Protocol found in the Appendix. Afterwards, consider sharing your interpretations with others.

Heartwood Path Axioms

Key Assertions From Waypoint 3.57

3.57.1.

Repetitively chant your name to bring forth pleasurable and gratifying associations from throughout your life.

3.57.2.

There are ways to bring abundant, authentic, and abiding happiness into your life and into the lives of others once you know the nature of gladness itself.

3.57.3.

With real effort you can also improve your happiness by working on the following internal circumstances: concerning your past, be satisfied, prideful, and serene; concerning the future, build within yourself hope, faith, optimism, and trust; and concerning the present, seek out joy, ecstasy, enjoyment and— most importantly—flow.

3.57.4.

Base your life more on gratifications—longer term inner world events that engage one fully, immerse one in the kind of absorption that seems to stop time, and result from skills matching challenges—than you do on bodily pleasures, which tend to lead to habituation and short-lived happiness.

3.57.5.

Those who dwell in pleasure typically have more fun but those who dwell in the gratifications typically achieve more and have later lives that are more successful.

Nocturnal Pilgrimage 3.57

For best results, write down your impressions of each night's dreams in your journal using the Heartwood Path Dreaming Time Protocols found in the Appendix. Afterwards, consider sharing your Dream Tending with others.

"Dreams become a kind of early warning system, telling of the (health) problem long before we are faced with actual symptoms." (Aizenstat, 2009, p. 190).

Aizenstat's statement is a good reminder of the need to continue to tend to your dreams daily.

After Dream Tending, move to the next waypoint: "Awesome Goodness." The next waypoint is a key step towards remarkable jubilation. Be sure not to diminish the elation that can be found at the next waypoint by convincing yourself that you do not have time to do the activity in nature. We slight nature at our own expense. By immersing ourselves in our attractions in nature we light up a specific portions of the brain, specifically the anterior portions of the parahippocampal gyrus, which is rich in opioid receptors. These receptors connect to the dopamine reward system and, therefore, have the ability to trigger feelings of wellness and the motivation needed for helpful behavioral modification (Selhub & Logan, 2014, p. 28).

58

Awesome Goodness

IDENTIFY AND USE YOUR OWN INDIVIDUAL STRENGTHS AND ENTER INTO A RELATIONSHIP

Gratifications require personal virtue and lead to the good life. Pleasures require nothing more than time and space and lead to a fun life. Unfortunately, modern day humans in industrialized countries all too often choose easy fun over daunting goodness. A good way to overcome this tendency is to identify and use your own individual strengths.

Everyone has a certain ranking of strengths (positive personal attributes) that serve him or her the best on their course to becoming a good person. We shall look at these two dozen possible strengths in terms of the virtues that these personal attributes lead towards: wisdom, courage, humaneness, justness, temperance, and transcendence:

Strengths that lead to *wisdom* include:

1. curiosity—the strong desire to know or learn something;

2. love of learning—the enjoyment of the acquisition of knowledge or skills;

3. judgment—critical thinking, the ability to make sensible conclusions;

4. ingenuity—the quality of being clever, original, and inventive;

5. intelligence—the ability to acquire and apply knowledge personally, socially, and emotionally; and

6. perspective—a way of looking at the world that makes sense to yourself and others.

Strengths that lead to *courage* (including, doing things in the face of adversity when the end is uncertain) include:

7. moral, psychological and physical valor—great courage in the face of danger;

8. perseverance—steadfastness in doing something despite difficulty or delay in achieving success; and

9. integrity—the state of being whole and undivided, the quality of being honest and having strong ethical principles, having one's intentions be consistent with one's behaviors.

Strengths that lead to *humaneness* include:

10. kindness—the quality of being generous, friendly, and considerate; and

11. giving and receiving love—the intense feeling of deep affection, the great interest and pleasure in something, and/or romantic and sexual attachment.

Strengths that lead to *justness* include:

12. citizenship—duty, team work, and loyalty;

13. fairness—equity, being in accordance with the rules or standards, justness, and/or the state of being appropriate); and

14. leadership—the action of leading a group or people or an organization.

Strengths that lead to *temperance* (the appropriate and moderate expression of appetites and wants) include:

15. self control—the ability to control ones emotions, desires, verbalizations and behaviors;

16. prudence—the state of being cautious or prudent; and

17. humility—modesty, humbleness.

Strengths that lead to *transcendence* (emotional strengths that reach outside and beyond oneself to something larger and more permanent) include:

18. the appreciation of beauty—having qualities that please the aesthetic senses and excellence—the quality of being outstanding or extremely good;

19. gratitude—the quality of being thankful, readiness to show appreciation for and to return kindness;

20. optimism—hopefulness and confidence about the future or the successful outcome of something;

21. spirituality—a sense of purpose and faith;

22. forgiveness—the action or process of forgiving or being forgiven, no longer being angry or resentful and mercy;

23. playfulness—being fun-loving, spirited, and full of humor; and

24. enthusiasm—zest, passion, eagerness, interest, and exuberance (Seligman,2011).

Develop each of these strengths to create the good life for yourself. To get there, rely most on your strongest individual strengths. Determine your best virtue-producing strengths by doing the activity in this waypoint.

Once you have determined your own venerable and enduring strengths, use them to develop your goodness. You might as well use your best tools. They will help you become wise, courageous, humane, just, temperate, and transcendent—the virtues that lead to a good life.

My experience shows me that identifying and using one's individual key strengths—one's most positive and enduring traits—will lead to more satisfaction than will trying to overcome one's greatest weaknesses. It may be helpful to both use key strengths and to correct significant weaknesses; but, to get the most out of a finite amount of time and energy, focus most on your strengths.

The Heartwood Path is designed to take its followers on a journey that uses the participants' key strengths to positively alter how they occupy their time, particularly in the main dimensions of life: love, raising children, and work. If desired, the program can be used, for example, to re-craft work into a calling. By this I mean that the program helps the participant change her vocation into an occupation—either compensated (as when one becomes an ecocentric life coach) or done on a volunteer basis (as when one becomes an eartHeart)—that is gratifying, puts her into the positive state of flow (the matching of assignments to strengths and virtues), and contributes to the greater good.

To One's Best Shot...

HumaNatureConnect Activity

Start-up Protocol

If this is not a day when you prefer to spend time in nature without an agenda, do the Heartwood Path Start-up Protocol found in the Appendix.

Picking Your Own Best Strengths Of Character To Increase Your Virtue

For this activity, look over the list of twenty-four strengths listed above in this waypoint. Pick and rank your top five strengths. If the ranking does not come to you automatically use the following set of criteria to choose your top five strengths (only one need apply): a sense of ownership and authenticity, a feeling of excitement while displaying this strength, rapid learning when first practicing this strength, continuous learning about how to enact this strength, a sense of yearning for how to use this strength, a feeling that using the strength is inevitable, a feeling of invigoration while using the strength, and/or a feeling of enthusiasm or joy while using the strength.

Follow-up Protocol

For best results, write down your impressions of this activity in your journal using the Heartwood Path Follow-up Protocol found in the Appendix. Afterwards, consider sharing your interpretations with others.

Heartwood Path Axioms

Key Assertions From Waypoint 3.58

3.58.1.

Overcome the tendency of modern day humans in industrialized countries too often choose easy fun over daunting goodness by identifying and using your own best individual strengths.

3.58.2.

Everyone has a certain ranking of strengths (positive personal attributes) that serve him or her the best on their course to becoming a good person.

3.58.3.

With real effort you can also improve your happiness by working on the following internal circumstances: concerning your past, be satisfied, prideful, and serene; concerning the future, build within yourself hope, faith, optimism, and trust; and concerning the present, seek out joy, ecstasy, enjoyment and—most importantly—flow.

3.58.4.

Base your life more on the flow that leads to gratifications—longer term inner world events that engage one fully, immerse one in the kind of absorption that seems to stop time, and result from skills matching challenges—than you do on the intermittent hodge-podge of activities that lead to bodily pleasures, which tend to lead to habituation and short-lived happiness.

Nocturnal Pilgrimage 3.58

For best results, write down your impressions of each night's dreams in your journal using the Heartwood Path Dreaming Time

Protocols found in the Appendix. Afterwards, consider sharing your Dream Tending with others.

What do you say? Do you want to now do something that is powerful and life-changing? It will be a bit tricky, but it will be time-tested, appropriate, and positive. I am speaking of a way to go directly from the waking state into a lucid dream without any gap in your consciousness. This technique is called Wake-Induced Lucid Dream—WILD, for short.

Tonight, I want you to make what may be your first attempt at watching your body go to sleep while your mind stays awake and aware. To fall asleep consciously requires a relaxed body and clear and aware mind. In doing so, you are not becoming lucid; you already are aware.

From an earlier waypoint, you may remember that lucidity is a spectrum. WILDs typically present a very high and stable form of lucidity. You will have full and conscious influence over the events, landscape, and Characters in your dream.

Crossing the threshold between waking and dreaming reminds me of the openings of my first Iron Butterfly, Led Zeppelin, Yes, or Pink Floyd concerts—full of strange lights and sounds. These productions seemed to borrow from the sensations that occur during *dorveille*—the twilight time between sleeping and waking. It is during this period that one's creativity and intuition soar.

Here's a few tips before we begin:

1. Get and stay relaxed.
2. Have fun.
3. Be playful. And
4. Set your own pace. Do not make it competitive.

Go WILD

1. Use your Wake-Back-To-Bed skills. Catch your last REM cycle by setting an alarm to two hours before you need to wake up.
2. Wake up for twenty minutes or so, doing whatever keeps your mind awake but your body relaxed.
3. Focus on your breath and release any tension you may be holding in your body as you lie back down. Let your thoughts pass without attaching your mind to them. In doing these things, you will enter into a stare of relaxed attentiveness.
4. Close your eyes and watch for the flashes of light or streaks of color that normally occur right before one drifts off to sleep.
5. Allow your body to gradually become numb, heavy, and temporarily paralyzed as your awareness of the outside world diminishes.
6. Keep watching the flashes and streaks until one of them becomes a clear image that will, after it or you moves to become closer, engulf you.
7. Congratulations! You are having a WILD. Think to yourself that you are having a dream, use your dream stabilization skills, and begin to explore the dream landscape. Talk with Dream Characters. Seek answers. Have fun.

More tips about WILD follow, beginning at Waypoint 3.72. In the mean time, sleep. Practice your WILD. Tend to your dreams.

After tending to your dreams, give yourself what amounts to a little drop of opium in the form of immersion in nature. Recalling that nature immersion stimulates the opioid receptors in the brain, go again into nature, not only to inhibit any pain you may be feeling, but also to create the following remarkable responses:

1. less perception of stress,
2. more likelihood to form emotional bonds,
3. less dwelling on negative memories,
4. greater focusing on the positive aspects of one's life, and

5. less depression (people with depression have decreased brain activity in the anterior parahippocampal gyrus, a part of the brain that is stimulated by immersion in nature. (Selhub & Logan, 2014, p. 28).

These findings alone ought to be enough reason to motivate you to spend more time in nature, but there are still more to come.

After making your entries into your dream journal you are ready to take another important step towards greater happiness by moving to the next Heartwood Path waypoint: "Romantic Relationships." Did you ever think that saving the environment could be this much fun?

59

Romantic Relationships

DEVELOP A LOVING RELATIONSHIP AND SECURE YOUR HAPPINESS

A main basis for happiness is whether the person is involved in a long-term romantic relationship. Those in long-term, committed, loving relationships tend to be happier than those who are not.

Feeling wholeheartedly bonded in love does not destroy one's unique individuality. "The experience of connectedness with a healthy community" writes Macy and Johnstone, " . . . brings out our latent, distinctive gifts" (2012, p.93).

The way we were loved as a child tends to make us in adulthood feel secure in love, avoidant in love, or anxious in love. It only takes one secure partner in a relationship to bring happiness and longevity to the couple, even if the other partner is either avoidant or anxious in love. You will be given ways to find a mate and ways to enhance your present relationship in the Heartwood Path For Couples book—**Eros.**

To The Seventh Of Many Touchstones Of People-Nature Inter-facing...

HumaNatureConnect Activity

Start-up Protocol

If this is not a day when you prefer to spend time in nature without an agenda, do the Heartwood Path Start-up Protocol found in the Appendix.

Generating Patterns Of Human-Nature Interaction # 7:
Moving One's Body Vigorously

For this activity, move your body vigorously. In doing this interaction pattern, you could be running to beat someone else for a ride in a cab (a perverse interaction pattern) or you could be running on the sidewalks of your hometown (a domestic interaction pattern). By choosing instead to hike on a wilderness trail (a wild interaction) you would be doing something that will have a positive psychological effect on you.

In your journal, write down what meaning you would derive from this wild interaction pattern; what joy, if any, it would produce; how, if at all, it would build within you a bond between your mind and nature; and how, if at all, the wild version of this interaction pattern would be better for you than the perverse or domestic instantiation of the same interaction pattern; and how not being allowed to participate in this sort of wild interaction pattern—running on a wilderness trail—would make you feel? How does interacting in this way in the presence of your attractive natural being make you feel? How would it feel to have this interaction without the presence of your attractive natural being? In writing down these responses you will be adding to our collective nature language, so important to rekindling the bond between humans and nature. Look over your impressions and think about them as you fall asleep tonight before dreaming.

Follow-up Protocol

For best results, write down your impressions of this activity in your journal using the Heartwood Path Follow-up Protocol found in the Appendix. Afterwards, consider sharing your interpretations with others.

Heartwood Path Axioms

Key Assertions From Waypoint 3.59

3.59.1.

Those in long-term, committed, loving relationships tend to be happier than those who are not.

3.59.2.

The way we were loved as a child tends to make us in adulthood feel secure in love, avoidant in love, or anxious in love.

3.59.3.

Your dreams can tell you that you need treatment for ailments even before you or your doctor can notice them.

Nocturnal Pilgrimage 3.59

For best results, write down your impressions of each night's dreams in your journal using the Heartwood Path Dreaming Time Protocols found in the Appendix. Afterwards, consider sharing your Dream Tending with others.

Dreams tell us of our capacity to heal. Write Aizenstat:

"The same bodily intelligence that knows how to fight off an in-
fection or generate new cells can also use dream imagery to give us
clues about how to cure whatever ails us. In fact, dreams will often
prescribe a means of complementary treatment even before we go to
a conventional physician" (2009, p. 190).

For dreams to work in this way, they need tending, as you are by
now doing between each Heartwood Path waypoint.

After you tend to your dreams, allow your brain to be aroused and
allow your brain to take a much needed rest from its extra exertion as
a result of processing information in nonnatural settings by immersing
yourself in nature. This requirement for a rest from urban mental
processing is more needed in those who have anxiety (Selhub & Logan,
2012, p. 29). When one's amygdala is amped up from processing urban
stimuli fear too often sets in. Nature helps one overcome this short-
circuiting. Fear often leads to guilt, shame, and melancholy. Nature
counters these unpleasant responses in the way it helps one develop
positive emotions such as joy, contentment, vitality, love, and interest
(Selhub & Logan, 2012, p. 30).

Bring positive emotions into play by moving to the next waypoint:
"Suggestions." Follow the advice at the next waypoint (to seek out or
secure a romantic relationship and to spend more time in nature) and
then chant some positive affirmations, as instructed in the next activity.
Take the next step down the Heartwood Path and you will discover
five ways to improve yourself.

60

Suggestions

USE FIVE PROVEN WAYS TO IMPROVE YOURSELF

There is always time to make improvements in your Self. To do so, use the next five suggestions on your loved ones and yourself:

1. Review what you liked about the past day or week.
2. Reflect on what positive occurrences are likely to happen in the next day and make a deal with yourself and others to promote positive behaviors.
3. Make New Year's resolutions and conduct midyear assessments of progress towards meeting goals.
4. Acknowledge when you are using your own key individual strengths to build up your virtue.
5. Chant positive affirmations, as described in the following activity.

To Powerful Pronouncements...

HumaNatureConnect Activity

Start-up Protocol

If this is not a day when you prefer to spend time in nature without an agenda, do the Heartwood Path Start-up Protocol found in the Appendix.

Chanting Positive Affirmations

For this activity, use your natural sense of hearing including resonance, vibrations, sonar, and ultrasonic frequencies, to chant positive affirmations. Write down a phrase about yourself using the present tense, such as "I am happy to be fit and trim." Generally, affirmations do not have to be about your individual self. Any positive statement, stated in the present tense, will do. For this exercise, we are focusing on affirmations about yourself. For our purposes here, it is not recommended that you affirm your desire for more money, a new car, a bigger house, or any other goals in the Realm of Exteriority. Focus instead on aspects of your Realm of Interiority, such as wanting inner peace, more confidence, or greater feelings of love. By focusing your attention inwardly, you are not giving up your desires for external objects or conditions. By focusing on your inner world you are simply concentrating on the source of external goodies—your own mind. Remember, everything begins in the mind. Focus your attention on your good vibrations pertinent to inner conditions, the quality and subject matter of your thinking. To practice making and experiencing the vibrations of a positive affirmation, repeat your phrase over and over, aloud. Play with the tones and rhythm until you find one that fits. Chant your phrase loud for several minutes. Then, whisper your chant for a while. Next, remember your chant in silence for a few minutes. While sitting in silence absorb the experience without trying to understand it. This sequence of chanting loudly, whispering, and attending to silence will be explained subsequently. For now, just try it. Then, in your journal, make and fill out a table like the one below.

Element Of Self-esteem Changed By This Activity	Yes	No	Unsure	My Impressions Of How This Activity Changed My Level Of Self-esteem
I put more value in my opinions and ideas.				
I focus more on my strengths.				
I give myself more credit for my skills and assets.				
I more strongly believe that I am capable and successful.				
I can more easily accept positive feedback.				

I am less fearful of failure.			
I feel less likely to boast as a way to cover up my inadequacies.			
I am more assertive in expressing my needs.			
I am more able to form secure and honest relationships.			
I am more realistic in my expectations.			
I am less likely to be overly critical of myself and others.			

I am more resilient and better able to weather stress and setbacks.			
I am less likely to experience feelings such as worthlessness, guilt or shame.			
I am less likely to develop eating disorders.			
Other			
Other			

Are you reasonably thankful of Nature? Are you beginning to trust Nature because of its lack of predetermined goals for you, or because it has been time-tested over the eons, or because it is composed of so many nonjudgmental actors? Write down what aspects of your self were changed by this activity. Perhaps you are, by now, becoming more trustful of nature because communing with it has allowed for the upwelling of sound guidance, or the receiving of kind treatment, or the provision of serene space where you can sort out matters of importance. If you like, in your journal, recreate and fill in the following table, adapted from a survey by Dan Oestreich, to determine your changed level of trust with Nature as a result of this activity (Oestreich Associates. www.teamtrustsurvey.com).

Ways To Trust Nature	Level Of Change In This Element Of Trust In Nature As A Result Of This Activity (5 For High Level Of Increased Trust, 3 For No Change, And 1 For Low Level Of Change)	Description Of Changes Level Of Trust in Nature As A Result Of This Activity
I felt like I got along well with Nature.		
Differences were worked out amicably.		
I felt like I received understandable and helpful feedback from Nature.		
I felt free of blame while communing with Nature.		
I felt comfortable taking risks in my interactions with Nature.		

Nature stayed with me despite the sensitive and conflictual issues presented.

Nature was free of cliques and alliances and was able to make me feel like it was on my side.

Nature remained vulnerable and supportive to my concerns.

I felt like the guidance I received was a shared responsibility.

Guidance happened in a timely fashion.

Nature presented no self-serving arguments.

Nature did not try to prove itself to be right, nor did it attempt to protect its interests over mine.

I felt the discussions were held in a spirit of cooperation and compromise.

I was able to come to conclusions I would not have been able to make alone.

I felt like my interests and sensibilities were respected.

I felt allowed to bring up any topic of discussion.

Other

Other

Follow-up Protocol

For best results, write down your impressions of this activity in your journal using the Heartwood Path Follow-up Protocol found in the Appendix. Afterwards, consider sharing your interpretations with others.

Heartwood Path Axioms

Key Assertions From Waypoint 3.60

3.60.1.

Review often what you liked about the past day or week and reflect on what positive occurrences are likely to happen in the next day or week.

3.60.2.

Make a deal with yourself and others to promote positive behaviors.

3.60.3.

Make New Year's resolutions and conduct midyear assessments of progress towards meeting goals.

3.60.4.

Acknowledge when you are using your own key individual strengths to build up your virtue.

Nocturnal Pilgrimage 3.60

For best results, write down your impressions of each night's dreams in your journal using the Heartwood Path Dreaming Time Protocols found in the Appendix. Afterwards, consider sharing your Dream Tending with others.

Sometimes it is hard to remember even tiny fragments of your dreams even if you wake up and do not move right away, as previously suggested. By slowly moving to the right side, or stomach, or back, or right side, you may roll into the memory of your dreams. The trick is to find the position you were in when you were dreaming. In finding it, you can use the dream to help heal your physical illness.

"The Dream Image linked to our bodily disorders are themselves often out of order, broken, malignant, or damaged in some way," writes Aizenstat. "In Dream Tending we treat the physical disorder by treating the wounded image. . . When the image returns to vitality, so do we." (2009, p. 191).

Improve your vitality by moving to the next waypoint: "Acts And Traits." When you get there, be sure to balance the reading with actively seeking out your attractions in nature. As usual, reading alone will not be enough. By getting out into nature you will create more activity in two important brain centers: the anterior cingulate, which, when active, creates emotional stability and a positive mental outlook, and the insula, which, like the anterior cingulate, heightens empathy but also plays a role in the development of the emotion of love. Urban scenes do not significantly activate either of these parts of the brain (Selhub & Logan, 2012, pp. 30-31). Enjoy the next adventure!

61

Acts And Traits

FIND HAPPINESS THROUGH ACTS OF KINDNESS

The Heartwood Path is not the best route to take if one solely wants to heal psychological damage. Rather, it is better used to promote positive emotions (confidence, hope, trust), positive traits (valor, courage, etc), and positive institutions (the family, democracy, etc.).

The quality of one's life is more than just the quantity of good moments minus the quantity of bad moments. Hedonism is a flawed attempt to find lasting happiness. It is the psychological strengths and virtues that entitle us to find authentic, abundant, and abiding happiness.

True happiness is not achieved through the pursuit of pleasure but rather through the pursuit of gratification. To illustrate how this works, do the following:

To A Juxtaposition Of Being Delighted And Being Considerate...

HumaNatureConnect Activity

Start-up Protocol

If this is not a day when you prefer to spend time in nature without an agenda, do the Heartwood Path Start-up Protocol found in the Appendix.

Comparing The Benefits Of Pleasure To The Benefits Of Kindness

For this activity, determine how you will engage in three acts of pleasure and three acts of kindness. Return home from your chosen NatureConnect site and conduct your acts of pleasure (eating, conversation, sex, entertainment) and kindness (doing charity work, giving anonymous gifts, visiting a shut-in person). Then, return to your chosen NatureConnect Site again, obtain your chosen being's consent again, and in your natural location write down how well, if at all, your acts of pleasure and kindness added to your abiding, abundant, and authentic sense of happiness. Compare how you felt when seeking pleasure as opposed to how you felt after acts of kindness.

Follow-up Protocol

For best results, write down your impressions of this activity in your journal using the Heartwood Path Follow-up Protocol found in the Appendix. Afterwards, consider sharing your interpretations with others.

Heartwood Path Axioms

Key Assertions From Waypoint 3.61

3.61.1.

Find happiness through acts of kindness.

3.61.2.

True happiness is not achieved through the pursuit of pleasure but rather through the pursuit of gratification.

3.61.3.

The Heartwood Path is best used to promote positive emotions (confidence, hope, trust), positive traits (valor, courage, etc), and positive institutions (the family, democracy, etc.).

Nocturnal Pilgrimage 3.61

For best results, write down your impressions of each night's dreams in your journal using the Heartwood Path Dreaming Time Protocols found in the Appendix. Afterwards, consider sharing your Dream Tending with others.

Sleep. Dream. If you cannot remember your dream, pay attention to your present emotions. They will often give you a clue about the nature of your dream.

After tending your dreams, head outside to commune with nature with the reassurance that comes from knowing the following information: another part of the brain, the basal ganglia, which is associated with voluntary motor control, the development of habits, and other cognitive and emotional functions, is activated by happy faces, the recollection of happy memories, and nature scenes. Also stimulated by nature scenes are the parts of the brain associated with addictions and rewards. These findings lead to the hope that nature can trump the computer screen as a way to satisfy one's cravings for the feelings of happiness, good memories, addictions, and rewards (Selhub & Logan, 2012, p.31).

Armed with Selhub and Logan's information as a stimulus, go further down the Heartwood Path by moving to the next waypoint: "Enduring Trumps Temporary." There, you will discover the relative benefits of positive traits over positive states.

62

Enduring Trumps Temporary

FIND TRIPLE-A HAPPINESS IN YOUR ENDURING TRAITS RATHER THAN IN YOUR TEMPORARY STATES

Generally, when one calls upon a set of personal strengths, one's day goes better than when one merely exposes oneself to mindless pleasure. Wellbeing comes from engaging one's enduring strengths and virtues. Focus on bolstering positive traits rather than on building up a storehouse of positive states. The enduring traits are abiding dispositions that lead to virtue. They offer a better payback than the temporary states that come from transitory pleasure. The trait of optimism, for example, helps a person feel that negative occurrences are temporary, controllable, and limited. No transient state can have such a widespread and lasting positive effect.

Of the two ways to build happiness—1) securing better shelter, finer clothes, and more prestigious friends and 2) mental development—the latter is definitely more abiding. No gains in the Realm of Externality

will be sufficient to secure happiness without a corresponding development of peace of mind.

When I was a child, from the Third Grade through High School,
whenever I needed more peace of mind (at least three times a week in
the Fourth and Fifth Grades), for some reason unknown to me then, I
found emotional comfort by perching myself high up in trees, usually
in tree houses of my own design and construction, some minimal,
some elaborate. It simply added to my peace of mind to be up in the
air with the leaves, the higher perspectives, the birds, and the freedom
from people with low empathy. Notice that I did not climb telephone
polls or buildings. I preferred the solitariness of the branches of thorny
locust trees, sycamore trees, and box elders. Investigations in Japan
have shown that climbing natural trees reduces tension, lowers anxiety,
improves mental clarity, and encourages one to engage in conservation
activities (Selhub, 2012, p. 120). I can attest to the fact that my tree
climbing had all of these effects on me. Tree climbing gave me a chance
to process my own pre-teen thoughts, which often drifted towards
conservation. Next, you will find a related activity.

To The Eighth Of Many Touchstones Of People-Nature Interfacing...

HumaNatureConnect Activity

Start-up Protocol

If this is not a day when you prefer to spend time in nature without an agenda, do the Heartwood Path Start-up Protocol found in the
Appendix.

*Generating Patterns Of Human-Nature Interaction
8:
Climbing*

For this activity, make a climb after you feel connected to your chosen attractive natural being. In doing this interaction pattern, you could be playing a video game of climbing (a perverse interaction pattern) or you could be climbing a rock wall in a gym (a domestic interaction pattern). By choosing instead to climb a tree, natural mountain, or cliff (a wild interaction) you would be doing something that will have a positive psychological effect on you.

In your journal, write down what meaning you would derive from this wild interaction pattern; what joy, if any, it would produce; how, if at all, it would build within you a bond between your mind and nature; and how, if at all, the wild version of this interaction pattern would be better for you than the perverse or domestic instantiation of the same interaction pattern; and how not being allowed to participate in this sort of wild interaction pattern—climbing a tree or a natural cliff—would make you feel? How does interacting in this way in the presence of your attractive natural being make you feel? How would it feel to have this interaction without the presence of your attractive natural being? In writing down these responses you will be adding to our collective nature language, so important to rekindling the bond between humans and nature.

Follow-up Protocol

For best results, write down your impressions of this activity in your journal using the Heartwood Path Follow-up Protocol found in the Appendix. Afterwards, consider sharing your interpretations with others.

Heartwood Path Axioms

Key Assertions From Waypoint 3.62

3.62.1.

Find TripleA happiness in your enduring traits rather than in your temporary states.

3.62.2.

Focus on bolstering positive traits rather than on building up a storehouse of positive states.

3.62.3.

Generally, when one calls upon a set of personal strengths, one's day goes better than when one merely exposes oneself to mindless pleasure.

3.62.4.

No gains in the Realm of Externality will be sufficient to secure happiness without a corresponding development of peace of mind.

3.62.5.

Of the two ways to build happiness—1) securing better shelter, finer clothes, and more prestigious friends and 2) mental development—the latter is definitely more abiding.

Nocturnal Pilgrimage 3.62

For best results, write down your impressions of each night's dreams in your journal using the Heartwood Path Dreaming Time Protocols found in the Appendix. Afterwards, consider sharing your Dream Tending with others.

Continue to tend to your dreams by doing one the the most important aspects of this task: write down notes about your dreams. So important is this topic to the quest for happiness in a sustainable environment, we shall in the waypoints that follow offer several tips for keeping a dream journal that are different from those listed in our After Dreaming Protocol. Here are two such tips:

1. prominent on your journal page for a specific dream in which you became conscious, write the word LUCID and describe what you may have done to facilitate this special event. Doing so will allow you to improve your lucid dreaming skills.
2. record your observations, thoughts, and feelings regarding the natural world. Be sure to include your afterthoughts and reflections that may arise in your dreams after you return from your time in nature.

To learn to value your awareness; to digest bad news; to become ready to care, act, and to be happy, move to the next waypoint: "Vital Aim." There, you will also learn how to uncover your core purpose.

63

Vital Aim

UNDERSTAND AND DO SOMETHING ABOUT THE HIGH LEVEL OF CONCERN ONE FEELS ABOUT THE FUTURE OF THE WORLD

It will not be possible to achieve the high and enduring level of happiness promised at the end of the Heartwood Path if one does not understand and do something about the high level of concern one feels about the future of the world. How can one be happy when it appears likely that, without a massive collective shift in consciousness and actions, our civilization will not endure? How can one sustain deep gladness when one knows that, barring big changes, it will not be possible for complex forms of life (this includes humans) to survive?

This is not a doomsday course, so we will not focus on the science behind the concern about global warming, water shortages, fuel availability, and bad or insufficient food. If you do not by now know about the bad track we are on, I suggest you look deeper. Our mission here will be to help the participants avoid feeling hopeless, and to learn what can be done to tackle global problems at their root. We will not, however, be offering blind hopefulness but will instead focus on making one's aims or desires, especially those that are good for all people and the planet, come to fruition.

With a clear view of reality, we offer a suitable response to the crisis of sustainability. We aim to help participants move in proper directions. We aim to help Heartwood Path pilgrims bring others along. And we aim to frame values in such a way that doomsday scenarios never come true.

I believe that a business-as-usual approach to life and the efforts to solve global environmental and social problems will not work because its assumptions are untenable:

1. Economic growth may be essential to prosperity of the elite but it worsens conditions for the poor and non-human beings;
2. Nature may be a commodity to be used for human purposes but there are limits in carrying capacity and ethics demand that we save some for future generations;
3. Promoting consumption may be good for the economy but it is inevitably bad for the world's ecology;
4. The central plot may be getting ahead, but this is only working out for the rich; and
5. The problems of other people, nations, and species may not be the concern of those who espouse the business-as-usual approach; but, in time, the plight of the many will be known, corrections will have to come, or trouble will brew.

Given the bankrupt basis for the business-as-usual approach, those who follow the Heartwood Path are given a novel alternative:

We dedicate the Heartwood Path to the mission of developing the vital aim of spreading a gladness that is deep enough to be both a response to and a cause of environmental sustainability.

In this regard, the Heartwood Path is compatible to what Macy and Johnstone call the "Great Turning" and the "Work that Connects" (2012, p.5). Since this work is largely done in groups, we will discuss group actions in greater details in the Heartwood Path book for groups—**Collectivos**.

The Heartwood Path course entitled **Collectivos** is important because of "how much more we can achieve working together than as separate individuals" (Macy & Johnstone, 2012, p. 7). Groups are made up of individuals. The distinct participant will be our focus here.

We will discuss here ways to overcome any feelings that arise from the notion that bad things have gone too far to be able to do anything about them. The Heartwood Path does not cross this point of no return. It instead provides directions to the essential adventure of our time: the Great Work! This noble job involves showing participants how it is possible to save the environment by reframing the views of individuals. It teaches participants how to work well with others. And it helps sustain participants in their efforts by finding the enchantment of everyday life at home.

For decades, thanks to the guidance of David Brower and others, I helped to save many non-humans, I saved some good parts of the non-human gene pool for future generations, I participated in the passages of most of the legislative environmental safety net, and, thus, I considered myself a successful professional environmentalist. My glee over such actions as helping to stop the Meramec Dam in Missouri or helping to protect wilderness in Illinois, Missouri, and Alaska was short-lived, however, because, for every law passed, I saw the need for more laws or I saw these laws improperly administered; for every place saved, I saw more destroyed; and for every species saved, I saw more threatened with extinction. I also saw most of my cohorts, my fellow protestors, become weary and disillusioned. Many saw our past actions as important, but they eventually began to regard the successes as insufficient holding actions. We protected lots of places we would reminisce, but realized that more needed to be done. So many of my conservation buddies turned to developing new economic and social structures such as municipal recycling programs and the promotion of appropriate technologies. When many of these were later seen as being co-opted by corporate interests, it seemed that the accomplishments were serving as public relations tools for sizable businesses rather than serving as tools for helping those without adequate voices. Impressive as some of the environmental advances were in my years of involvement in the Seventies, Eighties, and Nineties, another type of response seemed to be needed. That response to the global environmental predicament was —and is— this: the change in our perception, thinking, and values. Both the Heartwood Path and Macy and Johnston's the Spiral Of the Work that Connects undertake the important job of changing individuals' principles and standards of behaviors—in short, values.

While it is organized differently, the Heartwood Path supports and uses Macy and Johnstone's way to develop an active form of hope, which begins with "Gratitude," and then moves on to "Honoring Our Pain for the World," "Seeing With New Eyes," and "Going Forth" (2012, 37-40). Our spin on Macy and Johnston's Work That Connects is only slightly altered (ours mentions more about appreciation of natural beings, for example). We will put a slight Heartwood Path twist and elaborate on "Gratitude" and "Honoring Our Pain" here; and save "Seeing With New Eyes" for the next Heartwood Path book—**Ecos**—and "Going Forth" for the Heartwood Path book entitled **Remeos**.

Gratitude Is The First Great Turning Of The Spiral Of The Work That Connects

If you want to be happier and more satisfied, be grateful (Macy & Johnstone, 2012, p.43). To be appreciative, to be thankful, and to have a sense of wonder, are all ways to be grateful. Recognizing what is offered to you in life strengthens your character. By savoring what is bestowed upon you, a feeling of buoyancy emerges. This buoyancy maintains your balance and poise, even when the rough times come.

The resilience and strength that come from gratitude helps you face upsetting information.

As a builder of trust and generosity, very little beats gratitude. But, to reap its rewards, you will need to both become appreciative and recognize what others did to bring you your good fortune.

Being altruistic (helpful towards others) does not come about simply because a giver of help is nice. Doing for others is "influenced by the level of gratitude we experience" (Macy & Johnstone, 2012, p. 45). Unlike materialism, which brings about the possession of goodies but decreases happiness and life satisfaction, gratitude is an antidote to consumerism and increases happiness and life satisfaction (Macy & Johnstone, 2012, p. 46).

Advertising is meant to make you unhappy enough to yearn to buy something to ease the sense of lack. The buying of stuff to overcome one's advertising-inspired sense of lack unduly taxes the environment and makes people unhappy, in part, because, once one becomes a dissatisfied materialistic consumer, one can never get enough.

A remedy is readily available. Instead of focusing on the advertisements, one can direct one's mind to the gratefulness one feels for the attractiveness of natural beings and for the people in one's life who have one's well-being in mind. Doing so will not only reduce consumerism, it will also be an antidote to environmental destruction and depression.

Honoring Our Pain For The World Is The Second Great Turning Of The Spiral Of The Work That Connects

For psychological and social reasons, we often tend to state that all is well with ourselves and the world around us even when we know it isn't. In doing so, we fall into habits that tend to lower our survival responses by deadening our natural alarms and our willingness to sound them. According to Macy and Johnstone, our impulse to notice and say something about threats is diminished in the following ways:

1. we tend to downplay the seriousness of the threat;
2. we say it is not our role to solve the problem;
3. we remain quiet about threats so we do not stand out in a crowd;
4. we stay quiet to safeguard our financial or political interests;
5. we prefer not to think about threats;
6. we feel powerless to act on the issue, not knowing what to do; and
7. we feel that our individual actions will not make a difference (2012, pp. 60-64).

In our social situations it is taboo to talk too much about depressing topics. We do not want to be called overly negative or emotional so we remain quiet and alone, suffering in silence. The more we shy away from such psychological and emotional difficulties, the less confident we are to rise to the occasion and work for solutions. The habit of avoidance sets in and quickly spreads throughout the culture. In time, a systemic barrier develops that weakens our ability to cope, lowers our ability to perceive threats, prevents us from contemplating depressing facts, and makes us believe that we will not be able to overcome our released grief. This stifling of our pain for the world makes us feel less alive, less energetic, and less motivated to act.

It need not be like this. Thanks to Joanna Macy, there is a way to become strengthened by one's psychological pain regarding the mess we are in globally. It involves applying open alertness, opening the heart to the suffering of others, and undertaking a journey that begins uncomfortably but soon helps participants value their awareness; digest bad news; and become ready to care, act, and be happy. Participants are encouraged to openly speak what they already know (as in Part 3 of the activity below). As said by Macy and Johnstone:

Intellectual awareness by itself

is not enough.

We need to digest the bad news.

That is what rouses us to respond.

(2012, p. 71)

Try the activity below and notice how you allow feelings to move through yourself, notice how you feel less stuck in the mire, notice how you feel more space to allow for corrective actions, and notice how you feel a return or a heightening of happiness as your vital aim emerges, step by step, from your pain.

Find And Develop Your Vital Aim...

HumaNatureConnect Activity

Start-up Protocol

If this is not a day when you prefer to spend time in nature without an agenda, do the Heartwood Path Start-up Protocol found in the Appendix.

Flushing Out Your Purpose

For this activity, discover your core purpose. The process of fostering one's own vital aim that we will present in this activity is multi-fold:

1. Begin by *scanning your memories* and identifying events that happened during the last twenty-four hours that please you. With eyes closed, re-experience these events; notice the colors, smells, sounds, tastes and bodily sensations, plus how these events make you feel psychologically. Thank whoever or whatever gave you these happy moments.

2. Finish the following sentences regarding *gratitude*:

I love the following aspects of being alive on earth:...

My magical place when I was a child was...

These are my favorite activities:...

A person who helped me believe in myself was...

I appreciate the following aspects of myself:...

A natural being I owe a debt of gratitude to is...

Try thinking of your appreciated natural being as an extended member of your family. Sometimes one cannot rightly do anything to show gratitude to a long-lost natural being or person. In such cases, one can pay the debt forward to someone or something else. One can always receive from the past and give to the future. Such acts of gratitude block guilt and fear while, at the same time, increase one's motivation.

3. Finish the following sentences about *the pain of the world*:

Concerning the condition of the world, I would say things are getting ...

I am concerned about:...

The following feelings come up when I think about the condition of the world:...

One of my worst fears about the future is...

Here's what I do with these feelings:...

I avoid such painful feelings by...

Ways I use these feelings include:....

Find a place in nature to lay a stone that represents a concern you have for life on earth in the future. Walk away, think of another problem, and return with another stone. Lay it on top of the other stone. Whenever you have another worry, return to the pile of stones, and lay another stone on your cairn of concern. Do not at this point ponder fixing any of the problems. For your own concerns, and the concerns you hear from others, at first simply accept the validity and significance of the problems by laying another stone. Encourage others to do the same.

Think of your opening to the pain of the world as the beginning of a great, new adventure, one in which you step into new territory and develop new tools to meet the challenges that lie ahead (Macy & Johnstone, 2012, pp. 43-79).

Follow-up Protocol

For best results, write down your impressions of this activity in your journal using the Heartwood Path Follow-up Protocol found in the Appendix. Afterwards, consider sharing your interpretations with others.

Heartwood Path Axioms

Key Assertions From Waypoint 3.63

3.63.1.

Understand and do something about the high level of concern one feels about the future of the world.

3.63.2.

If you want to be happier and more satisfied, be grateful.

3.63.3.

For psychological and social reasons, we often tend to state that all is well with ourselves and the world even when we know it isn't.

3.63.4.

The more we shy away from psychological and emotional difficulties, the less confident we are to rise to the occasion and work for solutions.

3.63.5.

Going down the Heartwood Path helps participants value their awareness, digest bad news, and become ready to care, act, and be happy.

Nocturnal Pilgrimage 3.63

For best results, write down your impressions of each night's dreams in your journal using the Heartwood Path Dreaming Time Protocols found in the Appendix. Afterwards, consider sharing your Dream Tending with others.

Here are a two more dream journaling tips:

1. Do not include the meanings of dream signs from dream dictionaries. You are the only one who can assign such meaning; and, when you do, be open to changing the meanings as wider symbolism is revealed to you over time.

2. Go to bed calm so your dreams can come to you like reflections on a still lake—clearly.

As you prepare for sleep, express your gratitude and recall more ways to honor your feelings about the pain of the world. Sleep and dream. After you sleep, tend to your dreams, commune with nature, and record your impressions in your journal (keeping in mind the tips listed here).

When you are ready, move to the next waypoint: "Exemplary Compassion (Part One)." There, you will learn how to make yourself impeccable.

64

Exemplary Compassion (Part One)

PRACTICE TO MAKE YOURSELF IMPECCABLE (COMPLETE)

Unlike most of the waypoints along the Heartwood Path, this atypical four-part stop will take more than one day to complete. Take your time. Developing the integrity of wholeness and becoming more compassionate are not simple endeavors.

The Heartwood Path leads to the development of big-heartedness, not some wimpy form of pity, but exemplary compassion. There are three key ways to become commendably compassionate, each slow to develop:

1. morality (ethics, morals, and principles);
2. determined contemplation; and
3. understanding.

These three ways to compassion lead to a meaningful life. They are borrowed from the Dali Lama's book, **How to Practice** (2002). Each way to compassion is related, just as the roots, trunk and branches of a tree are all related. It takes morality and determined contemplation to achieve the enduring calmness that, when combined with the special insight that comes from understanding, leads to a meaningful life. In this way, each type of practice serves as the basis for the next. Understanding depends on the removal of distractions and faulty mental states. While this removal is achieved by determined contemplation, there can be no success with determined contemplation until one, metaphorically speaking, emulates the whole Heartwood Path Tree of Impeccability, as shown below and described in the next three waypoints.

Figure 6: Heartwood Path Tree of Impeccability

To Develop Empathy...

HumaNatureConnect Activity

Start-up Protocol

If this is not a day when you prefer to spend time in nature without an agenda, do the Heartwood Path Start-up Protocol found in the Appendix.

Generating Empathy Towards Others

For this activity, think about the keys to compassion, which need to be used in the following order:

1. The Development of Morality (ethics, morals, and principles)

   Think of a situation in your life that needs the application of some form of ethics, morals or principles.

2. The Practice of Determined Contemplation

   Think of one topic and only one topic that tends to make you calm.

3. The Exercise of Understanding

   Think of how one of your favorite natural beings such as a tree or a rock cliff and consider in depth how that being arose (how it came into being).

Do not be concerned if you are not fully versed in these components at this point. Just jot down your initial thoughts at this point. More on these topics follows in the next two waypoints.

Follow-up Protocol

For best results, write down your impressions of this activity in your journal using the Heartwood Path Follow-up Protocol found in the Appendix. Afterwards, consider sharing your interpretations with others.

Heartwood Path Axioms

Key Assertions From Waypoint 3.64

3.64.1.

Practice to make yourself impeccable (complete).

3.64.2.

Compassion comes from morality, intent contemplation; and understanding.

3.64.3.

It takes morality and determined contemplation to achieve the enduring calmness that, when combined with the special insight that comes from understanding, leads to a meaningful life.

Nocturnal Pilgrimage 3.64

For best results, write down your impressions of each night's dreams in your journal using the Heartwood Path Dreaming Time Protocols found in the Appendix. Afterwards, consider sharing your Dream Tending with others.

With the information you picked up in this waypoint and your impressions from the most recent activity, decide what you would like to dream about, and sleep. If you are not remembering your dreams perhaps they are being interrupted. Check with your doctor about the possibility that you may have sleep apnea (interruption of sleep).

Here is one more tip for your Dream journalling: write down any patterns that are emerging in your dreams, particularly recurring dreams or recurring Characters.

Tend to your dreams before going on to the next waypoint: "Exemplary Compassion (Part Two)." There, you will learn about anchoring your life on the roots of morality.

65

Exemplary Compassion
(Part Two)

ANCHOR A MEANINGFUL LIFE ON
THE ROOTS OF MORALITY

To do so, help others or, at least, do no harm to others; work
to do away with the Ten Non-virtues (these are the Physical Non-
virtues of killing, stealing, and sexual misconduct; the Verbal Non-
virtues of lying, senseless chatter, divisive talk, and insensitive speech;
and the Mental Non-Virtues of craving/coveting, ill-will, and, having
an incorrect world view). Also, free yourself from what is known as
"cyclical existence" which means, along with the endless round of birth,
aging, sickness and death, the seemingly endless struggle and suffering
that accompanies "striving" as opposed to the bliss that accompanies
"arriving."

To free yourself from the suffering of seemingly endless struggles,
get to know the Four Noble Truths, which are:

1. knowing the specific types of suffering;

2. discovering the sources of one's own suffering (or another person's suffering, especially if that person's hardships affect you or those you love);

3. knowing how to cease the suffering; and

4. stopping the suffering.

The types of suffering include pain, change, and pervasive conditioning. Pain is commonly known and the typical tendency is to seek to avoid or diminish it. The suffering of change occurs when something good (or appears to be good) changes into something that is bad. Pervasive conditioning is suffering that results from tendencies created by previous actions and afflictive or counterproductive emotions such as lust or hatred.

When examining these types of suffering, and especially when facing a difficulty, maintain a positive attitude. This becomes easier when you realize that when you undergo difficult situations with grace you are diminishing the negative consequences.

The source of pain is often afflictive emotions such as lust and hatred. Some of these emotions are best expressed and others are best left unexpressed. Telling the person who normally calls how you felt when she did not call is an example of a prudent time to express your afflictive emotions. Telling a person who has, over the course of your lifetime, made you feel like you did not matter but is unlikely or unwilling to make amends is a good example of when your afflictive emotions are best left unexpressed. For persistent sources of suffering, as opposed to one-time discrepancies, expressing your afflictive emotion will likely only cause stronger or more prevalent negative actions. In this case, it is best to focus on the disadvantages of orally engaging in afflictive emotions while displacing them with understanding and feelings of satisfaction and love.

Learning how to end suffering is mostly a matter of overcoming misconceptions. Ignorance is a primary source of suffering and, therefore, knowledge is a key way to diminish the struggles of one's life. A key point to learn that will help one diminish suffering has to do with the emptiness of all forms. I will return to this point in a moment.

To stop one's suffering involves the practice of putting down roots of morality so that, from this anchoring, one can later engage in determined contemplation and achieve understanding. This secure root system of morality has "ingredients"—chief of which are refraining from harm and helping others.

To The Ninth Of Many Touchstones Of People-Nature Interfacing...

HumaNatureConnect Activity

Start-up Protocol

If this is not a day when you prefer to spend time in nature without an agenda, do the Heartwood Path Start-up Protocol found in the Appendix.

Generating Patterns Of Human-Nature Interaction # 9:

Cooking Around The Fire Circle And Building An Outdoor Shelter

For this activity, build a shelter after you feel connected to your chosen attractive natural being. In doing this interaction pattern, you could be designing a house on a computer (a perverse interaction pattern) or you could be setting up a tent in a campground (a domestic interaction pattern). By choosing instead to create a space to sleep under a rock outcropping (a wild interaction), you would be doing something that will have a positive psychological effect on you.

Also, after you feel connected to your chosen attractive natural being, build a fire circle and cook a meal outdoors. In doing this interaction pattern, you could be cooking food in a microwave oven (a perverse interaction pattern) or you could be grilling food on your backyard barbecue set (a domestic interaction pattern). By choosing instead to cook food over an open fire in a natural setting (a wild interaction) you would be doing something that will have a positive psychological effect on you.

In your journal, write down what meaning you would derive from this wild interaction pattern; what joy, if any, it would produce; how, if at all, it would build within you a bond between your mind and nature; and how, if at all, the wild version of this interaction pattern would be better for you than the perverse or domestic instantiation of the same interaction pattern; and how not being allowed to participate in this sort of wild interaction pattern—cooking in your kitchen at home or sleeping under a natural rock outcropping, for example—would make you feel? How does interacting in this way in the presence of your attractive natural being make you feel? How would it feel to have this interaction without the presence of your attractive natural being? In writing down these responses you will be adding to our collective nature language, so important to rekindling the bond between humans and nature. Look over your impressions and think about them as you fall asleep tonight before dreaming.

Follow-up Protocol

For best results, write down your impressions of this activity in your journal using the Heartwood Path Follow-up Protocol found in the Appendix. Afterwards, consider sharing your interpretations with others.

Heartwood Path Axioms

Key Assertions From Waypoint 3.65

3.65.1.

Anchor a meaningful life on the roots of morality.

3.65.2.

Anchor a meaningful and moral life by doing no harm to others; doing away with non-virtues, freeing yourself from the seemingly endless struggle and suffering that accompanies "striving" as opposed to the bliss that accompanies "arriving."

3.65.3.

To free yourself from the suffering of seemingly endless struggles, get to know the Four Noble Truths, listed at the beginning of this waypoint.

Nocturnal Pilgrimage 3.65

For best results, write down your impressions of each night's dreams in your journal using the Heartwood Path Dreaming Time Protocols found in the Appendix. Afterwards, consider sharing your Dream Tending with others.

The next immediate section marks the beginning of several discussions about how to wake up in your dreams.

Ways To Perform A Reality Check

Number One: Ask The Question.
In doing a reality check by asking during your waking time "Am I dreaming?" you are not really trying to make sure you are awake. You probably already know that. By asking this question ten times at regular intervals during the day you are setting a behavior that will carryover into your dreams. When you can answer the question "Am

I dreaming?" with a "Yes" you can then begin your lucid dream. As previously described, great things happen while you are awake inside your dreams. After a day of performing reality checks, sleep and dream. Upon waking, tend to your dreams.

After making a journal entry about your dreams, move to the next learning station. As you begin the next activity, be sure to spend time outdoors, as instructed. In doing so, you will be learning about and strengthening your own Greater Self. The mortality of people, nations, and the planet depends of the widespread acceptance of the reality that nature is a part of us. Writes Selhub and Logan:

> "Our perception of stress, our mental state, our immunity, our happiness, and our resiliency are all chemically influenced by the nervous system and its response to the natural environment" (2012, p. 33).

To maintain your commitment to seeking the wholeness of spiritual maturity, work to increase both your merit and your understanding. Increase your merit by serving others, giving away material things, sharing love, giving teachings, and offering relief from negative situations. Increase your understanding by focusing on how phenomena arise and exist dependent on sources, causes, circumstances and conditions. One can move forward with the task of doing no harm, helping others, and seeking enlightenment for the sake of other sentient beings best when one spends enough time and energy to develop a trunk of determined contemplation at the next waypoint: "Exemplary Compassion (Part Three)."

66

Exemplary Compassion (Part Three)

DEVELOP A TRUNK OF DETERMINED CONTEMPLATION

Here, I am speaking of achieving enduring calmness by focusing the mind. Normally, the mind is too scattered for effective contemplation. By not allowing the mind to always be scattered and easily distracted calmness abides. Through enduring calmness, achieved by focusing the mind in determined contemplation, wisdom unfolds. To focus the mind, remove distractions and find a happy medium between excitement and lethargy. Use this wisdom whenever you generate a human-nature interaction, including in the next three important activities.

To The Tenth Of Many Touchstones Of People-Nature Interfacing...

HumaNatureConnect Activity

Start-up Protocol

If this is not a day when you prefer to spend time in nature without an agenda, do the Heartwood Path Start-up Protocol found in the Appendix.

Generating Patterns Of Human-Nature Interaction # 10:

Walking The Edges Of Nature

For this activity, walk the edges of nature after you feel connected to your chosen attractive natural being. In doing this interaction pattern, you could be walking the edge of a portion of a forest that has be clear-cut (a perverse interaction pattern) or you could be walking on a boardwalk at a beach-side home (a domestic interaction pattern). By choosing instead to walk along an undeveloped ocean beach or along a pristine river (both examples of wild interactions), you would be doing something that will have a positive psychological effect on you.

In your journal, write down what meaning you would derive from this wild interaction pattern; what joy, if any, it would produce; how, if at all, it would build within you a bond between your mind and nature; and how, if at all, the wild version of this interaction pattern would be better for you than the perverse or domestic instantiation of the same interaction pattern; and how not being allowed to participate in this sort of wild interaction pattern—walking along a pristine body of water—would make you feel? How does interacting in this way in the presence of your attractive natural being make you feel? How would it feel to have this interaction without the presence of your attractive natural being? In writing down these responses you will be adding to our collective nature language, so important to rekindling the bond between humans and nature. Look over your impressions and think about them as you fall asleep tonight before dreaming.

Follow-up Protocol

For best results, write down your impressions of this activity in your journal using the Heartwood Path Follow-up Protocol found in the Appendix. Afterwards, consider sharing your interpretations with others.

Heartwood Path Axioms

Key Assertions From Waypoint 3.66

3.66.1.

Develop determined contemplation.

3.66.2.

Develop determined contemplation by achieving enduring calmness, focusing the mind, removing distractions, and finding a happy medium between excitement and lethargy.

3.66.3.

To focus the mind, remove distractions and find a happy medium between excitement and lethargy.

3.66.4.

Wise sensitivity comes by generating patterns of human-nature interaction.

Nocturnal Pilgrimage 3.66

For best results, write down your impressions of each night's dreams in your journal using the Heartwood Path Dreaming Time

Protocols found in the Appendix. Afterwards, consider sharing your Dream Tending with others.

Ways To Perform A Reality Check

Number Two: Set An Alarm.

As a way to remind you to ask the question "Am I dreaming?" set a series of alarms on your mobile device. Each time you answer the question while awake you are increasing the chance that you will use the question to initiate a lucid dream.

After responding to several alarms, look over your most recent human-nature interaction as you recorded it in your journal. With your impressions of this interaction in mind, sleep and dream. Tend to your dreams.

After making a journal entry, move to the next waypoint: "Exemplary Compassion (Part Four)." As you move there think about how you may be becoming reliant on screen-based gadgets to the point that they are taking you away from a time-tested, powerful source of wellness; namely, nature. Do not become a slave to your screens. Turn off your electric ones on a daily basis, at least for a while, and use the added time you gain to move beyond the screens on your doors and windows to an attractive natural being outdoors. Then, after gaining consent and offering your gratitude, commune with that source of health, information, and guidance, as instructed.

67

Exemplary Compassion
(Part Four)

ON TOP OF THE TRUNK OF DETERMINED CONTEMPLATION, WHICH DEVELOPS FROM THE ROOTS OF MORALITY, LEARN FROM THE BRANCHES OF UNDERSTANDING

One way to do so is to study how living and nonliving beings arise. This is insightful practice because beings are not as they appear. One needs to determine how beings exist to most effectively offer help or, at least, do no harm.

Other ways to learn from the branches of understanding include learning how things are impermanent, extending compassion to the planet, becoming more empathetic with the wounded, opening your heart to others, facing the facts, and choosing your friends well.

To The Eleventh Of Many Touchstones Of People-Nature Interfacing...

HumaNatureConnect Activity

Start-up Protocol

If this is not a day when you prefer to spend time in nature without an agenda, do the Heartwood Path Start-up Protocol found in the Appendix.

Generating Patterns Of Human-Nature Interaction # 11:

Harvesting

For this activity, bring in the harvest after you feel connected to your chosen attractive natural being. In doing this interaction pattern, you could be using too many hardwoods from a rainforest (a perverse interaction pattern) or you could be picking vegetables from your home garden (a domestic interaction pattern). By choosing instead to digging up clams with indigenous people (a wild interaction), you would be doing something that will have a positive psychological effect on you.

In your journal, write down what meaning you would derive from this wild interaction pattern; what joy, if any, it would produce; how, if at all, it would build within you a bond between your mind and nature; and how, if at all, the wild version of this interaction pattern would be better for you than the perverse or domestic instantiation of the same interaction pattern; and how not being allowed to participate in this sort of wild interaction pattern—digging clams with the Eskimos— would make you feel? How does interacting in this way in the presence of your attractive natural being make you feel? How would it feel to have this interaction without the presence of your attractive natural being? In writing down these responses you will be adding to our collective nature language, so important to rekindling the bond between humans and nature. Look over your impressions and think about them as you fall asleep tonight before dreaming.

Follow-up Protocol

For best results, write down your impressions of this activity in your journal using the Heartwood Path Follow-up Protocol found in the Appendix. Afterwards, consider sharing your interpretations with others.

Heartwood Path Axioms

Key Assertions From Waypoint 3.67

3.67.1.

Determine how beings exist to most effectively offer help or, at least, do no harm.

3.67.2.

Develop a Trunk of Determined Contemplation by achieving enduring calmness, focusing the mind, removing distractions, and finding a happy medium between excitement and lethargy.

3.67.3.

Understand how things arise, how things are impermanent, how to extend compassion to the planet, how to stay healthy yourself, how to open your heart to others, how to face the facts, and how to choose your friends well.

3.67.4.

EartHearts are open to the feelings, pain, and suffering of others (empathy) and desire to alleviate such suffering (compassion) strongly enough to do something about it (altruism).

Nocturnal Pilgrimage 3.67

For best results, write down your impressions of each night's dreams in your journal using the Heartwood Path Dreaming Time Protocols found in the Appendix. Afterwards, consider sharing your Dream Tending with others.

Aizenstat presents three steps to healing through dreaming:

1. naming of any wounded image,
2. offering relief to the wounded image, and
3. practicing—doing the healing ritual repeatedly over time.

The application of each of these steps is a subtle and complex art. Each operation requires completion before moving on to the next" (Aizenstat, 2009, p. 192).

Ways To Perform A Reality Check

Number Three: Look For Reminders.

You can choose any kind you want; but, since you are practicing eco-psychology as you go down the Heartwood Path, you might as well look to nature to remind you to ask "Am I dreaming?" Perform this reality check whenever you move from sun to shade, whenever you pass under a big tree, whenever you see a squirrel, when you cross a creek, whenever you hear a bird song, or whenever you experience some pre-determined natural reminder.

When you do the activity at the next waypoint in nature try meditating with the image of your attractive natural being in your mind's eye or use a soft focus while you are sharing space with your attractive natural being. As your mind wanders, return your attention gently to this being or landscape. Work to withhold judgement. See if your sense of separation does not start to diminish during your meditating and space sharing. Look for signs that your are feeling more connected and comfortable in the presence of your natural attractive being.

Continuing with our nocturnal tradition, tend to your dreams, and then move to the next waypoint, "Scrutinize." There, you will learn about being a good follower and more.

68

Scrutinize

FOLLOW BUT KEEP YOUR EYES OPEN

Unless I am one of your cherished long-term buddies, you do not know me well enough for me to be a trusted model or mentor. Writing this book does not qualify me for being a sage. My experience tells me what things are impossible to achieve. While sounding like a skill, this perspective is a fault. It is far better to be so naïve that you go ahead and muddle your way to impossible achievement.

Unless you are one of today's youth, who tend to claim to know everything, don't try to give consultations. In most matters, be a coach rather than a consultant.

Fortunately you do not need to know everything to be a good life coach. That job requires an ability to ask questions, not to answer them.

Everyone ought to know that I would not make a good guru because I am not young enough to know everything. Still, what I write here deserves to be scrutinized and applied to your life in ways you determine to be suitable. Subject all that I say to critical analysis. And accept or reject my message on the basis of your own understanding.

To Enthusiastic Adherence...

HumaNatureConnect Activity

Start-up Protocol

If this is not a day when you prefer to spend time in nature without an agenda, do the Heartwood Path Start-up Protocol found in the Appendix.

Following With Open Eyes

For this activity, become a good follower by 1) recognizing the need for leadership, 2) making sure you are not wanting too much by managing your expectations, 3) thinking about your part in the enterprise plus whatever may be good for the whole enterprise, and 4) giving reasonable and helpful feedback.

Follow-up Protocol

For best results, write down your impressions of this activity in your journal using the Heartwood Path Follow-up Protocol found in the Appendix. Afterwards, consider sharing your interpretations with others.

Heartwood Path Axioms

Key Assertions From Waypoint 3.68

3.68.1.

Experience tells you what things are impossible to achieve.

3.68.2.

It is good to be so naïve that you go ahead and muddle your way to impossible achievement.

3.68.3.

Being a good life coach requires an ability to ask questions, not to answer them.

3.68.4.

Accept or reject any other person's message on the basis of your own understanding.

Nocturnal Pilgrimage 3.68

For best results, write down your impressions of each night's dreams in your journal using the Heartwood Path Dreaming Time Protocols found in the Appendix. Afterwards, consider sharing your Dream Tending with others.

Ways To Perform A Reality Check

Number Four: Be Present.

Two ways to do so come to mind, one positive for your dreaming time world and one negative for your waking time world. By getting in the habit of looking for nice things in your waking time you will carry that habit to your dreaming time. Doing so will, at once, make your dreams more pleasurable and remind you to wake up to your lucid dream. By getting into the habit of looking for unpleasant things in your waking time or dreaming time, you receive prompts that can lead to greater compassion.

The misery of millions is not a cause for pity but it is a cause for compassion that begins by reflecting on how your own actions affect other people's hearts. What a miracle it is to peer into the eyes of a brokenhearted person whom you are assisting!

You also have the option to do nothing; but, if this is your constant option, do not expect to find uncommon happiness. As we all know, if you don't seem concerned about the plight of the needy and anyone says you lack empathy just tell them that you do not care. True or not, employ dreams for healing purposes again.

When you are ready to continue, move to the next waypoint: "One's Shoes (Part One)." There, you will learn what it takes to become more empathetic—that is, capable of feeling and understanding the emotions of others.

69

One's Shoes (Part One)

CULTIVATE EMPATHY BY UNDERSTANDING CAUSES AND CONDITIONS

You now come to another waypoint that will likely take more than one day. Spend the next few days raising your ability to understand and share the feelings of another. To reach the kind of understanding that leads to an open heart, proceed in two ways:

1. the rational process of analysis and
2. the cultivation of empathy with your chosen object (being, person, place, or thing).

Of the two, along the Heartwood Path you will be repeatedly directed to use the latter. Settling the mind on a chosen object/being requires that you go beyond thoughtful analysis. One needs also to develop empathy with the object of attention. Focused, pinpointed empathy requires positive thinking that occurs over many hours. Empathy also requires the cultivation of compassion rather than hatred or fear. The goal of empathic meditation is for one's mind to become momentarily fused with the object of attention. You know the phrase: "You never know until you walk around in one's shoes." The result is enduring calmness.

To allow empathy to bring forth fulfillment and happiness one first needs to understand the concepts of causes and conditions. As a concrete example of the universal principle of "as within, so without," one's mental conditions are caused in much the same way that external objects (physical conditions) are caused in the Realm of Exteriority. For example, just as trees are caused when seeds are subjected to the conditions of being watered in soil and bathed in warmth, emotions are caused by inner world conditions. If one changes one's inner world causes one's inner world conditions change. In the Realm of Interiority, negative emotions such as stinginess, for example, can be changed into opposing inner world factors such as generosity. Negative inner world conditions have unpleasant outer world effects. Repeated bouts of anger in the Realm of Interiority, for example, prevent one from working efficiently in the Realm of Exteriority. To avoid such ill-effects, one needs to train one's Self to recognize in oneself negative emotions (vanity, for example) and trade them for positive emotions (such as humility). Similarly, in the Realm of Exteriority, one has the ability and the responsibility to act virtuously. The most virtuous of acts are those motivated, not by fear of being caught doing something bad, but by the motivation to end suffering. Acting on this motivation is the pathway to saintliness.

To eliminate negative emotions and the actions these emotions generate, one needs to reach understanding through listening (to respected teachers, for example), through contemplation (which leads to certainty of the subject matter) and through meditation (during which one's mind is absorbed into the subject matter). Success in compassion demands using listening, contemplating, and meditating to rid yourself of afflictive emotions of greed, jealousy, fear, hatred, and so forth.

Greater understanding leads to heightened convictions. Without such convictions there can be no fervor and, therefore, no excellence in action.

To The Presentation Of An Offering To A Dream Figure...

HumaNatureConnect Activity

Start-up Protocol

If this is not a day when you prefer to spend time in nature without an agenda, do the Heartwood Path Start-up Protocol found in the Appendix.

Making A Full-force Offering To A Wounded Dream Figure For Healing Purposes

For this activity, beef-up your offering to a Wounded Dream Figure for healing purposes. We will make this a two step process:

1. Look for the positive "silver-lining" in the wound, illness, or affliction of the imaginal Wounded Healer. And
2. "Discover what the wounded Dream Figure needs to heal?" (Aizenstat, 2009, 225). Then, if possible, give the Figure what it needs.

Follow-up Protocol

For best results, write down your impressions of this activity in your journal using the Heartwood Path Follow-up Protocol found in the Appendix. Afterwards, consider sharing your interpretations with others.

Heartwood Path Axioms

Key Assertions From Waypoint 3.69

3.69.1.

Cultivate empathy by understanding causes and conditions.

3.69.2.

Use compassion to alleviate suffering and use loving kindness to foster happiness.

3.69.3.

To understand with an open heart, proceed with a rational process of analysis and cultivate empathy with your chosen being, person, place, or thing.

3.69.4.

Make an offering to a wounded Dream Figure for healing purposes by looking for the silver-lining in the affliction and offering what is needed for a restoration of health.

Nocturnal Pilgrimage 3.69

For best results, write down your impressions of each night's dreams in your journal using the Heartwood Path Dreaming Time Protocols found in the Appendix. Afterwards, consider sharing your Dream Tending with others.

Before you prepare for sleep, think about what you will do to become more empathetic. Then sleep and dream. Do not move from your sleeping position as you begin to recall your dreams. Use your journal as you tend to your dreams.

Move to the next waypoint, "One's Shoes (Part Two)," to continue. Remember that by dallying for long hours at a computer screen or television set you are, most likely, merely skimming for information and taking time away from other more productive pursuits. Do not become a slave to your electronic screens. Find liberation outdoors.

70

One's Shoes (Part Two)

CULTIVATE EMPATHY BY
FOCUSING ON IMPERMANENCE

One of the most fruitful ways to wisdom is the understanding of impermanence. This understanding has to do with the rejection of the common idea that things have a concrete inherent existence that is separable and unaltered by one's own perception and perspective. The essential quality of a thing is not inherent in the phenomena. The observer imparts that quality.

Correcting the pervasive misconception about the permanence of things is a way of wisdom that reduces suffering. Hard as it may be, it is imperative to recognize the nonexistence (impermanence) of the qualities one gives to things psychologically. Doing so bolsters humility and reduces pride—especially when the topic of consideration is the ill-conceived self-grasping notion that one can be separated from the environment. One naturally becomes more humble when one understands that one is but a lesser part of a greater whole.

What better way to learn about impermanence than to commune and contemplate something as ephemeral and transient as water? Keep the fading, fleeting, and temporary aspect of water in mind as you do the next activity.

To The Twelfth Of Many Touchstones Of People-Nature Inter-facing...

HumaNatureConnect Activity

Start-up Protocol

If this is not a day when you prefer to spend time in nature without an agenda, do the Heartwood Path Start-up Protocol found in the Appendix.

Generating Patterns Of Human-Nature Interaction # 12:

Being Moved By Water

For this activity, be moved by water after you feel connected to your chosen attractive natural being. In doing this interaction pattern, you could think about tubing the Lazy River at a water park (a perverse interaction pattern) or you could think about floating on a raft on a lake in a residential area (a domestic interaction pattern). By choosing instead to ride a big wave on a surfboard (a wild interaction), you would be doing something that will have a positive psychological effect on you.

In your journal, write down what meaning you would derive from this wild interaction pattern; what joy, if any, it would produce; how, if at all, it would build within you a bond between your mind and nature; and how, if at all, the wild version of this interaction pattern would be better for you than the perverse or domestic instantiation of the same interaction pattern; and how not being allowed to participate in this sort of wild interaction pattern—surfing a big wave—would make you feel? How does interacting in this way in the presence of your attractive natural being make you feel? How would it feel to have this interaction without the presence of your attractive natural being? In writing down these responses you will be adding to our collective nature language, so important to rekindling the bond between humans and nature. Look over your impressions and think about them as you fall asleep tonight before dreaming.

Follow-up Protocol

For best results, write down your impressions of this activity in your journal using the Heartwood Path Follow-up Protocol found in the Appendix. Afterwards, consider sharing your interpretations with others.

Heartwood Path Axioms

Key Assertions From Waypoint 3.70

3.70.1.

Cultivate empathy by focusing on impermanence.

3.70.2.

Settling the mind on a chosen object/being requires that you go beyond thoughtful analysis and develop empathy with the object of attention.

3.70.3.

Negative inner world conditions have unpleasant outer world effects.

Nocturnal Pilgrimage 3.70

For best results, write down your impressions of each night's dreams in your journal using the Heartwood Path Dreaming Time Protocols found in the Appendix. Afterwards, consider sharing your Dream Tending with others.

Ways To Perform A Reality Check

Number Five: Carry A Reality Check Reminder.

After a few unpleasant experiences, my mother eventually began asking me to empty my own pockets after playing outside. No bigger than a large earthworm, the small ringneck snakes I brought home in my pants pockets were, in my mother's' way of thinking, unwelcome additions to our little family. I can still see in my mind's eye that dropped scattering of my day's prizes on the floor of the laundry area—motionless bottle caps, burr-oak acorns, and some pennies I would use to make snowflake patterns, plus a wiggling little friend.

"Get that snake out of here!" my mother would yell, as she crouched on her hands and knees on top the dryer. "Let the poor thing go."

Lesson learned? Do your own laundry. And, if you pick up anything in nature and bring it home, limit yourself to beings that will not be hurt when you forget to empty your own pockets before washing your clothes.

That is one reason why, for this Reality Check, I recommend carrying only a small rock in your pocket and, every time you encounter it during the day, asking the question "Am I dreaming?" Ask this question often enough and you will habitually repeat the question while you are dreaming, thus launching you into a lucid dream you can use to make progress toward the goal of arriving at Gladandgreen Junction.

With the various axioms of this waypoint in mind, cultivate a dream. Sleep. Dream. And tend to your dreams.

When ready, move to the next waypoint, "One's Shoes (Part Three)." Once there, put down your i-Somethings or other e-devices and go where there are no electrical sockets. Have you noticed the association between the number of gadgets and the timing and location of the rise of stress, mental health disorders, learning and behavioral disorders, sleep problems, lower IQ's, and lack of happiness? I, for one, am skeptical that there will be anything like a cyber-utopia. Don't you think you would flourish more by getting away from your screens and, at least for short periods of time each day, into the wild?

71

One's Shoes (Part Three)

CULTIVATE EMPATHY BY FOCUSING ON DEVELOPING A BROAD SENSE OF RESPONSIBILITY

The way to incorporate the most beneficial perception into one's view of the world is compassion. Feeling the suffering of others (empathy) and doing something about the misery (compassion and altruism) are the key components of the route to enlightenment. The more responsibility one feels for another (be it a person or a planet) the more one is unable to bear the other's suffering. Likewise, the more gratitude one feels towards others—recognizing that most of what one receives comes from others—the more appreciation one feels for others.

Stop indulging in a self-centered view of the world and you will reduce your own suffering and help to preserve both the happiness of others and the physical condition of the environment. Use compassion to alleviate suffering and use loving kindness to foster happiness. Focus on an individual—a certain person rather than on all others in a general way. Engage in formal meditation but also carry the contemplation with you in your daily rounds. An hour or so of meditation per day will probably not be enough to develop the compassion needed to effectively help alleviate suffering and heighten happiness. Preparing yourself to reduce suffering will not happen overnight so do not risk overworking yourself on an impossible timetable.

While it is helpful to focus one's compassion on one individual at a time it is not fruitful to only extend compassion to a few select individuals. Genuine compassion needs to be unconditional—extended even to those who make one feel angry or hateful. Such feelings, while understandable, are irrational since they do more harm to oneself that they do to others. Therefore, offer compassion to friends and enemies alike. (As we all know, loving your enemies will, at least, drive them nuts.)

Everyone wants to be happy and avoid suffering. Directly or indirectly, everyone provides a contribution to one's wellbeing.

To Wide Duties...

HumaNatureConnect Activity

Start-up Protocol

If this is not a day when you prefer to spend time in nature without an agenda, do the Heartwood Path Start-up Protocol found in the Appendix.

Developing A Broad Sense Of Responsibility

For this activity, consider how you can demonstrate broad responsibility by helping to protect the environment and then write in your journal your impressions for each of Kim McKay and Jenny Bonnin's ideas from their book **True Green: 100 Everyday Ways You Can Contribute To A Healthier Planet (2007)**.

Ways To Make The Planet Healthier	My Impressions, Reactions, Responses, Or Plans

Reduce your waste.

Reuse your waste.

Recycle your waste.

Shorten your showers.

Restrict water flow.

Reduce water used by your toilet by buying a high-efficiency toilet, by placing a bottle filled with water in the tank, or by buying a toilet that uses less water to flush liquids only.

Buy an Energy Star Dish Washer.

Use the sun to produce electrical energy or heat your water.

Beef up the insulation in your home.

Seal the cracks in your home.

Use fans more liberally.

Rely on natural light.

Use timers and movement sensors to turn off lights.

Use energy efficient light bulbs.

Cut down on the use of space heaters.

Use clothing to keep your self warm rather than crank up the heat.

Dry your clothes outside in the sun.

Think about your energy usage before using your washing machine —use cold water and wash more often with full loads.

Cut down on your use of plastics.

Buy recycled or used furniture.

Detoxify your home.

Use lumber certified by the Forest Stewardship Council.

Use recycled lumber.

Put movable insulation on your windows.

Use energy efficient windows.

Turn off power at the source to prevent the waste from standby power.

Switch to renewables.

Stick with native plants.

Put in multiple layers of habitat in your yard for all sorts of wildlife.

Cut down on irrigated lawns.

Shade your house with trees.

Use the "grey water" from your shower to water your garden.

Collect rainwater in tanks and use the collected water for your garden.

Use decals on windows and otherwise make your property suitable for migratory birds.

Use old-fashioned push mowers and rakes instead of power tools.

Grow your own fruits and vegetables.

Use organic pesticides.

Water the roots and not the leaves and air.

Compost your food waste.

Create water-efficient landscaping.

Use water permeable pavements.

Use an ionizing water purifier in your swimming pool.

Save money, cut down on waste by packing your own lunch in reusable containers.

Stop using disposable cups.

Refill your printer cartridges.

Create a paperless office.

Turn off lights.

Unplug your mobile device recharger.

Add plants to indoor spaces.

Turn off computers when not in use.

Wash your clothes yourself or use clean and green cleaning services.

Keep your investments green.

Work to make your employer green.

Buy less, borrow more. Buy secondhand clothes.

Use rechargeable batteries.

Avoid excessive packaging.

Use reusable shopping bags.

Eat more grains, fruits and vegetables.

Buy or make green personal care and cleaning products.

Wear chemical free fibers.

Buy local.

Check the environmental creden-
tials of every business you support.

Walk instead. Ride your bike. Or
car-pool.

Downsize your vehicle. Buy less
polluting vehicles. Consider a
hybrid or an electric vehicle. Use
bio-fuels.

Share your living space with others.

Spread love.

Follow-up Protocol

For best results, write down your impressions of this activity in your journal using the Heartwood Path Follow-up Protocol found in the Appendix. Afterwards, consider sharing your interpretations with others.

Heartwood Path Axioms

Key Assertions From Waypoint 3.71

3.71.1.

Cultivate empathy by focusing on developing a broad sense of responsibility.

3.71.2.

Feeling the suffering of others (empathy) and doing something about the misery (compassion and altruism) are the key components of the route to enlightenment.

3.71.3.

Genuine compassion needs to be unconditional—extended even to those who make one feel angry or hateful.

3.71.4.

Negative inner world conditions have unpleasant outer world effects.

3.71.5.

To eliminate negative emotions and the actions these emotions generate, one needs to reach understanding through listening (to respected teachers, for example), through contemplation (which leads to certainty of the subject matter) and through meditation (during which one's mind is absorbed into the subject matter).

Nocturnal Pilgrimage 3.71

For best results, write down your impressions of each night's dreams in your journal using the Heartwood Path Dreaming Time Protocols found in the Appendix. Afterwards, consider sharing your Dream Tending with others.

Name your inner world wounded healer. Make an offering to it. Engage in a ritual over time to bring forth the healing that is needed. Find the silver-lining in the affliction. With a wide sense of responsibilities in mind, sleep and dream. Save your reflections in your dream journal.

When you are ready, move to the next waypoint, "Self-occupied"—an important step down the Heartwood Path to Gladandgreen Junction. This waypoint is important because self-centeredness is the root cause of most suffering. I have never seen anyone, for example, more miserable than the one person I know who is the most self-directed, most self-absorbed, and most self-centered. This person, who shall remain nameless, thinks that her problems are making her unhappy. Really, her suffering is the result of her unwavering self-centered focus on her unmet needs, her unending desires, her continuous quest for more goodies, and her focus on her interests only.

72

Self-occupied

STIFLE SELF-CHERISHING

Most of what comes into one's life comes from the hard work and the variable vibes of close family members, friends, and colleagues. Even one's tolerance comes from the work one does to at least understand the poor choices of others. When considering the sources of such hard lessons one discovers the pointlessness of self-cherishing.

One can avoid self-cherishing by replacing it with a new other-cherishing orientation. Doing so helps one naturally aspire towards helping all sentient beings. Lack of patience is the main obstacle to exchanging self-orientation for others-orientation. Patience helps one develop a strong sense of equanimity and removes prejudice from one's mind.

To The Cessation Of Narcissism...

HumaNatureConnect Activity

Start-up Protocol

If this is not a day when you prefer to spend time in nature without an agenda, do the Heartwood Path Start-up Protocol found in the Appendix.

Stifling Self-cherishing

For this activity, stifle self-cherishing in any of the following ways, inspired by a book entitled **The Narcissism Epidemic** *by Twenge and Campbell (2009).*

1. Put narcissism in quarantine by 1) not dating the self-absorbed jerk, 2) not hiring the woman who is more interested in what the company can do for her than what she can do for the company, 3) not participating in celebrity gossip, and 4) not creating shallow friendships. Write out a statement about how you plan to do such things, if at all.
2. Quiet the Ego by honestly appraising yourself, showing compassion to yourself, and realizing that everyone is flawed. Write out a pertinent plan.
3. Realize that you do nothing totally by yourself, that you are interdependent on others and the world, and that you are similar to others (and not particularly special). Write out a pertinent plan.
4. In politics support both the left's emphasis on equality and the right's emphasis on self-reliance, support the left's community-level efforts and the right's family-level efforts. Write out a pertinent plan.
5. As parents, set limits, give up trying to be the perfect parent, emphasize working hard, and give specific advice rather than generalized praise. Write out a pertinent plan.
6. Notice the absence of narcissism in nature.

Follow-up Protocol

For best results, write down your impressions of this activity in your journal using the Heartwood Path Follow-up Protocol found in the Appendix. Afterwards, consider sharing your interpretations with others.

Heartwood Path Axioms

Key Assertions From Waypoint 3.72

3.72.1.

Most of what comes into one's life comes from the hard work and the variable vibes of close family members, friends and colleagues.

3.72.2.

Lack of patience is the main obstacle to exchanging self-orientation for others-orientation.

3.72.3.

Patience helps one develop a strong sense of equanimity and removes prejudice from one's mind.

3.72.4.

Rid yourself of narcissism in ways found along the Heartwood Path.

Nocturnal Pilgrimage 3.72

For best results, write down your impressions of each night's dreams in your journal using the Heartwood Path Dreaming Time Protocols found in the Appendix. Afterwards, consider sharing your Dream Tending with others.

Use the following technique soon as you begin your lucid dream as a way to keep it going:

Treat your dream body to a pirouette—that is, spin around. Doing so makes it difficult for your mind to wake up your body.

After tending to your dreams, move to the next waypoint: "Big Shot." You will need to visit the next waypoint because common sense is not so common and a mentor will come in handy. In choosing a leader, do not pick one who knows all things . . . only fools think they know everything.

When listening to your leader, remember that a good way to avoid falling for anything is to stand for something. As we all know, if your prospective mentor has a clear conscious he will also likely have a bad memory.

73

Big Shot

MEDITATE ABOUT YOUR CHOSEN LEADER

Improving oneself in the ways described in this book requires calmness and single-pointed concentration, developed in degrees over a time and motivated by the quest for virtue. The practice begins by focusing on the mental image of a leader (consider Jesus or Allah, or Buddha, or Moses, or Saint Francis of Assisi—you will get to know Saint Francis better in the activity that follows). Such focusing results in a sense of closeness, particularly when the image becomes stable (through lack of excitement and distraction) and clear (through meditation in a quiet environment and the putting aside of worldly preoccupations).

Sit in a formal meditation position with a straight back. Remain vigilant in your introspection. Maintain a joyful mood. Stay focused on the present, which occurs mentally in the "vacuum" created between the recollections of the past and the projections of the future. In time, the true nature of the mind, which is empty of thought processes but not blank as it is during deep sleep, will emerge. The true mind of awareness, as opposed to the cluttered mind full of judgments, negativity, and worthless "chatter," is marked by the clear experience of knowing and not by speculation. It is also focused often on "emptiness" as the object of concentration. This concept of "emptiness" has to do with the non-solid and impermanent aspect of things.

To Make Yourself Into A Mirror Of A Revered Torchbearer...

HumaNatureConnect Activity

Start-up Protocol

If this is not a day when you prefer to spend time in nature without an agenda, do the Heartwood Path Start-up Protocol found in the Appendix.

Emulating Your Chosen Leader

For this activity, pick a leader you admire, or that has done something to significantly change himself, others, and our viewpoint of the world at large, particularly our relations with all sentient beings. Create a two-column table in your journal. On the left side of the table, list a quality or action you would like to emulate. On the right column, list what you like about each quality or action and write down how you plan to do something similar or reminiscent. If you prefer, you can use Saint Francis, as I have done after reading the **Reluctant Saint: The Life of Francis of Assisi,** by Donald Spoto (2003). As you can see below, I have listed some aspects of this patron saint of the environmental movement. I believe Francis of Assisi is a worthy role model for eartHearts. Be inspired by Saint Francis of Assisi or choose another leader to emulate.

Quality Or Action Of An Admired Leader	What I Plan To Do In A Similar Or Reminiscent Way

" . . . saints are in fact heroically in love, and like lovers, they sometimes become eccentric, and even overstep themselves; holiness does not preclude humanity, after all. Above everything, however, saints keep God firmly in sight. They remain faithful, and that is why they are saints—not because they are invariably models of polite or even imitable conduct" (Spoto, 2002, p. 65).

(example: "I will allow myself to be considered eccentric in the following ways . . ."

"They found him constantly surprising" (Spoto, 2002, 74).

St. Francis "insisted on their dedicating themselves to poverty in their own lives" (Spoto, 2002, p. 74).

St. Francis "also admonished them 'not to look down upon or judge those who they see dressed in soft and fine clothes and enjoying the choices food and drink–rather, let everyone judge and look down upon himself. Judgement was the prerogative of God." (Spoto, 2002, p. 74).

"There was in Francis nothing of the sanctimonious censor; her rarely alluded to damnation, and unlike many wandering reformers of his hime, he pronounced no condemnations against any person or any specific belief" (Spoto, 2002, p. 74).

"If we had possessions . . . we would need arms for our protection—because disputes and lawsuits, as you know, usually arise our of possessions" (Spoto, 2002, p. 76).

Because they were bound by no vows or ties to any biship, much less to superiors in Rome, they faced none of the problems of organization, of structure or of churchly legality. They were simply working men who begged for food as compensation and devoted private time to prayer" (Spoto, 2002, p. 78).

"He did not love an impersonal universal force, nor did he salute a vague rhythm of life. He was drawn to the divine; he was in love with God.

Francis wrote "I want to write a new Praise of the Lord for his creatures, which we use every day and without which we cannot live." Through them, the human race greatly offends the Creator, and we are continually ungrateful for such great graces and good gifts, not praising, as we ought to do, our Lord the Creator and the Giver of all good. In his Canticle of the Creatures he writes" Praised be You, my Lord, with all Your creatures, especially Sir Brother Sun...Praised be You, my Lord, through Sister Moon and the stars...through Brother Wind...through Sister Water...through Brother Fire. Praised be You, my Lord, through our Sister, Mother Earth, who sustains and governs us, and who produces various fruits with colored flowers and herbs" (Spoto, 2002, pp. 200-202.

In the Spaces below, fill in another quote, attribute, or Action of St. Francis or someone else you admire.

Write in your own qualities and
actions of an admired leader in the
spaces that follow.

Follow-up Protocol

For best results, write down your impressions of this activity in
your journal using the Heartwood Path Follow-up Protocol found in
the Appendix. Afterwards, consider sharing your interpretations with
others.

Heartwood Path Axioms

Key Assertions From Waypoint 3.73

3.73.1.

**Focusing on a chosen leader results in a sense of closeness and
direction, particularly when the image becomes stable
(through lack of excitement and distraction) and clear
(through meditation in a quiet environment and the putting
aside of worldly preoccupations).**

3.73.2.

Stay focused on the present, which occurs mentally in the "vacuum" created between the recollections of the past and the projections of the future.

3.73.3.

The true mind of awareness, as opposed to the cluttered mind full of judgments, negativity, and worthless "chatter," is marked by the clear experience of knowing and not by speculation.

3.73.4.

The true mind is also focused often on "emptiness" as the object of concentration. This concept of "emptiness" has to do with the non-solid and impermanent aspect of things.

3.73.5.

Create a Dream Council to interact with your living dreams.

Nocturnal Pilgrimage 3.73

For best results, write down your impressions of each night's dreams in your journal using the Heartwood Path Dreaming Time Protocols found in the Appendix. Afterwards, consider sharing your Dream Tending with others.

Before moving to the next waypoint, sleep, dream, and tend to your dreams. Then, turn your attention to the following:

So important is the next Dream Tending practice that several of the next HumaNatureConnect Dream Activities will be devoted to it. I am speaking of engaging a Dream Council. I believe that the Dream

Council is an extremely fulfilling way to interact with living dreams. Like your list of friends, some members of the Dream Council will come and others will go, some will be easy to get along with and others will not.

If you do not have enough Dream Council members already, look for potential Dream Characters to serve on your Dream Council. Look for Dream Characters that stand out. In the selection process, use your intuition, suspend your judgement, and follow your wants. Once an inner world Dream Character is made into a three dimensional outer world figure (as you will be instructed to do) and added to your Dream Council, we will use the term "Dream Figure" for the outer world object instead of the term for the inner world image ("Dream Character").

When ready, move to the next waypoint, titled "Expanding Benevolence," There you will learn about altruism.

74

Expanding Benevolence

DEVELOP ALTRUISM IN STAGES

Whether one focuses on a respected model such as Jesus or the true nature of the mind, the result is typically the enduring calmness of single-pointed concentration and sustained, effective, and mutually beneficial compassionate altruism. Such altruism develops in nine stages:

1. directing the mind toward its object of concentration and over-coming inevitable initial distractions,
2. experiencing fleeting moments of mental stillness
3. re-establishing mental focus,
4. experiencing mental laxity and excitement,
5. overcoming laxity or excitement through awareness—not through thoughts but through the empty stage for one's thoughts (which is awareness),
6. powerful introspection,
7. ease of awareness,
8. single-pointed concentration, and
9. the blissful pliancy of body and mind that comes through single-pointed concentration.

Through these steps one penetrates into one's conception of emptiness, and in so doing, becomes wise. Through consistent, repeated meditation one undergoes a process of preparation and deep seeing. This process reveals the nature of life, prompts the desire to relieve suffering, and evokes loving-kindness. Through this process (described in more detail later), one develops responsibility, accumulates merit and wisdom, develops the responsibility to attain enlightenment, and eventually trades striving in selfishness for arriving in altruism.

Such arriving is persistent like a perpetually flowing river—a continuum of moments of knowing and compassion. The topic of getting to this high level of altruism comes later because there is much to do before one is ready to share the arrival of the light of persistent altruism, including the following activity.

To Picture Yourself As The Absolute Spirit Serving Others...

HumaNatureConnect Activity

Start-up Protocol

If this is not a day when you prefer to spend time in nature without an agenda, do the Heartwood Path Start-up Protocol found in the Appendix.

Imagining Yourself As The Absolute Spirit Acting In Service of Others

For this activity, meditate on your own body as if it were a divine being. Remember our earlier discussion of the emptiness of all things, notice the emptiness of your body. Notice also how you (and everything else, for that matter) do not arise independently. Combine in your consciousness your wisdom about the emptiness of existence and your dependent arising with your compassionate motivation. Visualize that you are being initiated as a divine being with particular positive attributes. Focus your mind on these attributes and how they might play out in your life. Pay particular attention to how you would use newly found positive attributes and principles in all aspects of life, especially those that serve others. Apply the notion of the emptiness of existence to any other aspect of your life and imaginatively walk yourself through how this application would play out in your real life.

Follow-up Protocol

For best results, write down your impressions of this activity in your journal using the Heartwood Path Follow-up Protocol found in the Appendix. Afterwards, consider sharing your interpretations with others.

Heartwood Path Axioms

Key Assertions From Waypoint 3.74

3.74.1.

Whether one focuses on a respected model such as Jesus or the true nature of the mind, the result is typically the enduring calmness of single-pointed concentration and sustained, effective, and mutually beneficial compassionate altruism.

3.74.2.

Altruism develops in nine stages, each described along the Heartwood Path.

3.74.3.

Through consistent, repeated meditation one undergoes a process of preparation and deep seeing—a process that reveals

the nature of life, prompts the desire to relieve suffering, and evokes loving-kindness.

Nocturnal Pilgrimage 3.74

For best results, write down your impressions of each night's dreams in your journal using the Heartwood Path Dreaming Time Protocols found in the Appendix. Afterwards, consider sharing your Dream Tending with others.

Continue to scan your dreams in search of potential members for your Dream Council. "Do not include human images only . . . include images of dream entities, animals, elements, machines, or whatever catches your attention and curiosity" (Aizenstat, 2009, p. 233).

After finishing your Dream Tending session, begin your next Heartwood Path waypoint: "Concealed." Do not minimize your opportunities by attempting to go down the Heartwood Path in your indoor chair. The most meaningful and life-enhancing experiences will come to those who commune regularly with Mother Nature on her home turf.

75

Concealed

DABBLE IN THE DARK

The dark side of one's personality does not fit with one's perfect image of one's Self. One keeps the dark side of one's personality away from the peace table in one's heart by denying it; but it still lurks elsewhere. The following are some ways one can discover where the dark side lurks in one's life, during: selfishness, anger, vindictiveness, uncontrolled sexual urges, self-loathing (the hemorrhaging of the Soul), making premature judgments, and distasteful or morally reprehensible behaviors.

The dark side flourishes when one engages in self-loathing. This seemingly inexhaustible capacity arises in many forms, including when one does not like the way one capitulates to the needs of others by disavowing one's own needs, when one ignores cruelty to keep the peace, or when one denies one's own unrequited desires.

Along with directing the negative aspects of the dark side toward one's self or other individuals, one sometimes lashes out at groups, transforming them into scapegoats or enemies. Usually one's negative images of other groups—minorities, homosexuals, political so-called "enemies," the homeless, etc.—are drawn from denied aspects of one's Self. Thus, grappling with one's dark images of other groups reduces the difference between one's idealized projected public image and one's actual imperfect inner image of one's Self.

Along with negative, prejudicial images of other groups, death and dying are considered by many people to be among the worst aspects of the Dark Side. Do not be afraid of death. Be concerned that your altruistic life will never begin.

The prospect of death can be a great motivator for those who care about how they will be remembered. The justification for an honorable epitaph on one's own gravestone is one way death brings goodness to the living. So live long but also live wide by putting a lot into each day and at least something for others.

To put the wisdom of this section of the Heartwood Path to work for you, do the following activity:

To Your Own Commemoration...

HumaNatureConnect Activity

Start-up Protocol

If this is not a day when you prefer to spend time in nature without an agenda, do the Heartwood Path Start-up Protocol found in the Appendix.

Writing Your Own Epitaph

For this activity, write down the words of commemoration (those words beyond your name, birth date and death date) that you would like to see on your grave marker.

Follow-up Protocol

For best results, write down your impressions of this activity in your journal using the Heartwood Path Follow-up Protocol found in

the Appendix. Afterwards, consider sharing your interpretations with others.

Heartwood Path Axioms

Key Assertions From Waypoint 3.75

3.75.1.

The dark side of one's personality does not fit with one's perfect image of one's Self.

3.75.2.

One keeps the dark side of one's personality away from the peace table in one's heart by denying it; but it still lurks elsewhere.

3.75.3.

The dark side lurks in the following aspects of one's life, during: selfishness, anger, vindictiveness, uncontrolled sexual urges, self-loathing (the hemorrhaging of the Soul), making premature judgments, and distasteful or morally reprehensible behaviors.

3.75.4.

Rather than being afraid of death, be concerned that your altruistic life will never begin.

3.75.5.

The justification for an honorable epitaph on one's own grave-stone is one way death brings goodness to the living.

Nocturnal Pilgrimage 3.75

For best results, write down your impressions of each night's dreams in your journal using the Heartwood Path Dreaming Time Protocols found in the Appendix. Afterwards, consider sharing your Dream Tending with others.

In choosing your Dream Council, do not pick "exclusively beautiful or happy images . . . Be sure to include those images that are repulsive, horrifying, or terrible" (Aizenstat, 2009, p. 233). Such images are often the most transformative.

After ending your Dream Tending session, move to the next waypoint, "Proof," to take your next step down the Heartwood Path. Engross yourself in the next waypoint by going outside, as directed. That way you can take in the beneficial fresh air and expose yourself to healthful full-spectrum light.

76

Proof

APPROPRIATELY TEST THE
VALIDITY OF CLAIMS

Greater depth means to unfold greater consciousness. Simply revealing more information is not adequate. Claims revealed by one's ever-growing perspective have to be validated. Fortunately, there is a specific way to do so.

The means to check on the validity of claims in the universe's individual, exterior quadrant—the upper right leaf on our symbolic Four Leaf Model of Integrity—is the determination of truth. In the outer world realm of individual behaviors truthful statements refer to an observable objective state of affairs.

The means to check on the validity of claims in the universe's individual, interior quadrant—the upper left leaf on our symbolic Four Leaf Model of Integrity—is beauty. Here, dialogue is used to determine subjectively whether the maker of a statement is expressing a beautiful intention (which, when one probes deep enough, is always the case).

The means to check on the validity of claims in the universe's plural, exterior quadrant—the lower right leaf on our symbolic Four Leaf Model of Integrity—are two-fold. First one can determine how holons nest or fit within the overall objective system (how one's hand is part of ones arm, and how one's arm is part of one's body, and how one's body is part of one's household, and how one's household is part of one's community, for example). Second, one can determine truthfulness of the behaviors of groups (such as whether a group bombed a church).

The means to check on the validity of claims in the universe's plural, interior quadrant—the lower left leaf on our symbolic Four Leaf Model of Integrity—is reaching a mutual understanding concerning meaning, appropriateness, goodness, and "rightness" or "justness." This "justness" is not just for humans. The environmental ethics of earthHearts reminds us that this reality claim needs to apply to holons at all stages of development within the quadrant, especially for all sentient beings.

By following these trails to truth, the Heartwood Path leads eartHearts to the "Three Ats," which need to be known and acted upon because they make us beautiful, good, and true (and what could be better, more whole, or more perfect than that?):

1. ATtunement—getting in tune with the universe;
2. ATonement—requital of previous wrongdoings and compensating for damages caused by inappropriate actions; and
3. "AT-onement"—cosmic consciousness.

Each of these are fortified when you become in tune with:

- the goodness of "we" (all sentient beings acting ethically in the Community of Spirit);
- the truth of "it" (the objective state of affairs, the manifestations of the Spirit); and
- the beauty of "I" (not the sense of a separate self, but an expanded self that includes the Kosmos).

Without bringing forth all the "Three At's" into one's life one will end up in the kind of trouble that occurs when there is no integrity because one will become either ugly, or evil, or untruthful, or some combination of the three.

To Guard Against Disinformation...

HumaNatureConnect Activity

Start-up Protocol

If this is not a day when you prefer to spend time in nature without an agenda, do the Heartwood Path Start-up Protocol found in the Appendix.

Testing The Validity Of Claims

For this activity, work on finding the facts and on guarding yourself against untruths in advertising and political rhetoric. Brooks Jackson and Kathleen Hall Jamieson, authors of **Unspun: Finding Facts In A World Of Disinformation (2007),** inspired the following list of warning signs of dubious messages we are bombarded with in our daily lives. For each warning, write an example of a similar fabrication masquerading as a fact from your own experience. Mention your impressions from the revelation of the disinformation, and what you plan to do about it, if anything.

Disinformation Warning Signs	Fabrication Masquerading As A Fact From My Own Experience. Impressions From My Revelation Of The Disinformation, And What I Plan To Do About It, If Anything.
If its scary, be wary.	

If it sounds to good to be true, its too good to be true.

Watch out for dangling comparatives such as "larger," "faster," and "better-tasting."

Watch out for superlatives such as "more," and "higher."

Watch out for pay-you-later scams.

Beware of the blame game, pointing a finger at an unpopular group. Consider the opposing view.

Be suspicious of misnomers or jargon phrases such as "Assault weapon ban (there already is one), or Venti instead of Extra Large. Ask " What is behind the name? What would be a more accurate name for it?

Look for weasel words such as "Up to 50% Off" or "You may already be a winner."

Do not be distracted by eye candy.

When you hear the word "average" find out if it really means "typical."

Determine if a cut really means a smaller increase.

Determine whether "is" means ever or at the moment, such as "there is no sex of any kind." Does that mean not ever or just not at the moment?

Watch out for between the lines messages such as "get rock hard abs with no sweat."

Be careful that you are not believing something just to prove that you are right.

Do not confuse anecdotes with data.

Remember that not all studies are equal.

Saying something does not make it truthful.

Look for extraordinary evidence behind extraordinary claims.

Check facts with FactCheck.org, cdc.gov, consumerreports.org, cbo.gov, kff.org, gao.gov, quackwatch.org, census.org, or bus.gov.

You may never be completely certain but you can be certain enough.

Look for general agreement among experts.

Research the primary sources of the information.

Check the definitions so you know what counts.

Look into the sponsor of the information.

Seeing is not necessarily believing.

Everything matters so cross-check everything.

Know the difference between being *skeptical* (dubious, doubtful, taking something with a pinch of salt, doubting; cynical, distrustful, mistrustful, suspicious, disbelieving, unconvinced, incredulous, scoffing; pessimistic, rightfully hopeless) and being *cynical* (doubtful, distrustful, suspicious, disbelieving; pessimistic, negative, world-weary, disillusioned, disenchanted, jaundiced, sardonic.) If you have to be either, be skeptical.

Follow-up Protocol

For best results, write down your impressions of this activity in your journal using the Heartwood Path Follow-up Protocol found in the Appendix. Afterwards, consider sharing your interpretations with others.

Heartwood Path Axioms

Key Assertions From Waypoint 3.76

3.76.1.

Claims revealed by one's ever-growing perspective have to be validated.

3.76.2.

The means to check on the validity of claims in the universe's individual, exterior quadrant—the upper right leaf on our symbolic Four Leaf Model of Integrity—is the determination of truth.

3.76.3.

The means to check on the validity of claims in the universe's individual, interior quadrant—the upper left leaf on our symbolic Four Leaf Model of Integrity—is beauty.

3.76.4.

The means to check on the validity of claims in the universe's plural, exterior quadrant—the lower right leaf on our symbolic Four Leaf Model of Integrity—are two fold: 1) determining how holons nest or fit within the overall objective system and 2) determining truthfulness (actuality) of the behaviors of groups.

3.76.5.

The means to check on the validity of claims in the universe's plural, interior quadrant—the lower left leaf on our symbolic

Four Leaf Model of Integrity—is reaching a mutual understanding concerning meaning, appropriateness, goodness, and "rightness" or "justness."

Nocturnal Pilgrimage 3.76

For best results, write down your impressions of each night's dreams in your journal using the Heartwood Path Dreaming Time Protocols found in the Appendix. Afterwards, consider sharing your Dream Tending with others.

When incubating a dream for your nocturnal pilgrimages, do not attempt to force the results. Instead, stay disciplined and relaxed.

Fifth Stabilization Technique For Lucid Dreaming

You learned about staying calm and having one foot in and one foot out as a dream stabilization techniques earlier in the Heartwood Path. Now, after more practicing with lucid dreaming initiation, it is time to make sure you can hold on to your nocturnal lucidity. Here's another tip, useful for when you want to keep a dream from fading:

Touch something in the dream and that dream will stabilize. The same goes for smelling it, or hearing it, or tasting it, or, for that matter, applying any of the Natural Senses. As you reach out in your dream, even by touching the fingers of your dream body, stay focused and you will increase the chances that the dream will not fade.

After finishing your current Dream Tending session, begin your next adventure in your waking expedition down the Heartwood Path by moving to the next waypoint: "Bounds." When asked to go into nature in the following activity, make intimate contact with other living beings and absorb the beauty of the natural landscape.

77

Bounds

DEVELOP HEALTHY INDIVIDUAL BOUNDARIES, AVOID UNHEALTHY ENMESHMENT IN RELATIONSHIPS, AND LET GO OF UNHELPFUL BOUNDARIES

One's personal boundaries are how far one can go comfortably in a relationship. They protect but they ought not create undue distance or separation. These imaginary lines define the Self. They are where interaction occurs with others. As the way to protect the sanctity of your Self while also being in relationship, boundaries are the foundation for healthy intimacy.

Giving up the sense of who you are inevitably causes resentment, which can cause conflict when you try to reestablish your imaginary zone of protection. Being a person who always cook's the dinner, for example, may cause resentment when you suggest that you and your partner could take turns. One's management of boundaries, working on where one's boundary ends and where another person's begins, is a vital task because how one relates to others determines how one protects and nurtures one's Authentic Self. In the activity that follows, we shall address four of the most important things maintaining proper boundaries does for you:

1. having enough time to do what is important,
2. protecting from hurtful remarks or behaviors,
3. protecting your time, inner peace, and invigorating activities, and
4. protecting family, friends, needs, and principles.

To Outline The Personal Self...

HumaNatureConnect Activity

Start-up Protocol

If this is not a day when you prefer to spend time in nature without an agenda, do the Heartwood Path Start-up Protocol found in the Appendix.

Setting Personal Boundaries

For this activity, fill out the chart below regarding your personal boundaries:

Type Of Personal Boundary	Value In Having This Boundary	Person Who Violates Boundary	What This Person Does	Plan
Time	Having enough time to do what is important.			

Time	Having enough time to do what is important.			
Time	Having enough time to do what is important.			
Time	Having enough time to do what is important.			
Emotions	Protection from hurtful remarks or behaviors.			
Emotions	Protection from hurtful remarks or behaviors.			
Emotions	Protection from hurtful remarks or behaviors.			
Emotions	Protection from hurtful remarks or behaviors.			

Energy	Protecting your alone time, free time, inner peace, and invigorating activities.			
Energy	Protecting your alone time, free time, inner peace, and invigorating activities.			
Energy	Protecting your alone time, free time, inner peace, and invigorating activities.			
Energy	Protecting your alone time, free time, inner peace, and invigorating activities.			

Personal Values And Areas Of Importance	Protecting family, friends, needs, and principles.		
Personal Values and Areas of Importance	Protecting family, friends, needs, and principles.		
Personal Values And Areas Of Importance	Protecting family, friends, needs, and principles.		
Personal Values And Areas Of Importance	Protecting family, friends, needs, and principles.		

Follow-up Protocol

For best results, write down your impressions of this activity in your journal using the Heartwood Path Follow-up Protocol found in the Appendix. Afterwards, consider sharing your interpretations with others.

Heartwood Path Axioms

Key Assertions From Waypoint 3.77

3.77.1.

As the way to protect the sanctity of your self while also being in relationship, boundaries are the foundation for healthy intimacy.

3.77.2.

Giving up the sense of who you are inevitably causes resentment, which can cause conflict when you try to reestablish your imaginary zone of protection.

3.77.3.

One's management of boundaries, working on where one's boundary ends and where another person's begins, is a vital task because how one relates to others determines how one protects and nurtures one's Authentic Self.

Nocturnal Pilgrimage 3.77

For best results, write down your impressions of each night's dreams in your journal using the Heartwood Path Dreaming Time Protocols found in the Appendix. Afterwards, consider sharing your Dream Tending with others.

Continue to look over your dream journal for candidates for your Dream Council. I always maintain a minimum of eight members and never more than fifteen. Twelve is ideal.

If you have not done so already, begin to establish your Dream Council. Do not put this off. They are too potentially important for you not to have them in your corner.

Once you have at least a few members in your Dream Council, move to the next waypoint: "Real You." Be sure to head outside to begin your next activity. Take in the tonic of wild nature—the primary source of your physical, psychological, and spiritual well-being.

78

Real You

NURTURE THE AUTHENTIC SELF

This Authentic Self is not the mystique one projects to the outside world. This mystique is created by the False Self, which is also known as the "Ego." Comparatively, the Authentic Self is one's being, one's consciousness, and one's genuine essence. The False Self is projected outward but hides behind a mask. The Authentic Self determines what is personally important and meaningful.

The False Self sometimes serves as an assistant who helps one deal with the world. The False Self also creates unhealthy boundaries that serve to unduly separate oneself from people, places, and things.

The Authentic Self is not the Higher Self. The Authentic Self is recalled through therapy with the help of a professional counselor or psychologist or it is done through personal reflection by yourself (considering who you are and what you stand for). The Higher Self is recalled through spiritual practice. The Authentic Self is individual; the Higher Self is More-Than-Individual. The False Self puts up walls. The Authentic Self creates healthy boundaries. The Higher Self helps one let go of them.

A personal boundary establishes who one really is, individually. It contains the collection of one's true feelings, thoughts, needs, wants, values, hopes, and dreams.

The main initial job of personal growth is to contact the Authentic Self and to live by it. A quick way to find your Authentic Self is to ask the following questions:

1. When you were very little, what did you want to be when you grew up?
2. What makes you laugh?
3. What clothes do you feel comfortable wearing?
4. What activities do you enjoy?
5. Around who can you be yourself? (mindbodygreen.com)

If you are developing yourself as an eartHeart, contacting and living by the Authentic Self is the first important step. From there, the next steps include:

1. climbing to higher branches of individual development where one can recall one's ever-present connection to the spiritual realm,
2. bringing forth the Higher Self, and
3. being sufficiently prepared to serve other sentient beings and preserve the Earth.

Review for a moment where you stand with each of the above steps. If deficiencies are noticed, make corrections so that you are on your way to developing your Authentic Self. The following activity will help.

The False Self, domineering in most people, emerges because of issues related to past rejection, abandonment, betrayal, and the pain of being open with others only to be treated poorly. When such negativities occur, as they will for almost everybody, the prevalent reaction is to conceal feelings, hopes, dreams and longings from, not only other people, but also from oneself.

To The Real You...

HumaNatureConnect Activity

Start-up Protocol

If this is not a day when you prefer to spend time in nature without an agenda, do the Heartwood Path Start-up Protocol found in the Appendix.

Highlighting The Real You

For this activity, write down a description of the real you, the one behind the mystique, the one behind the mask that keeps the world from really knowing who you are. Consider describing the elements that make up your personality and life. Try to remember a time that you lost what you felt was your authenticity and recall what you had to do to live again as your Authentic Self. Describe how you are or are not true to yourself. Does anything you do make you feel like an empty shell? How are you living up to your own standards of personal responsibility? How are you violating your personal responsibility? In what ways are you maintaining your integrity and genuineness? Where, if at all, are you experiencing a mismatch between your values and your actions? What biases, if any, are testing your authenticity? In what ways do your behaviors span from the absurd to the meaningful? What does this span say about the real you?

Follow-up Protocol

For best results, write down your impressions of this activity in your journal using the Heartwood Path Follow-up Protocol found in

the Appendix. Afterwards, consider sharing your interpretations with others.

Heartwood Path Axioms

Key Assertions From Waypoint 3.78

3.78.1.

The Authentic Self is one's being, one's consciousness, and one's genuine essence.

3.78.2.

The Authentic Self is recalled through therapy or personal reflection and the Higher Self is recalled through spiritual practice.

3.78.3.

The Authentic Self is individual, the Higher Self is More-Than-Individual, the False Self puts up walls, the Authentic Self creates healthy boundaries, and the Higher Self helps one let go of them.

3.78.4.

Contacting and living by the Authentic Self is the first important step for the developing eartHeart, the second step is climbing to higher branches of individual development where one can recall one's ever-present connection to the spiritual realm, the third step is to bring forth the Higher Self, and the fourth

step is being sufficiently prepared to serve other sentient beings and preserve the Earth.

Nocturnal Pilgrimage 3.78

For best results, write down your impressions of each night's dreams in your journal using the Heartwood Path Dreaming Time Protocols found in the Appendix. Afterwards, consider sharing your Dream Tending with others.

"In Dream Council we express our Dream Images in physical form," writes Aizenstat. "Manifesting Dream Images physically transports both them and us into the immediacy of the present moment" (Aizenstat, 2009, p. 235). Fear of embarrassment or the perception of lack of artistic ability will likely make you feel resistant to making your physical Dream Council members. While there will likely be some discomfort initially, creating the members of your Dream Council is a forceful and necessary action. Continue looking for Dream Council recruits and begin to assemble your construction materials. Consider rocks, feathers, twigs, nuts, leaves, bones, shells, and other natural objects as materials to use to construct your Dream Council members. No need to get too elaborate in your constructing. When you are ready, continue to the next waypoint: "Personal Space." Respect and follow any urges to connect with nature regularly. Either wander without an agenda and let nature do its magic on you or do the next activity, or both.

79

Personal Space

PAY ATTENTION TO THE SPACE
AROUND ONESELF AND OTHERS

Unnecessary suffering can also be diverted by taking heed of the arrangement of things around you through the application of the ancient Chinese method known as Feng Shui (pronounced "feng shway"). While a complete elaboration of Feng Shui is too complicated for the purposes of this book, a quick accounting of whether your life is arranged according to its principles will be helpful towards establishing health and success. For more details, consult two books in the references for this text: Mitchell (2002) and Too (1999). In the activity below, in the right column write down your impressions about your own setting in reference to the Feng Shui prescription in the left column.

To A Positive Self-concept...

HumaNatureConnect Activity

Start-up Protocol

If this is not a day when you prefer to spend time in nature without an agenda, do the Heartwood Path Start-up Protocol found in the Appendix.

Paying Attention To The Space Around Oneself And Others

For this activity, consider whether you are following some basic Feng Shui principle by filling out the right column below. Be sure to state if you are in compliance or out of compliance and what you plan to do, if anything, to improve the setting of your home, garden or office. Look over the following diagram, paying attention to the colors of the three-lined trigrams. These come from the ancient text the I Ching and represent the life zones, as indicated. If you want to enhance any zone of your life, such as children and creativity, put more of this associated color in the room of your house or part of your garden that correlates most closely on the Bagua (shown below).

The Bagua

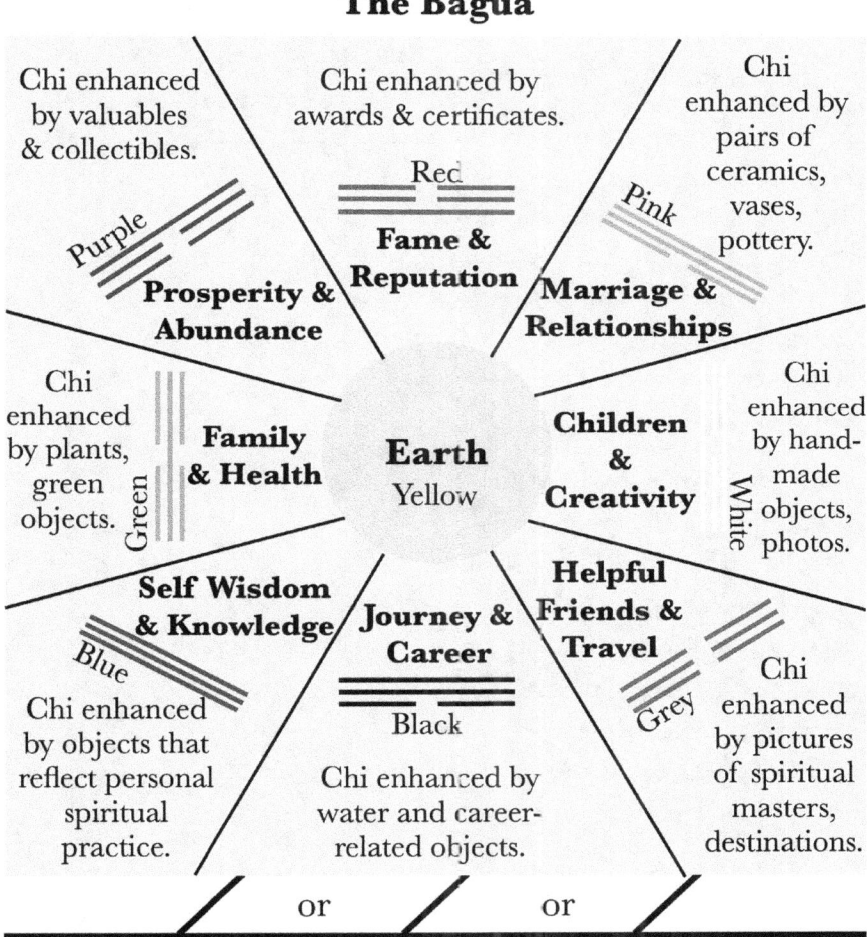

Chi enhanced by valuables & collectibles.

Chi enhanced by awards & certificates.

Chi enhanced by pairs of ceramics, vases, pottery.

Purple

Red

Pink

Prosperity & Abundance

Fame & Reputation

Marriage & Relationships

Chi enhanced by plants, green objects.

Family & Health

Earth
Yellow

Children & Creativity

Chi enhanced by hand-made objects, photos.

Green

White

Self Wisdom & Knowledge

Journey & Career

Helpful Friends & Travel

Blue

Black

Grey

Chi enhanced by objects that reflect personal spiritual practice.

Chi enhanced by water and career-related objects.

Chi enhanced by pictures of spiritual masters, destinations.

or   or

Entry to Room, House, or Garden

This will become more clear when you use the table below.

Soon you will be using the Bagua to determine where to place Dream Council figures. My favorite location is within the Self Wisdom and Knowledge zone, lower left in the Bagua illustration.

Basic Feng Shui Principle	My Alignment With Each Feng Shui Principle And My Plans To Make Pertinent Changes, If Any. Here Are My Impressions.
Balance Masculine Yang—masculine, assertive, light, hot, dry, and angular—with Feminine Yin—feminine, receptive, dark, cool, moist, and round—Qualities (Mitchell, 2002, pp. 14-40).	
Putting to use the Five Elements—Wood (growth and progress), Fire (heat and expansion), Earth (stability and dependability), Metal (strength), and Water (fluidity and movement). Think of the five elements as forces of creation (Mitchell, 2002, pp. 41-46).	

Map your home according to the different parts of your life—work, relationships, health, etc. This is done by using a type of map known as a "bagua" (Mitchell, 2002, pp. 57-73). Orient the Bagua according the position of the entry to your office, home, or garden—wherever you are doing a feng shui evaluation. Make a floor plan-type map of your office, garden or home. When you look at the entry way, note whether it is located on the left side (Self Wisdom and Knowledge zone of the Bagua, or the center (Journey and Career zone) or the right (Helpful Friends & Travel). Improvements can happen in any room or part of your garden.

Wood is associated with the color green. Its shape is columnar. Its direction is the East. Wood creates fire and destroys the Earth. It is also associated with being social and active in the community. Too much wood creates a lack of creative flow, over-expansion, and a feeling of being overwhelmed (Mitchell, 2002, p. 42).

Fire is associated with the color red. Its shape is pointed. Its direction is South. It creates Earth and destroys Metal. Earth is associated with the color yellow. Its shape is flat. Its direction is to the center. The Fire Element represents passion, energy and enthusiasm. Too much can burn and be destructive (Mitchell, 2002, p. 43).

Water is associated with the color black. Its shape is irregular. Its direction is north. Water creates Wood and destroys fire. Water represents learning, communication, and travel. It can be gentle or wild (Mitchell, 2002, p. 45).

Metal is associated with the colors white, silver, or gold. Its shape is arched. Its direction is the West. It creates water and destroys wood. The Metal Element indicates business, prosperity, and financial success. Too much leads to conflict and destruction (Mitchell, 2002, p. 45).

Earth creates metal and destroys water. It is associated with the color yellow. Its shape is flat and its direction is toward the center. Earth provides stability and grounding. Too much feels demanding, overly attentive, or suffocating (Mitchell, 2002, p. 44).

Ten easy ways to enhance the five elements in any room: Add red roses to introduce fire and wood. Add an indoor plant in a black pot to introduce more wood and water. Add a zebra or leopard print to introduce more fire. Add white candles in cut glass candlesticks to introduce fire, metal, and water. Add a bowl of goldfish to introduce water, metal, and fire. Add a painting of a desert landscape framed in wood to introduce wood and earth. Add a tabletop fountain to introduce more water. Add a chrome wind chime with a wooden clapper to introduce more metal and wood. Add ceramic tableware painted in yellows and blues to introduce the earth and water. Paint the walls yellow and cream tones to introduce more earth (Mitchell, 2002, p. 53).

No house, office, or garden has perfect Chi. Square or angular columns, ceiling beans, ceiling fans, and sharp corners are like poison arrows that need to be deflected by reflecting the bad energy with mirrors, plants or crystals. Make sure the front entry is attractive and functional. Brighten dark areas (which hold negative or under-activated energy) by adding light. Hang wind chimes in doors and hallways to slow down positive energy. Position your bed so that anyone lying there can have a view of the entire room and the door but not be in a direct path with the door. Keep doors to bathrooms closed (and the lid on the toilet) to prevent positive Chi from flowing down the drain. Use mirrors, crystals, and lighting to correct for portions of the Bagua that are miss-ing from your floor plan. More about cures is included in the next cell (Mitchell, 2002, pp. 75-89).

Light and brighten dark areas with cut glass and clean mirrors. Raise the energy of any space with pleasant music, bells, and wind chimes. Incorporate living things into your living area, especially fish and plants with lard round or oval leaves. Avoid using plants with thorns and plants with pointed leaves. Use heavy objects such as stones, fountains, or statues to anchor the Chi. Use more of the associated color with each zone in the Bagua to increase its positive effect. More importantly, use colors you enjoy. Consider how red uplifts, pink softens, purple enhances spirituality, orange enhances creativity, yellow lifts and brightens your mood and energy, green soothes, heals, and cools, brown relaxes; black evokes power; and white enhances spiritual attunement (Mitchell, 2002, pp. (92-97).

Do not worry if your home does not perfectly correlate with the Bagua. Since some feng shui schools require the bottom of the Bagua to face the South and other do not, let us not burden ourselves with particulars to the point of not using the Bagua as a general tool that encourages a systematic evaluation of ways to enhance energy in the various zones of your life—even if your floor plan is not perfectly aligned with the Bagua. Just be sure to bring in more colors in the life areas and enhance the Chi as the Bagua suggests, without undue concern if your kitchen seems to be in the Children and Creativity zone or your bathroom is in the Fame and Reputation zone. Life zone improvements can happen in any room or part of your garden. If your garage, for example, corresponds to the Marriage and Relationships zone on the Bagua (and you cannot see the association) just make some changes as prescribed on the Bagua, such as making vases and ceramic visible in the garage, or highlighting the color pink somewhere in your garage. Don't let the lack of explanations or your skepticism prevent you from trying out the recommended changes, just to see what happens, if anything. You will likely be positively surprised.

Follow-up Protocol

For best results, write down your impressions of this activity in your journal using the Heartwood Path Follow-up Protocol found in the Appendix. Afterwards, consider sharing your interpretations with others.

Heartwood Path Axioms

Key Assertions From Waypoint 3.79

3.79.1.

Creating a positive space for living is a way to prevent unnecessary suffering.

3.79.2.

Unnecessary suffering can also be diverted by taking heed of the arrangement of things around you through the application of the ancient Chinese method known as Feng Shui.

3.79.3.

Feng Shui enhances positive energy in one's environment through the proper arrangement of valuables, awards, pottery, photography, spiritual objects and plants.

Nocturnal Pilgrimage 3.79

For best results, write down your impressions of each night's dreams in your journal using the Heartwood Path Dreaming Time Protocols found in the Appendix. Afterwards, consider sharing your Dream Tending with others.

Use your imagination for creating your Dream Council figures. I personally like to incorporate natural objects/beings to represent my Dream Council Members. I collect small, flat, rounded, easily stackable stones, stack them into little cairns (piles of rocks often used for ceremonial purposes) or I make flat, mandala-like designs out of them. Just as I would new attendees of a meeting or workshop, I make a map of my Dream Council, with names of each figure, so I can distinguish each participating Dream Council Member. Begin making your Dream Council figures. The next step is to decide where to place them in your home. To help with this decision, look over the Bagua and Feng Shui material, presented earlier. To me, the lower left section of the Bagua seems most suitable for placement of Dream Council figures.

After you have decided where you will place your Dream Council figures in your home, move to the next waypoint: "Discernment." Be sure to take a break from your indoor existence by doing the next activity outdoors, as instructed. When doing so, get off the sidewalk or pavement and onto some grass or natural unimproved earth. That's where nature's tonic will likely be the strongest.

80

Discernment

DISTINGUISH NARCISSISM FROM SELF-CARE

Personal boundaries are rules or guidelines that a person creates to identify safe, reasonable and permissible ways for other people to behave towards them and how they will respond when someone crosses these imaginary lines. When such boundaries are unhealthy there is no space between you and the personal space of another person. Such overlapping of two peoples' personal boundaries is called "enmeshment."

Healthy boundaries foster growth rather than stagnation, intimacy rather than superficiality, and interaction rather than distancing. They also foster bonding rather than bondage, and relationships rather than no relationships.

Healthy boundaries foster self-caring rather than narcissism. Often inappropriately labeled by other people as narcissism, self-caring is a good thing. Self-caring evokes the Authentic Self, narcissism evokes the negative Ego. Self-caring is enlivening. Narcissism is toxic and draining. As we all know, you can go too far with being a narcissist. A sure sign is having so many facelifts you look like you are permanently frightened.

Your Authentic Self sets your boundaries; which, in turn, protects your Authentic Self. This pattern continues until something makes you feel upset, confused or scared and, instead of acting under the influence of your mature Authentic Self, you begin to act like a helpless child. Such "age regression," usually embarrassing and unproductive, can be a blessing if you use it to learn about your Authentic Self and make positive adjustments to your personal boundary. The following activity will help you make the best of this situation.

To Age-appropriate Actions…

HumaNatureConnect Activity

Start-up Protocol
If this is not a day when you prefer to spend time in nature without an agenda, do the Heartwood Path Start-up Protocol found in the Appendix.

Managing Age Regression

For this activity, think about a relationship in your life that is not going well. Admit to yourself that you are age regressing. Take purposeful slow breaths. Say to yourself: "I was hurt before. I am hurt now. I do not want to be hurt anymore. I am going to take a break from this hurtful relationship (for minutes, hours, days, weeks, a lifetime). I can free myself from this pain. I am learning from this age regression. In doing so, I am healing my Authentic Self."

Follow-up Protocol
For best results, write down your impressions of this activity in your journal using the Heartwood Path Follow-up Protocol found in the Appendix. Afterwards, consider sharing your interpretations with others.

Heartwood Path Axioms

Key Assertions From Waypoint 3.80

3.80.1.

Self-caring is enlivening while narcissism is toxic and draining.

3.80.2.

Acting like a helpless child, while embarrassing, can help one learn about one's Authentic Self and make positive adjustments to one's personal boundaries.

3.80.3.

Healthy boundaries foster growth rather than stagnation, intimacy rather than superficiality, and interaction rather than distancing.

3.80.4.

Healthy boundaries foster bonding rather than bondage, and relationships rather than no relationships.

Nocturnal Pilgrimage 3.80

For best results, write down your impressions of each night's dreams in your journal using the Heartwood Path Dreaming Time Protocols found in the Appendix. Afterwards, consider sharing your Dream Tending with others.

Continue to look for Dream Council participants in your dreams and in your dream journal. If you already have candidates, make the figures. Give them some sort of name and create a way to remember each name so you can distinguish them later. I do not like to look at name tags so I create a Dream Council seating chart, complete with the individual names of each Dream Figure/Council Member.

When ready, move to the next waypoint: "Mining For Gold." Before you do the next activity, go outside and spend some time in nature with no apparent purpose in mind. Doing so could result in some fruitful or interesting experiences in nature. Note how, if at all, having nothing to do in nature changes you. Repeat this activity often as a way to avoid thinking of nature as your own personal hospital or psyche lab.

81

Mining For Gold

GIVE BLESSINGS TO OTHERS

One gets what one gives. If one projects pain on to others, one gets back even more pain. If one extends love to others one gets more love in return. Benefiting from this "golden rule" would be easy if all the gold was on the surface. But, since so much of the gold in your Authentic Self is buried in your unconscious mind, you need to learn how to mine for it.

In any of the practices for revealing the Authentic Self (listed in the following activity) make sure you have a safe and supportive environment, including people who will accept your expressions without invalidating them. When the gold of your Authentic Self is pulled out of the mine of your unconscious mind, your expressions will likely be more elaborate and varied than the standard miner's call of "Eureka!" When the smoke clears, that too will be an apt expression.

Much of the preceding discussion has to do with recovery from pain, loss, or traumas. To work on such recovery, learn how to:

1. live often from your Realm of Interiority;
2. grieve, thus becoming free from chronic pain;
3. overcome age regression;

4. tolerate emotional pain, so you can stay with the current discomfort long enough to receive assistance from safe others and learn from the suffering;

5. get your needs met, by experiencing your life in relation to yourself, to safe others, and to a higher power; and

6. identify and rectify core issues—those which come up repeatedly, such as fear of abandonment, control issues, trust issues, being inauthentic, and incessantly engaging in all-or-nothing thinking.

It does not take long for one to begin the process of becoming codependent or wounded. It begins with the initial feeling of separation from the Source—that Source being God, a higher power, the Absolute Spirit, or all that is. While one is never truly separate from whatever you call the Absolute Spirit, it usually does not take long to feel like one has become alienated from one's Source. One is born into a family that does not meet all of one's needs. One begins to fear abandonment, one begins to feel like one does not matter, one idealizes parents to survive, one allows the False Self to run one's life, one distorts personal boundaries, one stunts one's personal development, and one begins to feel out of control. After a period of emptiness and frustration, one begins to feel stress and fear; one blocks grief (such blocking can lead to depression); and one may suffer from addictions, eating disorders, and physical illnesses.

Recovery begins as one becomes frustrated with repeated crises. Recovery continues as hope increases and as one admits to powerlessness in the face of the troubles. Then, the process of recovery goes on as one learns to set healthy boundaries, as one becomes properly assertive, as one discovers the child within, as one learns to grieve, as one becomes less tolerant of inappropriate behavior (by oneself and others), as one deepens spiritual practices, as one learns that the core of one's being is Love, as one enters into selfless service, and as one finds serenity.

As an individual, you have the right to: have numerous choices; to grieve; to develop and follow your own values and standards; to say "no;" to have needs and wants respected by others; to expect honesty; to own your own feelings; to be playful, relaxed and jovial; to change your mind; to change and grow; to live in a un-abusive and healthy environment; to trust others; and to give and receive unconditional love.

Along with feeling the need to have such rights fulfilled, eventually many people develop the need to have the direct experience of The Absolute. Those who have this need tend to not be fulfilled by a definition of The Absolute or God that limits It or Him to a divine being located solely "out there" or only up in Heaven. They search within for The Absolute. Sometimes they find God or divinity itself in the connections of one's relationships or in the psycho-spiritual space between themselves and others—where "I" and "Thou" meet.

This approach to spirituality goes beyond individualism (the main topic of this book) and collectivism (the main topic of the next Heartwood Path book). Eventually, go beyond the topic of the next book to understand how boundaries are bonding; and how when two people bond sexually, spiritually, and in a heartfelt manner they open up to each other without losing themselves as individuals. Go beyond Heartwood Path Book Five: **Ethos** to discover how to bring about the Authentic Self and enroll in the Heartwood Path for Groups book (the sixth in the series, entitled **Collectivos**) to bring about an authentic community. By the end of the Heartwood Path for Groups book, the reader will understand that The Absolute is both immanent in I-Thou Relationships and has an infinite and transcendent presence.

Through everyday contact with The Absolute (one's own Immanent and Transcendent God) one lives a life of immediate contact and connection. One lives a life that is intimate and united but not enmeshed or fused. Both closeness and separation are tolerable and healthy. Everyday contact with God or the Absolute unearths the Authentic Self, expands one's perspective, and allows for a wider range of incoming information.

To bring unconscious gold from the depths of your unconscious mind, engage in the following activity.

To The Gold Strike That Is You...

HumaNatureConnect Activity

Start-up Protocol

If this is not a day when you prefer to spend time in nature without an agenda, do the Heartwood Path Start-up Protocol found in the Appendix.

Mining For The Gold Of Your Authentic Self Deep Within The Unconscious Mind

For this activity, consider ways you would possibly benefit from each of the following (if you need more information about any of the following, resolve to make any necessary inquiries): risking, sharing, telling your own story, working on retrieving the pain you project onto others, psychodrama, attending self-help meetings, affirmations, breath work, guided imagery, eye-movement therapy, couples therapy, group therapy, art therapy, play therapy, movement therapy, prayer, meditation, journaling, writing un-mailed letters, and reading.

Follow-up Protocol

For best results, write down your impressions of this activity in your journal using the Heartwood Path Follow-up Protocol found in the Appendix. Afterwards, consider sharing your interpretations with others.

Heartwood Path Axioms

Key Assertions From Waypoint 3.81

3.81.1.

One gets what one gives.

3.81.2.

To recover from pain, loss, or traumas learn how to: 1) grieve, 2) overcome age regression; 3) tolerate emotional pain; 4) get your needs met, and 5) identify and rectify core issues—those which come up repeatedly, such as fear of abandonment, loss of control, loss of trust, being authentic, and engaging in all-or-nothing thinking.

3.81.3.

Recovery begins as one becomes frustrated with repeated crises and continues as one enters into selfless service and as one finds serenity.

3.81.4.

You have the right to have numerous choices, to live in a nurturing and healthy environment, to trust others, and to give and receive unconditional love.

3.81.5.

Both closeness and separation are tolerable and healthy.

Nocturnal Pilgrimage 3.81

For best results, write down your impressions of each night's dreams in your journal using the Heartwood Path Dreaming Time Protocols found in the Appendix. Afterwards, consider sharing your Dream Tending with others.

Locate a place in your home that will serve as the Temenos, or sacred space, for your Dream Council. This area can be a tabletop, a section of the floor, a shelf, the bottom of a window casing, or part of a counter. It could be the top of a chest or some kind of tray or box. Make this choosing in a playful, intuitive, and intentional way. More on the Dream Council placement decision-making process follows.

As you continue on your way to Gladandgreen Junction—waypoint by waypoint—physically touch the ground by planting your feet on the soil, by sitting on the sand, by laying down on the grass, or by striding across a natural landscape. Be receptive to the unmistakable flow of energy that will occur from the earth to your body. Consider this flow to be the encouragement and reassurance you will receive as you make contact with the earth as an attractive natural being. Ponder how the earth supports every one of us in ways no other surface can.

Expand your perspective by visiting the next Heartwood Path waypoint: "Highest View." There you will learn more about the typical worldview of EartHearts.

82

Highest View

ADOPT THE WORLDVIEW OF AN EARTHEART

See the world with a broad and penetrating perspective. From the subjective point of view, an eartHeart's cultural worldview needs to seek the greatest good. His or her intentions need to always be to seek to realize, protect, and restore the beauty of the Kosmos. From an empirical, objective point of view, eartHearts need to always seek the greatest depth of truth.

EartHearts seek the integration of mind, nature and culture by encouraging a shift from the present way of knowing—which is focused primarily on the objective observation of the surfaces of things—to an increased use of interpretation through dialogue to reveal more about the two realms of subjective, interior depth: namely, the realm of intentions and the realm of moral/ethics.

This last realm is the world where environmental ethics can and need to be interpreted. These ethics generally come in four sorts:

1. bio-equality (all living holons—things that are both parts and wholes—have equal value, worms are equal to apes, for example);

2. animal rights (all holons are not equal, value is determined by the possession of rudimentary feelings, depending on whether an animal can feel sensations);

3. hierarchical (each more complex living entity posses more rights, humans having the most rights but not the right to plunder other living things which also have basic rights); and

4. stewardship (humans alone have rights, but humans also have the responsibility to care for the Earth and its living inhabitants).

All of these schools of environmental ethics have to do with value which, in turn, also comes in sorts:

1. ground value (all holons are perfect manifestations of Emptiness or Spirit);

2. intrinsic value (value is determined by the level of depth intrinsic to the entity); and

3. extrinsic (value is determine by the number of other holons dependent on the entity; for example, an atom has more extrinsic value than a horse because if you destroy all horses less of the universe would be affected than if you destroyed all atoms).

To The Fourteenth Of Many Touchstones Of People-Nature Inter-facing...

HumaNatureConnect Activity

Start-up Protocol

If this is not a day when you prefer to spend time in nature without an agenda, do the Heartwood Path Start-up Protocol found in the Appendix.

Generating Patterns Of Human-Nature Interaction # 13:

Riding On An Animal

For this activity, imagine riding on an animal after you feel connected to your chosen attractive natural being. In doing this interaction pattern, you could think about riding an orca (killer whale) in an aquarium show (a perverse interaction pattern) or you could think about riding a horse on a ranch (a domestic interaction pattern). By choosing instead to think about riding a camel to explore a pristine desert (a wild interaction), you would be doing something that will have a positive psychological affect on you.

In your journal, write down what meaning you would derive from this wild interaction pattern (either doing it or imagining doing it); what joy, if any, it would produce; how, if at all, it would build within you a bond between your mind and nature; and how, if at all, the wild version of this interaction pattern would be better for you than the perverse or domestic instantiation of the same interaction pattern; and how not being allowed to participate in this sort of wild interaction pattern—riding a camel in a pristine desert—would make you feel? How does interacting in this way in the presence of your attractive natural being make you feel? How would it feel to have this interaction without the presence of your attractive natural being? In writing down these responses you will be adding to our collective nature language, so important to rekindling the bond between humans and nature. Look over your impressions and think about them as you fall asleep tonight before dreaming.

Follow-up Protocol

For best results, write down your impressions of this activity in your journal using the Heartwood Path Follow-up Protocol found in the Appendix. Afterwards, consider sharing your interpretations with others.

Heartwood Path Axioms

Key Assertions From Waypoint 3.82

3.82.1.

See the world with a broad and penetrating perspective: from the subjective point of view, an eartHeart's cultural worldview needs to seek the greatest good; his or her intentions need to always be to seek to realize, protect, and to restore the beauty of the Kosmos.

3.82.2.

EartHearts seek the integration of mind, nature and culture by encouraging a shift from the present way of knowing—which is focused primarily on the objective observation of the surfaces of things—to an increased use of interpretation through dialogue to reveal more about the two realms of subjective, interior depth: namely, the realm of intentions and the realm of moral/ethics.

3.82.3.

Ethics generally come in four sorts: 1) bio-equality, 2) animal rights, 3) hierarchical, and 4) stewardship.

3.82.4.

All schools of environmental ethics have to do with value which comes in three sorts: 1) ground value, 2) intrinsic value, and 3) extrinsic value.

Nocturnal Pilgrimage 3.82

For best results, write down your impressions of each night's dreams in your journal using the Heartwood Path Dreaming Time Protocols found in the Appendix. Afterwards, consider sharing your Dream Tending with others.

In deciding on a place for your Dream Council figures, follow your gut, with the following caveats: 1) the area ought to be away from heavy traffic, 2) pick an uncluttered space, 3) choose a space that is protected from disturbance over time, 4) decorate the space with candles or incense, 5) if disturbance is an issue, place the figure in some sort of special container.

With this knowledge, move to the next learning station. This and every other waypoint unfolds outside in nature. Something important happens when one touches the earth outside. Do not stay indoors long after you read the Heartwood Path text. Go outside. Feel your weight pressing down firmly on the undeveloped earth. Think about how the sensation of gravity outdoors evokes a feeling of security and how indoors the pull of gravity is simply not as satisfying.

When ready, move to the next waypoint: "Coverage." There, you will learn to appreciate both depth and span.

83

Coverage

PRESERVE AND APPRECIATE
BOTH DEPTH AND SPAN

The basic lesson of environmental ethics and values is that the vital needs of humans will be best served if we consume or destroy as little depth as possible. This simultaneously means doing as little harm to consciousness as possible and doing as little harm to the exterior environment as possible. This also means doing as little harm to intrinsic worth as possible. In a more positive tone, I offer the following key point: eartHearts encourage us all to preserve and enjoy the greatest amount of depth for the greatest amount of span.

Depth refers to the level of development: from Sprit to the physiosphere to the biosphere to the noosphere to the theosphere. Span refers to the number of entities at any given level of depth.

There are two reasons why eartHearts try to encourage both greater depth and the movement of attention to interior realms:

1. it will require a higher level of thinking to correct problems caused by thinking at a lower level of depth; and
2. considerations too often center on the exterior quadrants of behavior and systems (as represented on the right side of the Four

Leaf Cover Of Integrity) rather than the interior quadrants of intentions and values (on the left side).

Fortunately, we humans do not have to overcome cosmic inertia in our work to preserve and perfect both span and depth. The telos of the Kosmos—its inherent drive—can help eartHearts encourage greater depth (and thus more perfection) and, therefore, have a greater capacity to help preserve the environment. This cosmic drive nudges everything up an imaginary ladder (in our case we are using the metaphor of Jack's beanstalk) of increasing depth, leading to an expanded awareness.

This expanded awareness is very vital to the work of eartHearts. Since expanding awareness is an evolutionary process, the procedure is always to transcend and include. The result is greater depth (higher branches) and greater levels of consciousness capable of awareness expanded to include more of the Kosmos. Unfortunately, this incorporation of greater depth means that problems often occur. As the telos of the Kosmos—the universe's inherent drive to add depth to itself—nudges humans up the beanstalk to higher consciousness, parts of one's personhood is sometimes left behind on lower branches. Overcoming this untenable and unstable teetering between branches is a big part of the job of seeking perfection. One becomes more perfect—as we are describing perfect (that is, being whole, having integrity)—when one expands one's consciousness.

Expanded consciousness occurs in three steps:

1. the Self becomes aware of the level of consciousness it has at its disposal;
2. the Self begins to dis-identify or differentiate with its present consciousness level and can move beyond it, usually to the next level of depth; and
3. the Self includes and integrates itself to its new level.

When all works well, after climbing up the Beanstalk of Spiritual Growth, one is left with either greatness or saintliness or both. When incorporation of greater depth fails, one becomes, at best, mediocre or, at worst, a monster.

At each of the branches of consciousness there is a different type of Self-identity, a different type of Self-need, and a different type of moral stance. Adopting a fixed label of one's Self-identity, one's Self-needs, and one's moral stance is problematic because the process of moving up branches of development is almost never complete.

No Self is ever totally at one branch of consciousness development. Different aspects of the Self may leap forward or regress. Nevertheless, the Self does have a center of gravity that places it primary at one branch or another. Thus, so-called peak experiences are temporary "peeks" at higher stages of consciousness; but these are temporary states rather than permanent traits because one's center of gravity (one's enduring stage of development) pulls the consciousness down or up.

This description of levels of consciousness is important to eartHearts working to awaken themselves or any other person to their inherent wholeness because at times people might have aspects of their selves that are developed at higher levels but other aspects lingering behind at lower levels. Brilliant environmentalists without morals and moral environmentalists without self-motivation are but two examples. A person is a fully developed eartHeart when he or she has integrated the body, mind, and Spirit, using advanced powers of love, knowledge and the Will, to become Beautiful, Good, and True for the purpose of preserving and restoring the Greater Self which includes the "part-ness" of a holon seen as the individual ego/body and the "wholeness" of the holon which is the Earth or the universe.

With all of this development going on for them it is easy to see why eartHearts become so vital. Burnout is not a problem. Direction is a given. They are fully capable of leading the way to the New World of Environmental Sustainability. By example and deed, they encourage a greater emphasis on intentions and ethics, thus correcting the overemphasis on behaviors and physical systems. They have found a balance for themselves, and have the vitality, skill, and direction to encourage willing others to achieve their own highest level of development and balance.

EartHearts achieve this high level of development and balance by dealing with their inner world Addict and Blisshead Sub-personalities in the following ways:

1. Recognizing their former dependence on inner world Addicts and Blissheads.
2. Abstaining from addictions and patterns of escape.
3. Relying more on Spirit and the Soul.
4. Working the very things the Addicts and Blissheads have been helping them avoid; namely, their emotions, memories, and realities.
5. As is customary with all dealings with Sub-personalities, thanking them for their service.
6. Offering old addictive or escapist routines with healthy habits of presence, mature action, and encounters with Self. And
7. Looking behind patterns of addiction and escape for deep longings and acting on them.

Here is an activity that will provide you with another way to appropriately deal with your inner world Addict and Blisshead Sub-personalities—those aspects of our personalities that lead us to fleeting, inappropriate, or ineffective ways of being.

To Avoid Emotional Or Physical Pain...

HumaNatureConnect Activity

Start-up Protocol

If this is not a day when you prefer to spend time in nature without an agenda, do the Heartwood Path Start-up Protocol found in the Appendix.

Dealing With Your Addict And Blisshead Sub-personalities

This activity is adapted from an exercise developed by Bill Plotkin. Note the similarities and differences of his approach with Dr. Cohen's NatureConnect approach when he says to go "out and wander in a wild or semi-wild place until you come across a place or a nonhuman thing with which you can fall utterly in love." And when he says. "Once you find a natural being in a natural setting, sit there. Out loud, praise that place or thing, letting it know the ways it allures you" (2013, p. 198).

Plotkin suggests that you engage in a "fearless review" of the addictions and escapes that are still used by your Sub-personalities and "identify under which life circumstances they seem to be most active . . . and what draws you to these particular strategies . . . Then let him know that you . . . are choosing to be utterly present to the world because it's made of countless beguiling mysteries and numinous miracles . . ." (Plotkin, 2013, pp. 198-199). Do these things and then heed the Follow-up Protocol.

Follow-up Protocol

For best results, write down your impressions of this activity in your journal using the Heartwood Path Follow-up Protocol found in the Appendix. Afterwards, consider sharing your interpretations with others.

Heartwood Path Axioms

Key Assertions From Waypoint 3.83

3.83.1.

EartHearts encourage us all to preserve the greatest amount of depth (the level of development: from Sprit to the physiosphere to the biosphere to the noosphere to the theosphere)for the greatest amount of span (the number of entities at any given level of depth).

3.83.2.

One becomes more perfect—as we are describing perfect (that is, being whole, having integrity)—when one expands one's consciousness.

3.83.3.

Expanded consciousness occurs in three steps: 1) the Self becomes aware of the level of consciousness it has at its disposal; 2) the Self begins to dis-identify or differentiate with its present consciousness level and can move beyond it, usually to the next level of depth, and 3) the Self includes and integrates itself to its new level.

3.83.4.

A person is a fully developed eartHeart when he or she has integrated the body, mind, and Spirit, using advanced powers of love, knowledge and the Will, to become Beautiful, Good, and True for the purpose of preserving and restoring the Greater Self which includes the "part-ness" of a holon seen as the individual ego/body and the "wholeness" of the holon which is the Earth or the universe.

3.83.5.

EartHearts find balance for themselves, and have the vitality, skill, and direction to encourage others to achieve their own highest level of development and balance.

Nocturnal Pilgrimage 3.83

For best results, write down your impressions of each night's dreams in your journal using the Heartwood Path Dreaming Time Protocols found in the Appendix. Afterwards, consider sharing your Dream Tending with others.

A Dream Council is no ordinary meeting. Dream Council members engage in deep listening, focus on respecting all participants, and avoid quick reactions. Intelligent comebacks are not expected. Witnessing is more important than oration. The Dream Council figures are to be encouraged to speak on their own behalf, not ours. We will practice deep listening in the next Dream Activity. At your next opportunity, ask your chosen attractive natural being for guidance about the placement of your Dream Council Figures (your handmade committee that helps you tend to your dreams) in your home or garden and for the commencement of the First Dream Council. This meeting ought to be undertaken with an attitude of ritual. It ought to be given adequate time and space. It ought to be a secluded spot, far from the distractions of others, away from the noise of the television, and separated from the intrusion of the telephone. When starting the Dream Council you are reentering the dream world mindfully. In essence, the practice of Dream Council is to live in two worlds: the dreaming world and the waking world. This dual life allows for the development of the wisdom of our archetypal Ego. Palpably feel how the Dream Council engages your intuition and dreamlike knowing. When placing the figures, think about them and you, and how all will want to interact. You are not building a separate oracle. You are developing a tool for the expression of your More-Than-Individual inner world. Start by placing your figures in a semicircle and then rearrange them until the alignment feels right. Allow the figures to participate in their assigned locations and on the development of the agenda for the Council meeting. Determine what you are feeling about creating your first Dream Council. How are you feeling emotionally? How has your awareness changed? Do any of the Council members seem to be coming to life?

Be sure to answer these questions and write your responses in your journal. With good journaling, the interplay between your Heartwood Path waking activities and your Heartwood Path dreaming time activities is giving you an uncommon perspective, one that will be most useful as you develop into an eartHeart or a professional nature-centered life coach, or simply a happy person.

Make Your Dreams Come True

To make sure that you are getting the most from your dreams, follow the most common way to have a lucid dream. Before falling asleep, set an alarm to wake you up after your light sleep and deep sleep periods are over. Most people set there alarm for six hours after they fall asleep. When your alarm goes off, use the period we have been calling "The Watch" to incubate a certain dream. Also establish a sign within your dreams that lets you know it is time to ask the Question: "Am I dreaming?" The ways we have been telling you to initiate a lucid dream will work better after the six hours of light and deep sleep are behind you. Without delaying the prompting for lucid dreaming, your reminders would have to be held in your mind for hours, during which time they may fade away or fall victim to inner world distractions.

You are progressing well. Keep it going. Tend to your dreams. Keep going outside to let nature work its magic on you. And keep doing the activities.

After setting up and thinking about your Dream Council, move to the next waypoint: "From 'Me' To 'Us All.'" There, you will learn about transcending into super-consciousness.

84

From "Me" To "Us All"

DESPITE THE RISKS, TRANSCEND FROM INDIVIDUAL CONSCIOUSNESS TO COLLECTIVE SUPER CONSCIOUSNESS

Moving up the branches of depth/development has its risks. Each time one moves up another branch, there is more that can go wrong because more is included in the Self. The greater the depth of psycho-spiritual development, the greater the burden a person has to endure because more layers of depth need to be incorporated into the Self, need to be honored, and need to be expressed. As one develops spiritually, The Self becomes layered by wider circles of beings that have to be considered, respected, and accommodated. As one begins to embrace more of the universe into the Self, greater numbers of cherished beings can fall through any cracks that may exist in one's development. As a result, extra education is necessary at each level as people transform themselves as they move up the metaphorical beanstalk branches of spiritual formation.

Since essentially everyone has some area of their psycho-spiritual and physical development blocked at lower stages, it is vital to the effort of performing the Great Work! to increase the number of people consciously trying to increase their development. With more people seeking to become "perfect" (by having integrity and wholeness) the chances for success will go up. Only with greater numbers of people (span) achieving greater physical prowess and an expansion of consciousness (greater depth) will the effort to preserve the Earth be successful. For this reason, it is imperative that eartHearts work to encourage others to follow the Heartwood Path or other effective means to preserve the Earth.

The same progression that occurs when atoms turn into molecules that turn into cells that turn into organisms that turn into ecosystems needs to occur within the interior of the human domain—within human consciousness. There being nothing spooky about this, one needs to naturally transcend from individual consciousness to collective super consciousness by balancing intentions, ethics, behaviors, and physical systems as one climbs the Beanstalk of Spiritual Development.

To A Meeting With Your Dream Council—Your Handmade Dream Figures That Serve As A Mastermind Group (Wise, Cherished Advisors)...

HumaNatureConnect Activity

Start-up Protocol

If this is not a day when you prefer to spend time in nature without an agenda, do the Heartwood Path Start-up Protocol found in the Appendix.

Interacting With Your Dream Council

For this activity, go to the setting for the Dream Council, sit with your Council, slow down your mind, and begin to "listen" deeply. Within the definition of listening, in this case, is seeing, touching, smelling, tasting, and using the other natural senses. This listening is like when you paused to listen to your child tell of its day or when you listen to the birds in your backyard. As you continue to listen, the Dream Figures will become animated and grow in complexity. Sit at the perimeter of the Council group and then enter it. See one of your recalled dreams as if with the eyes of any one of the Dream Figures. Experience your chosen dream through its eyes. Note how you feel. Note what you learn. Note what any Dream Figure has to say. Note how your awareness changes.

Follow-up Protocol

For best results, write down your impressions of this activity in your journal using the Heartwood Path Follow-up Protocol found in the Appendix. Afterwards, consider sharing your interpretations with others.

Heartwood Path Axioms

Key Assertions From Waypoint 3.84

3.84.1.

Moving up the branches of depth/development has its risks because each time one moves up another branch there is more included in the Self and so more can go wrong.

3.84.2.

Only with greater numbers of people (span) achieving greater physical prowess and an expansion of consciousness (greater depth) will the effort to preserve the Earth be successful.

3.84.3.

**One needs to naturally transcend from individual conscious-
ness to collective super consciousness by balancing intentions,
ethics, behaviors, and physical systems as one climbs the Beanstalk of Spiritual Development.**

Nocturnal Pilgrimage 3.84

For best results, write down your impressions of each night's
dreams in your journal using the Heartwood Path Dreaming Time
Protocols found in the Appendix. Afterwards, consider sharing your
Dream Tending with others.

Whenever you feel the need, bring your concerns, problems, bad
feelings, and questions before your Dream Council. Doing so will help
you see things with a new perspective. It will help you gain confidence.
You will be guided and comforted. The Council is not really just about
finding answers. It is also an experience of deep belonging with your
Dream Characters. Use your Dream Council to feel reconnected to
your dream tribe. It is important to recall the dreaming time when
engaging your Dream Council figures. To get there, before engaging,
do the previously-outlined steps of the Dream Council Protocol: make
your Figures, place your Figures, choose your Dream Images to be the
topic of conversation, and listen deeply. I prefer my simple flat-stone
cairns as Dream Council members because I can move them easily.
Keep them outside in the fresh air. More often than not, I carry them
into the wild so that I can go through the steps again and, in so doing,
reenter the dreaming time. I also include a freshly chosen, attractive
natural being to augment the Dream Council by guiding its meeting
and, when asked, to offer the perspective of an amateur that exists in
the perpetual Now.

Whether carrying back a new Dream Council member or just aim-
less walking through nature, I often wear water shoes with no socks.

That way I can feel the water as I cross creeks or walk along the ocean. Without socks, it is easy to remove my shoes and feel the earth directly on the bottom of my feet. Safety demands that you leave your shoes on when walking into nature to find your attractive natural being, as you will be asked to do in the next activity. But, as soon as you deem it to be safe, remove your shoes and socks and feel the earth directly with your feet. Feel the temperatures and textures. Absorb the tonic of nature directly. Doing so seems to help me to sleep and have lucid dreams.

After tending to your dreams, continue to the next waypoint: "Dream Council." There, you will discover how I first learned about the increasing levels of complexity beyond the individual self.

85

Dream Council

MAKE A COMPLETE TRANSPERSONAL DEFINITION OF YOUR SELF

A revelation I once had in a backwater area along the Missouri River helped me make a more clear and complete transpersonal definition of the Self. In my canoe, I paddled off the main channel into the quiet water behind an island. Watching for birds, I slowly drifted into a perfectly still, shallow pool. A gentle breeze made scampering miniature ripples across the surface of the water. A kingfisher swooped down to pick up a minnow from just beneath the water. Leaves fell on the pool and then the leaves became a miniature armada sailing in the same direction as the scampering wind ripples. I thought of that pool as a "being," an "individual" Self just like myself. Different things happen to both of us, yet whatever happens to us occurs to a being that is called the "Self."

My own life was reflected in that pool. I thought of myself as a kind of pool of energy which can be thought of as "separated" from all other things, processes, and pools of energy in all realms of reality—physical and nonphysical. Even though it is possible to think of the pool and myself as separate entities, all entities are joined to others in ways too numerous and complex to comprehend. Just as wind, birds, and leaves touched the pool of water my own Self can catalogue many different thoughts, feelings, sensations, ideas, and other experiences. That pool gave my own consciousness a more complex notion of the Self. It "told" me that "selfdom" was not confined to the individual. Beyond the level of the individual self are ever-increasing stages of complexity. Just as one can develop to become conscious of the individual self, so too is it possible to develop in ways to be conscious of the More-Than-Individual-Self.

To See What Your Dreams Are Trying To Tell You About Your Individual Self And Your Kosmic Self…

HumaNatureConnect Activity

Start-up Protocol

If this is not a day when you prefer to spend time in nature without an agenda, do the Heartwood Path Start-up Protocol found in the Appendix.

Engaging The Dream Council And Employ A Dream Council Sentry

Ask your Dream Council and its Sentry whether there is anything in your dreams that indicate your relationship with your individual self and your Kosmic Self.

Follow-up Protocol

For best results, write down your impressions of this activity in your journal using the Heartwood Path Follow-up Protocol found in the Appendix. Afterwards, consider sharing your interpretations with others.

Heartwood Path Axioms

Key Assertions From Waypoint 3.85

3.85.1.

"Selfdom" was not confined to the individual.

3.85.2.

Beyond the level of the individual self are ever-increasing stages of complexity.

3.85.3.

Just as one can develop to become conscious of the individual self, so too is it possible to develop in ways to be conscious of the More-Than-Individual-Self.

Nocturnal Pilgrimage 3.85

For best results, write down your impressions of each night's dreams in your journal using the Heartwood Path Dreaming Time Protocols found in the Appendix. Afterwards, consider sharing your Dream Tending with others.

I cannot stress enough the importance of creating a special hand-made figure—called the Dream Council Sentry—and adding this figure to your Dream Council. The Dream Council Sentry serves as the host. It guards the proceedings. When asked, she offers the fruitful perspective of the idealistic amateur. I cannot count how many time in my life when I witnessed the idealistic amateur, not knowing how hard things can get, going ahead and doing the impossible. Had these amateurs known what they were getting into, numerous successful campaigns would have never started. Always listen to the advice of your helpful Dream Council Sentry. Its amateur advice helps to keep you from becoming jaded by your own experience, by your own knowledge of how hard the road will be, and by your fatigued willingness to give up before you start.

Most Heartwood Path waypoints end with two reminders: 1) to go again into nature and 2) to tend to your dreams. Here's a little more advice for each of these suggestions:

1. When asked to share space with an attractive natural being, linger for a while. Stop, stand, sit, or lie down. Look for other animals nearby as you remain still. Do not miss this opportunity to witness unobtrusive plants, and tiny inconspicuous flowers, and any other discreet fellow living beings that would remain beyond your awareness had you not slowed down.

2. When you ask "Am I dreaming?" before you answer look around to see if your setting is familiar or both familiar and strange. If it is completely out of your experience or familiar but strange, you are dreaming. "Strange" would be things like being able to poke your finger through your palm, or jumping up but slowly floating back down, or texts and clocks changing after a first glance.

With an appreciation of the importance of including a Sentry in your Dream Council, plus the advice about unobtrusive Natural Beings and ways to identify that you are dreaming, you are ready to continue your odyssey down the Heartwood Path by moving to the next waypoint: "Wisdom." There you will learn the importance of reducing judgments, restricting trivial notions, and avoiding group think.

86

Wisdom

REDUCE JUDGMENTS, TRIVIAL NOTIONS, AND GROUP THINK

The most noticeable thoughts come from the inner loud voice of judgment. One needs to lower this voice to allow for greater creativity.

The initial work an individual needs to do to affect the whole (the beginning work one person needs to do to preserve the Earth or remake the world, for example) is to increase awareness. One's own awareness is likely to be too often covered by wasted and trivial notions, judgments and groupthink (following the herd blindly).

Clarity of awareness is also clouded by the fact that one does not see the world as it is but rather as one is (and was). To counter this overwhelming distraction, focus on changing what is inside rather than on just what is seen as separate from you on the outside.

And do not minimize the importance of listening, for that is when you learn. Speaking is for sharing what you have already learned.

To Dream Council Adjournment...

HumaNatureConnect Activity

Start-up Protocol

If this is not a day when you prefer to spend time in nature without an agenda, do the Heartwood Path Start-up Protocol found in the Appendix.

Closing The Dream Council

For this activity, practice closing your Dream Council sessions. It is important to properly close the Dream Council sessions to insure that you do not end up feeling like you are in a state of suspended ambiguity —neither in the inner world nor in the outer world. To close a Council, look at each member, one at a time, and thank it for its participation. You can either leave your Dream Council members where they are, move them to their storage place, or respectfully dismantle ones you do not plan to use again. Give the whole Council one more look of gratitude as a whole before ending. Notice how you feel. Notice if your awareness has changed.

Follow-up Protocol

For best results, write down your impressions of this activity in your journal using the Heartwood Path Follow-up Protocol found in the Appendix. Afterwards, consider sharing your interpretations with others.

Heartwood Path Axioms

Key Assertions From Waypoint 3.86

3.86.1.

One needs to lower the inner loud voice of judgement to allow for greater creativity.

3.86.2.

The initial work an individual needs to do to affect the whole (the beginning work one person needs to do to preserve the Earth or remake the world, for example) is to increase awareness.

3.86.3.

One's own awareness is likely to be too often covered by wasted and trivial notions, judgments and groupthink (following the herd blindly).

3.86.4.

Clarity of awareness is also clouded by the fact that one does not see the world as it is but rather as one is (and was).

3.86.5.

Focus on changing what is inside rather than on just what is seen as separate from you on the outside.

Nocturnal Pilgrimage 3.86

For best results, write down your impressions of each night's dreams in your journal using the Heartwood Path Dreaming Time Protocols found in the Appendix. Afterwards, consider sharing your Dream Tending with others.

It is very important to include seemingly negative Dream Figures on one's Dream Council. Doing so creates the opportunity to "make peace with the darkest forces within us" (Aizenstat, 2009, p. 257). One can coax the negativity out of the shadows and into the light where it can be addressed with focus and clarity. Writes Aizenstat: "Better to be in continuous relationship with the horrific than to be blind to its presence" (2009, p. 257).

Fortify yourself to withstand the uncomfortable presence of nightmarish Dream Characters by absorbing the goodness of Natural Beings in nature or in your day dreams. Before or during your next outdoor activity, try meditating in nature. Sit cross-legged or rest your back against a tree or boulder. Be sure to sit still and consciously tune into the Earth. Maintaining this contact will increase your sense of spiritual connection with the Earth, a connection you can use like a shield of protection the next time you encounter Dream Demons.

With this advice, you are now ready to continue on your way to Gladandgreen Junction by moving to the next waypoint: "Crucible." There, you will be encouraged to steep yourself in a cauldron of awareness.

87

Crucible

ENTER THE CAULDRON OF AWARENESS

In this waypoint we are drawing an important distinction between thinking and awareness. We will be providing a way to become more aware and, in so doing, obtain better results. To focus on your awareness, form a sort of mental "container" in your mind wherein you suspend negative, old, habitual, outmoded thoughts. This metaphorical "container," really just a highly focused portion of your mind, will be the cauldron from which your own best awareness arises. We are simply using the metaphor of a cauldron because such a container allows in what you want to allow in—in our case, your awareness of what is going on around and with you—and keeps out what you want to keep out—namely, repetitive mental chatter, judgments, and and unproductive thinking.

Perhaps a personal example will be helpful. Sitting along a trail in the sunlight I notice a patch of poison ivy (poison oak in the West is a similar plant). In my mind, I bring up the mental image of a large cauldron made out of light-weight recycled cardboard (as a way to keep the mental image light in weight). I focus my mind inside the cauldron, where I find my awareness of the poison ivy. But I do not call it "poison ivy, nor do I think about the poison ivy. There is nothing there but my connection experience with the patch of plants. I do not worry about getting an itchy rash later. I do not remember the time I built a tree-house with the intention of keeping out younger kids by having it assessable only by climbing a big "hairy" vine. I do not remember how fantastically itchy I was days later, and how this experience taught me what mature poison ivy vines look like. It is just me being aware of a plant.

To understand what I am suggesting, try out your mental cauldron right now. Perceive something nearby, maybe something on a table or something else wherever you are. Simply create an image of a light-weight cauldron in your mind and, in that container, become aware of something without attaching any thinking to the awareness. No naming of the object, no reminiscing about the object, no worrying about anything. Just pure awareness goes on in your mental cauldron. Your purpose here is to receive information, guidance, and healing from the object of your awareness and not to bury these benefits under a pile of repetitive and unproductive thoughts. Pure awareness becomes easier with practice. And the "cauldron" will help.

In your mind, enter this mental cauldron whenever you wish. It is a way to protect yourself from the considerable disorientation that occurs from that which is outside of the container—one's obsessive thinking, for example. Your awareness of your own individual being and aspects of nature will be clearer from within the cauldron. **This clear awareness is a source of the guidance, information, and healing that you can receive from the object of your awareness.** Read that sentence again. It is very important to your success on the Heartwood Path and in life.

Nothing is physically happening (or nothing ought to be happening) in this cauldron. In this cauldron you become aware without attaching to your fleeting thoughts. This is a cauldron of mental awareness, not physical action and not obsessive thinking. If a thought arises simply let it pass and go back to pure awareness.

The metal cauldron of a witch is full and heavy. The sides of the container are made out of heavy iron metal. Comparatively, the mental cauldron of eartHearts is empty and light. I sometimes picture the mental cauldron of awareness to be made of black painted styrofoam. You will be served well by imagining the cauldron as being light in weight. Its emptiness (lack of thoughts) and lightness can remind you that, both figuratively and actually for all your sacred quests, the lighter your bag the heavier your rewards.

Suspend your old heavily-burdened life and enter into the lightness of the Cauldron of Awareness in order to make way for the first glimpse of new potions, new remedies, new possibilities—the first light of your new life. In doing so, you are upgrading your perspective and, thereby, beginning the Great Work! of remaking the world.

Once you are free of some of your old notions, look within for an intense longing to alleviate suffering. This longing comes from an awakened heart. Finding or cultivating this awakened heart, freeing oneself from the pain of ignorance and unworkable habitual patterns, freeing oneself from individual self-absorption, and helping others do the same so that they may more effectively work to become whole (aware of their perfection) and help to protect the environment are the primary purposes of the Heartwood Path.

Those who say that such a purpose leads to "mission: impossible" are missing the point. They are expressing an attachment to the ends (to the results), which is not recommended. It is the means (working towards wholeness and awareness of perfection) and the not the end (being whole or perfect) that is the focus of this series of books. More importantly, is your best shot at being happy in a beautiful and sustainable world.

There is gold in your awareness and fools gold in your chattering mind. Whenever you begin a new project, keep out largely repetitive and mostly worthless mental chatter by simply being aware of something in your mental cauldron. Good results will follow.

To put the wisdom of this section to work for you, empty yourself of old notions by doing the following activity:

To The Benefits Of Emptiness...

HumaNatureConnect Activity

Start-up Protocol

If this is not a day when you prefer to spend time in nature without an agenda, do the Heartwood Path Start-up Protocol found in the Appendix.

Emptying Yourself Of Old, Unworkable, And Unwanted Notions

For this activity, list five or more self-concepts that you once held that you are now ready to unload. (Examples: I am meant to be fat, I am stupid, I cannot write, I am separate from nature, I am a Republican . . .). Pick aspects of your thinking that will lighten your load, and clear the way to move towards remedies to problems you want to solve for yourself or the environment. List outmoded patterns of thinking regarding your own sense of self (do not list universal principles or ways for others to think or behave).

Follow-up Protocol

For best results, write down your impressions of this activity in your journal using the Heartwood Path Follow-up Protocol found in the Appendix. Afterwards, consider sharing your interpretations with others.

Heartwood Path Axioms

Key Assertions From Waypoint 3.87

3.87.1.

Form a sort of mental container in your mind where you suspend negative, old, habitual, outmoded thoughts.

3.87.2.

Suspend your old heavily-burdened life and enter into the lightness of the Cauldron of Awareness in order to make way for the first glimpse of new potions, new remedies, new possibilities—the first light of your new life.

3.87.3.

Upgrade your perspective and, thereby, begin the Great Work! of remaking the world.

3.87.4.

Finding or cultivating this awakened heart, freeing oneself from the pain of ignorance and unworkable habitual patterns, freeing oneself from individual self-absorption, and helping others do the same so that they may more effectively work to become whole (aware of their perfection) and help to protect the environment are the primary purposes of the Heartwood Path.

3.87.5.

There is gold in your awareness and fools gold in your chattering mind.

Nocturnal Pilgrimage 3.87

For best results, write down your impressions of each night's dreams in your journal using the Heartwood Path Dreaming Time Protocols found in the Appendix. Afterwards, consider sharing your Dream Tending with others.

Sixth Stabilization Technique For Lucid Dreaming

You have already learned many techniques to stabilize your lucid dreams. There are more. Use the the following recommended stabilization tip whenever your lucid dreams start to go out of focus:

Meditating while you are dreaming stabilizes your dreams, if you do it well. Here's how: sit and remind yourself that you are dreaming. Notice sounds and sensations. Simultaneously feel the solidity of the earth while also reminding yourself that it is not real. Remind yourself that dreaming occurs in your subconscious and that whatever seems to be appearing "out there" is really an aspect of yourself.

If you ever feel sleepy when moving outdoors in order to do the activities for this course, find a safe and appropriate location in nature and let yourself doze off. When you awaken, be sure to attempt to recall any vivid or striking images from your dreams. Then, record your impressions of your dreams in your journal, especially if you encountered striking, vivid, or negative images. "In a way, the shadow material (the negative Dream Figure) is the fire of the unconscious. That is, it can be a powerful force for creation or destruction" (Aizenstat, 2009, p. 258). Certainly the benefits and cautions surrounding the topic of negative Dream Images is something that is too important to keep to yourself.

As the following Dream Activity will demonstrate, a negative Dream Figure can heal us of our deepest psychological difficulties. It can be life-affirming if handled properly.

Before starting another nocturnal pilgrimage, proceed to the next waypoint, titled "Share." It has to do with sharing the information of this course.

88

Share

CONNECT WITH THE VERY BEST OF ONESELF AND HELP OTHERS DO THE SAME

As I say to you in this course, I encourage you to likewise say to others. In this way the message is spread and a better world emerges.

Like me, you need to wake up. We both need to free ourselves from our confused minds, especially from the mistaken notion that we are separate from one another. Each of us is unique **and** part of a greater whole. Each of us needs to share how to best work with our Inner Shadow—that which "our psyches repress (render unconscious), not what our Egos suppress (consciously hide from others) . . . The Shadow is what you fail to notice about yourself . . . Shadow characteristics can be either negative (what the Ego would consider beneath it) or positive (what the Ego would consider "above" it)" (Plotkin, 2013, p. 209-210). Following the adage "The Pot calls the kettle black," we sometimes learn about our Shadow by the way we project (unconsciously transfer) our own unconscious emotions, traits, or desires onto another person (in this case, the other person becomes your "screen." "The invaluable thing about projection and screens," writes Plotkin, " is that they provide the opportunity to discover something about yourself through what you see in others" (2013, p. 215). This often unconscious, un-comfortable, surprising, and self-revealing way to share unconscious aspects of yourself with others is one, albeit curious, way we become complete.

When we realize we are projecting unknown aspects of ourselves onto others and own up to the fact that we share in the aspects of the quality being projected, we become more empathetic, appreciative, compassionate and whole. Here's a Shadow exercise that will take you one big step closer to Gladandgreen Junction:

To Deal With That Part Of Yourself That Does Not Want To Be…

HumaNatureConnect Activity

Start-up Protocol

If this is not a day when you prefer to spend time in nature with-out an agenda, do the Heartwood Path Start-up Protocol found in the Appendix.

Dealing With Your Shadow

For this activity, learn how to benefit from your projections that reveal your Inner Shadow. Recall two people from your life: one you do not like and one you do like. These ought to be people to whom you over-react, both positively and negatively.

In your journal, list four traits that disturb you and four traits you admire As you list these traits, consider how each of them may be a characteristic of yourself. Look for characteristics in the others that you can use. Consider how you would change if you embraced your screens as allies in your life.

Follow-up Protocol

For best results, write down your impressions of this activity in your journal using the Heartwood Path Follow-up Protocol found in the Appendix. Afterwards, consider sharing your interpretations with others.

Heartwood Path Axioms

Key Assertions From Waypoint 3.88

3.88.1.

We all need to wake up.

3.88.2.

We all need to free ourselves from our confused minds, especially from the mistaken notion that we are separate from one another.

3.88.3.

While we may have parts of ourselves we keep in the shadows, each of us is unique and part of a greater whole.

Nocturnal Pilgrimage 3.88

For best results, write down your impressions of each night's dreams in your journal using the Heartwood Path Dreaming Time Protocols found in the Appendix. Afterwards, consider sharing your Dream Tending with others.

While often scary and unsettling, it is a good idea to include at least one Negative Dream Figure in your Dream Council. Being repugnant, horrific, repulsive, violent, depressing, or terrible, Negative Dream Figures bring up strong emotions like terror, despair, revulsion, or rage. Call a truce with this Negative Dream Figure and if the interactions are overwhelming take a break and ground yourself but do not try to stop, suppress, or ignore the emotions that arise. Find your inner strength and take good notes, especially noticing any good qualities exhibited by the Negative Dream Figure.

When closing the Council, remember that each Figure represents a living inner world being. For this reason, look at each member, offer your gratitude, and say something like, "I am closing this Council now but will see you in the next Council."

When doing the next activity, or any of the other subsequent activities, consider lying down for a while with your attractive natural being. From this position, look to the sky or to the canopy of trees overhead. Pay attention to the different perspective that lying down affords. Try using a new perspective for problem-solving, thought-sorting, and issue-pondering as you lie with your attractive natural being.

Armed with this advice, you are now ready to move to the next waypoint: "Unstuck Pleasure." There you will learn more about gratitude.

89

Unstuck Pleasure

EXPRESS GRATITUDE

Both you and I need to express our gratitude for our earthly joys and express respect for all sentient beings. Making a commitment to walk the entire Heartwood Path will be helpful here.

We need to express our humility and rouse our confidence. We need to free ourselves from self-centeredness, self-absorption, and self-importance so we may best serve others.

We need to go beyond our worldly pursuits and do God's work, the work of the Absolute Spirit. Part of the Absolute Spirit's work is seeking to end wars and resisting violence. Doing these things sets one on a course to true security, to a time for self-reflection, and to environmental protection.

We need to turn away from excessive comfort, conspicuous luxury, and other worldly seductions so that we do not become lulled into complacency or indifferent to the suffering of others. We need to seek an ideal balance between appropriate pleasure and lesson-giving pain.

We need to feel a sense of possibility. We need to feel a sense of potential. These things will give us a healthy appetite for difficulty.

We need to nurture the awakening of our hearts. To do so, it will be helpful to be in relationship with another person who serves as a witness when we expose ourselves to ourselves.

We each need a committed partner to hear us out without judging and without attempting to fix us. We each need someone to hear our confessions. We need to frame our confessions not as a means to condemn ourselves as a "bad me" but rather as a way to express regret with open-hearted tenderness, to express positive sadness about misdeeds, to demonstrate our basic wisdom, to state our intention to find a remedy, and to resolve to avoid making the same mistake again. For help finding and working with this significant other, enroll in the Heartwood Path for Couples course. In the meantime, you can proceed as a single person or share your thoughts and feelings with another.

We need to release our burdens. We need to make a fresh start. And we need to let go of the fixed version of ourselves.

We need to live our lives so that we may die with no regrets. To do so, we need to keep from acting on unwise impulses over and over again.

We need to take the pain when it is best to do so. Just as some inoculations are painful, pain always has within it an opportunity to learn and grow. Often the results of pain are well worth the momentary displeasure.

We need to experience pleasure when it is best to do so. A good time to seek pleasure is when you need to reduce tension or when you want to provide an inducement to encourage someone to spend time with you. Pleasure only causes problems when one becomes so attached to it that more and more thrill seeking is needed to obtain the same results. At some point, when allowed to go to extremes, any amusement will become a burden or counterproductive. So seek out pleasure without attachment and remember the benefits of moderation.

To The Crucial Urge…

HumaNatureConnect Activity

Start-up Protocol

If this is not a day when you prefer to spend time in nature without an agenda, do the Heartwood Path Start-up Protocol found in the Appendix.

Finding The Dream Figure's Essential Impulse

Find the essential impulse of your Dream Figures. You can do this by simply asking them to share. Simply ask about the intentions of your Dream Figures.

Follow-up Protocol

For best results, write down your impressions of this activity in your journal using the Heartwood Path Follow-up Protocol found in the Appendix. Afterwards, consider sharing your interpretations with others.

Heartwood Path Axioms

Key Assertions From Waypoint 3.89

3.89.1.

Express gratitude.

3.89.2.

Free yourself from self-centeredness, self-absorption, and self-importance so that you can best serve others.

3.89.3.

Take the pain when it is best to do so.

3.89.4.

Seek out pleasure without attachment and remember the benefits of moderation.

Nocturnal Pilgrimage 3.89

For best results, write down your impressions of each night's dreams in your journal using the Heartwood Path Dreaming Time Protocols found in the Appendix. Afterwards, consider sharing your Dream Tending with others.

As promised, we will now present a series of Wake Initiated Lucid Dream tips, scattered over many of the remaining waypoints.

First WILD Tip

Release tension and anxiety. Let your body do what it knows to do. Do not think too much. Clear your mind. Stay aware passively.

Your success along the Heartwood Path and in life will continue or increase the more you make physical contact with the surface of the unimproved planet. Seek ways during each outdoor activity to become grounded with the Earth. Doing so will cause your thoughts to become less scattered and less disconnected. As you sit on the surface of the wild earth your sense of Self will become broader and more solid. Watch how the flow of gravity pressing yourself against the wild earth makes your life more balanced and reality-based. Connecting with the earth in this way may impart to you a needed sense of rootedness and meaning. Carry this sense into your lucid dreams.

After tending to last night's dreams, find… a Dream Image (any recalled mental picture from your dream) in your (earlier recorded dream journal) that is either under construction, has been hand-crafted or machine-made, glows, or catches your eye. Notice the Dream Image's function, operation, and purpose. In making your Dream Council Figures, use natural materials such as sticks, twigs, grasses, bark, shells, and pebbles, along with a healthy dose of your own creativity, to make impressionistic and simple Figures that are full of vibrancy and placed in an outdoor remedy or special indoor space. In placing the Dream Figure amidst the members of your Dream Council, let their beauty mix with your own.

At one moment during your interaction with your Dream Council members, the Dream Sentry, and the new Dream Figure your breathing will change as you experience a sense of awe that comes when you realize that your creations have been personalized. Anything that is personalized can be played with, animated, and loved. After such engagement, close the Council and notice how your awareness is different.

After closing Council, move to the next waypoint: "Unlinked." There, you will learn about loosening your attachment to both pleasure and pain. You are making good progress.

90

Unlinked

LOOSEN YOUR ATTACHMENT TO PAIN OR PLEASURE

Always be vigilant not to become too attached to either pain or pleasure. A way to manage one's attachment to pain or pleasure is to do an exercise wherein you visualize with each inhalation the taking in of pain or pleasure and with each exhalation the distribution of relief from pain or the sharing of pleasure.

One way to become too attached to pleasure is to become overly driven to achieve psychological comfort. We do this by seeking false security rather than facing the hard facts. Chief among the facts that ought to be faced are the hard-to-grasp realities of groundlessness, emptiness, impermanence, and death.

Ask a guide or teacher to help you overcome your wrong views. Doing so will help you expand your merit and reduce your possessiveness.

We need to stop thinking about what we like and do not like. This propensity for constantly making judgments is a "misery-go-round." Unfortunately repeatedly thinking and doing things that do not have positive results is how most people spend most of their time. The source of discontent on one's typical, busy, unproductive ride to nowhere is the mistaken notion about one's separateness. This discontent arises because whatever one clings to as "me" or "mine"—be it a foot, a spouse, a possession, or a friend—causes suffering. The more we attempt to hold onto the groundless, impermanent, "ungraspable I," the greater the intensity of one's pain.

We need to harm no sentient beings, for doing so harms us more. We need to instead have fervent intentions to help others, recognize that others are essentially just like you and I, and understand that everyone wants to be free from discomfort and at home with themselves and their world. Since you and I and everyone else seek to be free from mental anguish we all have ample cause to prepare the ground for the awakening of our hearts.

Naturally, we want to be part of making things better. And we know that we need to get saner so we can do the work of improving relationships and protecting the environment. To become saner, we need to enter into the Cauldron of Awareness to rid ourselves of aggression, craving, ignorance, jealousy, envy and pride—the strong emotions that lead to suffering.

With awareness we can check our minds and, finding them full of opinions and preconceptions, engage in disciplines (such as yoga) that give relief from pain. We can engage in disciplines (such as meditation) that allow us to counter our addictive urges while there is still time. We can employ disciplines (such as contemplation) to help us use the eye of wisdom to tame what ought to be tame—by which I mean only the conceptual mind. And we can use disciplines (such as HumaNatureConnect Activities) that spur us to allow to remain wild that which ought to remain wild—by which I mean both the Earth's last remaining wilderness and each person's enduring inner world instinctive wildness.

To No More Excessive Focusing On Suffering and Amusement...

HumaNatureConnect Activity

Start-up Protocol

If this is not a day when you prefer to spend time in nature without an agenda, do the Heartwood Path Start-up Protocol found in the Appendix.

Loosing Your Attachment To Pain Or Pleasure

For this activity, loosen your attachment to pain or pleasure (which can disturb the mind, disturb the emotions, motivate unskilled actions, interfere with spiritual practice, and cause more attachment) by:

1. recognizing that suffering and enjoyment are two sides of the same coin and that coin is attachment,
2. recognizing that clinging to pleasure leads to the suffering of pain,
3. not lingering or trying to maximize pleasure as this leads to greater pain,
4. being impassive to pleasure but not apathetic to it,
5. not exacerbating hedonism nor extreme asceticism, and
6. being moderate and wise.

After pondering the subjects listed above, look around the natural landscape that contains your chosen natural being for evidence that animals feel pleasure or pain but do not become attached to their circumstances. See how they experience pain but seem to minimize their suffering about the pain or how they experience a blessing but do not seem to wallow in their pleasure. Look for examples of contentment, relief, comfort, and ease. Then look for examples of distress, heartache, misery, and affliction.

Follow-up Protocol

For best results, write down your impressions of this activity in your journal using the Heartwood Path Follow-up Protocol found in the Appendix. Afterwards, consider sharing your interpretations with others.

Heartwood Path Axioms

Key Assertions From Waypoint 3.90

3.90.1.

A way to manage one's attachment to pain or pleasure is to do an exercise wherein you visualize with each inhalation the taking in of pain or pleasure and with each exhalation the distribution of relief from pain or the sharing of pleasure.

3.90.2.

The propensity for constantly making judgments is a "misery-go-round" because whatever one clings to as "me" or "mine"—be it a foot, a spouse, a possession, or a friend—causes suffering.

3.90.3.

To become saner, we need to enter into the Cauldron of Awareness to rid ourselves of aggression, craving, ignorance, jealousy, envy and pride—the strong emotions that lead to suffering.

3.90.4.

We can use disciplines to spur us to allow to remain wild that which ought to remain wild—by which I mean both the Earth's last remaining wilderness and each person's enduring inner world instinctive wildness.

Nocturnal Pilgrimage 3.90

For best results, write down your impressions of each night's dreams in your journal using the Heartwood Path Dreaming Time Protocols found in the Appendix. Afterwards, consider sharing your Dream Tending with others.

Second WILD Tip

Stay put. The process of dream stabilization takes longer if you are fidgety. Feel the comfort around you.

Continue working with your Dream Council. It will bring you to a place where you can move seamlessly "between our outer lives and our inner lives, to the place where we no longer draw a sharp division between them" (Aizenstat, 2009, p. 276.)

Be sure to go outside for all of the following activities. Beyond these, develop the habit of going outside and communing with nature everyday. In doing so, nature will become an essential sanctuary for you, a place you look forward to visiting. Do not consider the outdoor activities to be an obligation. Make your sojourns into the wild outdoors the highlight of your day.

After your Dream Tending session, continue your expedition down the Heartwood Path by moving to the next waypoint: "Untamed And Tidy." There, you will learn about keeping your mind wild and uncluttered.

91

Untamed And Tidy

KEEP YOUR MIND WILD AND UNCLUTTERED

The wildness within is everything in one's inner world except for the chatterbox qualities of the mind filled with repetitive, judgmental, egotistical thinking. The wildness within that merits protection is a set of helpful and deep-seated yearnings. These yearnings may be for love or for freedom, for example.

Wisdom and compassion come from realizing the untamed, "non-conceptual" mind of awareness that is unsullied with trivial thinking. When our minds are thrown in random and trivial directions or when our minds are cluttered with repetitive thinking we have no means to maintain the most important of disciplines; namely, causing no harm, gathering merit and virtue, and serving others.

The unhelpful provocations that come from being alive in a modern culture—tendencies towards possessiveness and achieving for one's own self only, for example—can be countered by un-taming the mind—removing it from the cage formed by repetitive, judgmental, and trivial thinking. Our misperception about separateness—the notion that each of us is independent—creates tensions between you and me and others that lead to unhelpful, misery-producing concepts regarding what each of us like and do not like, what each of us are for and are not for, and what each of us want and do not want. Virtuous qualities, fresh insights, greater kindness, more relaxation, and heightened steadiness come to us when we "un-tame" our minds through awareness and meditation.

Without awareness we cannot observe the workings of our minds, we cannot be transformed through enlightened activity, and we cannot make the world a kinder place. With awareness we can let go of self-clinging and, thereby, find generosity, discipline, enthusiasm, patience, meditation, and wisdom.

We need to counter what is bad with the following of disciplines, such as meditation and toning, that lead to what is good. Patience, for example, is the primary antidote to aggression. It leads to tolerance. And staying present is the primary antidote for misery. Staying present leads to contentment.

To Rummage Around For Food...

HumaNatureConnect Activity

Start-up Protocol

If this is not a day when you prefer to spend time in nature without an agenda, do the Heartwood Path Start-up Protocol found in the Appendix.

Generating Patterns Of Human-Nature Interaction # 14:
Foraging

For this activity, forage for food after you feel connected to your chosen attractive natural being. In doing this interaction pattern, you could over-pick endangered wild leeks (a perverse interaction pattern) or pick strawberries at a farm (a domestic interaction pattern). By choosing instead to search for edible mushrooms in a forest (a wild interaction), you would be doing something that will have a positive psychological effect on you.

In your journal, write down what meaning you would derive from this wild interaction pattern; what joy, if any, it would produce; how, if at all, it would build within you a bond between your mind and nature; and how, if at all, the wild version of this interaction pattern would be better for you than the perverse or domestic instantiation of the same interaction pattern; and how not being allowed to participate in this sort of wild interaction pattern—search in a pristine woods for mushrooms—would make you feel? How does interacting in this way in the presence of your attractive natural being make you feel? How would it feel to have this interaction without the presence of your attractive natural being? In writing down these responses you will be adding to our collective nature language, so important to rekindling the bond between humans and nature. Look over your impressions and think about them as you fall asleep tonight prior to dreaming.

Follow-up Protocol

For best results, write down your impressions of this activity in your journal using the Heartwood Path Follow-up Protocol found in the Appendix. Afterwards, consider sharing your interpretations with others.

Heartwood Path Axioms

Key Assertions From Waypoint 3.91

3.91.1.

Wisdom and compassion come from realizing the "non-conceptual" mind of awareness that is unsullied with trivial thinking.

3.91.2.

When our minds are scattered and cluttered with scattered thinking we have no means to maintain the most important of disciplines; namely, causing no harm, gathering merit and virtue, and serving others.

3.91.3.

The unhelpful provocations that come from being alive in a modern culture—tendencies towards possessiveness and achieving for one's own self only, for example—can be countered by removing the mind from the cage formed by repetitive, judgmental, and trivial thinking.

3.91.4.

With awareness we can let go of self-clinging and thereby find generosity, discipline, enthusiasm, patience, meditation, and wisdom.

3.91.5.

We need to counter what is bad with disciplines that lead to what is good: patience, for example, is the primary antidote to aggression and staying present is the primary antidote for misery.

Nocturnal Pilgrimage 3.91

For best results, write down your impressions of each night's dreams in your journal using the Heartwood Path Dreaming Time Protocols found in the Appendix. Afterwards, consider sharing your Dream Tending with others.

Third WILD Tip

Stick 'em up! WILDs require that you fall asleep slowly and maintain your awareness. By lifting your forearm perpendicular to your upper arm you will be alerted that you are falling asleep because your arm will naturally fall on the bed. Try this approach with one arm and, on another night, try it with the other arm. By falling asleep while also noticing your falling arm you have reached the goal of moving directly from waking time to dreaming time. The falling arm is your reminder to begin lucidity within your dream.

In doing any of the activities that follow, try not to attach your communing with nature to a frenetic outdoor activity such as, for some people: kayaking, horseback riding, cross-country skiing, or any other outdoor endeavor that is so challenging it commands too much of your attention. You will commune with nature better when you refrain from overly attaching your awareness to overly active forms of outdoor recreation. And doing so before bedtime may help you sleep better.

By tending to our dreams after we sleep, we can reach inside of ourselves "to the deepest levels of the psyche and see our personal destiny as it unfolds" (Aizenstat, 2009, p. 276). After finishing another Dream Tending session, move to the next waypoint: "Ought To." Keep up your momentum. Try not to go too long between waypoints.

92

Ought To

REMAIN STEADY

We ought to not be aloof. Instead, we ought to stay aware of the environment and remain friendly.

When insulted, we need to not magnify it with thoughts that lead us into rage. Instead, we ought to simply acknowledge the insult, pay attention to the initial thoughts of the insult, and then let the thoughts fade away.

The main message of this waypoint has to do with countering the typical ambivalence many people feel towards nature and with countering your reactions to insults by achieving the sort of meditative stillness that comes from laying the groundwork for lucidity (thinking clearly). We will do so by helping you learn to engage in lucid dreaming.

To The Knowledge That You Are Dreaming While Doing So...

HumaNatureConnect Activity

Start-up Protocol

If this is not a day when you prefer to spend time in nature without an agenda, do the Heartwood Path Start-up Protocol found in the Appendix.

Dreaming Lucidly

Lay the groundwork for lucidity by understanding that in lucid dreams . . .

"you are aware, in real time, of the nature of the reality you are experiencing. You know that you are dreaming . . . You know that all of the phenomena of your dream—the scenery and participants— are the creations of your own mind" (Wallace, 2012, p. 1).

It is often difficult to make any sense out of one's dreams because the dreams have a lack of stability. To have lucid dreams, one's attention needs to be stabilized.

"Stability of attention is a crucial step to freedom—the freedom to transcend normal dream consciousness and recognize we are dreaming, then to maintain that lucidity, and to transform our dreams into a laboratory where we can carefully explore the mind" (Wallace, 2012, p. 1).

A system is needed, therefore, to focus one's attention, to replace confusion with ongoing coherence, and to develop a command over the dream environment. For this system to work, one has to be relaxed. One also has to have a stable and vivid mind. That is where Shamatha training comes in. If one has the relaxed mental clarity that comes from Shamatha one will have the mental clarity to awaken within the dream, to remember the importance of signs and symbols in dreams, and "to concentrate effortlessly on a chosen object . . ." (Wallace, 2012, p. 3).

The author of **Dreaming Yourself Awake**, Alan B. Wallace (2012), states that although "training in shamatha is not absolutely required, I highly recommend it." Taking his advice for this course, we will break down the shamatha training into three steps: 1) "Relaxing Through Mindfulness of Breathing," 2) Stabilizing One's Attention Through Settling the Mind in the Natural State," and 3) "Vividness of Attention Through Shamatha Without a Sign—which is awareness of awareness. Once these preparations are presented, subsequent Dream Activities will be devoted to lucid dreaming and putting everything together into a complete dream practice. These are wonderful trainings. Do them nightly or whenever you feel attracted to do so. Do not make them into a burden. Remembering the value of gratitude, express to someone how fortunate you are that you are learning how to awaken within a dream and, in so doing, find greater clarity for your life.

Relaxing Through Mindfulness Of Breathing

Begin by developing the intention of observing tactile sensations, of relaxing, and of returning to your tactile sensations when distracted. Find a comfortable position, sitting or lying down, back straight. Keep your stomach muscles and face muscles loose. Take three deep breaths, breathing through the nostrils and down into the abdomen. Expand the diaphragm and chest to full capacity with each inhalation. Pay attention to the sensations throughout the body that are associated with breath. Find a natural settled rhythm for your respiration. Breathe without forcing any control. Develop the positive attitude of patience. Rather than force the mind to be still, relax and let go of any turbulent body-mind energy. With every exhalation, feel a softening of the body. You will inevitably become distracted. Use mindfulness to remember what to do for this practice. Use introspection to notice when you need to guide yourself back to your tactile field of sensations.

Stabilizing One's Attention Through Settling The Mind

Develop the intention to train for stability. Settle into a natural posture, with back straight. Breathe with a natural rhythm. In the beginning, pay attention to your field of tactile sensations. Then focus on the rising and falling of the abdomen as you continue to breathe. Count your breaths from one to ten. Start over and continue for about twenty minutes. As you do this exercise soon you will discover there are two major types of distraction that cause one to forget one' task: agitation and dullness.

Concerning agitation, we are in the habit of thinking rapidly. We flit around from subject to subject.

Concerning dullness, when we try to meditate, we find our focus hazy. The object of attention lacks vividness.

It is best then to seek a middle ground between agitation and dullness. To do so, foster the attitudes of relaxation, stillness (which both counter agitation), and vigilance (which counters dullness).

Vividness Of Attention Through Awareness Of Awareness

Repeat relaxing through mindfulness of breathing and stabilizing one's attention trough settling the mind in a natural state, as previously described. Then, move into the third phase of mindfulness of breathing by elevating the focus of attention to the apertures of the nostrils or the area just above the upper lip or by counting the breathes.

Wallace likens the phases of mindfulness—relaxation, stability, and vividness—to the structure of a tree. The root is the whole practice of relaxation. The trunk is stability. The foliage is the vividness of shamatha.

"The overall strategy, then, is to allow stability to develop from relaxation and vividness to develop from stability" (Wallace, 2009, pp. 16-17).

Do not be surprised if, like beams of light breaking through the clouds, the three steps of shamatha lead to deeper layers of consciousness. You may even become prescient (prophetic, predictive, or farsighted).

Follow-up Protocol

For best results, write down your impressions of this activity in your journal using the Heartwood Path Follow-up Protocol found in the Appendix. Afterwards, consider sharing your interpretations with others.

Heartwood Path Axioms

Key Assertions From Waypoint 3.92

3.92.1.

One ought to stay aware of the environment and remain friendly.

3.92.2.

When insulted, we ought to simply acknowledge the insult, pay attention to the initial thoughts of the insult, and then let them fade away.

3.92.3.

Counter the typical ambivalence many people feel towards nature and counter your reactions to insults by achieving the sort of meditative stillness that comes from laying the groundwork for lucidity (thinking clearly) and from understanding your nighttime reveries through lucid dreaming.

Nocturnal Pilgrimage 3.92

For best results, write down your impressions of each night's dreams in your journal using the Heartwood Path Dreaming Time Protocols found in the Appendix. Afterwards, consider sharing your Dream Tending with others.

Play with or maintain your Dream Council Figures or call the Council to order. Add new members, if you feel the need and are able. Dream. Tend to your dreams. Make your interactions with your Dream Council a regular part of your day. Nightly, or whenever you feel the attraction to do so, employ the three steps of shamatha—relaxation, stability, and vividness—to prepare yourself for the engaging in lucid dreaming—the topic of the next Dream Activity (after the next daytime activity—"Being Like A Natural Being Or Natural Area").

Mountain-biking or using an All-Terrain Vehicle to get into the wild may not put you into the right frame of mind for doing Heartwood Path nature activities. Walking or canoeing fosters greater person-to-attractive natural being communion. Floating down a river in a self-powered boat such as a canoe can be one of life's most satisfying experiences. Canoeing on safe rivers while not drinking alcohol allows the canoeist to be enveloped in the river scene, connected to the water, exhilarated by the occasional rapids, and merged with the current. Other outdoor activities that do not get in the way of communing with nature include bird watching, wildlife tracking, swimming in safe water, dreaming while sleeping in nature, and soaking up the moonlight.

Fourth WILD Tip

Remember your intention to remain aware as your body drifts off to sleep. Don't bother counting sheep. Count "I'm dreaming" statements. Say that over and over as you drift off to sleep.

When you are ready, move to the next waypoint: "Stoneface." Doing so will help you make some progress on your pilgrimage to Gladandgreen Junction.

93

Stoneface

BE LIKE A BOULDER

When I was the Midwest Representative for Friends of the Earth I spent much time showing people, including the staff of members of Congress, the various woodlands that deserved to become congressionally designated wilderness areas. The wilderness coalitions (one in Missouri and one in Illinois) I co-founded wanted about fifteen areas protected by federal law from timber sales, off-road vehicle use, or mining. In time, such efforts resulted in preserving over one hundred thousand acres of forests in Illinois and Missouri. One such place not yet congressionally protected was Lower Rock Creek in the Ozarks of Missouri. One day in Lower Rock Creek, while resting near a large boulder, I became puzzled by my yearning to be as still and unfazed as my geological companion. I thought: "I wish I could be as calm and emotion-free as this big rock." While sitting in the proposed wilderness area, I thought that my desire to be like that rock was a curious yearning. I could not come up an explanation of the value of "being like a boulder" until I realized I was not wanting to repress all my emotions. Having over the years received much guidance from my Boulder Buddy, I wanted to, like him, refrain from building up the repetitive, judgmental concepts attached to emotions, be altruistic without overdoing it, work quietly for the benefit of others, be supportive, avoid obsessions, value diversity, and do the other things I so admired him for doing.

Refrain From Building Up The Repetitive, Judgmental Concepts Attached To Emotions

Now, just as that boulder is always hot in summer and always cold in winter, I can be similarly unfazed as I change my emotions. I can note my urges, thoughts, and futile strategies and continue to "be like a boulder." This allows me to use my honest, conscientious and diligent desires to serve others without being frantic about it.

Be Altruistic Without Overdoing It

I recommend the following simple actions: give away food and small change; think of others, particularly those who are social outcasts, as being just like yourself; identify with persons whom others tend to consider "lower" than yourself; while there is nothing wrong with possessions, visualize giving way cherished items; and then, as you begin to stretch a bit, give away enough possessions to come to the brink of regret. Start small. Do what is doable as a way to expand your courage and generosity. Eventually, you will be able to give and give to the point of being emotionally pinched by the action; but you will be able to do it anyway and overcome your regret. Repeated acts of consequential giving will help others but it will help you more. Acts of giving freely are significant steps on your path to wholeness. Benefiting others in this way leads to contentment. For this reason the Dali Lama calls such giving "wise selfishness." By contrast, hoarding is "foolish selfishness" which is selfish because it does not reflect concern for the welfare of others and it is foolish because it perpetuates one's own discontent.

Through giving one comes to recognize that richness is a state of mind. Not being generous, and holding back causes fear and neediness. To put an embargo on such consequences, give freely.

Thinking of that boulder in Lower Rock Creek—and, better yet, visiting that model of steadfastness—reminds me to . . .

Work Calmly For the Benefit Of Others

Like my "boulder buddy," I keep a suitable pace and relax while holding firm to my place on Earth. A suitable pace means not struggling and striving but nevertheless working daily with delight and joy and with the intention of awakening the soft heart of a saint in my self and others. My "boulder buddy" does not strive but, long ago, it arrived. In a similar manner, you and I ought to arrive, not by scurrying here and there in an exhaustive frenzy, but by applying the following priorities to your acts of compassion so that the workload is manageable: serving some of those who are in Hell on Earth—the so-called "despicable" ones living in desperate situations; serving some of those who seek to help others; protecting a portion of the environment upon which all depends; and doing all of this in tolerable intervals of delightful work and joyous rest. We are not obligated to help every so-called "despicable" person. Nor are we obligated to serve the whole community of helpers or solve every environmental problem.

We, being human, do have the charge of caring for our immediate families and others (including all sentient beings and the environment) nearby. Consider limiting the work by focusing on the nature of relationships rather than on all the agents in the environment—how a limited set of people relate to each other, how a manageable number of people relate to sentient beings, and how local or particular people relate to the environment. A friend of everyone is a friend of no one. Each of us determines for ourselves what we are willing and capable of doing.

Those who do not "be like a boulder" get ensnarled needlessly in life's petty dramas. They heighten their troubles by paying too much attention to their own individual story lines.

Be Supportive

My "boulder buddy" is never condescending nor disapproving. It teaches me that I too ought to develop these qualities.

Avoid Obsessions

Sitting by that igneous illustrator gives me rock-solid suggestions for how to live my life. For example, there is nothing obsessive, fanatical, or compulsive about my "boulder buddy." From this I learned that obsession is a way of wasting one's life.

In Valuing Diversity Gather The Virtues Of Devotion, Kindness, And Gratitude

While I do model some of my behavior on that mighty mineral, there are a few big differences between me and my "boulder buddy:" it has more time than me so it is reasonable that I feel I have less time to waste, I can be uplifted by my human dignity, I can smile, I can rejoice in the good qualities and good fortunes of others, I can generate warmth from heart-felt joy. It has all the virtue it needs. I, however, need to gather virtue; which I attempt to glean from observing good teachers, from those who have been kind to me, and from those who are suffering. From each of these sources I encourage you to gather the virtues of devotion, kindness, and gratitude.

Work Out Of The Limelight

Another lesson from by "boulder buddy:" never try to be better than your neighbors. From this guidance I have determined that to be happy I need to train myself to awaken my heart, to be kind only for the sake of my awakened heart, and to never attempt to prove that I am more virtuous than my neighbors. Most of what that stone does for others is invisible. You too may want to keep your good deeds out of the public eye.

Seek Fundamental Changes

I envy the way my boulder buddy cannot momentarily malfunction. Unlike my mineral model, I can have one tiny blip of rage and this event can destroy years of virtuous conduct. My "boulder buddy" does not bother with superficial acts of generosity that can be overcome in a flash of rage. From this I learned that good works are best when they produce a fundamental change of heart.

Put Anger To Use

Do not think that anger is always negative. Distinguish it from hatred, which is produced by ill will. Hatred is never justified. Never be caught in the trap of the bias of right or wrong that leads to hatred. My boulder buddy is never angry or hateful and does not appear to be getting very much done. I have seen my other role model, David Brower, use his anger—produced by good will—to generate profound acts of compassion, to stand firm against injustice, and to motivate others to do the impossible.

When faced with the rage of another person determine whether that rage is based on anger or hatred. If it is hatred, remove yourself from the presence of such ill will. If it is anger, look for the considerable tenderness that lies behind all anger. Hard as it may be, keep in touch with that vulnerability as a way to keep from responding destructively. Just as fire has heat and the sky has clouds, people have anger. When it comes your way simply pause, note the anger, shift gears, and move on. Remain like a boulder and do not retaliate. When faced with anger we have a choice: we can bolster our resentment or we can foster our understanding and empathy. We can widen the gap between our selves and others or we can narrow that gap. If you cannot choose, be resentful for a week and be understanding for a week. Then pick which alternative feels best.

Do What You Can

Boulder Buddy does what it can in its situation. What it cannot do, it does not get riled up about. This too has been a valuable lesson for me.

Be Patient

There may sometimes be years before I return to that boulder in Lower Rock Creek. During this time my boulder buddy undergoes subtle changes and remains seemingly patient about the pace of the change. Likewise, the changes you will make in yourself and in your situation in the world will occur gradually as you progress down the Heartwood Path. Be like a boulder and be patient with the pace of change. Think of your time on the Heartwood Path as a time of letting go of old unworkable patterns of thinking and doing. There is no way to get rid of such addictions without going through a "detox period" such as your time on the Heartwood Path. This course is designed to help sojourners realize that desires are endless and that trying to satisfy them with comfort and security creates that misery-go-round that I will give another name to in a moment. If, as you tread down the Heartwood Path, your patience wanes, think of an unshakable boulder and apply this steadfastness to your confidence.

Be Strong

My buddy weathers the seasons and stays steadfast through the eons. Witnessing this is inspiration to stand by your beliefs and to avoid being swayed by fads, public opinion, the advice of those who ought to mind their own boulder buddies.

Give Yourself Credit

My boulder buddy does not seem to care about praise or compliments, although it deserves them. Learning from this, I try not to be dependent on the whims other people's opinions to feel good about myself.

Recognize The Goodness In Troublemakers

I confess: it would be a bit boring to sit for long periods of time with my "boulder buddy" without all the trouble that goes on in its presence. Birds dive at snakes attempting to eat their eggs, winter water freezes and attempts to crack open the rock, people come but leave a trace, and hawks kill mice. What seems like trouble for some is, for me, a welcome opportunity to expand my patience. These troublemakers show me things I do not want to see. They remind me how I get trapped in sorrow over things I cannot and need not control. Having become fond of a little mouse only to watch it carried away in the talons of a red-tailed hawk teaches me to be relaxed even in provoking situations. The pain experienced by the mouse results in a needed meal for the hawk. Both are serving their own purposes. The mouse, the hawk, the snake, the person who left behind a tissue are all appreciated by me because each helps to advance me towards my own wholeness (awareness of perfection). They all gave me opportunities to wake up to my own inseparability. I learn that I am not unlike the troublemakers; for, like them, I too seek comfort, will always be subject to change, and will die. You too can find such value in the troublemakers in your life.

Even When You Cannot See The Way, Start

Despite all these troubles, my "boulder buddy" seems committed, steadfast, and unwavering. It didn't have any false starts. From it, one would think that I would have learned that it is better to not start than to start and then quit before completion. Yet this is not the case, for my continuing attendance with my boulder buddy demonstrates to me that it is indeed always in action. It is perpetually starting. It weathers all storms and faces all difficulties. Similarly, so will we, gladly; for the bigger the challenge the better!

Look For The Opposites

Like you and I, my boulder buddy is more than an individual agent. He is a being embedded in an environment—an environment that offers both challenges and opportunities. We will face such challenges by being as steadfast as the stone but also as nimble as the grass beside it. We will keep our sense of humor and catch ourselves when we get uptight.

Sometimes we can learn much from looking at opposites. Nothing seems more opposite from my "boulder buddy" than lightness and urgency. These qualities we ought to enthusiastically adopt, along with the main quality of the river otter I have occasionally seen in the creek below: playfulness.

Dump The Distractions

Nothing distracts my "boulder buddy." It never allows trivialities to destroy its presence. Being as present as my "boulder buddy" is a "mission: impossible" but emulating its lack of worldly concerns is a worthwhile practice nevertheless. We both, you and I, need to "be like a boulder" and put a rock solid check on the following worldly concerns: praise, blame, pain, pleasure, fame, obscurity, gain and loss. Paying too much attention to such matters results in the misery-go-round that the Buddhists call, and here is the other name I promised, "samsara:" which I shall define as the name for the endless cycle of busyness without differing results and without the intended outcomes.

To An Expanded Self...

HumaNatureConnect Activity

Start-up Protocol

If this is not a day when you prefer to spend time in nature without an agenda, do the Heartwood Path Start-up Protocol found in the Appendix.

Being Like A Natural Being Or Natural Area

For this activity, be like a natural being or natural area. After gaining permission to become involved with your chosen being or area, psychologically adopt the perspective of the being or natural area, and ask the natural being or natural area for guidance about discovering and maintaining your individuality.

Using any of the fifty-four natural attraction senses listed at Heartwood Path Waypoint # 3.4 (such as one's sense of appetite or one's sense of form and design), determine ways that aspects of nature in the area demonstrate and retain their unique attributes. Write down some attributes that you find attractive in a sentence such as "I find the tree's sturdiness attractive." Then, once you have at least five such sentences, in each sentence, replace the word you use for the natural attraction with labels you use for yourself, making the sentence something like "I find my own sturdiness attractive."

This will tell you a lot about what you find appealing about your own individuality. Then, look for ways in nature that entities remain distinct from one another such as "Brown creepers almost always feed below the bird feeder and nuthatches almost always feed up on the bird feeder."

Follow-up Protocol

For best results, write down your impressions of this activity in your journal using the Heartwood Path Follow-up Protocol found in the Appendix. Afterwards, consider sharing your interpretations with others.

Heartwood Path Axioms

Key Assertions From Waypoint 3.93

3.93.1.

Refrain from building up the repetitive, judgmental concepts attached to emotions.

3.93.2.

Work calmly for the benefit of others.

3.93.3.

Recognize the goodness in troublemakers.

3.93.4.

Even when you cannot see the way, start.

3.93.5.

Doing what you can expands the self.

Nocturnal Pilgrimage 3.93

For best results, write down your impressions of each night's dreams in your journal using the Heartwood Path Dreaming Time Protocols found in the Appendix. Afterwards, consider sharing your Dream Tending with others.

Tend to your dreams, as usual. Then, start your preparations for improving the chances for lucid dreaming—which is being conscious that you are dreaming.

This is not necessarily the easiest of all preparations. "Dullness and amnesia—which operate hand-in-hand—are the major obstacles to lucidity as we sleep. Dullness puts us in a daze . . . (and amnesia) keeps us from remembering while dreaming that we are asleep" (Wallace, 2012, p. 26). Five tips for how to purposefully enter into a lucid dream include:

1. motivating yourself to dream by stating forcefully beforehand, "Tonight, I will be aware that I am in a dream state,"
2. anticipating lucid dreaming during your waking hours,
3. developing the habit of lying still upon waking as a way to remember your dreams,
4. having to have something to say for your dream journal, and
5. having a collection of recorded Dream Images in a journal and picking out one of them, saying "the next time this image enters my dreams I will ask myself whether I am dreaming."

After tending to your dream, head to the next waypoint. Once there, you will take an important step toward self-perfection, which is self-surrender. Prepare to descend towards the Soul, to the lower part of the Self, where you can give birth to the nobler part of the Self. See from many points of view. Then, you can become both the composer and the symphony.

Make sure you are alone or with someone who will grant you some quiet time on your sojourns into nature for this book. I would not have been able to develop such a good relationship with my boulder buddy had I always visited my approachable monolith with chatty or distracting human companions.

Move to the next Heartwood Path waypoint: "Horizons." You are making great progress!

94

Horizons

MOVE FROM A "ME ONLY" PERSPECTIVE TO AN "ALL SENTIENT BEINGS" PERSPECTIVE

Heartwood Path books expand the participants perspective from "me only" to "me and my folks" to "all folks" to "all sentient beings." This series of books fosters this expansion in numerous ways, including:

1. by following numerous lines of intelligence such as naturalistic, interpersonal, verbal linguistic, and bodily kinesthetic (awareness of the position and movement of the body);
2. by understanding the use of Native American medicine wheels (as you will by doing the following activity);
3. by encouraging the creation of "childlife refuges;"
4. by going on vision quests;
5. by learning how to perceive ecological conditions;
6. by learning to attend;
7. by perceiving relations;
8. by adding context and processes to one's perception of material objects;
9. by maintaining flexibility of perception;

10. by perceiving depth;
11. by using the imagination;
12. by developing one's ecological identity through sense of place maps and personal property lists;
13. by understanding that any ethic is doomed if its practice causes those who live by it to perish and take their cherished moral notions with them; and
14. by learning to "let go" and
15. by evoking the authentic whole through The Eleven Directions Ceremony.

Each time one seeks an answer from a natural area the procedures employ any of the fifty-four natural attraction senses (such as the dreaming sense or the territorial sense) and have certain common elements, such as:

1. thinking about a question to bring to nature or asking "What can you help me with today?;"
2. thankfully gaining permission from an attractive natural area to visit it and to help you do this activity;
3. opening and closing the eyes to pick out various attractions in the scene;
4. using as many natural attraction senses as possible (such as touching a rock);
5. avoiding the use of names by calling the natural attraction a "connection experience;"
6. imagining becoming each attraction; psychologically adopting the perspective of the being's essence and then answering your own question(s);
7. returning to being yourself psychologically;
8. thanking this connection experience for being and for participating in your quest; and
9. writing down the answers to your questions and sharing them with others.

To The Knowledge In Dreams...

HumaNatureConnect Activity

Start-up Protocol

If this is not a day when you prefer to spend time in nature without an agenda, do the Heartwood Path Start-up Protocol found in the Appendix.

Dreaming Yourself Awake

For this activity, ponder the following ways to dream yourself awake, that is, to enter into lucid dreaming as a method of achieving insight and transformation:

1. awaken yourself in any dream where words change when looking back at them;
2. awaken yourself in any dream where clocks change when looking at them again;
3. awaken yourself in any dream where, after jumping up, you descend slowly;
4. extend your lucid dream by consciously giving it a longer story line;
5. when you see something unusual in a dream say to yourself "How odd is that?" or "Is this possible?"
6. setting an alarm during the last two hours of sleep (prime lucid dream hours) and then going back to your dream lucidly after you awaken;
7. purposefully inspecting a Dream Image by spinning it around and giving it a rub-down; and
8. on weekends, sleep a couple of extra hours and, thereby, extending the prime time for lucid dreaming.

Pick one or more of these devices to increase your chances of lucid dreaming.

Follow-up Protocol

For best results, write down your impressions of this activity in your journal using the Heartwood Path Follow-up Protocol found in the Appendix. Afterwards, consider sharing your interpretations with others.

Heartwood Path Axioms

Key Assertions From Waypoint 3.94

3.94.1.

Expand your perspective from "me only" to "me and my folks," then to "all folks," and finally to "all sentient beings."

3.94.2.

While communing with nature, always write down your impressions and avoid the use of names by calling the natural attraction a "connection experience."

Nocturnal Pilgrimage 3.94

For best results, write down your impressions of each night's dreams in your journal using the Heartwood Path Dreaming Time Protocols found in the Appendix. Afterwards, consider sharing your Dream Tending with others.

You can use lucid dreaming for flights of fantasy, for improving your skills, or to explore your mind. You can use lucid dreams to rehearse your interactions with people. Fears can be overcome. You can stretch the boundaries of your Ego or self-concept. Those engaged in lucid dreaming do so for a variety of reasons, "from an exotic hobby to a spiritual quest" (Wallace, 2012, p. 67). Perhaps most pertinent to this course, you can use lucid dreaming for "going beyond the dualism of 'self' and 'other'" (Wallace, 2012, p. 34).

Using what you now know, the next time you sleep, dream lucidly. Tend to your dreams. Then, continue with your pilgrimage by starting the next teaching.

Move to the next waypoint: "Sacred Hoop." While there, make sure the activity (and all subsequent activities) take place within the rich context of nature. If you are part of that half of the U.S. population that has or will have depression or some other mental disorder, use your time in nature as a remedy (Selhub & Logan, 2012, p. 40). If you are part of the other half you may be fine or you may be undiagnosed. Either way, even if you do not have a mental disorder now, use your time communing with nature as a preventative measure.

95

Sacred Hoop

BUILD AND USE A MEDICINE WHEEL

A medicine wheel is a graphic mystic symbol of the universe that is typically a circle of stones used as an aid to meditation and prayer. As a map of wholeness, the medicine wheel is said to:

1. help one recognize and fill any holes that jeopardize one's integrity;
2. give one a chance to strengthen one's connection with the Earth; and
3. increase one's understanding of oneself and one's relationship with all of creation.

Medicine wheels were usually placed by Native Americans in areas where the energy of the Earth could be felt strongly—sometimes in places called "*vortexes*" today.

Each quadrant of the medicine wheel has a specific function. The quadrant of the medicine wheel facing East corresponds with focusing the mind (intellect, intelligence, reason, and recollection). The South-facing quadrant of the wheel corresponds with guiding the will (decisions, desires, choice, determination, and resoluteness). The West-facing quadrant corresponds with using the intention (purpose, goals, aim and planning). And the North-facing quadrant of the medicine wheel corresponds with developing wisdom (common sense, prudence, understanding, and discretion). Each quadrant of the medicine wheel is said to present its insights best during a particular season: the East in Springtime, the South in Summer, the West in Autumn, and the North in Winter. In addition to the four quadrants pointing to the Cardinal Directions, medicine wheels also relate to the Sky above, Earth below, and the inner world within. Concerning the Above Direction of the medicine wheel, one embraces the unseen realms of Spirit, the heavenly realms, and the intangible forces in creation. In the Below Direction, one learns how to perceive unseen forces in the natural world, how spirit indwells in all living things, and how one brings forth or utilizes Spirit in the body. The Within Direction teaches one how to gain access to all life in the universe; how to access the inner realm; and how to behave in a state of awareness, without judgment or a sense of separation.

By figuratively or literally dancing with the medicine wheel, one can reach for knowledge of the mysteries and dangers inherent in life and learn how to bring balance to oneself and to the Earth. Look to the various parts of the medicine wheel, such as the Spirit Keepers or the Elemental Clans for the big picture, and the Moon Stones for the details (each aspect described subsequently).

The whole configuration of the medicine wheel appears as a circle within a circle that is divided into four quadrants. It is often manifested as a grouping of thirty-six rocks.

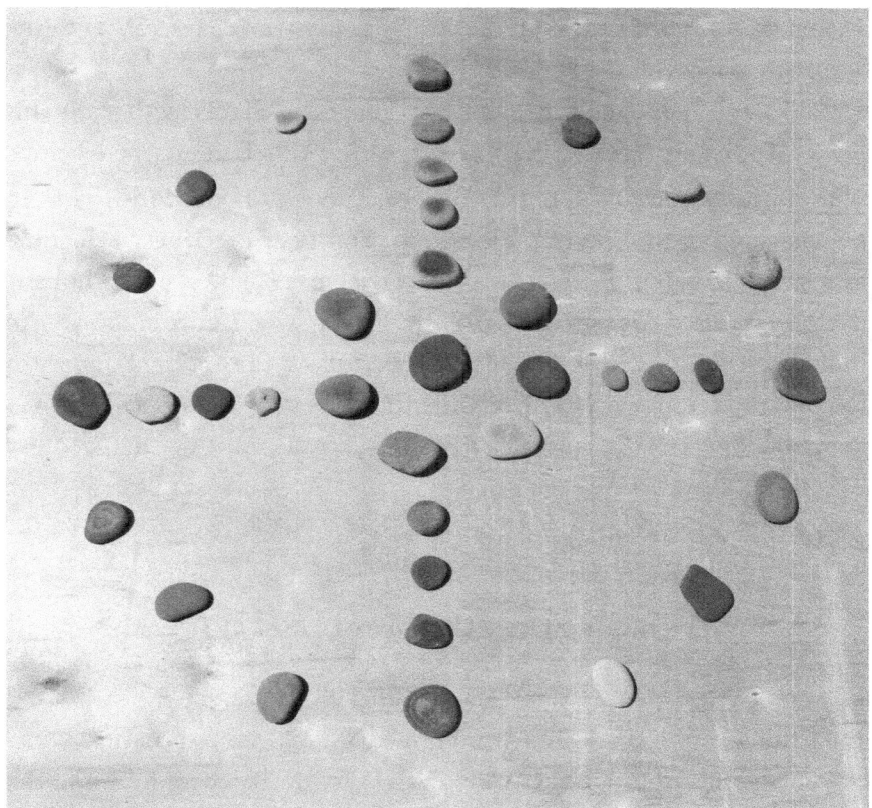

Each of the thirty-six rocks in a fully constructed medicine wheel has a specific function. As a whole, the medicine wheel represents a system of correspondences in terms of totems, seasons, and life lessons.

One need not associate magical powers with the medicine wheel or each of its stones (although that would be fine if you so desire). By building a medicine wheel, however, you will develop for yourself a comprehensive way to chart your own personal growth. There is no need to quibble about which Native American Tribe offers the best medicine wheel. All are but human interpretations of the Great Mystery, which can never be fully explained. If you prefer to think of the medicine wheel as a holistic way to chart one's personal growth (which it certainly is), then think (as I do) of the stones as representing various pertinent topics. If it helps you to regard each stone as a spiritual being with magical powers think of the stones as mystical characters with the ability to teach.

I like the medicine wheel author Sun Bear shares with us in his book **Medicine Wheel: Earth Astrology (1980)** (described below, without his associated totems which lead to more questions than can be answered in the present discussion). Sun Bear describes each stone as a spiritual being; I prefer to think of them as markers on a holistic chart to be used for personal growth. Either way, I encourage you to build a medicine wheel and then either follow the rational approach to contemplate at each stone or the original Native American or pagan approach of receiving guidance from the various stone deities.

To A Stronger Connection To The Earth...

HumaNatureConnect Activity

Start-up Protocol

If this is not a day when you prefer to spend time in nature without an agenda, do the Heartwood Path Start-up Protocol found in the Appendix.

Building And Using A Medicine Wheel

For this activity, gather up thirty-six rocks (trying not to use any used as hiding places by animals). Using Sun Bear's medicine wheel construction method, begin with the...

The Center Stone

Place a stone in the center of your space for the medicine wheel. This rock, the Father Stone, is known as the "Creator" because it is said to be the one that creates all or any elements, plants, minerals, animals and colors. The Creator, is to be viewed not as a noun but as a verb, indicating the movement, the activity, the motion, and the pulsations of the never ending source and force of the Creator. When contemplating at this stone, ask for help by evoking the power of the Absolute Spirit (or the Creator stone) when you feel fear about the creative abilities of the mind (or lack thereof), when you feel that you do not have a deep knowledge of the universe, when you feel unsure about your spiritual values, and when you feel the need for change. Questions to ask yourself in the presence of the Center stone include:

"Am I balanced?"

How do (or how can . . .) I bring beauty into the world?

and

How do (or how can . . .) I bring harmony into the world?"

The Center Circle

Seven rocks are arranged around the center Creator Stone. This circle of seven stones is known as the Center Circle. It is said to teach us about the basic elements of life. To find the location of each rock in the Center Circle begin with the stone (the Earth Mother Stone) located just southeast of the Center Stone, and then move in a sunwise /clockwise fashion.

Center Circle Mother Earth Stone

The Earth Mother stone represents the love of new beginnings, the nurturing female energy. Find solace at the Earth Mother stone when you feel sadness, anguish about the condition of the Earth, hopelessness, concern about infertility, and the need to become a better parent.

The Mother Earth Stone is said to represent (or give us) our home and our lives.

Earth Mother stone evokes the following question:

"How does (or how can . . .) my home enhance my life?"

Center Circle Father Sun Stone

Seek the active energy of the Father Sun Stone when you need energy or a place to pray about big issues such as nuclear weapons/energy. Contemplate at the Father Sun Stone when you need to ponder expansion in your life, when you need help with promoting or blocking masculine energy, when you need help learning how to accomplish something or finding courage, when you need help with expressing yourself, and when you need help in matters of discrimination. The Father Sun Stone represents that which warms and quickens our lives.

A question evoked by the Father Sun Stone is . . .

"What is my most effective source of energy?"

Center Circle Grandmother Moon Stone

This stone ought to be visited whenever you need help with your dreams and visions, help with intuitive powers and psychic abilities, help with discovering your own sensuality and sexuality, and help learning about your emotional side or the shadow side of your being. The Grandmother Moon Stone represents that which guides our dreams and visions.

Grandmother Moon Stone encourages us to ask . . .

"What is my biggest dream?"

and

"How would I describe my biggest vision?

Center Circle Turtle Clan Stone

The Turtle Clan Stone represents the following powers: organizational skills, deliberative action, solid growth; loyalty to the Earth and all her relations.

A question to pose at the Turtle Clan Stone is . . .

"What additional organizational skills or deliberative actions are needed for me to best express my loyalty to the earth?"

Center Circle Frog Clan Stone

The Frog Clan Stone represents that which teaches us how to expand the transformative, rejuvenating, and regenerating powers; how to change; how to feel one's emotions; and how to become aware of the reflective aspects of one's being.

A question for the Frog Clan Stone is . . .

"What do I need to clean up in my life?"

Center Circle Thunderbird Clan Stone

The Thunderbird Clan Stone represents the power of innovation, passion, transmutation; and observing all sides of reality.

The main question to be asked at the Thunderbird Clan Stone is . . .

"What do I feel most passionate about?"

Center Circle Butterfly Clan Stone

The Butterfly Clan Stone represents the powers of quickness and nimbleness; lightheartedness; open-mindedness to the point seeming to be indecisive; communicating with a wide variety of groups; and building bridges between the different realms of life: physical, mental, and spiritual.

At the Butterfly Clan Stone, ask . . .

"What in me needs to change for me to meet my goals?"

The Spirit Keepers

We move now to the stones at the four cardinal directions of the outer ring of stones. Power in all of its forms and lessons from the ethereal realm are to be found at each of the Spirit Keeper Stones.

Spirit Keeper Of The North Stone

This Spirit Keeper represents the message: "give it away." Give away your knowledge, give up your impatience, give away your fear of death, give away your unwillingness to take care of your body, and give away your reluctance to share all that has been given to you. The Spirit Keeper of the North represents that which influences all the moons in the Northeast quadrant (each discussed below). Go to the Spirit Keeper of the North when contemplating how to heal your body. Use wintertime to contemplate your life, the paradoxes in life, questions of life and death, and somatic healing.

At the North Spirit Keeper Stone, ask . . .

"What new knowledge do I need to meet my goals?"

and

"Do I question 'why' before acting on someone else's decision?"

Spirit Keeper of the East Stone

This Spirit Keeper represents innocence, awakening, new beginnings, spontaneity, playfulness, and truth-saying. Just as the Spirit Keeper of the North Stone represents the ability to heal the body, the Spirit Keeper of the East represents the ability to heal the mind.

At the East Spirit Keeper Stone, ask . . .

"What new beginning do I need to make to heal my mind?"

and

"Do I notice moments of inspiration?"

Spirit Keeper Of The South Stone

As the Spirit Keeper of Summer, the stone at the South Cardinal Direction represents rapid growth, energy, adaptability, maturity, self-assurance, attraction, falling in love, sensuality, sexuality, and humor.

As such, Summer is the time to heel the emotions and to correct problems in relationships.

At the South Spirit Keeper Stone, ask . . .

"In what way can I bring youthful energy to my relationships?"

"In what ways, if at all, do I enjoy physical work and using my body?"

and

"In what ways, if at all, do I enjoy dancing?"

Spirit Keeper Of The West Stone

This Spirit Keeper teaches us responsibility for the Self, the Earth, and all our relations on Earth. This sense of responsibility fosters self-lessness, which helps one heal spiritually. The West correlates with the Fall, a good time to balance looking within and acting without.

At the West Spirit Keeper Stone, ask . . .

"Of all my areas of responsibility, for which of them do I need to most look within for guidance?"

"In what ways, if at all, do my emotions get me into trouble?"

and

"Do I remember my dreams?"

The Four Spirit Pathways

The three stones that stretch from the Creator to each of the cardinal direction stones make up the Spirit Pathways. These lines of stones remind us of the gifts of the four Spirit Keepers and teach us about the gifts we need to return to the source, the Creator. Moving along the Spirit Paths, from the outside to the inside of the circle on a medicine wheel, is a symbolic trip from ordinary reality to sacredness. Spirit Paths or used to give thanks or to ask for help. They are also reminders of our gifts and responsibilities as humans.

Northern Spirit Pathway Cleansing Stone

This outermost rock in the northern Spirit Path, represents one's ability to:

1. detoxify the body by getting rid of impurities that are preventing good health,
2. clear out old ideas and to detach from former ways of thinking that no longer help,
3. discharge emotions that are blocked allowing for a true catharsis.

An important question to pose at the North Cleansing stone is . . .

"What do I most need to clean or purify in my life?"

Northern Spirit Pathway Renewal Stone

This middle stone in the northern path represents healing, rebuilding, and revitalizing one's physical body. This stone represents the following:

1. a healthier attitude concerning the way one views the world and one's place in it,

2. the value of opening up to new ideas and restructuring one's thinking,
3. how to love yourself more, how to be good to oneself, and how to take care of oneself regarding one's feelings.

This stone is used to renew one's belief in the Creator and in the goodness of life.

An important question to pose at the North Renewal Stone . . .

"How can I revitalize my body?"

Northern Spirit Pathway Purity Stone

Closest to the Creator on the North Spirit Path, this moon stone represents:

1. wholesomeness;
2. pristineness;
3. freshness;
4. the ability to see the world through the eyes of a child;
5. the ability to return to a sense of innocence;
6. the ability to rekindle enthusiasm;
7. the ability to get rid of misconceptions, preconceptions, cynicism, and sarcasm;
8. the ability to revitalize one's sense of integrity, honesty, spontaneity, and receptivity; and
9. self-realization.

A question to pose at the North Purity Stone is . . .

"What, if anything, do I have to renew in my life?

Eastern Spirit Pathway Clarity Stone

This moon stone is located first in from the Spirit Keeper Stone of the East. It represents:

1. how to simplify life and live without unnecessary complications;
2. how to see things clearly, have more awareness, and communicate more directly; and
3. how to have more unblocked emotional energy.

A question to pose at the East Clarity Stone is . . .

"What, if anything, do I need to bring into clearer focus in my life?"

Eastern Spirit Pathway Wisdom Stone

Midway toward the Creator on the East Spirit Pathway, this moon stone represents:

1. one's own limits and the limits of the world;
2. the ability to discern—the application of knowledge;
3. how to increase one's maturity and sense of stability; and
4. how to best express one's love or appreciation.

An important question to pose at the East Wisdom Stone is . . .

"Who or what do I need to appreciate more in my life?"

Eastern Spirit Pathway Illumination Stone

Closest to the Creator on the East Spirit Path, this moon stone represents how to:

1. let the sacred energy of the Creator flow vitally through oneself for the purpose of enlightenment;
2. relate to the world around oneself and thus help one see the truth of the universe;
3. allow one's emotions to be balanced and free-flowing;
4. explore the concept of unconditional love and peace; and
5. share with others the illumination one has received.

A question to pose at the East Illumination Stone is . . .

"Where in my life do I need foresight the most and how can I attain that intelligence?"

Southern Spirit Pathway Growth Stone

This first rock in from the South Spirit Keeper Stone, the Growth Stone represents:

1. change, development, unfolding, expanding, maturing and opening up oneself to all that is physical;
2. expansion of one's knowledge for the purpose of adding depth character;
3. the ability to experience a broad range of feelings; and
4. taking responsibility for one's own life.

A good question to pose at the South Growth Stone is . . .

"What in my life do I need to cast more light upon?"

Southern Spirit Pathway Trust Stone

Located midway to the Creator on the South Spirit Path, this moon stone represents:

1. confidence, being sure of oneself, accepting consequences, body acceptance, and surrendering to life;
2. letting go of suspicions, strengthening one's beliefs, increasing one's receptivity, and learning;
3. the capacity to give and receive love, express oneself completely, increase one's vulnerability, and learn about faith;
4. spiritual oneness, and
5. confidence in one's relationships.

A question to pose at the South Trust Stone is . . .

"What do I need to advance in my life?"

Southern Spirit Pathway Love Stone

This closest stone to the Creator in the South Spirit Path represents:

1. how the pleasure of love is expressed in sexual energy, affection, touching, eating, smelling, viewing, hearing, and in orgasm;
2. sensuality, union, touching, parenting, mating, and finding pleasure in one's relationship with the world and in one's body;
3. healing emotional problems, improving communication, accepting yourself and others, validating others, being honest, honoring

or cherishing others, devotion, tenderness, compassion, delight, joy, ecstasy, and passion;

4. harmony through nurturing, trust, and sharing; and
5. transcendence and selflessness through dedication to service.

A question to pose at the South Love Stone is . . .

"Who do I need to trust more in my life and how can I achieve that trust?"

Western Spirit Pathway Experience Stone

This outermost stone in on the West Spirit Path represents:

1. the value of concrete skills, body memory, trial and error, education, expertise, and hands-on learning;
2. how to increase stability, confidence, and involvement;
3. how to be selective;
4. how to know oneself better;
5. how to temper oneself; and
6. how to integrate and focus one's knowledge.

A question to pose at the West Experience Stone is . . .

"Where in my life do I need more experience, knowledge, and understanding?

Western Spirit Pathway Introspection Stone

Located midway on the Spirit Path of the West, this stone helps one look within. It represents how to:

1. reflect, contemplate, synthesize;
2. think before speaking; and
3. meditate, contain oneself, and communicate directly with the Creator.

A question to pose at the West Introspection Stone is . . .

"What do I need to be introspective about?

Western Sprit Pathway Strength Stone

Closest to the Creator in the West Spirit Path, this stone represents:

1. endurance, stamina, and power;
2. mental discipline and concentration; and
3. the courage of convictions;
4. increased determination and decisiveness; and
5. being centered, self-aware, balanced, courageous, aware of emotional limits and likes, and in control of one's actions.

A question to pose at the West Strength Stone is . . .

"Where in my life do I most need power in vigor of mind and how can I achieve that mental strength?"

The Moon Stones

Movement, change, growth and enrichment are all combined to form the essence of a medicine wheel. This essence is said to influence people throughout the year in various ways determined by the date of birth, the time of the year, and the contemplation of a particular moon stone.

It is said by those that believe in the magical powers of the medicine wheel that on the day you are born you come under the influence of your particular moon stone, one of twelve arranged to form, along with the Spirit Keepers, the Outer Circle of the medicine wheel. One's birth stone on the medicine wheel is said to determine how a person will be as a child and how they will act during times of transition in their lives. The qualities associated with one's birth stone are said to be the ones that make one feel most comfortable. Therefore, it is to your moon stone that you can return when you need familiarity, security, or confidence. You are not, however, bound to the qualities of your birth stone. You may contemplate other moon stone qualities as you attempt to change or grow. This statement brings up an important point:

Like the passing of the seasons,

people pass through many phases

during their lives.

Lessons can be gleaned from each moon. You may consider the lessons from any moon stone at any time, but it is recommended that you pay special attention to your birth stone and to the stone that corresponds to the current time of the year.

Earth Renewal Moon Stone

Beginning with the winter solstice on December 22—the time the Suns returns from its journey to the South and begins to bring the warmth that speeds growth—the Earth Renewal Moon (a so-called birth stone for those born between December 22 and January 19) is placed at the first of three positions moving clockwise between the North Stone and the East Stone. The lessons of this moon are:

1. how to be clear in receiving and transmitting universal energy;
2. how to be a good communicator of important information; and
3. how to be respectful of tradition and ritual.

People under the influence of this Moon Stone (or contemplating its associated lessons) have added potential for great power, keen vision, good ceremonial abilities, adaptability, prudence, and wisdom.

The question to pose while at this stone is . . .

"In what ways, if at all, am I a logical person?"

Rest And Cleansing Moon Stone

This stone (a birth stone for January 20 - February 18) is placed halfway between the North and East Cardinal direction stones. People experiencing this stone are reminded to learn the value in being:

1. valuable,
2. light-hearted, and
3. playful.

This stone represents what it takes to help one like people, oneself included; be more humanitarian in one's views; excel in communication; develop one's intellect; be more romantic; develop psychic abilities; and uncover bold or gentle aspects of one's being. Those under the influence of this stone (or remembering to contemplate its associated lessons) need to guard against dreaming so much that none of their noble ideas ever become reality.

Questions to seek answers for at the Rest and Cleansing Moon Stone is . . .

"In what ways, if at all, am I mentally disciplined?"

and

"In what ways, if at all, do I have a sense of oneness with all life?"

Big Winds Moon Stone

The Big Winds Moon (February 19 - March 20) is the last moon of the Spirit Keeper of the North. This stone, located clockwise three-thirds of the way toward the East, represents the teaching of the meaning of value; the value of healing abilities; the need to establish safe territory; psychic abilities; the value of sensitivity; the value of spirituality; the value of expressing one's true feelings; and the value of being grounded on the Earth. Those contemplating this stone are reminded to guard against:

1. moodiness (as we all know, never argue with a woman when she is tired....or rested),
2. melancholia,
3. hyper- sensitivity, and
4. being unrealistic.

A question to seek and answer for at the Big Winds Moon Stone is . . .

"In what ways, if at all do I have personal experiences in my relation-ship to the Absolute Spirit?"

Budding Trees Moon Stone

This stone (March 21 - April 19) is the first moon of the Spirit Keeper of the East. This stone is located one-third of the way clockwise between the Eastern and Southern stones in the outer circle.

This stone represents the following teachings:

1. the need for tempering fiery emotions;
2. the advantages of being grounded as well as soaring to new heights;
3. the joy and freedom of a long, clear perspective;
4. energy;
5. intensity;
6. catalyzing change;
7. fearlessness;
8. optimism; and
9. leadership.

A question to attempt to answer at the Budding Trees Moon Stone is . . .

"In what ways, if at all, do I sense shifts of energy around me?"

Frogs Return Moon Stone

This stone (April 20 - May 20) is placed halfway between the stones of the East and South.

This stone represents the value of:

1. balancing the Earth and the sky within oneself,
2. sustaining oneself and others,
3. making all environments as pleasing as possible,

4. stability,
5. perseverance,
6. patience, and
7. practicality.

Those contemplating this Moon Stone are reminded to guard against being too stubborn, overindulging, and holding back all of their feelings.

Questions to attempt to answer at the Frogs Return Moon Stone are . . .

"In what ways, if at all, do I feel drawn to the mysteries of life?"

Corn Planting Moon Stone

This location on the medicine wheel (May 21 - June 20), placed three-thirds of the way in a clockwise direction between the East and the South, represents the value of teaching about:

1. the link between the plant and animal kingdom,
2. cleansing and strengthening,
3. the beauty and grace of quick movement,
4. the beauty in yourself, others, and the environment,
5. one's own healing abilities,
6. the cutting edges in one's personality,
7. the necessity of balancing time and energy, and
8. one's ability to create.

Those contemplating this stone are reminded of the need to guard against inconsistencies, being overly suspicious, and not being willing to show deep feelings.

A question to attempt to answer at the Corn Planting Moon Stone is . . .

"In what ways, if at all, do I like regular exercise?"

Strong Sun Moon Stone

This stone (June 21 - July 22) is located one-third of the way between South and West. People encountering this stone learn about:

1. heart-felt connections,
2. personal abilities to heal and inspire,
3. the personal desire for expression,
4. intuition,
5. wildness,
6. the conservative aspects of one's personality,
7. the love of home and the need for a strong home-base,
8. the law of relationship, and
9. nurturing the family.

When contemplating at this location in the medicine wheel, guard against emotional groveling and the fear of taking a position.

A question to attempt to answer at the Strong Sun Moon Stone is . . .

"In what ways, if at all, do I like gardening?"

Ripe Berries Moon Stone

This location in the medicine wheel (July 23 - August 22) is located midway between South and West represents the value of teaching people:

1. about their own strength,
2. about their sweetness and the thorns they extend to protect the vulnerable part of themselves,
3. about their depth and need to teach,
4. about working from the heart center to demonstrate affection,
5. about how to face fears,
6. about ways to develop leaderships skills, and
7. about the development of courage and power.

People encountering the Ripe Berries Moon stone are reminded of the need to guard against impulsiveness, arrogance, and an inclination to dominate any situation.

A question to attempt to answer at the Ripe Berries Moon Stone is . . .

"In what ways, if at all, do I like my body?"

Harvest Moon Stone

This stone (August 23 - September 22) is the last rock moving clockwise before the West cardinal direction stone. Those contemplating at this moon stone are reminded:

1. to use good judgment and seek justice,
2. to develop the personal power needed to pierce the heart and soul,
3. to use their creative wonder,
4. to be discriminating,

5. to make fair decisions,
6. to have good sense,
7. to persevere,
8. to have confidence, and
9. to be practical and understand the concept of work and duty.

Contemplators at the Harvest Moon are reminded of the need to guard against being too critical of others and cynical about life.

At question to attempt to answer at the Harvest Moon Stone is . . .

"In what ways am I an emotional person?

Ducks Fly Moon Stone

This stone (September 23 - October 23) is the first moon moving clockwise from the Spirit Keeper of the West stone. People experiencing the Ducks Fly Moon are reminded of the value of learning:

1. how to draw in the energy from both the Earth and Sun to understand the messages of the heart;
2. about their abilities to soothe and irritate;
3. what it takes to understand their relationships in groups;
4. about the value of balance,
5. how they can go rapidly from one idea, concept, or mood to its opposite, and
6. how to show physical affection.

People associating with the Ducks Fly Moon stone are reminded of the need to guard against being indecisive and so changeable they confuse even themselves.

A question to attempt to answer at the Ducks Fly Moon Stone is . . .

"In what ways, if at all, do I welcome change?"

Freeze Up Moon Stone

This Moon Stone (October 24 - November 21) is halfway between West and North. People experiencing this stone are reminded to learn how to:

1. be sensitive and to focus their energies;
2. heal and be versatile
3. be adaptable and silently travel to places others might fear to go;
4. travel to other realms of existence and how to become a messenger for the spiritual aspects of life,
5. know the extent of one's energy and ability to create change, be inquisitive, desire truth, and see well.

Freeze Up Moon contemplators are reminded of the need to guard against not being grounded and becoming too suspicious.

A question to pose at the Freeze Up Moon Stone is . . .

"Do I enjoy shaking things up?"

Long Snow Moon Stone

The last location before the North cardinal direction, this Moon Stone (November 22 - December 21) reminds contemplators of the value of learning about:

1. one's ability to perceive and mirror the thoughts and feelings of others,

2. being soft and strong at the same time,

3. the power of beauty, majesty, and cooperation,

4. the desire for justice,

5. one's ability to live with the dualities of life,

6. mental strength,

7. fear of emotions,

8. teaching, and

9. communicating.

Although people at the Long Snow Moon stone are reminded to be insightful, independent, fearless, determined and openhearted, they will do well to guard against being too argumentative and erratic in intimate relationships.

A questions to pose at the Long Snow Moon Stone are . . .

"Do I question authority?"

Follow-up Protocol

For best results, write down your impressions of this activity in your journal using the Heartwood Path Follow-up Protocol found in the Appendix. Afterwards, consider sharing your interpretations with others.

Heartwood Path Axioms

Key Assertions From Waypoint 3.95

3.95.1.

Medicine wheels are said to strengthen one's connection with the Earth and to increase the degree of understanding of oneself and one's relationship with all of creation.

3.95.2.

By figuratively or literally dancing with the medicine wheel, one can reach for knowledge of the mysteries and dangers inherent in life and learn how to bring balance to oneself and to the Earth.

3.95.3.

By building a medicine wheel you will develop for yourself a comprehensive way to chart your own personal growth.

Nocturnal Pilgrimage 3.95

For best results, write down your impressions of each night's dreams in your journal using the Heartwood Path Dreaming Time Protocols found in the Appendix. Afterwards, consider sharing your Dream Tending with others.

We have already discussed tending to your dreams and dreaming lucidly. Now we will add the topic of dream yoga. Our purpose for developing a proficiency in dream yoga is nothing less than helping all sentient beings end their suffering and helping all humans achieve relative bodhichitta or near enlightenment. I say near enlightenment because the aim here is to become a saint rather than a sage—the latter being fully enlightened. We are looking for the source of great compassion towards all sentient beings. This search is not a matter of faith alone, for that is not enough. The search is more practical, a quest for degrees of realization. We will be continuing on this path by recognizing that our "normal waking experience is just as deluded and fantastic as our dreams (meaning that) phenomena exist interdependently" (Wallace, 2012, p. 80).

"Dream yoga seeks to go beyond the psyche, eventually to the primordial consciousness, which, when fully realized, is synonymous with the ultimate goal of . . . enlightenment. Before one arrives there, however, we encounter a state of consciousness more subtle than the psyche, though not as transcendent as primordial consciousness. This second mental field, substrate consciousness, is different from the subconsciousness of Freud and the collective consciousness of Jung" (Wallace, 2012, pp.70-71). Similar to a computer chip, substrate consciousness stores previous inputs (behaviors and thoughts). Like software, the substrate consciousness uses these inputs to moderate the present and condition the future. "Our fears, misconceptions, memories, latent tendencies, and so forth are all stored in the substrate consciousness . . . This space is vividly cognized when one experiences deep, dreamless sleep, lucidly . . . Explored wisely, the . . . substrate consciousness (becomes) the gateway to wisdom and to enlightenment. Dream yoga provides direct access to this realm and a means of transforming it. (Wallace, 2012, p. 72).

To begin the practice of dream yoga, after stopping at the next waypoint, engage in the next Dream Activity. It will have two parts: one on daytime dream yoga practice and the other on nighttime dream yoga.

Continue to the next waypoint: "Splendid Expectations." Get outside to do the next activity. Remember that any fears about insects, wolves, bears, or snakes are usually completely out of proportion to the actual danger. The chances of being attacked by any wild animal are miniscule. Just be careful and watchful and you will be fine.

96

Splendid Expectations

MOVE TO MAKE A MAGNIFICENT FUTURE

Metaphorically speaking, to get to a magnificent future, we need to move through some gates unlocked by a magical key. Some of the most significant gateways to this magnificent future are the Natural Systems Thinking Process (described in more detail in the next Heartwood Path book entitled **Ecos**) a physiological condition known as coherence, the development of environmental ethics, and the spread of certain valued traits in humans (all described in a subsequent Heartwood Path book entitled **Ethos**).

None of the benefits of the Natural System Thinking Process, coherence, environmental ethics, and certain valued human traits are put to good use without the magical key. That magical means, so critical to human happiness and a sustainable environment, is the requisite foundation for the creation of eco-centric elders. That magical means, that key to a magnificent future, is gratefulness.

Before examining the key to the gateway to a magnificent future, spend some time examining current problems in your life by doing the following activity:

To The Best Choices...

HumaNatureConnect Activity

Start-up Protocol

If this is not a day when you prefer to spend time in nature without an agenda, do the Heartwood Path Start-up Protocol found in the Appendix.

Examining Preferred-scenario Possibilities

For this activity, write down a description of a problem in your life or a missed opportunity. Ask yourself some future-oriented questions concerning your problems or missed opportunities:

1. What would your problem or missed opportunity look like if you were dealing with it better?
2. How would your lifestyle change once this problem is solved?
3. What will you do differently with people once this problem is solved?
4. What other behavioral pattern(s) would be in place when you solved this problem?
5. Regarding your chosen situation, what would be happening in your life once the problem is solved that is not happening now?
6. What would you have that you do not have now once this problem is solved?
7. What decisions would you have already made once this problem is solved?
8. What accomplishments would you have made once this problem is solved that are not in place now?
9. Concerning missed opportunities, what would the opportunity look like once it is developed?

10. Who do you know that has solved a similar problem or reaped a similar opportunity or developed a similar missed opportunity?
11. Why did you choose this person?
12. What did this person do to solve a similar problem or develop a similar opportunity?
13. Describe why this person's handling of a problem situation or missed opportunity appeals to you in terms of what this person has that meets your aspirations. Concerning your problem situation or missed opportunity, review a time in your life that you did not have similar problems or faced missing similar opportunities.
14. What was it about this better time in your life that is instructional to you now in correcting your current situation?

Decide how you can explore new possibilities by getting involved in new experiences, including volunteering, possibly moving to a new place of residence, or helping others face situations similar to the one or ones bothering you.

Follow-up Protocol

For best results, write down your impressions of this activity in your journal using the Heartwood Path Follow-up Protocol found in the Appendix. Afterwards, consider sharing your interpretations with others.

Heartwood Path Axioms

Key Assertions From Waypoint 3.96

3.96.1.

Four significant gateways to a magnificent future include the Natural Systems Thinking Process, the physiological condition

known as "Coherence," environmental ethics, and certain valued human traits.

3.96.2.

The key to all of the gateways to a magnificent future is gratefulness.

Nocturnal Pilgrimage 3.96

For best results, write down your impressions of each night's dreams in your journal using the Heartwood Path Dreaming Time Protocols found in the Appendix. Afterwards, consider sharing your Dream Tending with others.

Fifth WILD Tip

Make sure you are not fooled when you wake up. WILDs are very vivid and, if not too weird, may seem familiar enough to you for you to believe that you are awake when you are not. To guard against this occurrence, do Reality Checks, as instructed previously.

If you are actually awake, set an intention for tonight's dream. Associate with your dreams. Amplify your Dreams. Animate your dreams. Add to your Dream Council. Play with your Dream Council Figures. Add a Dream Council Sentry to the mix. Take your Dream Council with you when you visit a chosen attractive natural being.

When ready, move to the next waypoint: "Acknowledgement." None of the benefits of the Natural System Thinking Process, coherence, or valued human traits are put to good use without the acknowledgement of gratefulness.

97

Acknowledgement

SHOW GRATITUDE

To avoid a common misconception, let me first distinguish appreciation from gratitude. For our purposes here, let us define appreciation as the recognition and enjoyment of the good qualities of someone or something and gratitude as the quality of being thankful, readiness to show appreciation, and the returning of kindness. Note that only the latter, gratitude, comes with a sense of obligation, the returning of kindness. Later on, particularly in the section on the Natural Systems Thinking Process in the following book, I will discuss ways to appreciate natural attractions. Here I want to focus on the gratefulness, the thankfulness, and the sense of welcome obligation one has to return the kindness to the person or thing one appreciates. Unlike books like **The Secret**, I will not be talking about using gratitude to gobble up goodies. Consumerism causes "affluenza," the "emotional distress that arises from a preoccupation with possessions and appearance" (Macy and Johnstone, 2012, p. 46). Instead, I will, after a general discussion of gratitude, focus on the More-Than-Individual benefits that come from thankfulness to both wildness itself and the effort to preserve the environment.

According to Macy and Johnstone, "our willingness to act on behalf of others isn't just attributable to some people being good-natured and others less so. "Our readiness to help others is influenced by the level of gratitude we experience" (Macy and Johnstone, 2012, p. 45).

Gratitude "pulls us out of the rat race. It shifts our focus from what's missing to what's there" (Macy and Johnstone, 2012, p. 48) It is a free way to experience " a sense of well-being and contentment on an on-going basis" (Ryan, 1999, p. 13). Like the Natural Systems Thinking Process, gratitude is often discounted because it is uncomplicated and simple. All you have to do is notice a goodness in your life and feel the uplift of gratefulness. It helps one feel that, at least for the moment, one has all that one needs. In this way, gratitude opens the heart, a prerequisite to compassion. Gratitude also blocks fear and anger. Turning one's attention to the recollection of gifts received turns one toward the light, toward contentment, toward acceptance, toward order, toward peace, and toward clarity, especially towards one's view of the future. With gratitude, and the resulting widening of one's frame of vision, what was common becomes miraculous, what was discouraging becomes uplifting, and what made one repellent to others (one's thanklessness) makes us attractive to others (one's gratitude-induced exuberance). Gratefulness helps one overcome perfectionism, as one begins to see that oneself and the world are good enough. This state of thankfulness makes *having* less important than *being* and *presents* less important than *presence*. The quality of one's presence becomes more openhearted, especially as acts of gratitude, starting small and working up, gradually makes one trust, increasingly, the goodness of the universe. Showing gratitude in this way, in manageable but escalating steps, engenders the courage needed for the growth of generosity. This courage is reinforced as one notices that the more one gives the more one gets. As courage leads to the kind of generosity that results in various forms of payback one begins to see how much connection and reciprocity there is in the world. This sense of connection is joy-producing, especially as one practices the Natural Systems Thinking Process and environmentalism. These two monumentally important means are two ways to garner the notion, joyous because they feel like a loving embrace, that, as the following activity reinforces, one cannot live outside of the web of life.

I stress the importance of gratitude because, with all it gives in return, if you do nothing more than feel thankful and act on your gratitude, doing that alone will likely be good enough. Try it.

It is not enough to know the problems faced by nature. It is not enough to suffer in sympathy with the birds and bunnies. Count your concerns, girdle your guilt trips, and let go of fear. But do not stop there. One is more than one's suffering. Count also your blessings. One also can be wonderfully full of wonder and awed by the bountifulness and diversity in nature. See the world afresh, as if for the first time, everyday. Lay your arms open, not only to delight and fervor, but also to acceptance. To be fully happy in one's own fullest development, one has to both feel the suffering of others, human and non-human, and return the kindness nature imparts on us all.

As part of your grateful experience and action, change what you see that is not working. Change the way you see your commonplace world. Appreciate what you have and who you are. Trade taking aspects of the living earth for granted for being grateful for your thoughts and reciprocating actions. Be grateful for each positive thing in your scope of influence and concern and for each positive behavior in your range of experience and thought.

Shrink life's little annoyances with regular expressions of gratitude. When one faces all situations with gratitude, no matter what happens, one is free to choose to be happy.

The relationship between you and the earth is a comfortable two-way street, made even more reciprocal through gratitude. If you cannot think of anything to be grateful for, hold your breath as long as possible and you will be inspired to remember a very important gift. In times of trouble, look for the hidden opportunity, the newly revealed gift. If nothing else, learning and growing are always hidden within any tribulation. For the good times, adopt a sort of prayer in which you dedicate the positive moments to someone or something in need.

Always, live as if every day is your last and honor those who came before you (Ryan, 1999, p. 180). Doing so, builds "a sense of belonging and wholeness" (Ryan, 1999, p. 164).

Showing gratitude may not produce immediate material returns on one's investment, but it will offer the best feeling one can experience, for it is the mother of all other good feelings. Along with this immediate gratification, it will also result in fewer regrets in the future. Gratitude glues the positive to one's life.

Ingratitude makes one feel deprived and thus robbed of the energy to develop the valued traits so necessary for an eco-centric elder. Comparatively, when one finds one's great fullness of gratitude one has the fuel to act for the benefit of oneself AND others.

Learning universal principles and anchoring one's sense of an individual self—the topics of this and the previous Heartwood Path book—do not together necessarily mean that a person will end up with valued traits. Unless a person expands their own sense of Self outward to include the whole, it is likely that that person will be self-centered and self-serving. It is also doubtful that that person will be community-minded, unless that person develops a self-sense perspective that includes neighbors, the community, and the earth as a whole. Writes Winter and Koger:

"A clean delineation between self and environment is arbitrary and artificial . . . Much of our present difficulty stems from our having considered ourselves separate from, or even above, our natural environment. Instead, our actions are both a product and a cause of the environment in which we behave" (Winter and Koger, 2004, p. 117-119).

We shall now turn to a discussion aimed at promoting an end to this capricious and unnatural delineation.

To A Correspondence With Wholeness...

HumaNatureConnect Activity

Start-up Protocol

If this is not a day when you prefer to spend time in nature without an agenda, do the Heartwood Path Start-up Protocol found in the Appendix.

Cultivating One's Relationship With The Whole

For this activity, determine how each seemingly separate element has ties of relationship with the whole. We will work on making this determination in two ways: 1) Making a Relationships in Nature Map and 2) Feeling the Pain of the World.

Making A Relationships In Nature Map

Draw a kind of map of all the relationships in nature. Be sure to include yourself in this exercise. Map out numerous ties of attraction in words or as a drawing that looks like a web of relationships with lines between each relating part. On the lines label the nature of the relationship and how it is attracted to other aspects of nature. Notice the intelligence of the whole web, its attractiveness, and the love it displays by maintaining the whole. Share your notes or drawing of the web with others.

Connecting With The Pain Of The World

Take a moment to express gratitude more fully and to experience the pain of the world. Give thanks for the oxygen you are using which would not be there had it not been for the tireless work plants have done to make our atmosphere breathable. Thank the plants in your immediate environment for doing their part in absorbing carbon dioxide and, thereby, reducing the greenhouse effect that contributes to the

global climate change that, if unchecked, could make the planet danger-
ously overheated. After showing your gratitude extensively, experience
the flip side of gratitude, which is fear and anguish. Write down in
your journal what troubles you about the plight of the environment,
locally, nationally, and globally. Then turn to your responses to these
problems. How, if at all, is it your role to work on solutions? How,
if at all, are you reluctant to get involved for fear of standing out in
a crowd? How, if at all, does knowledge of the information about environmental problems threaten your political or commercial interests?
In what ways, if at all, are your worries about the environment too
upsetting to think about? What do you know, if anything, that you can
do to correct environmental problems? In what ways, if at all, do you
feel that your actions on behalf of the environment will not make any
difference anyway? Write down in your journal anything pertaining to
your pain for the world. Include any feelings of outrage, alarm, grief,
dread, and despair. As you write down your comments about your
pain for the world, if any, imagine that the planet is feeling these pains
through you. Imagine the feelings of pain for the world coming into
you from the planet and then out from you so they do not stick to
you in a way that is debilitating. Instead of just paying attention to
your normal inhalations and exhalations, image that the incoming air
is filled with the pain of the world. Allow this pain-filled air to move in
through your mouth or nose. Then, imagine that you are passing this
pain-filled air through your heart before it reconnects with the wholeness of the web of life. Feel the countless hardships coming in through
your nose and moving through your heart before returning to the environment. Just create in your mind the sensation of this flow, both in
and out. Allow the sorrows to ripen in your heart before passing them
back to the web of life. Do not worry that you will be harmed by all of
this grief. Your heart is as big as the world. Use these ripening sorrows
as fertile mulch in which you expand your knowing. If you feel no pain
but only numbness or if you feel only your own sorrows, note these
thoughts in your journal and try this activity again. Recall the words of
Thich Nhat Hanh:

"What we need most to do is to hear within us the sounds of the Earth crying"

(Macy and Johnstone, 2012, pp. 60-75).

Follow-up Protocol

For best results, write down your impressions of this activity in your journal using the Heartwood Path Follow-up Protocol found in the Appendix. Afterwards, consider sharing your interpretations with others.

Heartwood Path Axioms

Key Assertions From Waypoint 3.97

3.97.1.

Gratitude is a free way to experience a sense of well-being and contentment.

3.97.2.

Showing gratitude in manageable but escalating steps engenders the courage needed for the growth of generosity.

3.97.3.

As part of your grateful experience and action, change what you see that is not working.

3.97.4.

**Showing gratitude—the mother of all other good feelings—
glues the positive to one's life.**

3.97.5.

**When one finds one's great fullness of gratitude one has the
fuel to act for the benefit of oneself AND others.**

Nocturnal Pilgrimage 3.97

For best results, write down your impressions of each night's
dreams in your journal using the Heartwood Path Dreaming Time
Protocols found in the Appendix. Afterwards, consider sharing your
Dream Tending with others.

Sometimes your worst nightmare can be a blessing in disguise. If
you allow a lucid bad dream to happen, rather than ending it, you
can examine the evil character and perhaps determine that the evil
character is just like yourself—full of joys and sorrows, hopes and fears.
By offering compassion to the evil character, which may be a representation of some lost part of your Ego, you can possibly repair some hole
in your psyche.

Through lucid dreaming you can also repair some unfinished business with people and situations that cannot be approached directly. To
do so, conjure up the pertinent party, ask questions, offer forgiveness,
release feelings of guilt, or do whatever is cathartic.

You can use lucid dreaming to improve performance by lucidly
practicing without an actual audience. Similarly, you can use lucid
dreaming to improve creativity by lucidly manipulating mental objects
and situations. Sleep. Dream lucidly. Tend to your dreams.

As is our custom, do the next activity outdoors, for being in nature
is a way to buffer the stress of the man-made world, being in nature

provides an opportunity for deep contemplation, and being in nature enhances altruism (Selhub & Logan, 2012, p. 44).

When you are ready, move to the next waypoint, the last one in this course: "Unfolding." What you are achieving is monumental!

98

Unfolding

LEARN WHAT IT TAKES TO GET PEOPLE TO DO THE RIGHT THING ENVIRONMENTALLY

In any effort wherein people endeavor to reawaken to their wholeness, there is inevitably a certain amount of unfolding involved. The unfolding I speak of is the gentle change of awareness marked by a focus on yourself as an individual, to a focus that adds to your sense of Self a broader and deeper focus on one's place in the ecosystem, to a focus on one's affiliations, and to a focus on one's relationships.

As a child I remember my grandfather saying that the house being built next door would be unstable because it was built on fill-dirt that was not tamped down adequately nor given time to settle properly. Sure enough, within two years of being completed, that house literally cracked down the middle, as the back half slumped due to its improper footing. The inch-wide crack, that ran from gable to foundation, has always been an adequate reminder to me of the importance of a proper foundation.

The lesson learned is clear: one cannot build a stable More-Than-Individual-Self, full of rich relationships and suitable for environmental advocacy, until one has an Individual Self set on a firm footing. In person-construction, as in house-construction, there has to be a solid foundation.

To avoid sinking due to a weak foundation, the individual self, which is the foundation for the More-Than-Individual-Self (and the topic of the next Heartwood Path book) has to have at least the following four components:

1. self-confidence,
2. the ability to accept criticism,
3. the ability to obtain goals, and
4. the willingness to take risks and try new experiences.

Zen Habits, Inc. offers the following twenty-five ways to develop self-confidence (you don't need to do them all):

1. groom yourself,
2. dress nicely,
3. change your self-image,
4. think positive,
5. kill negative thoughts,
6. get to know yourself,
7. act positive,
8. be kind and generous,
9. be prepared,
10. live your principles,
11. speak slowly,
12. stand tall,
13. increase competence,
14. set a small goal and achieve it,
15. change a small habit,
16. focus on solutions
17. smile,
18. volunteer,
19. be grateful,

20. exercise,
21. empower yourself with knowledge,
22. get active,
23. stop procrastinating
24. work on small things, and
25. clear your desk (http://zenhabits.net/25-killer-actions-to-boost-your-self-confidence/).

Zen Habits, Inc. also has tips for how to accept criticism with grace and appreciation:

1. let the anger that develops run its course before you respond;
2. find the positive in the negative, such as finding new approaches to criticized actions;
3. thank all critics;
4. learn from criticism;
5. be a better person by delegating the criticism to your actions and not to your self-concept; and
6. rise above what feels like an attack by never attacking back (http://zenhabits.net/how-to-accept-criticism-with-grace-and-appreciation/).

Forbes contributor Molly Cain offers six ways to obtain your goals:

1. make them visible,
2. tell other people about them,
3. break your goals up into manageable steps, and
4. set a deadline.
5. be realistic, and
6. recommit to yourself each time you falter (http://www.forbes.com/sites/glassheel/2013/03/14/6-ways-to-achieve-any-goal/2/#7b6c3ed83c71).

To help yourself try new things and take risks:

708 | DON PIERCE

1. feel like you do not want to be left behind by developing yourself through risk-taking and novelty,
2. allow yourself to fail at first,
3. make repeated attempts, and
4. build up your courage by:

   - stopping underestimating yourself,

   - considering the risks of settling,

   - remembering that risk is relative (no need to compare your risk-taking to others),

   - being realistic about what could go wrong,

   - letting go of what others think,

   - picturing everything going well,

   - starting small,

   - facing your biggest fear,

   - doing what makes you happier,

   - allowing yourself to back out,

   - avoid recklessness,

   - weighing the risks and the benefits,

   - maintaining a safety net,

   - planning for failure, and

   - considering others

   (http://www.wikihow.com/Take-Risks).

By gently reminding others of the ways to develop the solid foundation of a an individual self-identity, we eartHearts help others to grow. EartHearts ought not, however, force a person to awaken to his or her own personal or broader identity. A flower opens at its own right time.

We eartHearts will not be involved in coercion—that is, getting people to grow or unfold by force. Nor will be spending much time in politics (as it is now practiced), which, when you think about it, is the culture's legitimate form of prodding others to support candidates and public policy.

We will, however, help political allies seeking environmental protection to become more effective and enduring; and, we will use a means to gently further the cause of creating an appealing and sustainable environment—namely: behavioral psychology, which can be used to change environmentally inappropriate behavior. Winter and Koger write:

> "The wizardry of technological solutions might be impressive, but if we do not develop a behavioral technology to change what people actually do, we will not be successful" (2004, p. 88). They are referring to being successful in extricating ourselves from "our ecological predicament" (Winter and Koger, 2004, p. 88).

According to behavioral psychology, ecologically inappropriate behaviors can be changed by:

1. reducing the interval between short-term reward and long-term punishment by making, for example, long-term goals clearer;
2. adding "reinforcers for environmentally appropriate behavior" such as "instituting tax breaks for conservation behavior;
3. adding punishers such as taxes for inappropriate behavior;
4. modeling appropriate behaviors; and

5. complimenting others for appropriate behavior (Winter and Koger, 2004, pp. 107-108).

These points hint at some of the things you will be doing in the next Heartwood Path book. But, for now, lets review what you said about your positive self-concept and what you said about what you expected to obtain by reading this book.

To The Envelop You Set Aside At The Onset Of This Book...

HumaNatureConnect Activity

Start-up Protocol

If this is not a day when you prefer to spend time in nature without an agenda, do the Heartwood Path Start-up Protocol found in the Appendix.

Opening Your Envelop Containing Your Personal Assessment Of Your Positive Self Concept And A Statement Of What You Hoped To Achieve By Taking This Book

At the onset of this book you were encouraged to create and fill out two tables and place them in a sealed envelope. In the first table, there are statements pertaining to what it takes to have a positive self-concept. Look at the statements made at the beginning of the book and then write down statements now that you have completed this part of the Heartwood Path. Compare.

Statements That Apply To People With Positive Self-concepts.	How, If At All, The Statements Apply To You At The Beginning Of This Course.	How, If At All, The Statements Apply To You At The End Of This Course.
I have self-confidence.		
I accept criticism and I do not become defensive.		
I can set obtainable goals.		
I am willing to take risks and to try new experiences.		

Now is your chance to react to what you stated at the onset of this course regarding your overall course expectations. Look over the second form you included in your sealed envelop. Compare your expectations to your results. Write down your reactions now that you have completed this course (answering the question on the right in the following table).

What would you like to get out of this course concerning your own individual self-concept?	What did you actually get out of this course concerning your own individual self-concept?

Follow-up Protocol

For best results, write down your impressions of this activity in your journal using the Heartwood Path Follow-up Protocol found in the Appendix. Afterwards, consider sharing your interpretations with others.

Heartwood Path Axioms

Key Assertions From Waypoint 3.98

3.98.1.

Prompt people to do the right thing environmentally.

3.98.2.

One tool for gently prompting people is behavioral psychology.

3.98.3.

The wizardry of technological solutions might be impressive, but if we do not develop a behavioral technology to change what people do, we will not be successful.

3.98.4.

Behaviors can be changed by: 1) reducing the interval between short-term reward and long-term punishment; or 2) adding reinforcers for appropriate behavior; or 3) adding punishers for inappropriate behavior; or 4) modeling appropriate behaviors; or 5) complimenting others for appropriate behavior.

Nocturnal Pilgrimage 3.98

For best results, write down your impressions of each night's dreams in your journal using the Heartwood Path Dreaming Time Protocols found in the Appendix. Afterwards, consider sharing your Dream Tending with others.

During lucid dreaming you can emanate or reproduce your Dream Images and you can purposefully transform them to your liking. Dream phenomena are entirely fluid. You can change characters in a nightmare. Or you can allow frightening dreams to continue, knowing that they are unreal and, therefore, no real threat.

Either way, get a good night's rest. Tend to your dreams.

In doing all the activities in the next Heartwood Path book, remember to move outside. The activities can be done in your backyard or in the back country; the wilder the landscape the better. If you can, do your activities in wilderness—relatively pristine wildness. Communing with nature in a wilderness area (as opposed to a manicured back yard) is adventurous and grippingly immediate. In essentially unspoiled wildness you can find the largest array and best balance of wild beings. You may want to start getting into the habit of bringing appropriate gear (raincoat, hat, sunscreen, appropriate shoes or boots) as you head out into nature for the subsequent activities.

You have now spent ample time anchoring your individual self and, in so doing, protecting for the world your unique gifts. Next, you will endeavor to expand yourself outward to take advantage of the ecological portion of your Self, that portion of your Self that is more-than-individual and appears, to most people, to be nature. By awakening to your More-Than-Individual-Self you will discover abilities that you did not know you have, you will begin to see nature preservation as self-preservation, and you will minimize your own suffering. You are making great progress in your pilgrimage down the Heartwood Path. Keep going. More great insights and treasures are in store as you continue this journey of a lifetime. Do not spend so much time in front of empathy-killing computer screens. Empathy is grown outdoors. Narcissism, by contrast, is built-up as you sit in front of an electronic screen. Empathy, by contrast, is grown outdoors. Writes Selhub and Logan, "any tilt from empathy to narcissism has enormous consequences for society and the natural environment" (2012, p. 44).

Congratulations on your progress. It is our hope that in taking this course you have been able to better anchor your own individuality. Prepare now to awaken to the unfolding of your awareness of your More-Than-Individual-Self. This unfolding will be a crucial stage in the quest to find enduring personal happiness and environmental sustainability.

When you are ready, move to the next book: **Ecos**. We will be there with you.

References

Abram, David. (1987) The perceptual implications of Gaia, Revision, 9(2), 7-15).

Access to Insight Website: http://www.accesstoinsight.org/lib/authors/silananda/bl137.html

Aizenstat, Stephen, Ph.D. (2009). Dream tending. New Orleans, Louisiana: Spring Journal, Inc.

Barrett, Julie Langdon. Website: http://julielangdonbarrett.com/2011/08/11/how-to-tell-the-difference-between-intuition-and-your-imagination-or-ego/

Babauta, Leo. (2009) The power of less: the fine are of limiting yourself to the essentials . . . in business and in life. New York, New York: Hyperion.

Barasch, Marc, Ian. (2000). Healing dreams: exploring the dreams that can transform your life. New York, New York: Riverhead Books.

Beck, Larry and Cable, Ted (2002). Interpretation for the twenty-first century. Urbana, Illinois: Sagamore Publishing, Incorporated.

Beck, Martha (2012). Finding your way in a wild new world. New York, New York: Free Press

Bernard, Patrick. (2004). Music as yoga: discover the healing power of sound. San Rafael, CA: Mandala Publishing.

Borden, Richard, J. (2014). Ecology and experience: reflections from a human ecological perspective. Berkeley, California: North Atlantic Books.

Bosnak, Robert. (1986). A little course in dreams. Boston, Massachusetts: Shambala Publication, Inc.

Bosnak, Robert. (1996) Tracks in the wilderness of dreaming. New York, New York: Delacorte Press

Boston, John Website: (https://www.american.edu/spa/cep/upload/jonathan-boston-lecture-american-university.pdf).

Bowden, Jonny, Ph.d, C.N.S. (2009). The 150 most effective ways to boost your energy. Beverly, Massachusetts: Fair Winds Press.

Buddy, Cathal Br. ofm. Website: www.praying-nature.com.

Buechner, Frederick. (1993). Wishful thinking. A theological abc. San Francisco, California: Harper.

Buhner, Stephen Harrod. (2004). The secret teaching of plants. Rochester, Vermont: Bear and Company, Inner Traditions International.

Bunzl, John M. (2004). Evolutionary Biology and Simultaneous Policy: Vision-Logic for the Next Stage in our Evolutionary Future, Website: http://www.integralworld.net/bunzl.html

Byzant Kabblah Website (www.byzant.com/mystical/kaballah/Path.aspx?number=31)

Care2.com

Cairns, John Jr. (2001) Equity fairness, and the development of a sustainability ethos. Blacksburg Virginia : Ethics in Science and Environmental Politics, February 1., Blacksburg Virginia. www.mnforsustain.org/cairns_j_equity_and_a_sustainability_ethos.htm

Cameron, Julie. (2006). Finding water: the art of perseverance. New York, New York: Jeremy P. Tarcher.

Cannon, Walter B. (1963). The wisdom of the body. New York, New York: W.W. Norton & Company, Inc.

Cengagesites Website: http://www.cengagesites.com/academic/assets/sites/4713/Chapter%2015.pdf

Capra, Fritjof. (1996). The web of life. New York, New York: Anchor Books, Random House.

Castro, Dr. Anthony J. (2009). Creating space for happiness: the secret of giving room. Amherst, New York: Prometheus Books.

CGJungPage Website: http://www.cgjungpage.org/learn/articles/technology-and-environment/683-robert-romanyshyn-on-technology-as-symptom-a-dream

Chakra Tones and Notes Website: http://www.wingmakers.co.nz/ Chakra_Tones_and_Notes.html

Chalquist, Craig, editor (2010). Rebearths: conversations with a world ensouled. Walnut Creek, Caliifornia: World Soul Books.

Chapman, Alan. (2003) website: http://www.businessballs.com/maslowtest.pdf

Childre, Doc and Martin, Howard. (1999). The heartmath solution. San Francisco, California: Harper Collins Publishers, Inc.

Chopra, Deepak. (2000). How to know god: the soul's journey into the mystery of mysteries. New York, New York: Harmony Books.

Chopra, Deepak. (2004). The book of secrets: unlocking the hidden dimensions of your life. New York, New York: Three Rivers Press.

Millaka Chopra Website: http://www.huffingtonpost.com/mallika-chopra/ finding-serenity_b_868151.html

Cialdini, Robert B. (2009) Influence: science and practice. Boston, Massachusetts: Pearson Education, Inc.

Clark, Rawn. (2002) Journal of Wester Mystery Tradition, No. 3, Vol 1 (Website www.jwmt.org/v1n3/32 paths.)

Cohen, Michael J. Ecopsych Website: http://www.ecopsych.com/iupsm-swaiver.html.

Cohen, Michael J. Ecopsych/Ecopsychology Journal Website: http://www.ecopsych.com/ecopsychologyjournal.html.

Cohen, Green Wave, ecopsych.com

Cohen, Michael J. Ecopsych/Lifeweb Website: www.ecopsych.com/lifeweb.html.

Cohen, Michael J. Ecopsych Thesis Quote Website: www.ecopsych.com/the-sisquote.html.

Cohen, Michael J. (1993) Integrated ecology: The process of counseling with nature. Humanistic Psychologist, 21(3), 277-295.

Cohen, Michael J, Ed.D. Personal email dated December 23, 2010.

Cohen, Michael J, Ed.D. Project NatureConnect Website: http://www.ecopsych.com/insight53senses.html.

Cohen, Michael J, Ed.D. Project NatureConnect Website: http://www.ecopsych.com/earthstories101.html).

Cohen, PNC Website: www.ecopshych.com/universealive.html

Cohen, Michael J, Ed.D. Green Wave Information: (Project NatureConnect Website: http://www.ecopsych.com/journalaliveness.html and personal email June 8, 2016)Comaford-Lynch, Christine. (2007). Rules for renegades. New York, New York: McGraw-Hill.

Cohen, Michael J. (2018). Principles of Organic Psychology. The Eco-Arts and Science of Unconditional Love Friday Harbor, Washington: Project Nature Connect

Cook, Charles. (2001). Awakening to nature: renewing your life by connecting with the natural world. New York, New York: Contemporary Books, MacGraw-Hill

Cope, Stephen. (1999) Yoga and the quest for the true self. New York, New York: Bantam Books.

Copenhagen Qabalah Website: www.qabalah.dk/paths.html.

Csikszentmihalyi, Mihaly. (1993) The evolving self: a psychology for the third millennium. New York, New York: HarperCollins Publishers, Inc.

Csikszentmihalyi. http://psychology.about.com/od/PositivePsychology/a/flow.htm)

Dangerfield, Dr. J. Mark Website. https://www.smashwords.com/.../how-to-love-nature-when-you-live-in-the city.

Delaney, Gayle, Dr. (1994) Sexual dreams: why we have them, what they mean. New York, New York: Fawcett Columbine.

De Stefano, Matias, Three Earth Chakra Videos on You Tube. https://m.youtube.com/watch?v=IcfOwlVQGec.

Discovery Fit and Health Website. http://health.howstuffworks.com/wellness/stress-management/finding-serenity-in-your-life2.htm

DreamTending Website: http://dreamtending.com/naturedreaming.pdf

Dyer, Wayne, Ph.D. (2005) The power of intentions: learning to co-create your world your way. Carlsbad, California: Hay House.

Dwoskin, Hale. (2009). The Sedona Method. Sedona, Arizona: Sedona Press.

Eat, Taste, Heal: an Ayurvedic Guidebook website: http://www.eattasteheal.com/ETH_6tastes.htm

Edge Magazine Website: http://www.edgemagazine.net/1995/11/robert-sardello/

E-How. http://www.ehow.com/how_2338305_develop-character.html.

EnglishClub.com Website: http://www.englishclub.com/vocabulary/fl-making-request.htm

Evernden, Neil. (1985). The natural alien. Toronto, Canada: University of Toronto Press.

Ewolt, Dave and Weeks-Ewolt, Alison. (2001) Rational spirituality: evidence of the web of life, Attraction Retreat Website: http://www.attractionretreat.org/Writings/RationalSpirituality.html

Farley, Kent M. (2002) Developing character traits through sport/athletic participation. The Sport Digest- ISSN: 1558-6448. The United States Sports Academy Website: http://thesportdigest.com/archive/article/developing-character-through-sportathletic-participation

Ferlic, K. (2007). Tapping and sustaining the source. Website: http://ryuc.info/common/creation_process/tap_sustain_source.htm

Ferlic, K (2009) A bottom line about sex and our creativity. Website: http://ryuc.info/creativesexuality/bottom_line_about_sex.htm

Fitness Health Zone Website: http://www.fitnesshealthzone.com/meditation/walking-meditation-and-its-benefits/

Fiorenza, Nick Anthony (2010). Planetary harmonics & Neurobiological resonances, Website: http://www.lunarplanner.com/Harmonics/planetary-harmonics.

Flickstein, Matthew. Online Website: Swallowing the River Ganges: http://innerself.com/Meditation/mindfulness.htm?phpMyAdmin=1IAC4WZXEVp9XvKg-Nokyjpr3el1.

Franden, Nathaniel. (1996). Taking responsibility. New York, New York: Simon and Schuster.

Franklin Institute Website: http://www.fi.edu/learn/brain/exercise.html.

Gallup, Inc: (http://www.gallup.com/poll/190916/americans-identification-environmentalists-down.aspx)

Gardner, Howard. (1999) "Intelligence reframed: multiple intelligences for the 21st century." New York: Basic Books.

Garon, Henry A. (2006). The cosmic mystique. Maryknoll, New York: Orbis Books.

GDRC Website: https://www.gdrc/uem/ee/Tbilissi.html.

George, James. (1995) Asking the Earth. Saftsbury, Dorset; Element Books Limited.

Goldman, Jonathan. (2002) Healing sounds: the power of harmonics. Rochester, Vermont: Healing Arts Press.

Goodreads Website: www.goodreads.com. Alan_Wilson_Watts

Grand, David, (2001) Emotional healing at warp speed. New York, New York: Harmony Books.

Gunther, Folke, and Folke, Carl, "Characteristics of Nested Living Systems," Journal of Biological Systems, 1:3, Stockholm: Sweden. Website: http://library.uniteddiversity.coop/Systems_and_Networks/Nested%20Living%20Systems%20(Holons)%20.pdf

Hargrove, Eugene C. (1988) Foundations of environmental ethics, Englewood Cliffs, New Jersey: Prentice Hall.

Hawkes, Joyce Whiteley, Ph.D. (2012) Resonance, nine practices for harmonious health and vitality, Carlsbad, California: Hay House, Inc.

Henning, Sequoia. Website: http://www.feelingsoulgood.com/index.php?id=2

Howerton, Mari and Sorensen, "Maya." Website: http://www.singandhum.com/educational-development/humming-for-health.html

Inner.org. The Gal Einai Website: http://www.inner.org/Institute of HeartMath. Online Website. Global Coherence Initiative. http://www.glcoherence.org/about-us/about.html

Hauser, Marc D. (2006) Moral minds: the nature of right and wrong. New York, New York: Harper Collins.

Helm, Russell Buddy. (2001). The way of the drum. St. Paul, Minnesota: LLewellyn Publications.

Hindu Temples and Gods Website: http://hindutemplesandgods.blogspot.com/2013/03/sri-yantra.html

Hubbard, Barbara Marx. (2001). Emergence: the shift from ego to essence. Charlottesville, Virginia: Hampton Roads Publishing Company

Huning, Barb. (2-28-11) Personal email: "Re: Editorial Help with Instructions and Marketing."

InnerVision Yoga Website: http://www.innervisionyoga.com/what-is-my-sacred-work/

Institute of Human Conceptual and Mental Development. Online Website. Experiences and Feelings: http://www.ihcmdonline.com/mentalproblems/experiences.htm.

Institute for Social Ecology Website: www.social-ecology.org/199.

Jackson, Brooks and Jamieson, Kathleen Hall. (2007). Unspun: Finding Facts In A World Of Disinformation. New York, New York: Random House Trade Paperbacks

Jensen, Derrick. (2000) A language older than words. White River Junction, Vermont: Chelsea Green Publishing Company

Jensen, Derrick. (2006) Endgame volume I: the problem of civilization. New York, New York: Seven Stories Press.

Jensen, Derrick. (2006). Endgame volume II: resistance. New York, New York: Seven Stories Press.

Jung Atlanta: http://www.jungatlanta.com/articles/winter02-decoding-hillman.pdf

Jurado, Anthony. (2010) Cracked.com Website: http://www.cracked.com/article_18405_7-insane-ways-music-affects-body-according-to-science_p2.html

Kahn , Pete3r H Jr. and Hasbach Patricia H. (2012) Ecopsychology: science, totems, and the technological species, Cambridge, MA: MIT Press.

Kawasaki, Guy (2004). The art of the start. New York, New York: the Penguin Group.

Kawasaki, Guy. (2012). Enchantment. New York, New York: Penguin Group.

Kaza, Stephanie. (1993) The attentive heart: conversations with trees. New York, New York: Fawcett Columbine.

Kittleswon, Mary Lynn. (1996). Sounding the soul: the art of listening. Einsiedeln, Switzerland: Daimon.

Kohn, Alfie (1990). The brighter side of human nature. New York, New York: Basic Books, Inc.

Kroeber, Theodora. (1961) Ishi: in two worlds. Berkeley, California: University of California Press.

Krutch, joseph Wood. (2009) The voice of the desert. New York, New York, General Books.

Kundalini Yoga Info Website: http://www.kundalini-yoga-info.com/humming.html.

Lachance, Albert (1997). "The Architecture of the Soul: Sacred Process Ecopsychology," from the book The Greening of religion: god, the environment, and the good life, edited by Carrol, John E., Broclelman, Paul, and Westfal, Mary. Hanover, New Hampshire: University Press of New England

Lama Dalai. (2011) How to be compassionate. New York, Neew York: Atria Books..

Lame Deer and Erdoes, John. (2009). Lame deer: seeker of visions. New York: New York: Simon and Schuster.

Leopold, Aldo. (1949) . A sand county almanac. London, England: Oxford University Press.

Leopold, Aldo and Flader, Susan L. (editor). (1991) The river of the mother of god and other essays by aldo leopold. Madison, Wisconsin: University of Wisconsin Press.

Lesser, Elizabeth. (2009). The seeker's guide. Website: www.oprah.com/spirit/10-Signs-of-Progress-on-Your-Spiritual-Path/10 - God is Optimistic - Oprah.com.

Lessmann, Kevin. (2004) Emotions of the Musical Keys Website: http://www.gradfree.com/kevin/some_theory_on_musical_keys.htm

Lewis, Dennis. Website: http://www.authentic-breathing.com/breathing_tips.htm

Levey, Joel and Michelle. (2003). The fine arts of relaxation, concentration & meditation: ancient skills for modern minds. Somerville, Massachutsetts: Wisdom Publications.

Levi, Renee. (2003). Group magic; an inquiry into experiences of collective resonance, doctoral dissertation executive summary: http://resonanceproject.org/execsum.cfm

Lovelock, James. (2010) The vanishing face of gaia. New York, New york: Basic Books.

Luks, Allen and Payne, Peggy. (1991). The healing power of doing good. New York, New York: Fawcett Columbine.

Luskin, Fred and Pelletier, Kenneth R. (2005) Stress free for good. San Francisco, California: Harper Collins Publishers.

Maathai, Wangari. (2010). Replenishing the earth. New York, New York: Random House.

MacGregor, Catriona. (2010). Partnering with nature: the wild path to reconnecting to the earth. New York, New York: Atria Paperback.

Macy, Joanna and Johnstone, Chris. (2012) Active home: how to face the mess we're in without going crazy. Novato, California: New World Library.

Mander, Jerry (1979) as quoted in the website: http://www.eco-action.org/dt/elimtv.html

Marc and Angel Website Practical Tips for Productive Living: http://www.marcandangel.com/2013/04/21/8-effective-ways-to-let-go-and-move-on/

Mayo Clinic/Ranges of Self-Esteem. www.mayoclinic.org

McCraty, Rollin Ph.D., Atkinson, Mike, Tomasino, Dana and Bradley, Trevor Raymond, Ph.D. (2006). The coherent heart: heart-brain interaction, psychophysiological coherence, and system-wide order. Boulder Creek, California: Institute of Heartmath.

McCraty, Rollin Ph.D. and Tomasino, Dana. (2006). Emotional Stress, Positive Emotions and Psychophysiological Coherence, Institute of HeartMath Website: alternativeworldwidehealth.com, Heartmath_Stress_chapter.pdf

McKay, Kim and Bonnin, Jenny. (2007) True green. Washington D.C: National Geographic Society.

McKay, Pip. (2009). Website: http://www.evolvenow.com.au.

McIntosh, Steve (2007) Excerpt from Integral consciousness and the future of evolution. Website: http://www.stevemcintosh.com/books/integral-consciousness/chapter-five-integral-politics/

McTaggart, Lynne. (2002). The field: the quest for the secret force of the universe. New York, New York: HarperCollins Publishers, Inc.

Mellick, Jill. (1996). The art of dreaming. Berkeley, California: Conari Press.

Michigan Online Website. http://web1.msue.msu.edu/4h/charcoun.html

Mindbodygreen Website: mindbodygreen.com

Mitchell, Shawne and Gunning, Stephanie. (2002). Creating Home Sanctuaries with Feng Shui: Sacred Spaces, Altars, and Shrines. New Page Books.

Montgomery, Pam. (2008) Plant spirit healing. Rochester, Vermont: Bear and Company.

Morris, Jill. (1985). The dream workbook: discover; the knowledge and power hidden in your dreams. Boston, Massachusetts: Little, Brown, and Company.

Murray, William H. From the website: http://innerself.com/content/social-a-political/environment/3934-for-those-who-would-save-the-earth.html

Myersbriggs.org

Myth-Dream-Symbols Website: http://www.mythsdreamssymbols.com/432.html

Nahko Bear (Medicine for the People). Song lyrics to "Aloha Ke Akua," (Onecommunityglobal.org).

Naiman, Rubin R. Ph.D. (2006). Healing night: the science and spirit of sleeping, dreaming, and awakening. Minneapolis, Minnesota: Syren Book Company.

National Catholic Reporter Website: http://ncronline.org/blogs/eco-catholic/fr-thedreamoftheearth.

Neubauer, Joan, R. (1985). Dear diary: the art and craft of writing a creative journal. Nashville, Tennessee: Turner Publishing Company.

New Oxford American Dictionary. Online Edition.

Noll, Doug. Website: http://lawyertopeacemaker.com/heartmath.html

Norbu, Namkhai. (2002). Dream yoga and the practice of natural light. Ithaca, New York: Snow Lion Publishing.

Nordhaus, Ted and Shellenberger, Michael. (2010). Break through: why we can't leave saving the planet to environmentalists. New York, New York: First Mariner Books.

Oelschlaeger, Max. (1991). The idea of wilderness. New Haven, Connecticut: Yale University Press.

Oestreich Associates. www.teamtrustsurvey.com

Oktar, Adnan. website: http://www.secretbeyondmatter.com/ourbrains/the-worldinourbrains3.html

Orloff, Judith (2003) Website: Trust your hunches: 5 steps to develop your intuition - Intuitive Advice: http://findarticles.com/p/articles/mi_m0NAH/is_8_33/ai_108786014/

Ortiz, John M., Ph.D. (1997) The tao of music: sound psychology. York Beach, ME: Samuel Weiser, Inc.

Ortner, Nick. (2013). The tapping solution: a revolutionary system for stress-free living. Carlsbad, California: Hay House, Inc.

Ouderkirk, Wayne and Hill, Jim editors. Land, value, community: Callicott and environmental philosophy. State University of New York Press. Internet: Callicott_My_Reply_to_Land_Value_Community.pdf

Parker, Jonathan (2011). The soul solution: enlightening meditations for resolving life's problems. Tiburon, California: H J Kramer.

Partridge, Ernest, Ecological morality and nonmoral sentiments. Internet: 60477.pdf.

Partridge, Ernest and Holmes, Ralston III. (1984 ad 1996) The Online Gadfly: http://gadfly.igc.org/papers/values.htm

Peaceful Mind. (2011) Website: http://www.peacefulmind.com/music_therapy.htm

Peaceful Rivers Online Website. Eckhart Tolle Quotes: http://peacefulrivers.homestead.com/EckhartTolle.html

Pearson, Carol S. (1991) Awakening the heroes within: twelve archetypes to help us find ourselves and transform our world. New York, NY: HarperCollins Publishers.

Peat, F. David. Nature and Ethics. http://www.paricenter.com/library/papers/peat23.php

Plotikin, Bill (2008). Soul craft: crossing into the mysteries of nature and the psyche. Novato, California: New World Books.

Plotkin, Bill. (2010). Nature and the human soul: cultivating wholeness and community in a fragmented world. Novato, California: New World Books.

Plotkin, Bill (2013). Wildmind: a field guid to the human psyche. Novato, California: New World Books.

Pratt, Vernon (Unknown) website: http://www.vernonpratt.com/211/

Reverso Online English Dictionary and Thesaurus: http://dictionary.reverso.net/english-cobuild/linear

Ricard, Matthieu. (2006) Happiness: A guide to developing life's most important skill. New York, NY: Little, Brown and Company.

Robbins, Stephen P. Organizational behavior, Chapter Six: website: http://www.go-bookee.net/organizational-behavior-stephen-p-robbins-14th-edition/

Root-Bernstein, Robert and Michele. (1999). Sparks of genius. Boston, Massachusetts: Houghton-Mifflin Company.

Rudd, Vols, Aaker Website: http://faculty-gsb.stanford.edu/aaker/pages/documents/TimeandAwe2012_workingpaper.pdf

Scull, J (n.d.) Eco-psychology: Where does it fit in psychology? Website: http://www.island.net/~jscull/ecopsych.htm

Scully, Matthew. (2002), Dominion. New York, New York: St. Martin's Press.

Second Journey Website, "Itineraries:" http://www.secondjourney.org/newsltr/NDX/Sullivan_frameset.htm

Selhub, Eva M. and Logan, Alan C. (2012). Your brain on nature: the science of nature's influence on your health, happiness, and vitality. Ontario, Canada: John Wiley and Sons Canada Ltd.

Seligman, Martin E.P. (2011). Flourish: a visionary new understanding of happiness and wellbeing. New York, New York: Free Press, Simon and Schuster.

Sewell, L. (1995). The Skill of ecological perception, In T. Roszak, M.E. Gomes, & A.D. Kanner (Eds.). Eco-psychology: Restoring the earth, healing the mind (pp. 201-215). San Francisco, California: Sierra Club.

Sewall, Laura Ph.D. (1999). Sight and sensibility: the ecology of perception. New York, New York: Jeremy P. Tarcher/Putnam.

Shannahoff-Khalsa, David S. (2006) Kundalini yoga mediation. New York, New York: W.W. Norton & Company

Sharp, Jonathan. (2002). Diving your dreams. New York: Simon & Shuster.

Silva Therapy Website: http://www.silvamindbodyhealing.com/articles/mind-body-healing/healing-colors/

SingingToThePlants Website: http://www.singingtotheplants.com/2014/01/dreaming-with-open-eyes/

Songwriting-guide.com Website: http://www.songwriting-guide.com/basic-music-theory.html

Sound Essence Website: http://www.soundessence.net/chakras.php

Sound-PHYSICS.com: http://www.sound-physics.com/Sound/Resonance-NaturalFrequency/

Spoto, Donald (2003). Reluctant saint: the life of francis of assissi. New York, New York: Penguin Books

Spurgeon, C.H. (1871) http://www.spurgeon.org/sermons/1005.htm

State of California, Department of Education, Regional Occupation Centers, and Department of Developmental Disability. (2014). Student Resource Guide: Direct Support Professional Training. http://www.dds.ca.gov/DSPT/Student/Student-Year1_FullVersion.pdf

Steep Path Online Website: http://www.steeppath.com/article.php?ID=6

Sun Bear. (1980). Medicine wheel: earth astrology. Austin, Texas: Touchstone.

Sunstein, Cass, R. and Nussbaum, Martha C. (2004) Animal rights. Oxford, England: Oxford University Press.

Székely, Edmond Bordeaux. The Essene Gospel of Peace. International Biogenic Society, 1981.

Tebra's Writer's Blog Website: http://www.thepensters.com/tebra/secular-saints-philosophy.html.

Templin, Steven, D.O.M Website. http://www.innerbalanceconsulting.com/wp-content/uploads/2011/11/HeartMath-Guide.pdf

Tharp, Twyla. (2003). The creative habit. New York, New York: Simon and Schuster.

Thomashow, Mitchell. (1996). Ecological identity: becoming a reflective environmentalist. Cambridge, Massachusetts: MIT Press.

Thompkins, Peter and Bird, Christopher. (1973) The secret life of plants. New York, New York: Harper and Row, Publishers.

Thoms, Justine. (2008) Small pleasures: finding grace in a chaotic world. Charlottesville, Virginia: Hampton Roads Publishing Company.

Thornton, James. (1999). A field guide to the soul: down-to-earth handbook of spiritual practice. New York, New York: Bell Tower

Thoreau, Henry David. (1965) Walden and on civil disobedience. New York, New York: Harper and Rowe.

Thoreau, Henry David. Excerpt from Journal, quoted from online website: http://www.mothwingarts.com/waldenvisionquest/excerpts.html

Thorncraft, Sylvan. 2006. Website: http://www.emeraldspritestudio.com/articles_toning_and_sacred_sound.htm.

TotalWellnessWorldwide Website: www.totalwellnessworldwide.com/ions.html

Twenge, Jean M. and Campbell, Keith, W. (2009). The narcissism epidemic. New York, New York: Free Press, Simon and Schuster. United States Conference of Catholic Bishops, Themes from Catholic Social Teaching" Washington, D.C., 2005. Website: http://www.cchdbaltimore.org/soc-teach-color-inst.pdf

Uphanishads. Uphanishads quotes and sayings. Website: http://spiritquotes.com/quotes/upanishadsquotes/upanishads_quotes1.htm.

Van Dyke, Deborah.Mantras Sacred Sounds Website: http://www.kirtancommunity.com/html/mantras_sacred_sound.html

Vedicyagyacenter Website: http://www.vedicyagyacenter.com/mantras-chant/Devi-Khadgamala-Stotram-lyrics-with-meaning.pdf

Veracious. Wikihow.com Website: http://www.wikihow.com/Choose-the-Right-Life-Coach

W, Karen. How to overcome fear. Website: http://www.wikihow.com/Overcome-Fear.

Wallace, Alan B. (2012). Dream yourself awake. Boston, Massachusetts: Shambala Publications, Inc.

Webster's Online Dictionary. http://www.websters-online-dictionary.com/definitions/Ethos

Weissman, Darren, R. (2005). The power of infinite love and gratitude. Carlsbad, California: Hay House, Inc.

Whitfield, Charles, L., Whitfield, Barbara H., Park, Russell, and Prevatt, Jeneane. (2006). The power of humility. Deerfield Beach, Florida: Health Communications, Inc.

Whitworth, Laura, Kimsey-Shouse, Karen, Kimsey-House, Henry, and Sandeahl, Phillip. (2007). Co-active coaching: new skills for coaching people toward success. Mountain View, California: Davies-Black Publishing.

Wholistic Healthworks Website: www.wholistichealthworks.com/healing%20with%20colors.htm

Wilber, Ken. (1995). Sex, Ecology, and Spirit: the spirit of evolution. Boston, Massachusetts: Shambala Publications, Inc.

Wilber, Ken, (1998). The essential ken wilber: an introductory reader. Boston, Massachusetts: Shambhala Publications, Inc.

Wilber, Ken (2007) Chapter 14. Integral Politics, or Our of the Prison of Partiality ... KenWilber.com Website: http://www.kenwilber.com/Writings/PDF/14-integral%20politics.pdf

Wilber, Ken; Patton, Terry; Leonard, Adam; and Morelli, Marco. (2008) Integral life practice: a 21st –century blueprint for physical health, emotional balance, mental clarity and spiritual awakening. Boston, Massachusetts: Integral Books.

Williams, Ernest H. Jr. (2005). The nature handbook: a guide to observing the great outdoors. New York, New York: Oxford University Press.

Wikia Website: http://synchromystic.wikia.com/wiki/432

Wiki-How. http://www.wikihow.com/Strengthen-Character

Wikipedia. David Hume. website: http://en.wikipedia.org/wiki/David_Hume

Wikipedia. Theory Z: webssite: http://en.wikipedia.org/wiki/Theory_Z

Wilderness Survival Sills for Save Wilderness Travel Website: http://www.wilderness-survival-skills.com/how-to-predict-weather.html

Wilson, Carol. (1997) Online Website. Mindfulness: Gateway Into Experience: http://www.dharma.org/ij/archives/1998b/carol_wilson.htm

Wilson, Edward O. (2002). The future of life. New York, New York: Vintage Books.

Winter, Deborah Du Nann and Koger, Susan M. (2004) The psychology of environmental problems. New York: Psychology Press

Wohlforth, Charles. (2010). The fate of nature: rediscovering our ability to rescue the earth. New York, New York: Thomas Dunne Books: St. Martin's Press.

You Tube: Caposiena, Nicholas. (2011) You Tube Podcast: https://www.youtube.com/watch?v=o-r_sMYzW_w

Zeleski, Inessa. North Star Wellness Center Website: http://www.calmness.com/chakras.htm

Zohar, Dana and Marshal, Dr. Ian. (2000). Spiritual intelligence: the ultimate intelligence. New York, New York: Bloomsbury Publishing.

Appendix

Online Resources

Your senses and the Heartwood Path will all come alive as you use the following online resources:

Read the **Glossary** and watch your sense of reason come alive. (www.heartwoodpath.com/glossary)

Use your sense of language when you connect online with other EartHearts at a variety of locations:

- **EartHeart Networking Forum** (www.heartwoodpath.com/connect)
- each **online waypoint** (learning station)
- our **Instagram** account (@heartwoodpath)
- our **Facebook** Page (Heartwood Path)

Your sense of light and sight will be activated when you watch our informative and visually appealing podcasts on **YouTube** (www.youtube.com/user/heartwoodpath).

Inside or outside, online or offline, the Heartwood Path helps you overcome any breaches in your well-being that hinder increasing your happiness and the sustainability of the natural environment.

HumaNatureConnect Activity Protocols

The full meaning of each protocol is revealed as you progress, waypoint by waypoint.

Start-up Protocol

- Read The Text — Use your literary sense, your mind sense, and your reason sense to move towards happiness and sustainability by reading the Heartwood Path text but also go outdoors to the backyard or to the backwoods, where the higher levels of negative ions in the air will improve your mood and well-being.
- Attention Restoration — With a pen and journal in hand, go to a natural area that is attractive, has a variety of plants and animals, and is tranquil enough to leave room for reflection.
- Source — Spend time wandering without an agenda in nature or, if you don't have time to receive nature's magic in this way, follow the instructions in the text at each learning station.
- Attractive Natural Being — Once you are in a natural area (the wilder, the better), look to find a natural being that is attractive to you and remain near that being until the end of the activity.
- Appreciation And Gratitude — While communing with your chosen natural being, appreciate it as you inhale and show it gratitude as you exhale.
- Consent — Once you find an aspect of nature that is attractive to you continuously for at least ten seconds, think of your continued attraction as your consent to have a connection experience that will help you function optimally; receive information, guidance, and healing; and establish in your mind a more helpful egalitarian relationship with the natural being.
- The Natural Senses — Beyond seeing, hearing, and the three other commonly recognized senses, use as many of the fifty-four

Natural Senses as you see fit and prepare to document the ones that you use in your journal.

- Great Trustable Truth — Experience what is happening at the present moment in nature, paying particular attention to the role of both beauty and balance; remember that the impressions you form about attractive natural beings and natural areas, coming from your experiencing of them in the Now, are trustable; and recognize that the natural processes and features witnessed are a source of special, substantial, and irreplaceable truthfulness about both nature and yourself.
- Recall — Place the great trustable truth and any other insights that you discover in a mental lock-box so you can later record them in your journal.

Follow-up Protocol

- Date — Write down the date of your outdoor nature-communing experience.
- Activity — Write down the waypoint title and number each time each you do an activity.
- Location — Write down the location of your outdoor nature-communing experience.
- Natural Being Indicator — Draw a picture or write down in your journal a nameless way to remember your chosen attractive Natural Being; for example, call it your "____ ____ Connection Experience."
- The Natural Senses Used — Write down all of the Natural Senses you used for this activity.
- General Description — Write a general description of how you did the activity and what happened.
- Freeform — Write, in freeform, what you found attractive about your natural being.
- Three Qualities — Write down three qualities you found attractive about your natural being.

- Three Learnings — Write down three things you learned from this activity.
- Self-esteem & Trust — Write down how, if at all, this activity changed your self-esteem or trustfulness of NNIAAL (Namelessness, Now, Intelligence, Alive, Attraction, and Love).
- Changes To Self — Write down what aspects of your Self, if any, were changed by this activity.
- Honor Yourself — Praise yourself and your commitment to making another stop along the Heartwood Path good for yourself and the world.
- I'm A Person Who. . . — Write down three different so-called "G/G Statements" using the following format: "This connection experience tells me that I am a person who_____."
- Feelings If Activity Taken — Write down a sentence about how you would feel if you lost your ability to experience this connection.
- Nature Compared To Self — Create a sentence that reads: "I love this (insert words that identify the attractive natural being) because it is (insert words that refer to the qualities you like about the natural being); then, create a parallel sentence that reads: "I love (insert the word "myself") because I am (insert the same qualities as before)."
- Ride The Green Wave — Determine whether you understand and agree with **all** of the Ten Green Wave Validation Statements.
- Name Your Discomforts — Make a list of aspects of your negative emotional residue, if any, that lifted simply by being in nature.
- Integral Immersion — Improve your journal writing by addressing what is, what could be, and what ought to be.
- Love Letter — Write a letter of gratitude to a natural being and another love letter from a natural being.
- Two-word Summary — Write down two words that summarize your response to this activity.

Heartwood Path Exchange

- Comment — Post your impressions and photos in the Comments section of this waypoint—the place for on-going discussion regarding this waypoint.
- Join — Engage with others in a Heartwood Path course or salon.
- Create — Start your own Heartwood Path salon that meets regularly online, by phone, or in person.
- Talk — Share your impressions with trusted family members and friends.
- Network — Post your impressions and photos on our EartHeart Networking Forum.
- Post — To see what conversations you can ignite, upload on social media your photos and impressions about anything pertaining to your journey down the Heartwood Path.
- Connect — Follow our account on Instagram, Like our Page on Facebook, Subscribe to our Channel on YouTube, and use hashtags such as "#heartwoodpath", "#eartHeart", and "#waypoint(insert book)(insert waypoint number) i.e."#waypointegos5").

Dreaming Time Protocols

The full meaning of each protocol is revealed as you progress, waypoint by waypoint.

Before Dreaming Protocol

- Dream Prep — Prepare yourself for productive dreaming by decluttering your mind before sleeping.
- Journal Ready — Prepare to record your dream impressions by placing your journal so that you can make initial recordings in it without changing your dreamtime sleeping position.

Dreaming Protocol

- Remember This — Look to your dreams to tell you what you need to remember.
- Open To Dream — Be receptive, fluid, interactive, and grounded as you dream.
- Lucid Dreaming — Be aware that you are dreaming and have an impact on what happens in the dream.
- Wake-Back-To-Bed — Wake up after six hours of sleep, staying awake for twenty minutes, then go back to sleep.
- Stabilize Your Dreams — Prolong your lucidity by making your dreams stable like the real world.
- Shape-shifters — Watch characters that change in your dream to see into the possibilities of your own transformation.
- World Dreams — Consider that your dreams may be tapping into the dreams of your chosen attractive natural beings or the wholeness of Nature.

After Dreaming Protocol

- First Off — Recall your dream by staying in your sleeping position as you make your first attempt to remember your dream.
- Book Of Dreams — Create an entry in your dream journal using the following linguistic tools: 1) talking in the present tense, 2) using verbs ending in "ing," 3) removing articles such as "an" or "the," and 4) using capital letters when naming the Dream Characters—which can be any notable people, places, or things that show up in your dream.
- Title — Give your dream a memorable title.
- Date — Write down the date of your dream.
- Description — Write down a short, general summary of your dream.
- Mood — Write down how the dream affected your mood upon waking.
- Life Event Affecting Dream — Write down any events in your life that may have influenced your dream.
- Dream Characters — List all remembered notable "actors" in your dream, whether they are people, places, or things.
- Setting — Describe the location of your dream.
- Statement Of Problem — Write down the complication, challenge, predicament, situation, obstacle, plight, quandary, or misadventure presented in your dream.
- Culmination Or Response To The Problem — Describe what you or another Dream Character did in your dream to respond to the problem presented in the dream.
- Conclusion — Describe how your dream ended.
- Beings Revealed — Write down how your dream seemed to be, if at all, linked in some way to your chosen attractive natural beings.
- Freud's Approach — Associate the actions of your Dream Characters with latent, infantile, repressed, or sexual drives.

- Jung's Approach — Amplify your Dream Characters into Archetypes that are global in scale, symbolic, pervasive, positive, and helpful.
- Hillman's Approach — Recognize your Dream Characters as animated, living beings by honoring their presence, place, and body.
- Right Information — Ask yourself the two main questions for Dream Tending: "Who is visiting now?" And "What is happening here?"
- The Richest Treasures — Do not force narrow interpretations upon the natural being impressions that reappear in your dream by condensing them into limited signs when it is more fruitful to simply engage with them as living beings that reside in your dream, possibly with infinite symbolic value.
- Privacy — Store your dream journal in a safe place and, where appropriate, share your dream with others.

Dream Council Protocol

- Create Dream Figures — Periodically create physical representations of select Dream Characters using natural materials, give them some form of identification, and gather them together.
- Pick Dream Council Members — Designate eight to fifteen of your most revered Dream Figures to serve on your Dream Council, which is your most honored dream advisory group.
- Convene A Dream Council Meeting — Whenever you desire, ceremoniously hold conversations with the Dream Figures that make up your Dream Council and write down any guidance you receive.
- Listen Deeply — If what you come across during your occasional interactions with Dream Figures does not make sense to you, write down your impressions so you can consider them at another time (when more experience can be brought to bear).

Green Wave Validation Statements

1. It is true what I experienced in the Heartwood Path HumaNatureConnect Activity.
2. Both myself and the natural attraction I experienced have at least some form of sensation and are, therefore alive.
3. Natural attraction is the essence of spirit, love, unity, and life.
4. There are ways of knowing that rely on scientifically valid sensations, there are ways of knowing that rely on stories, and happiness and sustainability are reduced when our subjective stories do not accurately reflect our AttractiveNaturalBeingImpressions;.
5. Humanity inherits fifty-four natural senses that enable us to register and relate reasonably to Nature's attractive aliveness and intelligence, in and around us today; **and I used, or considered the use of, all of these senses while doing this Heartwood Path HumaNatureConnect Activity.**
6. It is reasonable and intelligent to recognize that science is needed to clean up the mess made by believing that nature is an object to be exploited.
7. We suffer a wide range of disorders because, unreasonably, we live out of tune and balance with the purity of our AttractiveNaturalBeingImpressions. Without these impressions we habitually practice an artificial way of life whose nature-disconnected stories violate and injure the inherent natural wisdom that we share with the nature.
8. The whole of life deteriorates and we humans produce and suffer our discontents when our literate-story is inaccurate/imaginary/unreasonable and our consciousness is bonded to it and its nature-disconnected flaws.
9. HumaNatureConnect Activities improve our relationships by making space for NNIAAL (Now's Nameless, Intelligent, Alive, Attractive Love) to safely operate as we "Ride the Green Wave."

10. In any given moment we can come into balance and increase personal, social and environmental well-being by learning to empower our thinking and relationships through connecting with nature as we "Ride the Green Wave."

Natural Senses

The Radiation Senses

- Sense of light and sight, including polarized light.
- Sense of seeing without eyes such as heliotropism or the sun sense of plants.
- Sense of color.
- Sense of moods and identities attached to colors.
- Sense of awareness of one's own visibility or invisibility and consequent camouflaging.
- Sensitivity to radiation other than visible light including radio waves, X rays, etc.
- Sense of temperature and temperature change.
- Sense of season including ability to insulate, hibernate, and winter sleep.
- Electromagnetic sense and polarity which includes the ability to generate current (as in the nervous system and brain waves) or other energies.

The Feeling Senses

- Hearing including resonance, vibrations, sonar, and ultrasonic frequencies.
- Awareness of pressure, particularly underground, underwater, and to wind and air.
- Sensitivity to gravity.
- The sense of excretion for waste elimination and protection from enemies.
- Feel, particularly touch on the skin.
- Sense of weight, gravity, and balance.
- Space or proximity sense.

- Coriolis sense or awareness of effects of the rotation of the Earth.
- Sense of motion, body movement sensations, and sense of mobility.

The Chemical Senses

- Smell with and beyond the nose.
- Taste with and beyond the tongue.
- Appetite or hunger for food, water, and air.
- Hunting, killing, or food obtaining urges.
- Humidity sense including thirst, evaporation control and the acumen to find water or evade a flood.
- Hormonal sense, as to pheromones and other chemical stimuli.

The Mental Senses

- Pain, external and internal.
- Mental or spiritual distress.
- Sense of fear, dread of injury, death or attack.
- Procreative urges including sex awareness, courting, love, mating, paternity and raising young.
- Sense of play, sport, humor, pleasure, and laughter.
- Sense of physical place, navigation senses including detailed awareness of land and seascapes, of the positions of the sun, moon, and stars.
- Sense of time.
- Sense of electromagnetic fields.
- Sense of weather changes.
- Sense of emotional place, of community, belonging, support, trust, and thankfulness.
- Sense of self including friendship, companionship, and power.
- Domineering and territorial sense.

- Colonizing sense including compassion and receptive awareness of one's fellow creatures, sometimes to the degree of being absorbed into a superorganism.
- Horticultural sense and the ability to cultivate crops, as is done by ants that grow fungus, by fungus who farm algae, or birds that leave food to attract their prey.
- Language and articulation sense, used to express feelings and convey information in every medium from the bees' dance to human literature.
- Sense of humility, appreciation, and ethics.
- Senses of form and design.
- Sense of reason, including memory and the capacity for logic and science.
- Sense of mind and consciousness.
- Intuition or subconscious deduction.
- Aesthetic sense, including creativity and appreciation of beauty, music, literature, form, design, and drama.
- Psychic capacity such as foreknowledge, clairvoyance, clairaudience, psychokinesis, astral projection, possibly certain animal instincts, and plant sensitivities.
- Sense of biological and astral time, awareness of past, present, and future events.
- The capacity to hypnotize other creatures.
- Relaxation and sleep including dreaming, meditation, and brain wave awareness.
- Sense of pupation including cocoon building and metamorphosis.
- Sense of excessive stress and capitulation.
- Sense of survival by joining a more established organism.
- Spiritual sense, including conscience, capacity for sublime love, ecstasy, a sense of sin, profound sorrow, and sacrifice.
- Sense of homeostatic unity, of natural attraction aliveness as the singular essence-diversity attraction dance of all our other senses (NNIAAL). (Cohen, website: http://www.ecopsych.com/insight53senses.html).

Acknowledgments

I would like to thank everyone who helped me blaze the trail that has become the Heartwood Path. Initially, David Brower got me going, after asking me to "write a piece" to combat "burnout" in environmentalists. Roger Fritz helped me with my conversion from corporate executive to author. Paula Badger was a good listener on our frequent walks. Michael J. Cohen helped me to add nature's intelligence to the methodology. "Forest Maiden" Sylvia Shelton served as my "muse"—always with humor, tenderness, intelligence, and love. I started out thinking I was writing traditional books. My daughter Courtney Logue converted my text into an interactive website. Without her efforts—in editing, in creating the format, and in providing important encouragement—there would not be a Heartwood Path. To these people, and many more, I am forever grateful.

About The Author

Pierce has spent nearly his whole life working to protect the environment. After decades of work as a professional environmentalist, Pierce concluded that a new approach—one focused on the environmentalist and not just the environment—was needed.

When famed conservationist David Brower asked him to write "a piece" to show environmentalists how to persevere, the result was a series of books and courses that are good for both environmentalists and anyone seeking happiness and the preservation of nature. This series—the Heartwood Path—helps people to develop spiritually, helps people discover the benefits of communing with nature, and helps people find the abundant, abiding, and authentic happiness that comes from helping others, including natural beings.

Pierce formed his first environmental group—a tree planting club—when he was nine. After that, he was president of both his high school and college environmental organizations. After a few years as a professional river conservationist, he was hired by Brower to be the Midwest Representative of Friends of the Earth. Pierce has led numerous conservation groups, including the Illinois Chapter of the Sierra Club. He was a governor-appointed member of the Illinois Nature Preserves Commission.

He has a Bachelor's Degree in environmental science, a Master's Degree in political science, and Master's Degree in social work. When he was not working to protect the environment or guiding people down the Heartwood Path, Pierce—a qualified life coach and mental health practitioner—served those who needed his care—including those who are young, aged, mentally ill, or mentally disabled.

Currently working on his PH.D in eco-psychology, Pierce divides his time between Santa Barbara, California and St. Louis, Missouri. He is a professional drummer, an avid canoeist, and a photographer. He loves to walk in nature. He has two grown daughters (one, the mother of his two granddaughters, in Missouri and another one somewhere on a sailboat that is often close to Santa Barbara).

Heartwood Path One-On-One Guidance

(30 minute or 60 minute sessions)

Don Pierce will move you to an extraordinary awakening of personal happiness and ecological sustainability.

"Make a difference, happily."

To do so, go down the Heartwood Path under the skilled guidance of its creator, Don Pierce. Don's education and experience will help you turn your advocacy into a source of abiding, abundant, and authentic happiness. His years as an active environmentalist will enable him to teach you how to become both happy and effective in your own causes. His years as a social worker will help you fit better into your own environment. His experience as a life coach will help you set your own agenda towards meeting your goals. His years as a mental health practitioner will enable him to help you achieve the integrity that comes when your inner world enables you to be "glad" as you endeavor to make the outer world "green." By signing up for guidance, you will have Don at your side to answer questions, provide encouragement, and avoid wrong turns.

In productive and easy-to-afford steps, Guidance moves you to an extraordinary awakening of personal happiness and ecological sustainability. Guidance moves you beyond a common state of separation to an extraordinary awakening of oneness that is experienced as personal happiness, ecological sustainability, and spiritual maturity.

Sessions, which are purchased in thirty minute and one hour segments, occur online, on the phone, or in person with Heartwood Path creator Don Pierce. Elements of Heartwood Path guidance include:

- making checklists of topics or actionable items
- establishing guidelines
- setting and reviewing deadlines
- explaining and reviewing practices
- responding and questioning journal entries
- instructing
- providing individualized templates of models
- supporting individuals and teams in the field
- defining terminology and elaborating on Heartwood Path text
- mentoring on related subjects and
- assistance in interpreting signs and symbols.

Complementary Guidance sessions are available when you sign up for any Heartwood Path course.

Further Action

REVIEWS APPRECIATED AND OTHER HEARTWOOD PATH BOOKS

If you enjoyed reading **Egos**, please leave a review on Amazon. I would appreciate any comments you may wish to share. Positive reviews go a long way in spreading our important message.

For further reading, the next book in the Heartwood Path series is **Ecos**, on the important topic of connecting with the Ecological Self.

All Heartwood Path books are available on Amazon, including **Kosmos**, the Overture and **Logos**, which presents universal principles aimed at helping you avoid swimming upstream in life. Together, Heartwood Path books provide important personal preparations necessary for the creation of happiness and a regenerated environment.

In recognition for all that you do along the Heartwood Path, I say "thank you" and "Great Work!"

www.ingramcontent.com/pod-product-compliance
Lightning Source LLC
Chambersburg PA
CBHW060847120626
46553CB00001B/3